Records of
North American
Elk and Mule Deer

Records of North American Elk and Mule Deer

A book of the Boone and Crockett Club containing tabulations
of elk, mule deer, and blacktail deer of North America
as compiled from data in
the Club's Big Game Records Archives.

Edited by Jack and Susan Reneau

Second Edition
1996
The Boone and Crockett Club
Missoula, Montana

Records of North American Elk and Mule Deer

Second Edition - 1996

Library of Congress Catalog Card Number: 96-84237
ISBN Number for softcover: 0-940864-25-8
ISBN Number for hardcover: 0-940864-27-4

Published October 1996

Published in the United States of America
by the
Boone and Crockett Club
250 Station Drive
Missoula, MT 59801

(406) 542-1888
(406) 542-0784 (fax)

Prologue
Vision of the Past Brings Success for the Present

Paul D. Webster

As we near the 21st century, it is altogether fitting and appropriate that the Boone and Crockett Club publish this second edition of Records of North American Elk and Mule Deer. It stands as a fitting tribute to the 19th and early 20th century conservationists who founded the Boone and Crockett Club in 1887 and gave birth to the conservation movement. Theodore Roosevelt, George Bird Grinnell, and many other early Club members worked to preserve the natural resources of America for future generations to experience and enjoy.

Elk and mule deer have always held a soft spot for members of the Club. In fact, a distinct subspecies of elk that inhabits coastal areas from California to Alaska, the Roosevelt's elk, is named after Theodore Roosevelt, the Club's founder and 26th President of the United States.

This second edition of Records of North American Elk and Mule Deer provides hunters, wildlife biologists, and game managers of state, provincial, and federal wildlife agencies a clear picture of the health and strength of the elk and mule deer populations of North America. It stands as a permanent tribute to the efforts of early Club members.

As an example, the National Elk Refuge in Jackson Hole, Wyoming, was increased to its current size of more than 20,000 acres in large part due to the tireless efforts of Club members George Bird Grinnell, Kermit Roosevelt, Charles Sheldon, Horace M. Albright, George Shiras III, John C. Merriam, and T.S. Palmer.

The refuge, located a mile northeast of Jackson Hole, Wyoming, was created in 1912 after local ranchers and conservationists, including Club members, worked to preserve the historic wintering grounds of the elk that summered in Yellowstone National Park and the surrounding land that eventually became Teton National Park. In 1927, The Commission on the Conservation of the Jackson Hole Elk, chaired by the Club's Vice President, Charles Sheldon, was created by the President of the United States with the purpose of studying and reporting on the plight of the elk herd in that region. The Commission made lengthy recommendations that ultimately resulted in a Congressional appropriation of $6 million that expanded the refuge in 1935 by 16,400 acres.

The establishment of Teton National Park, with its substantial populations of elk, mule deer and other big-game species, was a direct result of conversations Horace M. Albright had with John D. Rockefeller, Jr., who asked Albright if the Tetons and surrounding land should be preserved. Albright said yes, and the rest is history. Rockefeller wrote a check that purchased the Tetons, and by an Act of Congress became Teton National Park in 1929.

Time and time again, the quiet conversations of Club members became the framework for new and/or expanded parks and refuges. Such is the ongoing work of the Club today as it funds research at its Theodore Roosevelt Memorial Ranch (TRMR), which has become an important elk and mule deer wintering range on Montana's Eastern Front. More is now known about the migration routes of big game in the vicinity of the TRMR because of Club-funded, graduate research studies at the University of Montana where the Club has endowed a Boone and Crockett professor. The vision and passion of early Club members lives on through the work of today's Club members.

This edition of Records of North American Elk and Mule Deer is an entertaining way to pay tribute to the thousands of wildlife managers and millions of hunters who work to insure that these magnificent creatures will be around for future generations to enjoy. If it were not for the contributions of hunters and the sound wildlife management practices created, espoused, and implemented by Club members, there would be no reason to publish a second edition of this book for there would be no healthy big game populations about which to write.

Paul D. Webster of Wayzata, Minnesota, is the current president of the Boone and Crockett Club and the Boone and Crockett Foundation. He served as its treasurer from 1993 to 1994 and is active in all aspects of the Club and Foundation. Paul is president of Webster Industries Incorporated, managing partner of Webster Wood Preserving Company and president of Bangor Equipment Company. He is a sustainer of the World Wildlife Fund and life member of the Foundation for North American Wild Sheep, The Grand Slam Club, International Sheep Hunters Association, Amateur Trapshooting Association, National Skeet Shooting Association, Rocky Mountain Elk Foundation and Texas Bighorn Society. Paul also supports and is active in many other wildlife conservation and hunting organizations.

Contents

STATE/PROVINCE/MEXICO	TYPICAL	NON-TYPICAL
Arizona	147	151
California	155	157
Colorado	159	173
Idaho	181	187
Iowa	—	193
Kansas	195	197
Montana	199	203
Nebraska	207	209
Nevada	211	215
New Mexico	217	221
North Dakota	225	—
Oregon	227	231
South Dakota	233	235
Utah	237	243
Washington	249	251
Wyoming	253	259
Alberta	263	265
British Columbia	267	269
Saskatchewan	271	273
Mexico	277	—

STATE/PROVINCE

Illustrations

Photographs of American Elk Record Trophies

STATE/PROVINCE/MEXICO	TYPICAL	NON-TYPICAL
Arizona	48	54
Colorado	56	60
Idaho	62	66
Iowa	68	—
Kansas	—	70
Montana	72	78
Nevada	80	82
New Mexico	84	88
Oregon	90	—
South Dakota	92	—
Texas	94	—
Utah	96	—
Washington	98	100
Wyoming	102	108
Alberta	110	114
British Columbia	116	118
Manitoba	120	122
Saskatchewan	124	—

Photographs of Roosevelt's Elk Record Trophies

STATE/PROVINCE

Photographs of Mule Deer Record Trophies

STATE/PROVINCE/MEXICO	TYPICAL	NON-TYPICAL
Arizona	146	150
California	154	156
Colorado	158	172
Idaho	180	186
Iowa	—	192
Kansas	194	196

Photographs of Columbia Blacktail Deer Record Trophies
STATE/PROVINCE

Photographs of Sitka Blacktail Deer Record Trophies
STATE/PROVINCE

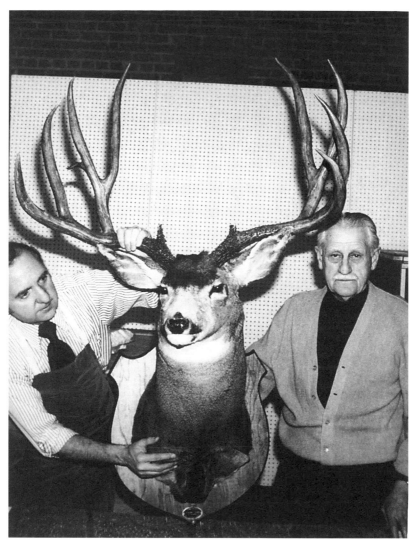

Photograph by Wm. H. Nesbitt

B&C Judges Bernard A. Fashingbauer, left, and Elmer M. Rusten, pose with Doug Burris, Jr.'s, World's Record typical mule deer (226-4/8 points) at the 15th Awards Program. Doug took this buck in Colorado in 1972, and it received the coveted Sagamore Hill Award in 1974.

Introduction
The Story of This Book

Jack and Susan Reneau

The Boone and Crockett Club is universally recognized as the source for records book data on native North American big game. The creation of *Records of North American Elk and Mule Deer* was the brainchild of Boone and Crockett Club members and wildlife biology staff in the late 1980s, who knew hunters wanted concise statistics of all Boone and Crockett Club elk and mule deer records accepted into the B&C Awards Programs.

The Boone and Crockett Club first published *Records of North American Elk and Mule Deer* in 1991. The first edition recognized the 1,803 outstanding elk and mule deer trophies accepted in the Club's Archives through December 31, 1988, the close of the 19th Awards Program. This second edition includes all the listings in the first edition plus 747 new elk and mule deer entries accepted during the 21st and 22nd Awards Programs (1989-1994).

This second edition of *Records of North American Elk and Mule Deer* contains the statistical details of 390 typical American elk, 66 non-typical American elk, 144 Roosevelt's elk, 640 typical mule deer, 430 non-typical mule deer, 769 Columbia blacktail deer, and 110 Sitka blacktail deer. Any argument with friends over which trophy is largest from each state or province is settled when a reader turns to that section of the book. Every trophy is listed under the state or province where it was taken along with basic statistics on rack size, final score, name of hunter and trophy owner, date and location of kill, all-time rank, and state or provincial rank. The top-ranked trophy from each state or province is featured with a full-page photograph at the start of each section. The top ten trophies from each category are listed at the front of their section of the book to enable readers to locate them quickly in the trophy listings.

The book is designed to fit neatly into a backpack. The sturdy cover offers double protection against rough hunting and weather conditions in the field. Convenient for any outdoorsman or outdoorswoman are reproductions of the official elk and mule deer score charts so hunters can score their own trophies and compare them to the listings in the book.

The score charts reproduced in this book include the data for the World's Record typical American elk taken by John Plute that scores 442-3/8 points; the World's Record Roosevelt's elk taken by Wayne Coe that scores 388-3/8 points; the World's Record non-typical American elk taken by James R. Berry that scores 447-1/8 points; the World's Record Columbia blacktail deer taken by Lester H. Miller that scores 182-2/8 points; and the World's Record non-typical mule deer taken by Ed Broder that scores 355-2/8 points.

This specialized records book was not the first such book published by the Boone and Crockett Club. Whitetail and Coues' deer are highlighted in the book, *Records of North American Whitetail Deer*, which is now in its third edition. This specialized whitetail deer records book contains more than 4,000 typical and non-typical whitetail and Coues' deer listings and hundreds of full-page photographs of state and provincial records. As with the elk and mule deer book, field photographs showing the hunter and trophy in the field are a popular component of the whitetail deer book.

New in 1996 is the first Boone and Crockett Club records book of wild sheep, goats, and pronghorn titled, *Records of North American Sheep, Rocky Mountain Goats and Pronghorn*. This specialized records book provides the latest in big-game statistics and photographs for the avid outdoorsman and outdoorswoman. This book lists all accepted Boone and Crockett Club sheep, goats and pronghorn and organizes them by the state or province where they were taken. The book also features full-page field and portrait photographs of Boone and Crockett trophies. Basic horn measurements, final B&C score and world rank, location and date of kill, and name of hunter and owner are listed for each trophy. For this first edition, the editors have compiled the key statistics for 709 bighorn sheep, 544 desert sheep, 336 Stone's sheep, 339 Dall's sheep, 601 Rocky Mountain goats, and 1,412 pronghorn that are fully accepted in the Boone and Crockett Club through the 22nd Awards Program (1992 to 1994).

No other set of specialized records books contains such a compact and concise method of analyzing where the big ones are found and hunted. The records books for elk and mule deer; whitetail and Coues' deer; and sheep, Rocky Mountain goats, and pronghorn; offer the game biologist and hunter the quickest way to focus on areas they want to study or hike to locate the best of the best in each of those big-game categories. Knowledge of animal behavior, time spent scouting an area, and lots of good luck play important roles in a successful hunt, but these specialized records books give the reader an extra edge.

The current copyrighted Boone and Crockett Club scoring system dates from its adoption by the Records Committee in 1950 and has been in continuous usage, without major change, since then, which is testimony to its reliable method of measuring big-game antlers, horns, and skulls. The strength of the Boone and Crockett Club scoring system is the ability to repeat the measurements time and time again. Should someone question an individual measurement or the scoring of an entire trophy, the measurements and scoring can be repeated to demonstrate correctness, even years after the original scoring takes place. This is possible because the Boone and Crockett Club scoring system bases its measurements on durable horns, antlers, and skulls that do not disintegrate. Using body length or weight -- or a combination of these measurements – as a basis for a score, could not be repeated because flesh, muscle, body mass, and fur disintegrate as an animal decomposes. The Boone and Crockett Club's scoring system relies upon objective measurements of enduring animal characteristics, which has assisted in its universal acceptance as the measuring system for all native North American big-game trophies.

Typical or Non-Typical?

Non-typical categories are described for both American elk and mule deer. No non-typical category exists for Roosevelt's elk, Columbia blacktail deer, and Sitka blacktail deer. The non-typical category differs from the typical in the recording of the abnormal points that are beyond the usual pattern of antler development. Abnormal points are subtracted from typical big-game categories as a penalty from the final score but such points are added into the final score on a non-typical trophy measurement. Boone and Crockett Club scores are higher in the non-typical categories because abnormal points are added to the final score. The Boone and Crockett Club scoring system has no set definition of how much non-typical material must be present to classify a trophy as non-typical. That decision lies with the trophy owner who may decide to have the rack measured as non-typical to gain a higher final score.

Non-typical American elk and mule deer require a separate score chart from their typical counterparts. Columbia and Sitka blacktail deer are measured using the same score chart as a typical mule deer. Roosevelt's elk also have a separate score chart for their measurements. Roosevelt's elk are subspecies of the American elk, and Columbia and Sitka blacktail deer are subspecies of the mule deer so their geographic boundaries are clearly defined by the Boone and Crockett Club. The geographic boundaries are needed to prevent their larger cousins from being erroneously entered into the records program. For example, a small mule deer could be a large "Columbia blacktail deer" if there were no such boundaries. The general boundaries of these subspecies are outlined at the start of their data sections in this book.

Scoring of Trophies

The first step in scoring a trophy is to read the instructions on the Boone and Crockett Club score charts reproduced in this book. If a trophy seems to receive a rough score that comes close to the minimum entry for that big-game category, a hunter or owner can call the Boone and Crockett Club's national headquarters at (406) 542-1888 to order their own score chart. If a preliminary measurement suggests the need for closer scrutiny, the Club's staff can send a complete list of official measurers in the caller's state or province. The measurer will officially measure a trophy for possible entry into the all-time, or awards records books published by the Boone and Crockett Club.

If an official measurer determines that a trophy meets the minimum score requirements, he or she will assist the hunter or owner in submitting the official score chart with a hunter, guide, and hunt information sheet; a signed Fair Chase statement; a copy of his or her hunting license; and a processing fee of $25 made out to the Boone and Crockett Club. Photographs of the front and right and left sides of the antlers must be submitted with the paperwork. After several weeks of review, Boone and Crockett Club staff determine if a trophy is eligible for acceptance into the Boone and Crockett Club records keeping program. A certificate and letter of congratulations is sent to the trophy owner when a trophy is fully accepted into the Club's archives.

An official measurement cannot be made until the antlers have dried for at least 60 days under normal atmospheric conditions after the kill. Trophies in velvet must have the velvet removed before official measurements are taken. Boone and Crockett Club official measurers donate their time to measure all trophies and do not charge for their services, but a trophy must be taken to them at their convenience since they are volunteers. Premeasurement of a trophy by the owner is helpful to determine if an official measurer should be called.

Every three years, new entries into the Boone and Crockett Club's records keeping program are organized by an awards period. The first Awards Program, called the First Competition, was in 1947. Annual competitions were held until 1951 when the Boone and Crockett Club instigated biennial competitions beginning with 1952 through 1953. The biennial competitions continued until the 14th Competition when triennial competitions were begun in 1968. The Competitions were renamed Awards Programs beginning with the 15th Awards Program (1971 to 1973) to better reflect their intent. The Boone and Crockett Club has completed twenty-two Awards Programs since 1947, and is currently in the 23rd Awards Program that closes on December 31, 1997.

Starting with the 18th Awards Program (1980 to 1982), the Boone and Crockett Club published a specialized awards program records book that featured the full-page photographs and hunting stories of all award-winning trophies from that triennial period. All officially accepted trophies from the recognized big-game categories are listed in charts with key trophy measurements, final score, Award Program rank, location and year of kill, and name of hunter and owner. Field photographs of some of the trophies from that Awards Period are included in these hardcover books with colored dust jackets. The 18th, 19th, 20th, and 22nd Awards Program books are currently available for sale from the Boone and Crockett Club while supplies last. The 21st Awards Program book is out of print.

The top-ranking trophies in each three-year Awards Program of trophy entry are recognized with medals and/or certificates. Owners of the top-ranking trophies are invited to send their antlers, skulls, and horns to the triennial Awards Program. At the Awards Program, a select panel of B&C Official Measurers remeasure and certify the invited trophies and give recognition to each trophy based upon its final score from the Judges' Panel. If a trophy owner decides not to send the antlers, skull, or horns to the Judges' Panel, its records book listing will be asterisked without final rank, pending submission of additional verifying measurements by other official measurers. In the case of a potential World's Record, the trophy must come before the Judges' Panel to be certified as the new World's Record. There is no exception to this rule.

Trophies invited to an Awards Program are on display for an extended period of time preceding the Awards Banquet. Displays are often held at natural history museums in major U.S. metropolitan areas where tens of thousands of people view them before trophies are returned to their owners.

Records of North American Elk and Mule Deer, 2nd Edition, is a testament to the outstanding wildlife management practices of the fish and game professionals in the United States, Mexico, and Canada who, along with hunters, do more to enhance wildlife populations and habitats than any other group of individuals. The sale of hunting licenses and hunting equipment to hunters is the single most important financial contribution to our wildlife heritage. This book is a permanent record of strong and healthy elk and mule deer herds thanks to those contributions.

Jack Reneau is a certified wildlife biologist and the director of big-game records for the Boone and Crockett Club, a position he has held since January of 1983. He holds a B.S. in wildlife management from Colorado State University and a M.S. in wildlife management from Eastern Kentucky University. He was responsible for the day-to-day paperwork of the Boone and Crockett Club's records keeping program from 1976 through 1979 as the information specialist for the Hunter Services Division of the National Rifle Association (NRA) when NRA and the Boone and Crockett Club cosponsored the North American Big Game Awards Program as it was known during that time. He is the co-author of the book, Colorado's Biggest Bucks and Bulls, *and the co-editor and designer of sixteen Boone and Crockett Club books.*

Susan Reneau is the author of The Adventures of Moccasin Joe: True Life Story of Sgt. George S. Howard, 1872 to 1877, *and co-author of* Colorado's Biggest Bucks and Bulls. *She is the co-editor and designer of seven Boone and Crockett Club books and 28 books for other publishers. She also produces three to five hours of live radio talk shows per day for Super News Talk 1290 KGVO Radio in Missoula, Montana. Susan holds a B.A. in education and speech communications from the University of Northern Colorado and a M.S. in business marketing and public relations from American University, Washington, D.C. Jack and Susan live in Missoula, Montana, with their three teen-age sons and two black Labrador retrievers.*

Photograph by Leo T. Sarnaki

Elmer M. Rusten, left, and Frank Cook admire an American elk they scored at the 14th Awards Competition held at the Carnegie Museum in Pittsburgh, Pennsylvania, in 1971.

Photograph Courtesy of Jim Zumbo

Jim Zumbo with one of several bull elk he's taken in limited entry areas. These are the easiest of the economical hunts. Fewer hunters, more quality elk, and often easier access.

How to Get an Easy Elk

Jim Zumbo

Of all the animals I've hunted in North America, elk get my vote as the toughest. Goats live in more treacherous terrain; whitetails are smarter; moose are bigger; but day in and day out, an elk hunt on public land without the services of an outfitter can be downright miserable. Even with an outfitter's assistance, plenty of hunters go home each year without an elk. To be specific, if you average all the Western states, 25 percent of the total elk hunters are successful. That might not seem too bad, but look at it from another perspective: 75 out of 100 hunters *don't* get their elk each year. That's a bunch of folks going home with an unfilled tag.

To be sure, making a kill isn't necessarily a requirement of having a successful hunt. Plenty of folks who hunt elk country end their hunt smiling, whether they get an elk or not. Just being in the high elevations with the associated sights, sounds, and smells is enough of a reward.

But, the fact is, the objective of a hunt is indeed to bag an elk. If you've got a bull tag, you obviously would love a crack at the Boss Bull of the Woods. Unfortunately, few of us get that chance because elk are too often being elk, usually living in impossible country and staying under cover during shooting hours. Most of us who hunt elk with more than casual interest have been outsmarted and frustrated more than we care to admit. Elk hunting often becomes an ordeal, an endurance contest that pushes our bodies to the limit. Every year we may swear off elk hunting forever, but we know we don't really mean it. Once the aches and pains wear off and are forgotten, we make plans for next year's hunt, even though we know what we're getting into – Gluttons for punishment, as they say.

With this being the case, is there really such a thing as an easy elk? Many folks will argue that the critter doesn't exist. No, elk is easy, they claim.

I suppose that depends on how you define "easy." It's a relative term, depending on what you compare it with. My intent here is to look at the elk hunt from every angle, delve into it intensely, and determine all the ways it can be done. I'm convinced that the easy hunt exists, but again, it's all a matter of perspective.

A major consideration in defining the easy hunt is the necessity of transporting the elk from where it fell to a road or vehicle. No matter how much, or how little effort you've expended, you must always deal with a carcass that may weigh up to a half ton, more commonly 600 to 700 pounds in the case of the average mature bull. Elk are big. Removing several hundred pounds of meat is not usually easy, especially if your quarry lies in the bottom of an unroaded canyon and your vehicle is parked on top of the ridge. Always beware of Murphy's Law!

So, to truly define an easy hunt, we must first deal with getting the meat out. We're putting the cart before the horse because we aren't yet considering the effort to get a shot at the elk in the first place. In terms of physical effort, meat removal is almost always the cause of most misery. Of course, the easiest way to do this is to hire someone else to do it for you. Enter the outfitter, guide, wrangler, or packer. You pay him for his services; your elk ends up magically at the meat processing plant or at your front door, depending on your arrangements.

The obvious way to get an easy elk, then, is to buy it. It follows that the best way to avoid going through a major physical campaign to get an elk is to hunt where there's comparatively less walking and hiking. Looking at all the options, the easiest of all the elk hunts is, without question, the game farm hunt. These elk are contained within an escape-proof fence; many of the bulls are enormous; your hunt is guaranteed; and, you don't need a hunting license to pursue one.

There are a few problems with this easiest-of-all-hunts. First and foremost, realize that your bull cannot be entered in the Boone and Crockett Club's all-time records book because the hunt does not conform to the rule of Fair Chase that pertains to hunting animals within an escape-proof fence. Second, expect a big hit in your bank account since these hunts are expensive. Third, depending on your circle of hunting friends, you probably won't be doing much bragging about where and how you got your elk. Some folks just aren't too fond of game farm hunting.

Since this book is a Boone and Crockett Club publication, why am I mentioning game farm hunting in the first place? Because it's reality. Remember, I'm discussing all the ways you can hunt elk. Since game farm hunting is legal in several states, and since there are hunters who have no problem with the concept, it needs to be addressed. Each of us has different values. What doesn't appeal to us may appeal to the next person.

Other less controversial ways to buy an elk hunt are to hire outfitters who will take care of most of your needs, and, hopefully, get you into

Photograph by Jim Zumbo

These resting bulls were photographed in a lottery draw, limited entry area during hunting season.

good elk country. The word "hopefully" implies that there's a bit of a question here. Indeed there is, and you'll wholeheartedly agree if you've hired many outfitters over the years.

Unfortunately, there are unethical outfitters out there as well as the good ones. Regardless, elk hunting can be so unpredictable that you may hire one of the top outfitters in the country and still go home without an elk. All sorts of factors, primarily weather, can work against you.

Your "easy" outfitted hunt, whether you're successful or not, may end up being a major ordeal, particularly if you're on a backcountry wilderness trip. To some folks, the mere requirement of sitting atop a horse for several hours is a huge effort. Then you must consider the need to follow a guide afoot around steep mountains every day, from long before daybreak to after dark. Chances are your guide will be a tough cowboy much younger than you, who asks that you perform the impossible by just staying within sight of him as you trudge up and down some terribly rugged terrain. You may find yourself sitting on a big rock, gasping for air in the oxygen-depleted high country, rubbing fatigued muscles, and wondering what in the world you're doing there. You'll quickly learn that mountain elk hunting is far from easy.

Another option is to sign on with an outfitter who hunts private land where you can get around easily and shoot your elk fairly close to a road. Many outstanding hunts are available on Indian reservations, most of them in Arizona and New Mexico, or on large ranches that are located in every Western state. Be aware, though, that some private ranch hunts may not be everything they're cracked up to be. For example, New Mexico has five, five-day hunts each fall. If you book into the fourth hunt, and have no snow to move elk around you may see few, if any, decent bulls, most of them having been already shot or thoroughly spooked by earlier hunters. It happens all the time.

Bottom line in buying your hunt is to have reasonable expectations. Be willing to come home with something less than you anticipated, though that's tough to do when you're spending good money on a hunt. With the exception of game farm hunts, no outfitter should guarantee a hunt. If he does, you should take a hard look at his operation.

My first outfitted elk hunt was a Montana affair many years ago. With high hopes I drove to Montana, hauling a big meat box in back of my truck and nurturing lofty dreams of the giant bull I was going to bring home. It didn't quite work out that way. I returned home empty-handed after being thoroughly fleeced by an outfitter who was drunk and had little knowledge of elk hunting.

Another way to get an easy elk is to simply be lucky. Best case scenario is to walk out of your tent or camper, spot an elk sneaking along, and shoot it next to your pickup truck. That, unfortunately, doesn't happen very often, but most of us have heard of cases where lucky incidents occur.

I was told about a hunt that began with a lengthy poker game the evening prior to opening day. The participants received little sleep that night, and all but one doggedly got up at the prescribed time and headed for the elk woods prior to daybreak. The lone hold-out remained in his sleeping bag until mid-morning, crawled into his truck around noon, and drove a half mile down the road, where he pulled over and promptly fell asleep in the cab. An hour later, he woke up to see a grand six-point bull trotting toward him, whereupon the hunter eased out of his truck, rested his rifle on a fencepost, and downed the elk. With help from other passing hunters, he loaded the bull in his truck, winched it up a tree branch next to camp, and had dinner ready when his pals got in that night. Imagine their surprise when they returned to that scene, especially since none of them had seen so much as a spike bull that day.

On a recent Colorado hunt with Gen. Chuck Yeager, we had to cope with blizzards and poor visibility. Elk hunting was practically shut down, but one morning, while I walked away from camp, a small herd of elk ran down a ridge toward me. One of them was a five-point bull that I immediately collected, counting myself extremely lucky to see any elk. Unbeknown to me at the time, Chuck had kicked the elk off the ridge, and I happened to be at the right place at the right time. The bull cooperated nicely by falling 20 yards away from the road.

Another way to get an easy elk is to win it. By applying for one of the many limited entry elk tags offered in states where elk is hunted, you can beat the dismal general season odds and have an opportunity at a good bull. Happily, many of these units are in accessible areas where you often can do an economical hunt on your own. Private landowners within those units are quite often willing to allow free access or they might charge a modest trespass fee. Since the tags are issued in a computer draw, they can't lease their lands to groups of hunters as they commonly do in general hunt areas.

You'd think that hunters would be chomping at the bit to apply for these limited entry tags, but it's surprising how few take advantage of the opportunity. For the last fifteen years, I've been giving seminars on western big-game hunting. At the Kingdome Show in Seattle, I routinely show a slide of 22 mature bulls in a single herd. The audience typically gasps at the sight of these bulls, and commonly believe that the elk were photographed in Yellowstone or another prime elk area. They're shocked when I tell them the bulls were photographed near Mt. St. Helens, Washington, which is just a two-hour drive from downtown Seattle. They're also amazed that the bulls were photographed in a hunting unit during hunting season.

The bulls inhabit a limited entry unit with a very high hunter success rate, far higher than the general hunt rate. Yet less than 5 percent of the hunters in the audience claim that they apply for those outstanding limited areas. I think there are a few reasons why this is so. Many hunters believe they're too unlucky to draw a tag. They don't bother filling out the application. Some hunters don't want to hunt an unfamiliar area, preferring instead to hunt the same units with their pals that they've been hunting for years. Other hunters are so fed up with some of the complicated application forms that they simply refuse to consider limited entry hunts.

To help draw a tag, many states now offer preference or bonus points. The concepts are simple. The preference point system awards a point if you fail to draw a tag. The points accumulate each year until you have enough to draw a tag. No longer is luck a matter of winning a tag; it's simply perseverance. On the down side, some of the units are popular enough that it might take several years to draw a tag.

Some years ago I drew a limited entry elk tag in Colorado after having accumulated four points. The hunt was in relatively low country, had plenty of access, and much of the unit was public land where I camped. I took a nice six-point bull after having passed up several others. The elk fell within 200 yards of a road, and I saw only a couple of other hunters that day. Other than the cost of the nonresident tag and some food and gasoline, I had no major expenditures.

This might not seem to be terribly exciting, but when you consider that elk hunting on Colorado's public lands is woefully crowded with hordes of hunters, and your chances of seeing a mature six-point bull are slim to none in heavily hunted areas, you'd appreciate the ease with which I took my bull. Interestingly enough, I make the same survey among my audiences in Denver as I do in Seattle, and very few hunters apply for those units. This baffles me, especially since Colorado offers the win-win preference point system.

Some states give bonus points if you don't draw a tag. These points also accumulate, but instead of being applied to one application as the preference points are, each bonus point allows an extra application in the hopper. In other words, if you have three bonus points, you have three applications working for you in the computer. Obviously, your odds greatly increase as your bonus points accumulate. This system allows anyone to draw, even the first year, which is impossible with high demand units made available by preference points.

A basic premise in elk hunting is the very clear fact that competition among hunters is a primary reason that success rates are low. And, if you're looking for a mature bull, you might have a long search on public land in general units. It's quite possible that there are no mature bulls where you hunt because they simply don't live long enough. It takes several years for an elk to develop massive antlers; in many heavily hunted areas, a three-year-old bull is ancient.

Another aspect of getting an easy elk, or even in getting any elk, is knowing about elk behavior. It's always a good idea to know the habits of your quarry, as well as the place it calls home. Your success rate will improve markedly once you understand and become familiar with behavioral characteristics of elk.

Who ever said hunting for elk was easy? And, when it gets right down to it, who really wants to hunt elk the easy way? The best elk hunts I remember are the ones that made me work for my goal. That's what hunting is all about.

Jim Zumbo of Cody, Wyoming, is the author of fifteen books and more than 1,000 magazine articles. He is a regular keynote speaker at national and regional conventions and on television. He is the hunting editor for Outdoor Life. *His newest book,* To Heck with Moose Hunting, *is available now and contains humorous tales similar to his other bestsellers,* To Heck with Elk Hunting *and* To Heck with Deer Hunting. *Other new books by Zumbo include* Amazing Venison Recipes *and* The Big Game Hunter's Bible. *Jim has two college degrees in forestry and wildlife management and worked as a forester and wildlife biologist for 15 years before joining the* Outdoor Life *staff in 1978. Recently, Jim designed his own elk call and produced a 30-minute video on its use. To order any of Jim's books or outdoor items, call or write to Wapiti Publishing Co., P.O. Box 2390, Cody, WY 82414 or (800) 673-4868.*

Photograph Courtesy of Rocky Mountain Elk Foundation

Elk and other wildlife species roam southwestern Montana's Porcupine Drainage where Rocky Mountain Elk Foundation has joined a partnership dedicated to acquiring and consolidating critical lands for these animals of the Greater Yellowstone Ecosystem.

The Rocky Mountain Elk Foundation
Ensuring Great Habitat for Great Elk

Robert W. Munson and Richard A. Gooding, M.D.

The pages of this book honor one of North America's most breathtaking, magical creatures – the elk. These great elk came to be for a variety of reasons, including good luck and good genetics. But, the biggest reason for their existence is tied to the land they inhabit. Our privilege to enjoy seeing these majestic animals continues today only because somebody, many years ago, realized the importance of good habitat.

In the late 1800s, as many species of North American wildlife came close to extinction, the founders of the Boone and Crockett Club – starting in 1887 – and other conservationists stepped forward to effect change. Their concern for the future of wildlife guided them through their efforts to institute game laws and work for habitat conservation.

Their accomplishments helped reverse the downward spiral among wildlife populations and set the conservation standard for future generations. One thing these early conservationists could not do was ensure that their work would continue in the decades to come. Most of them could probably never have predicted the incredible challenge of continuing their legacy in the face of rapid human population growth and the spread of development.

Fast-forward to 1984, to Troy, Montana. A couple of brothers, Bob and Bill Munson, and two of their friends, Dan Bull and Charlie Decker, living amidst some of North America's most spectacular elk country, took a long look around them. Even in this remote corner of one of the most sparsely populated states in America, they recognized a frightening trend. New subdivisions, roads, and other developments were swiftly consuming elk habitat, and, along with it, habitat for moose, cutthroat trout, bears, turkeys, and many other species. At the time, the four friends realized, no one organization existed specifically to put a stop to the disappearance of elk habitat.

And, so, in May of 1984, the Rocky Mountain Elk Foundation

(RMEF) was born. The founders conceived a magazine about elk, called *BUGLE*, and, later, a member newspaper, dubbed, *WAPITI*. They formed a small, diehard staff and set out in search of others who cared about the future of wildlife habitat. In a few short years, the enthusiasm of the four elk hunters began to draw in more and more folks who shared their concerns.

In 1988, the small staff made a big move, packing up the RMEF's headquarters to relocate to Missoula, Montana. Today, with just 12 years gone by since four friends hatched an idea about doing something good for elk habitat, the RMEF now claims more than 100,000 members. Those members have enabled the organization to generate $50 million for the conservation and enhancement of more than 1.8 million acres of North American wildlife habitat.

RMEF members come from all walks of life, all parts of the United States and Canada, and around the world. They all share a deep commitment to the RMEF mission. It's a simple mission, followed by four straightforward goals:

The mission of the Rocky Mountain Elk Foundation is to ensure the future of elk, other wildlife and their habitat.

In support of this mission, the RMEF is committed to:
- *Conserving, restoring, and enhancing natural habitats;*
- *Promoting the sound management of wild, free-ranging elk and other wildlife, which may be hunted or otherwise enjoyed;*
- *Fostering cooperation among federal, state and private organizations and individuals in wildlife management and habitat conservation; and*
- *Educating members and the public about habitat conservation, the value of hunting, hunting ethics, and wildlife management.*

The RMEF's conservation successes over the last 12 years depend in large part upon that mission, with words like cooperation, education, and conservation forming the backbone of what the RMEF does.

By not taking sides in divisive political issues and focusing on creating partnerships, the RMEF has devoted most of its energy toward conserving critical habitat. When the RMEF does occasionally enter the arena of resource conflicts, dealing with issues like cattle and elk sharing the range, it seeks the role of facilitator and mediator, bringing together divergent viewpoints in a spirit of cooperation.

Most of the funds raised by the RMEF support habitat enhancement

Photograph Courtesy of Rocky Mountain Elk Foundation

In May 1995, elk set foot on Wisconsin soil for the first time in more than 130 years – a historic reintroduction effort spearheaded by Rocky Mountain Elk Foundation members and volunteers in the state. Projects like these have made RMEF famous for its work to restore historic elk herds to their natural habitat.

Photograph Courtesy of Rocky Mountain Elk Foundation

Rocky Mountain Elk Foundation sponsors the "Becoming an Outdoors-Woman" program that creates a relaxed environment for women to learn outdoor skills to share with their families.

and conservation efforts, along with a solid dose of conservation education and hunting heritage. The RMEF cooperates with agencies, private individuals, industry, and other conservation groups to fund several categories of conservation projects, as well as land protection efforts. Conservation projects are chosen by project advisory committees made up of state and federal land managers, RMEF field directors and state chairs, wildlife biologists and resource experts who scrutinize various proposals before recommending priorities and funding levels. To date, RMEF has cooperated on more than 1,300 conservation projects in 41 states and five Canadian provinces.

The projects funded by the RMEF fall into one of five categories: research, management, habitat enhancement, conservation education, and hunting heritage. Research projects generate information about habitat conditions and wildlife use. For example, in Colorado, human/elk interaction studies are helping guide biologists toward finding the delicate balance between the competing habitat needs of people and elk.

Management projects create a better balance of wildlife and available habitat and help restore elk in their native habitats. These projects include efforts to increase elk security by selectively closing or obliterating non-essential roads, as well as historic elk reintroductions. In 1995, the RMEF and its members helped return wild elk to Wisconsin for the first time in 130 years. And in 1996, a transplanted herd of elk set foot in Kentucky, where the last native elk disappeared 150 years earlier.

Habitat enhancement projects improve the necessary components of habitat for elk – food, water, and shelter. These habitat improvements include prescribed burns to rejuvenate decadent forage, water developments that help redistribute animals away from sensitive riparian areas, and seedings to jumpstart native plant communities severely damaged by wildfire.

The need for and results of all these conservation projects are communicated through conservation education programs, nurturing the next generation of conservationists. The RMEF funds a variety of education programs, and also creates its own. With "WILD About Elk," a classroom education program put together in cooperation with the national Project WILD organization, the RMEF has found a way to reach thousands of teachers and even more students. The program consists of a workbook, loaded with natural history information about elk and their habitat, along with several fun, educational activities for teachers to share with their students. A video and posters complement the program. The

Photograph Courtesy of Rocky Mountain Elk Foundation

The excitement of Rocky Mountain Elk Foundation big game banquets and national conventions draws enthusiastic crowds of people committed to the future of wildlife in North America.

14

most exciting part for most teachers comes in a big gray trunk. The RMEF provided each state Project WILD coordinator with an "elk trunk" to loan to teachers. These trunks contain hides, skulls, antlers, and other hands-on items and activities.

Children aren't the only audience targeted by the RMEF. Through hunting heritage programs, the RMEF helps educate people of all ages about safety and ethics, while promoting a tradition that has generated so many conservationists and sustained conservation programs for wildlife. Many women across North America are gaining new confidence in themselves while learning outdoors skills through the "Becoming an Outdoors-Woman" program. By supporting this program at both the state and national levels, the RMEF helps open up the worlds of hunting, outdoor recreation, and conservation to thousands of women and their families.

In addition to these five categories of conservation projects, the RMEF remains committed to helping stem the tide of habitat loss through land protection projects. Using habitat acquisitions, land donations, and conservation easements, the RMEF protects vital habitats at risk from development. Lands purchased by the RMEF for conservation purposes, like the 6,182-acre Porcupine acquisition in southwestern Montana's Gallatin drainage, usually become public ground, managed and cared for by state and federal agencies for everyone to enjoy.

Because, in many areas, private land sustains as much wildlife as public ground, the RMEF has stepped up its efforts to work with private landowners to place conservation easements on their land. These easements allow landowners to retain ownership of land that's sometimes been in the family for several generations. The family can continue some of their traditional land uses, like cattle grazing, as long as those uses stay compatible with maintaining quality wildlife habitat. And, best of all, the land's wildlife values remain protected forever, no matter who may own the property in the future.

From habitat acquisitions to conservation education projects, getting all these things done depends on the RMEF's most important resource – people. Thousands of enthusiastic volunteers from more than 425 RMEF chapters throughout the United States and Canada organize local fund-raising banquets. Banquets give many folks from British Columbia to South Carolina, a chance to express their commitment to the future of the wildlife and wild lands they love.

Twice each year, many RMEF members also take advantage of a

chance to gather with elk enthusiasts from throughout North America at one of the RMEF's annual conventions. The Eastern Rendezvous draws folks from throughout the East and Midwest, while the International Elk Camp and Exposition hosts thousands more in the West. Thousands more visit RMEF's Wildlife Visitor Center in Missoula, Montana.

In addition to member and volunteer support, the RMEF owes much of its success to its partners. These partners run the gamut, from large timber companies, which cooperate with the RMEF to improve the wildlife values on their lands, to outfitters who donate hunts and trips for fund-raising purposes, to individual donors who become RMEF Habitat Partners so that they can contribute something more towards a project or acquisition near and dear to their hearts.

Amidst the daily storm of gloomy news from the world of resource management, the RMEF has been able to generate a new reason for optimism. Once bitter enemies, the livestock and wildlife communities have joined together in the spirit of compromise thanks to the "Seeking Common Ground" program. Winter ranges and migration corridors that seemed all but lost to encroaching subdivisions remain open, unchanged, and full of wildlife. Women are joining the ranks of hunters and conservationists faster than ever.

There are still many habitat enhancements to complete, audiences to reach with the conservation message, and thousands of acres to protect. But, thanks to the devotion of thousands of caring people, the RMEF will continue meeting its mission, leaving a legacy of great habitat for great elk.

For more information about the Rocky Mountain Elk Foundation and its programs, call or write: Rocky Mountain Elk Foundation, 2291 W. Broadway, Missoula, Montana 59802; Call 1-800-225-5355.

Robert W. Munson of Missoula, Montana, is president and co-founder of the Rocky Mountain Elk Foundation. Richard A. Gooding, M.D., a plastic and reconstructive surgeon from Albuquerque, New Mexico, is chairman of the board of RMEF and a regular member of the Boone and Crockett Club. Dr. Gooding is a member of the board of directors, Class of 1996, for the Boone and Crockett Foundation and chair of the Boone and Crockett Club's Conservation Committee. Jennifer Knox, conservation information manager for the Rocky Mountain Elk Foundation, assisted with this chapter.

Photograph by Jack Reneau

Thousands of visitors each year enjoy the Rocky Mountain Elk Foundation's museum, gift shop and art gallery in Missoula, Montana. The museum includes an impressive display of B&C top-ranking trophy elk. (Inset) A larger-than-life-size bugling bull elk bronze greets visitors at the entrance.

17

Craig Boddington, left, and Lad Shunneson with a "suburban mule deer" taken literally on the outskirts of Boulder, Colorado. As the eastern front of the Rocky Mountains gets developed, mule deer are learning to adapt.

What Mule Deer Hunting Is All About

Craig Boddington

I have never shot the kind of mule deer you will see listed in this volume. Part of the reason, quite possibly, is because I'm simply not as good a hunter as those whose bucks have "made" these hallowed listings. A good part, undoubtedly, is because I haven't been quite so lucky – provided, of course, that you accept the hunter's definition of luck as, "when preparation and opportunity meet."

Certainly, a good part of it is due to the simple fact that I have never made a science of attempting to be in the right place at the right time for big mule deer; meaning that I haven't studied the listings and done exhaustive research to determine the exact areas that seem to have the best antler-producing genetics, feed, and minerals. Nor have I made a similar science of determining exactly when the rut should kick off in these best areas, making the older and wiser bucks just a wee bit more vulnerable.

These are the things one must do if a monster mule deer is the goal, and I simply haven't done them – at least not on a consistent enough basis to pay off. On the other hand, I have enjoyed my mule deer hunting immensely, and I've done quite a lot of it over the last 30 years. Some of these hunts have been in the "right" places. Others have been at the right times. Once or twice I believe I've even combined the right places with the right times. Even so, I'm not sure I've ever even seen the kind of mule deer that you see listed herein.

No, that's a lie. I saw one once. Yep, sure did. Missed him, too. It was more than a quarter-century ago, on one of those early timberline deer seasons in Colorado's Maroon Bells Wilderness Area. I was sitting on top of an endless grassy slope, stretching down a quarter-mile at a 45-degree angle to some aspen thickets. Although it was late August the aspen were already starting to turn due to the 12,000-foot elevation. A huge buck stepped out of the quakies at the bottom of the slide and stood for long moments.

The buck was high, wide, heavy, and handsome. It was still in velvet, of course, so probably wasn't as big as I thought it was, but it was a long distance outside its ears, very tall, and the light was good enough that I believe the buck sported a perfect four-by-four rack with eye guards. For sure it was the only mule deer buck I have ever seen that was well outside the magical 30-inch mark.

It was very far away, but in those days, with teenage eyes and reflexes and altogether too much confidence, it wasn't a difficult shot. I had too much confidence, too, in my .264 Winchester Magnum – a good enough caliber for sure, but in those prechronograph days I thought it had almost mystical properties. Chances are I could shoot better then I ever will again; years would pass before it occurred to me that such a thing was difficult. But what I had in youthful ability I lacked in experience. I didn't know how to figure the effects of extreme altitude and a steep angle. In fact, I didn't even try. I held where I knew I had to in order to drop the 129-grain Hornady into his shoulder. The hold was dead steady, and undoubtedly the bullet hit exactly where I aimed – right over its withers. It stood for a moment while I waited in vain for it to drop. Then it walked into the aspens and vanished forever, leaving an image etched into my memory forever.

Back then, if I'd known how to make that shot I could have made it. Today I know how. In fact, I've known since that day that I should have held a bit low instead of high. But today I'm no longer as sure as I was then that I could make such a shot. And, so it goes!

Over the years I've missed a few other mule deer, and I've hit and carried home many more. The fact that that long-ago Colorado buck is the only "for-darn-sure" Boone and Crockett buck I've ever seen speaks volumes about several things. First, it undoubtedly suggests that I'm not exclusively a trophy hunter of mule deer. That's true; I enjoy a wide variety of hunting, and consider myself very much a generalist, a jack-of-all-trades and master of absolutely none. But, it also points up the simple fact that truly huge mule deer are among the most scarce commodities in North American big-game hunting today.

When I was a kid, mule deer numbers were quite high across much of the West, and hunter numbers were low. I grew up in Kansas at a time when our state had no deer season at all, so I missed those halcyon years of mule deer hunting, but I read about it in all the magazines. In those days, it seemed, you could find a big buck bedded under each and every piece of rimrock. Even the big ones always looked back, and getting a huge mule deer was just a matter of going to a reasonably good area and being choosy.

20

Photograph by Craig Boddington

Mule deer are not as adaptable as whitetail, but they do occupy a wide variety of habitats. This is typical of the Sonoran Desert, one of the great trophy hotspots of the 1990s.

Mule deer hunting like that seems almost a myth today, but in the 1950s and on into the 1960s it was darn near that good. No more. There are still tremendous numbers of mule deer in the West, but the truth is the huge bucks are few and far between today. In fact, mule deer numbers as a whole are simply not what they were in those golden years, and may never be again.

Most biologists today are in a quandary as to exactly why this is, let alone what to do to reverse the trend. Undoubtedly, there are many contributing factors. One is certainly greatly increased human population and development throughout the West. This translates into competition with livestock, loss of winter range, and, of course, increased hunting pressure, among other things. Not insignificant is management for quantity rather than quality, which has skewed the age class of the buck herd in many areas. Sagebrush eradication may be another important factor, with many biologists now believing sagebrush is far more important to mule deer than was formerly believed.

Right now the elk population explosion throughout the Rocky Mountain states is having an adverse effect. As a microcosm, Colorado is a prime example. Historically, at least during the tail end of the "good old days" of mule deer hunting, Colorado hosted about 100,000 elk and a half-million mule deer. Today the elk herd has more than doubled, but the deer herd has plummeted by some 40 percent. It's simply a matter of carrying capacity, born out by the fact that mule deer have increased substantially out in the plains units where there are few or no elk.

Periodic bad winters hurt, too, but bad winters are part and parcel to classic mule deer habitat. The problem today is that the mule deer's ability to rebound appears slower than was the case in decades gone by. It's a complex issue, and it certainly doesn't indicate that mule deer as a species are in trouble. They aren't, but the easy pickings for big mule deer have gone the way of the bison.

I'm sorry I missed the good old days, but there's still a lot of great mule deer hunting out there, and it still offers some of North America's most enjoyable sport. The opportunity to see the western mountains, plains, and badlands when crisp nights bring on the fall colors is a matchless experience. I'll never forget that one huge buck that I missed, but every buck I've brought to bag is, in its way, just as memorable.

Hunting the high country is hard work. The crisp, clean air and beautiful vistas more than make up for the sweat, but most mule deer are earned in hard coin and are all the more valued because of it. To me at least, the country and the style of hunting more than make up for a few inches of antler here and there.

Just a few years ago, when my Dad was 68, he shot his first mule deer ever. We were hunting with Keith Atcheson in the Missouri Breaks of Montana, hardly high-mountain habitat but breathtaking in its own rugged way. Pop is mostly a bird hunter. He's hunted a bit with his .308 for many years, and is a competent rifle shot, but he's never achieved any real confidence in his ability with a rifle. He's also permanently a bit stiff courtesy of a bad spill off a horse some years ago. Keith and I had hoped we could find him a reasonable and reasonably easy buck.

It didn't work that way. The rut was just beginning, and we found a lovely plains buck tending some does in some rolling country. Unfortunately, it led us over several hills, and ultimately Pop had to crawl quite a distance on his hands and knees to get in position for a shot. By now the buck had laid down, does all around him. The buck jumped up and faced us, and the second shot centered the white throat patch. Although he's shot moose, bear, and a few other things, Pop has two mounted trophies – his first good pronghorn and that mule deer.

Of course mule deer don't always come hard. Sometimes, as is the case with hunting, you just blunder into what you're looking for or a buck blunders into you. A first of anything is always memorable, thus my own first mule deer certainly is. The truth, however, is that I was lying in my sleeping bag, in the open on a groundcloth, along a willow-lined creek north of Lusk, Wyoming. We'd gotten in late and dawn had come and gone when I stuck my head out of the goose down and looked around. A nice buck was ambling past just 100 yards or so away, and I wasted no time finding my rifle. In fact, it took longer to find and lace my boots so I could go field-dress him.

Mostly, though, mule deer hunting is a very deliberate sport. I love all deer hunting, and, of course, I'm entranced by the whitetail deer. But, much whitetail hunting is stand-hunting, with most of the actual hunting done through scouting and stand placement. Sitting in a stand is a passive form of hunting, and although I've learned to deal with it, I don't like it. Mule deer hunting, along with most western hunting, is a very active sport. My first mule deer notwithstanding, chances are a buck won't come to you. You have to find him and then go get him, and that's part of the charm of mule deer hunting.

Most of my early mule deer hunting consisted of simply covering ground, hoping to spot a buck before he spotted me or, more likely, jump one out of cover close enough for a shot. This is a poor way to hunt any animal that lives in big country – possibly a poor way to hunt any big-game animal. In thick country with limited visibility, hunting from well-placed stands is clearly the method of choice. In heavy oak brush or timber this can be a very productive way to hunt both mule deer and his far-west cousin, the blacktail deer. Fortunately, though, most mule deer country is open enough to practice my favorite hunting technique of all – glassing.

Glassing with good optics is far and away the most productive and, at least for me, the most enjoyable way to hunt not only mule deer but also all western deer. I like to get high and get comfortable and use good optics until I find what I'm looking for. It takes a bit of technique with the glasses; you have to learn how to get steady, and it takes practice to learn what you're looking for. Mostly, though, it takes patience and confidence. If you're glassing correctly, you're glassing a whole lot more than you're walking. You might glass a given hillside a half-dozen times, thoroughly, before moving on. That's the patience part, and the only way you can have such patience is to truly believe that what you're looking for is there and it's simply your job to find it. That kind of confidence is twofold: first, in your ability to use your optics effectively and, second, from doing your homework. You simply have to believe you're in the right spot. Such confidence can come from pre-season scouting, from map reconnaissance, from hiring a good outfitter, from discussions with local hunters and biologists, and probably from a combination. But, it's essential that you know you're in the right place. Then just get comfortable and keep looking.

Chances are you'll see several times the game from a good vantage point than you ever would traipsing about in rough country. The other advantage is that the game you see will generally be undisturbed. If something looks interesting you can plan a careful approach and make a stalk. Of course the animal may not be there when you arrive or it may not be as big as you'd hoped. But I know that is the best way to hunt western deer.

There are wrinkles. If you know the rut is in progress or just coming on, keep your eyes on groups of does. This was a favorite trick of the late Jerry Hughes, a great Nevada outfitter. He would often watch small groups of does for days, and his clients took a number of truly great mule deer as reward for their patience.

Sometimes nothing works no matter how well you do it, and other

Photograph by Craig Boddington

California outfitters Jim and Rory Schaafsma glassing from a high point. Coastal fog like this is common in much of blacktail country.

times just plain dogged persistence pays off. The last time I hunted with Jerry Hughes we just couldn't put it together. We were hunting the Monitor Peak range in north central Nevada, wonderful big buck country. The rut should have started, but it was too darned hot and the moon was full. We glassed endlessly from high points and we watched a couple of doe herds day after day. Nothing.

The last day of the hunt we took our horses in a skirmish line and simply covered ground, over ridges and across deep drainages. It was midafternoon when rocks clattered in the bottom of a juniper-choked canyon. Two fine bucks came out and skylined on the opposite edge and we got them both.

Although it's a question I'm often asked, I simply can't tell you where to go to get a really great Rocky Mountain mule deer today. The best odds, most likely, are to be found in some of the limited-permit units scattered through the West. The Paunsaugunt Plateau in Utah is as good as they say but it's weather sensitive. Arizona's Kaibab is even more weather sensitive, but when conditions are right, it's just like the good old days. Most Nevada units, all on permit draw, are pretty darned good, with western Nevada in particular offering reasonable odds for very big mulies.

The eastern front of the Rockies in Colorado is amazingly good, and while the plains units are perhaps best for big whitetails, anywhere on the plains today you may see a mule deer no one could pass. My good friend Lad Shunneson has guided mule deer hunters on a little place just north of Boulder, Colorado, for more than 20 years. Today, it's darn near a suburb, but for some reason remains a buck funnel. Last year, after sending his clients home with deer, Lad went out on the last evening of the season to take a "freezer buck" and shot an absolutely fabulous high-scoring typical mule deer buck.

Of course there are still some very big bucks in all the traditional big buck areas. Northern New Mexico's mule deer are making a comeback, and although the permits are quite costly, the Jicarilla Reservation still holds monsters. However, most of these traditional areas – western Colorado, western Wyoming, northern New Mexico – have experienced such a tremendous elk population explosion that mule deer simply aren't as plentiful as they used to be.

On a recent elk hunt in northwestern Colorado I was seeing, honestly and literally, 300 elk a day. I doubt I saw more than 25 mule deer altogether in the same period, but I did see a couple of pretty good bucks. They're still there, but to my mind for numbers of mule deer today you need to look outside of elk country. Unfortunately, this generally means the plains and badlands on either side of the Rockies. And, that usually means drier conditions, poorer feed, and bucks that average a bit smaller. But, if you hunt them for what they are, there are still plenty of good bucks and great hunting.

For really enjoyable mule deer hunting and the chance to see lots of deer, lots of bucks, and plenty of nice, mature, respectable four-by-fours, my pick today would be eastern Wyoming and eastern Montana. Once in a while these regions will produce great bucks but there remain plenty of very nice, fully mature bucks, the kind of bucks that are reasonable goals for Rocky Mountain mule deer hunters today.

Although the largest and most sought-after, the Rocky Mountain mule deer is just one of several mule deer subspecies. The other, smaller subspecies offer hunting opportunities just as enjoyable and with surprisingly excellent trophy opportunities.

To the south of the Rocky Mountain mule deer, one finds the desert subspecies, currently lumped together with Rocky Mountain deer for records keeping purposes at the Boone and Crockett Club. Hunting for them varies considerably. West Texas is actually a sleeper for very fine mule deer hunting. The numbers are high and the hunting most enjoyable, though, in general, the antlers are similar to Great Plains mulies, perhaps smaller yet. Desert mule deer in southern Arizona and New Mexico vary considerably both in density and size, but remote desert units in both states, as well as southeastern California, all produce the occasional true monster.

The hot spot for desert mule deer, however, is Sonora in old Mexico. Why the desert mule deer in Sonora get as big as they do is a total mystery to me, but they surely do. The hunting is shockingly different, too. The Sonoran desert is a living, brushy desert. The deer are wandering nomads, and they seem to inhabit the desert floor more than the dry, rocky hills. Tracking is the method of choice, and the Mexican cowboys are the finest trackers I have ever seen. The African trackers are justifiably legendary and I've been amazed at their powers of observation. And, the Mexican cowboys I've hunted with are better!

My own very best mule deer is actually not a Rocky Mountain mulie, but rather a desert mule deer from Sonora. We rode out across the desert at dawn, looking for tracks. We found them in the early morning, just faint impressions in the rocky ground. My guide assured me they were fresh and of a big buck, so we followed across granite tailings, hard-packed clay, through grassy washes. After about six hours I shot the buck in his bed at 60 yards.

The blacktail of the Pacific Northwest, small cousin to the mule deer, also offers hunting that can vary considerably. In the coastal jungles hunting it can be very like whitetail hunting, with trail-watching and even tree stands darn near the only way to get a shot. But, in northern California and southern Oregon, we hunt them by glassing, just as you would hunt mule deer but in country that somehow seems tighter, more compressed.

The great secret is that, right now, blacktail offer the best trophy hunting odds of any deer in North America. And, it's equal-opportunity hunting. There are wilderness areas and special-draw units in both Oregon and northern California where a tough hunter can backpack in and should come out with a record-class buck. There are well-managed private lands where a very few guides can offer surprisingly good odds on bucks of the same class.

Although diminutive by mule deer standards, the blacktail is a truly beautiful deer, with striking white throat patch and ears and face scaled down in keeping with his antlers. In the better areas the hunting is particularly enjoyable because you can expect to see a number of good bucks and a great blacktail is a truly beautiful trophy.

Farther north yet, the Sitka blacktail also offers wonderful deer hunting opportunities. Hard to get to, this deer is ignored by all but those who live there, plus a few trophy collectors. This is unfortunate, because this northernmost mule deer actually offers the most exciting deer hunting in North America. On Kodiak Island and some of the other really good areas it's possible, no exaggeration, to see more than 100 bucks a day!

Of course, the hunting varies. In heavily timbered southeastern Alaska and northwestern British Columbia the deer are there, but the cover is so thick you won't see many. Calling and antler rattling are the methods of choice there. Farther north, especially late in the season when the winds and rain beat down the summer grass, you find the deer out on the open slopes and can glass to your heart's content.

Like all game, you must hunt Sitka deer for what they are – not what you wish they could be. Their antlers are modest, thick, and compact, and you must know what you're looking for. Relatively few Columbia blacktails ever reach the typical four-by-four with eye guard configuration, and even fewer Sitka deer do. The Sitka deer, however, are larger in body than the Columbia blacktails – undoubtedly an adaptation to their harsh climate. They also store much fat in the fall, and are far and away the tastiest deer I've ever eaten.

I grew up on the Kansas prairies, and I get claustrophobic in close cover. I like broad vistas and big horizons, and I can find all the mule deer subspecies in such country. I like hunting them all, and I can't tell you which I like the most. The enjoyment to me, whichever subspecies I hunt and wherever I pursue them, is to hunt them for what they are, not for what they used to be, or what they might be over the next mountain range. But that's me. In the listings in this book you'll find proof positive that the big ones are still out there. They won't come easy, but they're there. If such a buck is your dream, I won't wish you luck. You'll have to make that for yourself. But, I do wish you success.

––––––––––

Craig T. Boddington of Paso Robles, California, is a professional member of the Boone and Crockett Club and the senior field editor for Petersen's HUNTING *and* GUNS & AMMO *magazines. He is a regular contributor to the Boone and Crockett Club's national magazine,* FAIR CHASE: The Official Publication of the Boone and Crockett Club. *Craig is the author of nine books including* Deer Hunting Coast to Coast, Safari Rifles, North American Rifles, *and* From Mt. Kenya to the Cape: Ten Years of African Hunting. *For ordering information about his many books, write Safari Press, 15621 Chemical Lane, Suite B, Huntington Beach, CA 92649 or call (714) 894-9080. In May of 1996, Craig was promoted to Colonel in the U.S. Marine Corps Reserve. Craig has 22 years of service in the U.S. Marine Corps as an infantry officer.*

Emmett Burroughs, left, founder of the Mule Deer Foundation, signed a memorandum of understanding with the U.S. Forest Service and the U.S. Bureau of Land Management in 1989. Bob Nelson, director of wildlife and fisheries, (seated at far right) represented the U.S. Forest Service.

The Mule Deer Foundation
A Look at its Brief History

Rich Fletcher

During the summer of 1986, Emmett Burroughs spent many hours in mule deer country filming wildlife videos. As he filmed mule deer and other wildlife, his eyes were opened to vast changes taking place in mule deer habitat.

His discussions with state fish and game departments, U.S. Bureau of Land Management, and U.S. Forest Service personnel convinced him that no one was looking after the interests of the deer. Interests such as livestock grazing, mining, gas exploration, and real estate development were attacking mule deer habitat from the edges and from the center.

In the vast Nevada desert, drought was crowding deer into limited habitat with the threat that at any time a long cold winter could decimate the herds. Habitat was changing on a broad scale throughout the West, as if a mighty force had decided that the mule deer, a species long taken for granted in sagebrush country, was no longer worthy of prominence.

At one point he found the remains of four great bucks, heads loped off and capes removed, the hideous results of poachers, trespassers who killed for personal gain with no conscience.

During the fall of 1986, Emmett went mule deer hunting with a friend as they had done many times before. While sitting around an evening campfire, the men discussed their love for the country and the reverence of mule deer hunting. They told stories and recounted the bucks they had personally taken, taken but not replaced.

With a deep sense of respect for mule deer and a personal need to give back some of what he had taken, the harvested bucks became Emmett Burroughs' motivation to help deer, and his partner agreed to provide support. In 1987, Emmett Burroughs, founder of the Mule Deer Foundation, began the search for the key elements of what was to become the Foundation. From his personal data base he selected top candidates for positions on the board of directors. He created the administrative organization for the group with his own time, effort, and money.

From the response to his search for board members he selected nine men. Together with Burroughs' attorney, the group met in July of 1988

31

at the Holiday Inn in Redding, California. On that weekend, Emmett gathered together with the men who were to become the Mule Deer Foundation's original board of directors. They approved the bylaws and articles of incorporation and they discussed the purpose and goals of the organization as proposed by Emmett. Per Emmett's instructions, they named the organization the Mule Deer Foundation, and a new wildlife conservation foundation was formed.

The first board of directors consisted of Emmett Burroughs of Redding, California; George Bettas, Pullman, Washington; Larry Green, Redding; George Cook, Poulsbo, Washington; Rich LaRocco, Wellsville, Utah; Tom Tietz, Conifer, Colorado; Gary Holtz, Estes Park, Colorado; and, Bill Brenz, Salt Lake City, Utah.

These men were convinced they could provide sportsmen and conservationists with a wildlife organization unlike any other. When the Foundation's principle plan was accepted, Emmett was named the executive director and chairman of the board for two years. The organization was patterned after other successful conservation groups with a chapter-based membership. Detailed instructions for planning and conducting a fund-raising banquet, raffle, and auction were created.

Fundraising began immediately with a "founding benefactor" program. The first fund-raising banquet was held in Redding, with 400 people in attendance and proceeds that exceeded $55,000. The Redding Chapter held a second banquet on May 5, 1990. Once again a crowd of 400 generated funds for mule deer, with gross proceeds of more than $60,000 and a net profit of $25,000. The Mule Deer Foundation set lofty goals, including a commitment to make every effort to put 50 percent of banquet and auction proceeds to habitat and wildlife programs, which became a financial challenge for the young group.

During the early years, the Mule Deer Foundation was located in Redding but after leading the organization for two years, Emmett stepped down as chairman of the board and executive director to become involved with politics and wildlife issues, especially consumptive-user education. George Bettas was his successor in both capacities.

In 1990, the Mule Deer Foundation published its first magazine, a 64-page glossy color magazine with interesting stories about mule deer and mule deer hunting. Although the magazine content and quality were a big hit, distribution problems sidetracked the project and it was four years later that the next issue of *Mule Deer* magazine would reach the membership. Along with the demise of the first magazine, came a miserable performance by the Foundation at the mule deer convention, which was held at the San Jose Convention Center. Scaled down from three days to one, to minimize losses, the convention sported an impressive display of antlers and an evening banquet. The convention also set the stage for the formation of the Central Coast Chapter of the Mule Deer Foundation that was to become one of the organization's most productive chapters – a chapter whose productivity would carry the organization through several lean years.

After the 1990 convention ended, the Mule Deer Foundation's assets were liquidated to pay bills. Board member David Stevens, along with Emmett and other major contributors, debated the future of the organization. With an infusion of new enthusiasm, David Stevens took over as chairman. David was a successful Washington State wheat farmer with an interest in mule deer and conservation. The "Ranching for Wildlife" program on his 35,000-acre wheat farm was beginning to produce big deer and David Stevens knew from firsthand experience that the decline of mule deer populations could be reversed if the Mule Deer Foundation could survive.

Three banquets were accomplished in the next year. Personnel problems and financial pitfalls seemed destined to destroy the organization, but the membership's understanding of the desperate plight of mule deer held the Mule Deer Foundation together, along with the stubborn will of the board of directors.

In 1992, the Foundation began publishing *Insights*, a 16-page newsletter. In its original form, the newsletter was printed in black and white and was produced with volunteer help. That same year, the Foundation held a national convention at Bally's Hotel-Casino in Reno. Major promotions and donations were generated to attract new members and potential new chapter chairmen to Reno. A major effort on the part of the board of directors and the membership at large produced a successful convention that generated 37 new life members and sowed the seeds that would produce several new chapters.

Along with the convention came a move of the headquarters from Redding to Reno and hiring of new staff who would lead the Mule Deer Foundation through a year of modest success. In 1992, seven successful banquets were conducted; however, underlying the success was concern that the financial strain of expanding the membership and completing projects could jeopardize the Foundation.

With a clamoring for more project dollars, the Mule Deer Foundation board of directors made the decision to name Board Chairman David Stevens acting president in an emergency situation. The intent was to reduce overhead and use as much of the Foundation's funds as possible for fieldwork. During this time period, despite many failures, the roots of success began to take hold. Between January and September of 1994, the Mule Deer Foundation conducted 17 banquets, in five Western states. Unrest with some successful chapters was overshadowed by membership expansion, project success, and an infusion of new blood from new chapters.

In 1994, the Foundation's newsletter, *Insights*, took major steps forward, providing the membership with a timely and reliable source of information and feedback. The eight to twelve page, two-color newsletter was attractive, but many members lobbied for a full-fledged magazine. In early 1994, the Mule Deer Foundation board of directors, under Chairman Stevens, agreed to expand the board from six to fifteen members. This expansion of the board made room for the addition of members with a variety of expertise and added extra manpower to the board. In addition, several chapter chairmen were named as board members, a first within the Mule Deer Foundation.

In 1995, the Foundation's magazine, *Mule Deer*, was revived with 36 pages in the Fall 1995 issue and expanded to 44 pages for the Winter 1995 issue. The magazine remains a quarterly publication. A major expense and major commitment by the board of directors created a magazine that expressed both the beauty of mule deer and the problems they faced. The magazine was an instant success with much of the membership and gave the organization more stability and exposure than it had experienced in past years.

By 1995, the Mule Deer Foundation held more than 20 successful banquets in five states. Larry Minkler was hired in late 1995 as president and C.E.O. of the Mule Deer Foundation. Under his leadership the number of chapters grew to 43 by 1996. The organization focused on growth, and, for the first time, chapter development became an organizational strength. In 1996, with field directors in six regions and events scheduled as far east as Missouri, the Mule Deer Foundation expanded numerically and geographically to more than 5,000 paid members who paid annual membership fees of between $25 for regular membership to $800 for life membership. Corporate and outfitter membership categories are also available.

Despite the continued growth and obvious successes, the Mule Deer

Foundation still has miles to travel before it can truly be a force for the preservation of mule deer. The realization of the dream of two mule deer hunters has come to involve many thousands of others. They have worked together and sometimes disagreed on visions of the route to success, but a great call has prevailed. The same emotions that moved two deer hunters to create a foundation for the protection of the species has propelled many others into the effort.

The Mule Deer Foundation will last beyond those who created it, nurtured it, and endured. In an ever-changing world, it will continue to be a conservation voice for mule deer and their allies. Only those with strong wills and a clear vision can overcome the adversity of a complex society where some will select preservation over conservation. The sacrifices that many individuals have made for the benefit of mule deer will yield returns for many years to come.

Rich Fletcher of Livermore, California, is editor of MULE DEER *magazine, the official national publication of the Mule Deer Foundation. Rich organized the Livermore-Pleasanton Chapter of the Mule Deer Foundation in 1992 and spent two years as its chairman. He joined the MDF board of directors and in 1995 was asked to edit* MULE DEER *magazine. He has written two books about hunting. For more information about The Mule Deer Foundation, write them at 1005 Terminal Way, Suite 140, Reno, NV 89502. Call them at (800) 344-2825.*

Records of North American
Big Game

BOONE AND CROCKETT CLUB

250 Station Drive
Missoula, MT 59801
(406) 542-1888

Minimum Score: Awards All-time
360   375

**TYPICAL
AMERICAN ELK (WAPITI)**

Detail of Point
Measurement

Abnormal Points	
Right Antler	Left Antler
2 5/8	

	Right Antler	Left Antler
Subtotals	2 5/8	
Total to E	2 5/8	

SEE OTHER SIDE FOR INSTRUCTIONS				Column 1 Spread Credit	Column 2 Right Antler	Column 3 Left Antler	Column 4 Difference
A. No. Points on Right Antler	8	No. Points on Left Antler	7				
B. Tip to Tip Spread	39 6/8	C. Greatest Spread	51 6/8				
D. Inside Spread of Main Beams	45 4/8	(Credit May Equal But Not Exceed Longer Antler)		45 4/8			
E. Total of Lengths of Abnormal Points							2 5/8
F. Length of Main Beam					55 5/8	59 5/8	4
G-1. Length of First Point					20 5/8	20 5/8	--
G-2. Length of Second Point					27 3/8	25 5/8	1 6/8
G-3. Length of Third Point					20	18 5/8	1 3/8
G-4. Length of Fourth Point					22 4/8	21 5/8	7/8
G-5. Length of Fifth Point					15 7/8	15 4/8	3/8
G-6. Length of Sixth Point, If Present					11 7/8	7 3/8	4 4/8
G-7. Length of Seventh Point, If Present							
H-1. Circumference at Smallest Place Between First and Second Points					12 1/8	11 2/8	7/8
H-2. Circumference at Smallest Place Between Second and Third Points					7 5/8	7 5/8	--
H-3. Circumference at Smallest Place Between Third and Fourth Points					7 7/8	8	1/8
H-4. Circumference at Smallest Place Between Fourth and Fifth Points					8	9	1
			TOTALS	45 4/8	209 4/8	204 7/8	17 4/8

ADD	Column 1	45 4/8	Exact Locality Where Killed: Dark Canyon, Colorado
	Column 2	209 4/8	Date Killed: 1899 Hunter: John Plute
	Column 3	204 7/8	Owner: Ed Rozman
	Subtotal	459 7/8	Owner's Address:
SUBTRACT Column 4		17 4/8	Guide's Name and Address:
	FINAL SCORE	442 3/8	Remarks: (Mention Any Abnormalities or Unique Qualities)

I certify that I have measured this trophy on ___8 February___ 19 _62_

at (address) __American Museum of Natural History__ City _New York_ State _NY_

and that these measurements and data are, to the best of my knowledge and belief, made in
accordance with the instructions given.

Witness: _____ Signature: ___Elmer M. Rusten___

B&C Official Measurer ⬚⬚⬚⬚

I.D. Number

INSTRUCTIONS FOR MEASURING TYPICAL AMERICAN ELK (WAPITI)

All measurements must be made with a 1/4-inch wide flexible steel tape to the nearest one-eighth of an inch. Wherever it is necessary to change direction of measurement, mark a control point and swing tape at this point. (Note: A flexible steel cable can be used to measure points and main beams only.) Enter fractional figures in eighths, without reduction. Official measurements cannot be taken until the antlers have air dried for at least 60 days after the animal was killed.

A. Number of Points on Each Antler: To be counted a point, the projection must be at least one inch long, with length exceeding width at one inch or more of length. All points are measured from tip of point to nearest edge of beam as illustrated. Beam tip is counted as a point but not measured as a point.

B. Tip to Tip Spread is measured between tips of main beams.

C. Greatest Spread is measured between perpendiculars at a right angle to the center line of the skull at widest part, whether across main beams or points.

D. Inside Spread of Main Beams is measured at a right angle to the center line of the skull at widest point between main beams. Enter this measurement again as the Spread Credit if it is less than or equal to the length of the longer antler; if greater, enter longer antler length for Spread Credit.

E. Total of Lengths of all Abnormal Points: Abnormal Points are those non-typical in location (such as points originating from a point or from bottom or sides of main beam) or pattern (extra points, not generally paired). Measure in usual manner and record in appropriate blanks.

F. Length of Main Beam is measured from lowest outside edge of burr over outer curve to the most distant point of what is, or appears to be, the main beam. The point of beginning is that point on the burr where the center line along the outer curve of the beam intersects the burr, then following generally the line of the illustration.

G-1-2-3-4-5-6-7. Length of Normal Points: Normal points project from the top or front of the main beam in the general pattern illustrated. They are measured from nearest edge of main beam over outer curve to tip. Lay the tape along the outer curve of the beam so that the top edge of the tape coincides with the top edge of the beam on both sides of point to determine the baseline for point measurement. Record point length in appropriate blanks.

H-1-2-3-4. Circumferences are taken as detailed for each measurement.

FAIR CHASE STATEMENT FOR ALL HUNTER-TAKEN TROPHIES

FAIR CHASE, as defined by the Boone and Crockett Club, is the ethical, sportsmanlike and lawful taking of any free-ranging wild game animal in a manner that does not give the hunter an improper or unfair advantage over such game animals.

Use of any of the following methods in the taking of game shall be deemed **UNFAIR CHASE** and unsportsmanlike:

I. Spotting or herding game from the air, followed by landing in its vicinity for the purpose of pursuit and shooting;

II. Herding, pursuing, or shooting game from any motorboat or motor vehicle;

III. Use of electronic devices for attracting, locating, or observing game, or for guiding the hunter to such game;

IV. Hunting game confined by artificial barriers, including escape-proof fenced enclosures, or hunting game transplanted solely for the purpose of commercial shooting;

V. Taking of game in a manner not in full compliance with the game laws or regulations of the federal government or of any state, province, territory, or tribal council on reservations or tribal lands;

VI. Or as may otherwise be deemed unfair or unsportsmanlike by the Executive Committee of the Boone and Crockett Club.

I certify that the trophy scored on this chart was taken in **FAIR CHASE** as defined above by the Boone and Crockett Club. In signing this statement, I understand that if the information provided on this entry is found to be misrepresented or fraudulent in any respect, it will not be accepted into the Awards Program and all of my prior entries are subject to deletion from future editions of *Records of North American Big Game* and future entries may not be accepted.

Date: _____ Signature of Hunter:_____
(Signature must be witnessed by an Official Measurer or a Notary Public.)

Date: _____ Signature of Notary or Official Measurer:_____

37

Records of North American
Big Game

BOONE AND CROCKETT CLUB

250 Station Drive
Missoula, MT 59801
(406) 542-1888

Minimum Score: Awards All-time
385   385

NON-TYPICAL
AMERICAN ELK (WAPITI)

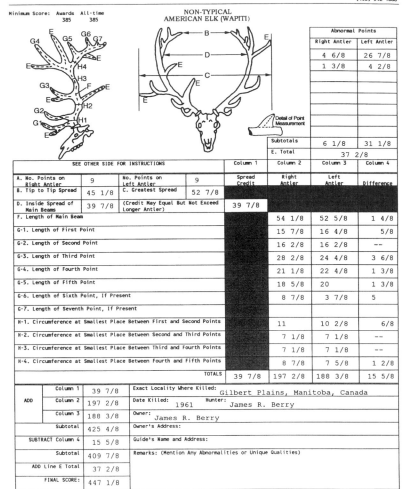

Abnormal Points		
	Right Antler	Left Antler
	4 6/8	26 7/8
	1 3/8	4 2/8
Subtotals	6 1/8	31 1/8
E. Total	37 2/8	

SEE OTHER SIDE FOR INSTRUCTIONS				Column 1	Column 2	Column 3	Column 4
				Spread Credit	Right Antler	Left Antler	Difference
A. No. Points on Right Antler	9	No. Points on Left Antler	9				
B. Tip to Tip Spread	45 1/8	C. Greatest Spread	52 7/8				
D. Inside Spread of Main Beams	39 7/8	(Credit May Equal But Not Exceed Longer Antler)		39 7/8			
F. Length of Main Beam					54 1/8	52 5/8	1 4/8
G-1. Length of First Point					15 7/8	16 4/8	5/8
G-2. Length of Second Point					16 2/8	16 2/8	--
G-3. Length of Third Point					28 2/8	24 4/8	3 6/8
G-4. Length of Fourth Point					21 1/8	22 4/8	1 3/8
G-5. Length of Fifth Point					18 5/8	20	1 3/8
G-6. Length of Sixth Point, If Present					8 7/8	3 7/8	5
G-7. Length of Seventh Point, If Present							
H-1. Circumference at Smallest Place Between First and Second Points					11	10 2/8	6/8
H-2. Circumference at Smallest Place Between Second and Third Points					7 1/8	7 1/8	--
H-3. Circumference at Smallest Place Between Third and Fourth Points					7 1/8	7 1/8	--
H-4. Circumference at Smallest Place Between Fourth and Fifth Points					8 7/8	7 5/8	1 2/8
			TOTALS	39 7/8	197 2/8	188 3/8	15 5/8

ADD	Column 1	39 7/8	Exact Locality Where Killed: Gilbert Plains, Manitoba, Canada
	Column 2	197 2/8	Date Killed: 1961 Hunter: James R. Berry
	Column 3	188 3/8	Owner: James R. Berry
	Subtotal	425 4/8	Owner's Address:
SUBTRACT Column 4		15 5/8	Guide's Name and Address:
	Subtotal	409 7/8	Remarks: (Mention Any Abnormalities or Unique Qualities)
ADD Line E Total		37 2/8	
FINAL SCORE:		447 1/8	

I certify that I have measured this trophy on ___6 May_____ 19 _92___

at (address) __Milwaukee Public Museum___ City _Milwaukee_____ State _WI_
and that these measurements and data are, to the best of my knowledge and belief, made in
accordance with the instructions given.

Witness: ___C. Randall Byers_____ Signature: ___John O. Cook III_____

B&C Official Measurer

I.D. Number

INSTRUCTIONS FOR MEASURING NON-TYPICAL AMERICAN ELK (WAPITI)

All measurements must be made with a 1/4-inch wide flexible steel tape to the nearest
one-eighth of an inch. Wherever it is necessary to change direction of measurement, mark a
control point and swing tape at this point. (Note: A flexible steel cable can be used to measure
points and main beams only.) Enter fractional figures in eighths, without reduction. Official
measurements cannot be taken until the antlers have air dried for at least 60 days after the
animal was killed.
   A. Number of Points on Each Antler: To be counted a point, the projection must be at least one
inch long, with length exceeding width at one inch or more of length. All points are measured
from tip of point to nearest edge of beam as illustrated. Beam tip is counted as a point but not
measured as a point.
   B. Tip to Tip Spread is measured between tips of main beams.
   C. Greatest Spread is measured between perpendiculars at a right angle to the center line of
the skull at widest part, whether across main beams or points.
   D. Inside Spread of Main Beams is measured at a right angle to the center line of the skull at
widest point between main beams. Enter this measurement again as the Spread Credit if it is less
than or equal to the length of the longer antler; if greater, enter longer antler length for
Spread Credit.
   E. Total of Lengths of all Abnormal Points: Abnormal Points are those non-typical in location
(such as points originating from a point or from bottom or sides of main beam) or pattern (extra
points, not generally paired). Measure in usual manner and record in appropriate blanks.
   F. Length of Main Beam is measured from lowest outside edge of burr over outer curve to the
most distant point of what is, or appears to be, the main beam. The point of beginning is that
point on the burr where the center line along the outer curve of the beam intersects the burr,
then following generally the line of the illustration.
   G-1-2-3-4-5-6-7. Length of Normal Points: Normal points project from the top or front of the
main beam in the general pattern illustrated. They are measured from nearest edge of main beam
over outer curve to tip. Lay the tape along the outer curve of the beam so that the top edge of
the tape coincides with the top edge of the beam on both sides of point to determine the baseline
for point measurement. Record point length in appropriate blanks.
   H-1-2-3-4. Circumferences are taken as detailed for each measurement.

FAIR CHASE STATEMENT FOR ALL HUNTER-TAKEN TROPHIES

FAIR CHASE, as defined by the Boone and Crockett Club, is the ethical, sportsmanlike and
lawful pursuit and taking of any free-ranging wild game animal in a manner that does not give
the hunter an improper or unfair advantage over such game animals.
   Use of any of the following methods in the taking of game shall be deemed UNFAIR CHASE
and unsportsmanlike:

   I. Spotting or herding game from the air, followed by landing in its vicinity for the
       purpose of pursuit and shooting;

   II. Herding, pursuing, or shooting game from any motorboat or motor vehicle;

   III. Use of electronic devices for attracting, locating, or observing game, or for guiding
         the hunter to such game;

   IV. Hunting game confined by artificial barriers, including escape-proof fenced
        enclosures, or hunting game transplanted solely for the purpose of commercial
        shooting;

   V. Taking of game in a manner not in full compliance with the game laws or regulations
       of the federal government or of any state, province, territory, or tribal council on
       reservations or tribal lands;

   VI. Or as may otherwise be deemed unfair or unsportsmanlike by the Executive Committee of
        the Boone and Crockett Club.

I certify that the trophy scored on this chart was taken in FAIR CHASE as defined above by the
Boone and Crockett Club. In signing this statement, I understand that if the information
provided on this entry is found to be misrepresented or fraudulent in any respect, it will not
be accepted into the Awards Program and all of my prior entries are subject to deletion from
future editions of Records of North American Big Game and future entries may not be accepted.

Date: _____ Signature of Hunter:_____
                           (Signature must be witnessed by an Official Measurer or
                           a Notary Public.)

Date: _____ Signature of Notary or Official Measurer:_____

39

Records of North American
Big Game

BOONE AND CROCKETT CLUB

250 Station Drive
Missoula, MT 59801
(406) 542-1888

Minimum Score: Awards 275 All-time 290

ROOSEVELT'S ELK

Crown Points		
	Right Antler	Left Antler
	11 2/8	12 7/8
	2 5/8	
	2	
	7 2/8	
I. Crown Points Total	36	

Abnormal Points		
	Right Antler	Left Antler
	1 5/8	

Detail of Point Measurement

Total to E	1 5/8

SEE OTHER SIDE FOR INSTRUCTIONS

				Column 1 Spread Credit	Column 2 Right Antler	Column 3 Left Antler	Column 4 Difference
A. No. Points on Right Antler	11	No. Points on Left Antler	8				
B. Tip to Tip Spread	39	C. Greatest Spread	46 4/8				
D. Inside Spread of Main Beams	36 1/8	(Credit May Equal But Not Exceed Longer Antler)		36 1/8			
E. Total of Lengths of Abnormal Points							1 5/8
F. Length of Main Beam					44 2/8	46 7/8	2 5/8
G-1. Length of First Point					15 7/8	18 1/8	2 2/8
G-2. Length of Second Point					16 6/8	17 1/8	3/8
G-3. Length of Third Point					19 6/8	20 4/8	6/8
G-4. Length of Fourth Point					17	15 5/8	1 3/8
G-5. Length of Fifth Point					12 2/8	12 2/8	
G-6. Length of Sixth Point, If Present					--	3 7/8	
G-7. Length of Seventh Point, If Present							
H-1. Circumference at Smallest Place Between First and Second Points					11 2/8	11 2/8	--
H-2. Circumference at Smallest Place Between Second and Third Points					7 7/8	7 3/8	4/8
H-3. Circumference at Smallest Place Between Third and Fourth Points					7 3/8	7 5/8	2/8
H-4. Circumference at Smallest Place Between Fourth and Fifth Points					7	6 4/8	4/8
			TOTALS	36 1/8	159 3/8	167 1/8	10 2/8

ADD	Column 1	36 1/8	Exact Locality Where Killed: Tsitika River, British Columbia, Canada
	Column 2	159 3/8	Date Killed: 4 Nov. 1989 Hunter: Wayne Coe
	Column 3	167 1/8	Owner: Wayne Coe
	Total of I	36	Owner's Address:
	Subtotal	398 5/8	Guide's Name and Address:
SUBTRACT Column 4		10 2/8	Remarks: (Mention Any Abnormalities or Unique Qualities)
FINAL SCORE		388 3/8	

I certify that I have measured this trophy on   6 May   19 92

at (address) Milwaukee Public Museum   City Milwaukee   State WI

and that these measurements and data are, to the best of my knowledge and belief, made in

accordance with the instructions given.

Witness: Larry Streiff   Signature: Michael C. Cupell

                                          B&C Official Measurer

                                          I.D. Number

INSTRUCTIONS FOR MEASURING ROOSEVELT'S ELK

All measurements must be made with a 1/4-inch wide flexible steel tape to the nearest one-eighth of an inch. Wherever it is necessary to change direction of measurement, mark a control point and swing tape at this point. (Note: A flexible steel cable can be used to measure points and main beams only.) Enter fractional figures in eighths, without reduction. Official measurements cannot be taken until the antlers have air dried for at least 60 days after the animal was killed.

A. Number of Points on Each Antler: to be counted a point, the projection must be at least one inch long, with length exceeding width at one inch or more of length. All points are measured from tip of point to nearest edge of beam as illustrated. Beam tip is counted as a point but not measured as a point.

B. Tip to Tip Spread is measured between tips of main beams.

C. Greatest Spread is measured between perpendiculars at a right angle to the center line of the skull at widest part, whether across main beams or points.

D. Inside Spread of Main Beams is measured at a right angle to the center line of the skull at widest point between main beams. Enter this measurement again as the Spread Credit if it is less than or equal to the length of the longer antler; if greater, enter longer antler length for Spread Credit.

E. Total of Lengths of all Abnormal Points: Abnormal Points are those non-typical in location (such as points originating from a point or from bottom or sides of main beam) or pattern (extra points, not generally paired), occurring before the G-4 point. Measure in usual manner and record in appropriate blanks.

F. Length of Main Beam is measured from lowest outside edge of burr over outer curve to the most distant point of what is, or appears to be, the main beam. The point of beginning is that point on the burr where the center line along the outer curve of the beam intersects the burr, then following generally the line of the illustration.

G-1-2-3-4-5-6-7. Length of Normal Points: Normal points project from the top or front of the main beam in the general pattern illustrated. They are measured from nearest edge of main beam over outer curve to tip. Lay the tape along the outer curve of the beam so that the top edge of the tape coincides with the top edge of the beam on both sides of point to determine the baseline for point measurement. Record point length in appropriate blanks.

H-1-2-3-4. Circumferences are as detailed for each measurement.

I. Crown Points: From the well-defined Royal on out to end of beam, all points other than the normal points in their typical locations are Crown Points. This includes points occurring on the Royal, on other normal points, on Crown Points, and on the bottom and sides of mainbeam after the Royal. Measure and record in appropriate blanks provided and add to score below.

FAIR CHASE STATEMENT FOR ALL HUNTER-TAKEN TROPHIES

FAIR CHASE, as defined by the Boone and Crockett Club, is the ethical, sportsmanlike and lawful pursuit and taking of any free-ranging wild game animal in a manner that does not give the hunter an improper or unfair advantage over such game animals.

Use of any of the following methods in the taking of game shall be deemed **UNFAIR CHASE** and unsportsmanlike:

    I.   Spotting or herding game from the air, followed by landing in its vicinity for the purpose of pursuit and shooting;

    II.   Herding, pursuing, or shooting game from any motorboat or motor vehicle;

    III. Use of electronic devices for attracting, locating, or observing game, or for guiding the hunter to such game;

    IV.   Hunting game confined by artificial barriers, including escape-proof fenced enclosures, or hunting game transplanted solely for the purpose of commercial shooting;

    V.   Taking of game in a manner not in full compliance with the game laws or regulations of the federal government or of any state, province, territory, or tribal council on reservations or tribal lands;

    VI.   Or as may otherwise be deemed unfair or unsportsmanlike by the Executive Committee of the Boone and Crockett Club.

I certify that the trophy scored on this chart was taken in **FAIR CHASE** as defined above by the Boone and Crockett Club. In signing this statement, I understand that if the information provided on this entry is found to be misrepresented or fraudulent in any respect, it will not be accepted into the Awards Program and all of my prior entries are subject to deletion from future editions of *Records of North American Big Game* and future entries may not be accepted.

Date: _____   Signature of Hunter:_____

                                    (Signature must be witnessed by an Official Measurer or a Notary Public.)

Date: _____   Signature of Notary or Official Measurer:_____

Records of North American
Big Game

BOONE AND CROCKETT CLUB

250 Station Drive
Missoula, MT 59801
(406) 542-1888

Minimum Score:	Awards	All-time
mule	180	190
Columbia	125	135
Sitka	100	108

TYPICAL
MULE DEER AND BLACKTAIL DEER

Kind of Deer: __Mule__

Detail of Point Measurement

Abnormal Points		
	Right Antler	Left Antler
	2 5/8	
Subtotals	2 5/8	
Total to E	2 5/8	

SEE OTHER SIDE FOR INSTRUCTIONS					Column 1	Column 2	Column 3	Column 4
A. No. Points on Right Antler	6	No. Points on Left Antler	5		Spread Credit	Right Antler	Left Antler	Difference
B. Tip to Tip Spread	28 5/8	C. Greatest Spread		33 2/8				
D. Inside Spread of Main Beams	30 7/8	(Credit May Equal But Not Exceed Longer Antler)			30 1/8			
E. Total of Lengths of Abnormal Points								2 5/8
F. Length of Main Beam						30 1/8	28 6/8	1 3/8
G-1. Length of First Point, If Present						2 3/8	2 6/8	3/8
G-2. Length of Second Point						22 4/8	22 3/8	1/8
G-3. Length of Third Point, If Present						14 2/8	14 3/8	1/8
G-4. Length of Fourth Point, If Present						14 6/8	13 6/8	1
H-1. Circumference at Smallest Place Between Burr and First Point						5 2/8	5 3/8	1/8
H-2. Circumference at Smallest Place Between First and Second Points						4 4/8	4 4/8	--
H-3. Circumference at Smallest Place Between Main Beam and Third Point						4	4 1/8	1/8
H-4. Circumference at Smallest Place Between Second and Fourth Points						4 2/8	4 4/8	2/8
				TOTALS	30 1/8	102	100 4/8	6 1/8

ADD	Column 1	30 1/8	Exact Locality Where Killed: Dolores Co., Colorado
	Column 2	102	Date Killed: 19 Oct. 1972 Hunter: Doug Burris, Jr.
	Column 3	100 4/8	Owner: Doug Burris, Jr.
	Subtotal	232 5/8	Owner's Address:
SUBTRACT Column 4		6 1/8	Guide's Name and Address:
	FINAL SCORE	226 4/8	Remarks: (Mention Any Abnormalities or Unique Qualities)

I certify that I have measured this trophy on ___27 February___ 19 _74_

at (address) _____ City _Atlanta_____ State _GA_

and that these measurements and data are, to the best of my knowledge and belief, made in accordance with the instructions given.

Witness: ____B.A. Fashingbauer_____ Signature: ___Arnold O. Haugen____

B&C Official Measurer

I.D. Number

INSTRUCTIONS FOR MEASURING TYPICAL MULE AND BLACKTAIL DEER

All measurements must be made with a 1/4-inch wide flexible steel tape to the nearest one-eighth of an inch. Wherever it is necessary to change direction of measurement, mark a control point and swing tape at this point. (Note: A flexible steel cable can be used to measure points and main beams only.) Enter fractional figures in eighths, without reduction. Official measurements cannot be taken until the antlers have air dried for at least 60 days after the animal was killed.

A. Number of Points on Each Antler: To be counted a point, the projection must be at least one inch long, with length exceeding width at one inch or more of length. All points are measured from tip of point to nearest edge of beam as illustrated. Beam tip is counted as a point but not measured as a point.

B. Tip to Tip Spread is measured between tips of main beams.

C. Greatest Spread is measured between perpendiculars at a right angle to the center line of the skull at widest part, whether across main beams or points.

D. Inside Spread of Main Beams is measured at a right angle to the center line of the skull at widest point between main beams. Enter this measurement again as the Spread Credit if it is less than or equal to the length of the longer antler; if greater, enter longer antler length for Spread Credit.

E. Total of Lengths of all Abnormal Points: Abnormal Points are those non-typical in location such as points originating from a point (exception: G-3 originates from G-2 in perfectly normal fashion) or from bottom or sides of main beam, or any points beyond the normal pattern of five (including beam tip) per antler. Measure each abnormal point in usual manner and enter in appropriate blanks.

F. Length of Main Beam is measured from lowest outside edge of burr over outer curve to the most distant point of what is, or appears to be, the Main Beam. The point of beginning is that point on the burr where the center line along the outer curve of the beam intersects the burr, then following generally the line of the illustration.

G-1-2-3-4. Length of Normal Points: Normal points are the brow tines and the upper and lower forks as shown in the illustration. They are measured from nearest edge of beam over outer curve to tip. Lay the tape along the outer curve of the beam so that the top edge of the tape coincides with the top edge of the beam on both sides of point to determine the baseline for point measurement. Record point lengths in appropriate blanks.

H-1-2-3-4. Circumferences are taken as detailed for each measurement. If brow point is missing, take H-1 and H-2 at smallest place between burr and G-2. If G-3 is missing, take H-3 halfway between the base and tip of G-2. If G-4 is missing, take H-4 halfway between G-2 and tip of main beam.

FAIR CHASE STATEMENT FOR ALL HUNTER-TAKEN TROPHIES

FAIR CHASE, as defined by the Boone and Crockett Club, is the ethical, sportsmanlike and lawful pursuit and taking of any free-ranging wild game animal in a manner that does not give the hunter an improper or unfair advantage over such game animals.

Use of any of the following methods in the taking of game shall be deemed **UNFAIR CHASE** and unsportsmanlike:

   I.   Spotting or herding game from the air, followed by landing in its vicinity for the purpose of pursuit and shooting;

  II.   Herding, pursuing, or shooting game from any motorboat or motor vehicle;

 III.   Use of electronic devices for attracting, locating, or observing game, or for guiding the hunter to such game;

 IV.   Hunting game confined by artificial barriers, including escape-proof fenced enclosures, or hunting game transplanted solely for the purpose of commercial shooting;

  V.   Taking of game in a manner not in full compliance with the game laws or regulations of the federal government or of any state, province, territory, or tribal council on reservations or tribal lands;

 VI.   Or as may otherwise be deemed unfair or unsportsmanlike by the Executive Committee of the Boone and Crockett Club.

I certify that the trophy scored on this chart was taken in **FAIR CHASE** as defined above by the Boone and Crockett Club. In signing this statement, I understand that if the information provided on this entry is found to be misrepresented or fraudulent in any respect, it will not be accepted into the Awards Program and all of my prior entries are subject to deletion from future editions of *Records of North American Big Game* and future entries may not be accepted.

Date: _____ Signature of Hunter: _____
(Signature must be witnessed by an Official Measurer or a Notary Public.)

Date: _____ Signature of Notary or Official Measurer:_____

43

Records of North American
Big Game

BOONE AND CROCKETT CLUB

250 Station Drive
Missoula, MT 59801
(406) 542-1888

Minimum Score: Awards All-time
215   230

**NON-TYPICAL
MULE DEER**

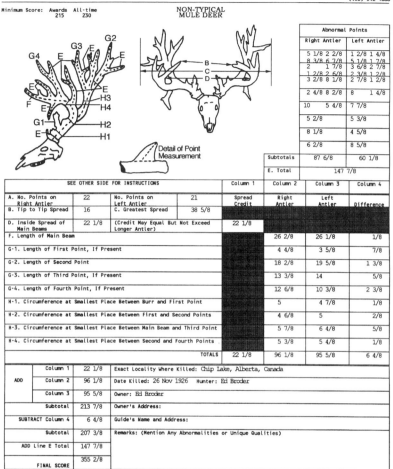

Detail of Point
Measurement

Abnormal Points		
	Right Antler	Left Antler
	5 1/8 2 2/8	1 2/8 1 4/8
	8 3/8 6 7/8	5 1/8 1 7/8
	2 1 7/8	3 6/8 2 7/8
	1 2/8 2 6/8	2 3/8 1 2/8
	3 2/8 8 1/8	2 7/8 1 2/8
	2 4/8 8 2/8	8 1 4/8
	10 5 4/8	7 7/8
	5 2/8	5 3/8
	8 1/8	4 5/8
	6 2/8	8 5/8
Subtotals	87 6/8	60 1/8
E. Total	147 7/8	

SEE OTHER SIDE FOR INSTRUCTIONS				Column 1	Column 2	Column 3	Column 4
A. No. Points on Right Antler	22	No. Points on Left Antler	21	Spread Credit	Right Antler	Left Antler	Difference
B. Tip to Tip Spread	16	C. Greatest Spread	38 5/8				
D. Inside Spread of Main Beams	22 1/8	(Credit May Equal But Not Exceed Longer Antler)		22 1/8			
F. Length of Main Beam					26 2/8	26 1/8	1/8
G-1. Length of First Point, If Present					4 4/8	3 5/8	7/8
G-2. Length of Second Point					18 2/8	19 5/8	1 3/8
G-3. Length of Third Point, If Present					13 3/8	14	5/8
G-4. Length of Fourth Point, If Present					12 6/8	10 3/8	2 3/8
H-1. Circumference at Smallest Place Between Burr and First Point					5	4 7/8	1/8
H-2. Circumference at Smallest Place Between First and Second Points					4 6/8	5	2/8
H-3. Circumference at Smallest Place Between Main Beam and Third Point					5 7/8	6 4/8	5/8
H-4. Circumference at Smallest Place Between Second and Fourth Points					5 3/8	5 4/8	1/8
			TOTALS	22 1/8	96 1/8	95 5/8	6 4/8

ADD	Column 1	22 1/8	Exact Locality Where Killed: Chip Lake, Alberta, Canada
	Column 2	96 1/8	Date Killed: 26 Nov 1926 Hunter: Ed Broder
	Column 3	95 5/8	Owner: Ed Broder
	Subtotal	213 7/8	Owner's Address:
SUBTRACT Column 4		6 4/8	Guide's Name and Address:
	Subtotal	207 3/8	Remarks: (Mention Any Abnormalities or Unique Qualities)
ADD Line E Total		147 7/8	
		355 2/8	
FINAL SCORE			

I certify that I have measured this trophy on __24 February_____ 19 _62___

at (address) __American Museum of Natural History__ City __New York_____ State __NY__
and that these measurements and data are, to the best of my knowledge and belief, made in
accordance with the instructions given.

Witness: _____Grancel Fitz_____ · ___ Signature: ____John E. Hammett_____

B&C Official Measurer

I.D. Number

INSTRUCTIONS FOR MEASURING NON-TYPICAL MULE DEER

All measurements must be made with a 1/4-inch wide flexible steel tape to the nearest
one-eighth of an inch. Wherever it is necessary to change direction of measurement, mark a
control point and swing tape at this point. (Note: A flexible steel cable can be used to measure
points and main beams only.) Enter fractional figures in eighths, without reduction. Official
measurements cannot be taken until the antlers have air dried for at least 60 days after the
animal was killed.

A. Number of Points on Each Antler: To be counted a point, the projection must be at least
one inch long, with length exceeding width at one inch or more of length. All points are measured
from tip of point to nearest edge of beam as illustrated. Beam tip is counted as a point but not
measured as a point.

B. Tip to Tip Spread is measured between tips of main beams.

C. Greatest Spread is measured between perpendiculars at a right angle to the center line of
the skull at widest part, whether across main beams or points.

D. Inside Spread of Main Beams is measured at a right angle to the center line of the skull at
widest point between main beams. Enter this measurement again as the Spread Credit if it is less
than or equal to the length of the longer antler; if greater, enter longer antler length for
Spread Credit.

E. Total of Lengths of all Abnormal Points: Abnormal Points are those non-typical in location
such as points originating from a point (exception: G-3 originates from G-2 in perfectly normal
fashion) or from bottom or sides of main beam, or any points beyond the normal pattern of five
(including beam tip) per antler. Measure each abnormal point in usual manner and enter in
appropriate blanks.

F. Length of Main Beam is measured from lowest outside edge of burr over outer curve to the
most distant point of what is, or appears to be, the main beam. The point of beginning is that
point on the burr where the center line along the outer curve of the beam intersects the burr,
then following generally the line of the illustration.

G-1-2-3-4. Length of Normal Points: Normal points are the brow tines and the upper and lower
forks as shown in the illustration. They are measured from nearest edge of main beam over outer
curve to tip. Lay the tape along the outer curve of the beam so that the top edge of the tape
coincides with the top edge of the beam on both sides of point to determine the baseline for point
measurement. Record point lengths in appropriate blanks.

H-1-2-3-4. Circumferences are taken as detailed for each measurement. If brow point is
missing, take H-1 and H-2 at smallest place between burr and G-2. If G-3 is missing, take H-3
halfway between the base and tip of G-2. If G-4 is missing, take H-4 halfway between G-2 and tip
of main beam.

FAIR CHASE STATEMENT FOR ALL HUNTER-TAKEN TROPHIES

FAIR CHASE, as defined by the Boone and Crockett Club, is the ethical, sportsmanlike and
lawful pursuit and taking of any free-ranging wild game animal in a manner that does not give
the hunter an improper or unfair advantage over such game animals.
Use of any of the following methods in the taking of game shall be deemed UNFAIR CHASE
and unsportsmanlike:

    I.   Spotting or herding game from the air, followed by landing in its vicinity for the
        purpose of pursuit and shooting;

   II.   Herding, pursuing, or shooting game from any motorboat or motor vehicle;

 III.   Use of electronic devices for attracting, locating, or observing game, or for guiding
        the hunter to such game;

  IV.   Hunting game confined by artificial barriers, including escape-proof fenced
        enclosures, or hunting game transplanted solely for the purpose of commercial
        shooting;

   V.   Taking of game in a manner not in full compliance with the game laws or regulations
        of the federal government or of any state, province, territory, or tribal council on
        reservations or tribal lands;

  VI.   Or as may otherwise be deemed unfair or unsportsmanlike by the Executive Committee of
        the Boone and Crockett Club.

I certify that the trophy scored on this chart was taken in FAIR CHASE as defined above by the
Boone and Crockett Club. In signing this statement, I understand that if the information
provided on this entry is found to be misrepresented or fraudulent in any respect, it will not
be accepted into the Awards Program and all of my prior entries are subject to deletion from
future editions of *Records of North American Big Game* and future entries may not be accepted.

Date: _____ Signature of Hunter:_____
(Signature must be witnessed by an Official Measurer or
a Notary Public.)

Date: _____ Signature of Notary or Official Measurer:_____

TOP 10 AMERICAN ELK LISTINGS INDEX

Tabulations of Recorded American Elk

The trophy data shown on the following pages are taken from score charts in the records archives of the Boone and Crockett Club. A comparison of the rankings of this book with those of the first edition of *Records of North American Elk and Mule Deer* will reveal many significant differences. This is primarily due to the addition of numerous trophies from the 21st (1989-1991) and the 22nd (1992-1994) Awards Programs, including 13 new state/provincial records.

American elk (wapiti) are found in many Western states and are a favored trophy species by hunters. Geographic boundaries are not described, as elk racks can be easily distinguished from the other deer categories. Geographic boundaries are described for the smaller antlered Roosevelt's elk, to prevent entry of American elk into the Roosevelt's elk category.

The scores and ranks shown are final, except for the trophies shown with an asterisk (*). The asterisk identifies entry scores subject to final certification by an Awards Panel of Judges. The asterisk can be removed (except in the case of a potential World's Record) by the submission of two additional, independent scorings by Official Measurers of the Boone and Crockett Club. The Records Committee of the Club will review the three scorings available (original plus two additional) and determine which, if any, will be accepted in lieu of the Judges' Panel measurement. When the score has been accepted as final by the Records Committee, the asterisk will be removed in future editions of this book and the all-time records book, *Records of North American Big Game*. In the case of a potential World's Record, the trophy must come before a Judges' Panel at the end of an entry period. Only a Judges' Panel can certify a World's Record and finalize its score. Asterisked trophies are unranked at the end of their category.

Photograph by Wm. H. Nesbitt

ARIZONA STATE RECORD (NEW)
TYPICAL AMERICAN ELK
SCORE: 421⁴⁄₈
Locality: Gila Co.   Date: 1985
Hunter: James C. Littleton

ARIZONA
TYPICAL AMERICAN ELK

Score	Length of Main Beam R	L	Inside Spread	Greatest Spread	Circumference at Smallest Place between First and Second Points R	L	Number of Points R	L	Total of Lengths Abnormal Points	All-Time Rank	State Rank
	◆ Locality / Hunter / Owner / Date Killed										
421⁴⁄₈	55⁴⁄₈	58²⁄₈	39	45¹⁄₈	11²⁄₈	10⁶⁄₈	7	7	0	3	1
	◆ Gila County / James C. Littleton / James C. Littleton / 1985										
405⁷⁄₈	53⁴⁄₈	55⁵⁄₈	44⁶⁄₈	48⁷⁄₈	8⁵⁄₈	8⁵⁄₈	6	8	7⁵⁄₈	15	2
	◆ Ft. Apache Res. / Roy R. Blythe / Roy R. Blythe / 1970										
401⁷⁄₈	57⁴⁄₈	58⁴⁄₈	42⁴⁄₈	48⁴⁄₈	9⁴⁄₈	9²⁄₈	6	7	2⁷⁄₈	20	3
	◆ Apache County / Bruce R. Keller / Bruce R. Keller / 1987										
399³⁄₈	58³⁄₈	58	49³⁄₈	55⁶⁄₈	9²⁄₈	9¹⁄₈	6	6	0	30	4
	◆ Coconino County / Terry J. Rice / Terry J. Rice / 1979										
396⁶⁄₈	56¹⁄₈	56³⁄₈	43⁴⁄₈	47³⁄₈	9⁷⁄₈	10⁶⁄₈	6	6	0	38	5
	◆ Volunteer Canyon / Lamar Haines / Lamar Haines / 1960										
395	59⁴⁄₈	59	44⁶⁄₈	50	7⁷⁄₈	7⁷⁄₈	7	7	0	44	6
	◆ Apache County / R. Steve Bass / R. Steve Bass / 1993										
393⁷⁄₈	57¹⁄₈	58	43⁷⁄₈	48⁷⁄₈	8	8	6	6	0	54	7
	◆ Apache County / T.R. Tidwell / T.R. Tidwell / 1983										
392³⁄₈	54	54⁶⁄₈	41⁷⁄₈	46³⁄₈	9⁴⁄₈	10	6	6	0	64	8
	◆ Apache County / McLean Bowman / McLean Bowman / 1989										
390⁶⁄₈	57³⁄₈	57²⁄₈	51²⁄₈	53¹⁄₈	8⁶⁄₈	8⁴⁄₈	6	6	0	72	9
	◆ Apache County / Robert M. Brittingham / Robert M. Brittingham / 1990										
388³⁄₈	53⁵⁄₈	55	47¹⁄₈	50²⁄₈	9	9³⁄₈	7	6	0	91	10
	◆ Coconino County / Picked Up / Tim Cotten / PR 1982										
388²⁄₈	52⁵⁄₈	51³⁄₈	39	48⁷⁄₈	10¹⁄₈	10¹⁄₈	6	6	0	92	11
	◆ Gila County / Fred B. Dickey / Fred B. Dickey / 1984										
386⁴⁄₈	56²⁄₈	54⁶⁄₈	44	50¹⁄₈	8⁵⁄₈	8⁶⁄₈	6	6	0	117	12
	◆ Coconino County / Lee Clemson / Lee Clemson / 1974										
386¹⁄₈	55¹⁄₈	54²⁄₈	53¹⁄₈	54	7³⁄₈	7¹⁄₈	6	6	0	122	13
	◆ Apache County / Don K. Callahan / Don K. Callahan / 1993										
385⁶⁄₈	52⁴⁄₈	56	41³⁄₈	48¹⁄₈	9	8⁴⁄₈	7	8	1⁷⁄₈	128	14
	◆ Apache County / Jay A. Kellett / Jay A. Kellett / 1993										
385⁵⁄₈	59⁶⁄₈	56⁶⁄₈	41²⁄₈	45³⁄₈	8⁷⁄₈	9³⁄₈	7	8	2⁷⁄₈	130	15
	◆ Ft. Apache Res. / Glen Daly / Glen Daly / 1957										
385²⁄₈	53³⁄₈	52²⁄₈	41¹⁄₈	48¹⁄₈	10¹⁄₈	9⁷⁄₈	6	7	1⁷⁄₈	137	16
	◆ Apache County / Herman C. Meyer / Herman C. Meyer / 1991										
384⁶⁄₈	54	54	50	62⁷⁄₈	10¹⁄₈	10	7	6	9⁶⁄₈	143	17
	◆ Hualapai Indian Res. / Tod Reichert / Tod Reichert / 1975										

Score	Length of Main Beam R	L	Inside Spread	Greatest Spread	Circumference at Smallest Place between First and Second Points R	L	Number of Points R	L	Total of Lengths Abnormal Points	All-Time Rank	State Rank
	♦ Locality / Hunter / Owner / Date Killed										
384 6/8	56 2/8	58 4/8	44	49	9 4/8	9 6/8	6	6	0	143	17
	♦ *Ft. Apache Res. / Jim P. Caires / Jim P. Caires / 1978*										
384 6/8	60	60 2/8	44 3/8	47 1/8	9 5/8	10	7	7	4 1/8	143	17
	♦ *Apache County / H.C. Meyer & J.T. Caid / Herman C. Meyer / 1982*										
384 5/8	57 6/8	56 6/8	40 5/8	43 7/8	8 7/8	8 7/8	6	6	0	147	20
	♦ *Graham County / Laura R. Williams / Laura R. Williams / 1986*										
384 2/8	61 7/8	64 6/8	40 6/8	45	11	10 4/8	6	8	2	154	21
	♦ *Ft. Apache Res. / Ralph C. Winkler, Jr. / Ralph C. Winkler, Jr. / 1977*										
384 2/8	58 1/8	60 6/8	49 3/8	52 7/8	10	8 3/8	6	7	1 1/8	154	21
	♦ *Apache County / Roy W. Baker / Roy W. Baker / 1980*										
383 5/8	54 6/8	55 3/8	54 4/8	58 5/8	8 2/8	8	6	7	6 5/8	163	23
	♦ *Apache County / Randall S. Ulmer / Randall S. Ulmer / 1987*										
383 2/8	55 5/8	53 1/8	45	50 2/8	10 3/8	10 5/8	6	7	0	166	24
	♦ *Coconino County / Jay E. Elmer / Jay E. Elmer / 1979*										
383	55	55	52 2/8	55 3/8	9 3/8	8 6/8	6	8	0	169	25
	♦ *Coconino County / Gene Bird / Gene Bird / 1972*										
382 6/8	56 7/8	55 4/8	48	50 6/8	9 3/8	10 5/8	6	6	0	173	26
	♦ *Apache County / William E. Moss / William E. Moss / 1985*										
382 3/8	49 6/8	52 1/8	35 5/8	42 1/8	11	10 1/8	6	6	0	180	27
	♦ *Morman Lake / Wayne A. Barry / John E. Rhea / 1965*										
382 2/8	58 4/8	62 6/8	48	53	8	7 4/8	6	6	0	182	28
	♦ *Williams / Oscar B. Skaggs / Oscar B. Skaggs / 1954*										
382 2/8	48	49 5/8	39 2/8	41	8 6/8	8 2/8	7	7	0	182	28
	♦ *Apache County / R. Steve Bass / R. Steve Bass / 1992*										
381 5/8	59 6/8	58	39 7/8	48 5/8	9 5/8	9 2/8	6	6	0	198	30
	♦ *Coconino County / George E. Long / George E. Long / 1985*										
381 5/8	58 2/8	57 2/8	39 5/8	47 2/8	9 7/8	10 1/8	6	6	0	198	30
	♦ *Apache County / McLean Bowman / McLean Bowman / 1990*										
380 5/8	54 3/8	53 4/8	42 3/8	53 3/8	10 2/8	9 3/8	6	6	0	216	32
	♦ *Apache County / Don L. Corley / Don L. Corley / 1984*										
380 4/8	52 4/8	52 6/8	41	49	9	8 6/8	6	6	0	220	33
	♦ *Payson / Harold Foard / Harold Foard / 1947*										
380 2/8	56 2/8	54 1/8	45	51 5/8	8 5/8	8 7/8	7	6	0	224	34
	♦ *Coconino County / Doug Kittredge / Doug Kittredge / 1975*										
380	53 2/8	56 2/8	50 3/8	55 1/8	10 3/8	9 7/8	7	6	1 7/8	230	35
	♦ *Ft. Apache Res. / George E. Crosby / George E. Crosby / 1957*										

ARIZONA TYPICAL AMERICAN ELK *(continued)*

Score	Length of Main Beam R	Length of Main Beam L	Inside Spread	Greatest Spread	Circumference at Smallest Place between First and Second Points R	Circumference at Smallest Place between First and Second Points L	Number of Points R	Number of Points L	Total of Lengths Abnormal Points	All-Time Rank	State Rank
♦ *Locality / Hunter / Owner / Date Killed*											
380	50 4/8	50 3/8	35	42 5/8	8	8 2/8	7	7	0	230	35
♦ *Navajo County / Gerry J. Tod / Gerry J. Tod / 1990*											
379 7/8	56 7/8	56 2/8	42	48 2/8	8 1/8	8 4/8	8	6	3 7/8	234	37
♦ *Graham County / Gerald Williams / Gerald Williams / 1985*											
379 3/8	60 1/8	61 1/8	45 5/8	49	8 7/8	8 3/8	6	6	0	245	38
♦ *Coconino County / Tammy J. Otero / Tammy J. Otero / 1984*											
379 2/8	58 3/8	57 2/8	41 6/8	45 3/8	9	9 4/8	6	6	0	249	39
♦ *Sierra Blanca Lake / Joseph A. Rozum / Joseph A. Rozum / 1965*											
379 2/8	56 3/8	57 1/8	56	53	8 6/8	8 3/8	6	0	0	249	39
♦ *Coconino County / Fred Williams / Fred Williams / 1990*											
379 1/8	56 6/8	56 1/8	45 5/8	49 3/8	9 5/8	9 3/8	6	7	0	256	41
♦ *Coconino County / Charles M. Krieger / Charles M. Krieger / 1992*											
378 4/8	56 3/8	57 3/8	50 6/8	54 1/8	10 1/8	9 1/8	6	6	0	266	42
♦ *Apache County / Robert E. Sterling / Robert E. Sterling / 1991*											
378 1/8	53 4/8	54 7/8	52 5/8	54 3/8	7 5/8	7 5/8	7	6	0	274	43
♦ *Navajo County / Stanford H. Atwood, Jr. / Stanford H. Atwood, Jr. / 1987*											
377 5/8	54 2/8	54 5/8	40 6/8	45 6/8	8 6/8	8 1/8	6	7	12 1/8	282	44
♦ *Apache County / A.C. Goodell / A.C. Goodell / 1963*											
377 4/8	52 2/8	53 1/8	42 2/8	48 2/8	8 1/8	8 6/8	6	6	0	284	45
♦ *Ft. Apache Res. / Picked Up / Gary Marsh / 1971*											
377 2/8	55 4/8	60 1/8	50 6/8	52 1/8	9 7/8	10 3/8	6	6	0	292	46
♦ *Show Low / Michael Pew / Michael Pew / 1964*											
377 2/8	54 2/8	54 2/8	44 2/8	50 7/8	8 2/8	8 1/8	7	7	0	292	46
♦ *Apache County / Donald E. Franklin / Donald E. Franklin / 1981*											
377	45 6/8	46 4/8	42 2/8	53 2/8	7 4/8	7 2/8	7	7	0	297	48
♦ *Navajo County / Melvin Nolte, Jr. / Melvin Nolte, Jr. / 1983*											
376	47 5/8	50 1/8	48 6/8	51	10 1/8	10 1/8	7	8	4 4/8	317	49
♦ *Apache County / William C. Moore / William C. Moore / 1983*											
375 7/8	52	54 6/8	37 3/8	41 4/8	9	8 5/8	6	6	0	320	50
♦ *Apache County / McLean Bowman / McLean Bowman / 1986*											
375 3/8	59 2/8	60 4/8	45 2/8	49 5/8	8 7/8	8 5/8	6	7	4 3/8	335	51
♦ *Apache County / Michael S. Muhlbauer / Michael S. Muhlbauer / 1989*											
375 3/8	58 1/8	59 1/8	37 3/8	44 7/8	8 4/8	8 6/8	6	6	0	335	51
♦ *Apache County / Picked Up / H. Jack Corbin / 1989*											
375 1/8	58 4/8	58 5/8	37 3/8	51	10 2/8	9 7/8	7	7	0	348	53
♦ *Tonto Lake / Louise F. Campbell / Louise F. Campbell / 1967*											

Score	Length of Main Beam R	L	Inside Spread	Greatest Spread	Circumference at Smallest Place between First and Second Points R	L	Number of Points R	L	Total of Lengths Abnormal Points	All-Time Rank	State Rank
	◆ *Locality / Hunter / Owner / Date Killed*										
375	57 7/8	57 5/8	49 4/8	51 4/8	6 7/8	7 3/8	6	6	0	350	54
	◆ *Coconino County / Arthur D. Ortiz / Arthur D. Ortiz / 1993*										
372	57 6/8	57 2/8	39 6/8	45 6/8	9 4/8	9 2/8	6	6	0	360	55
	◆ *Mohave County / David A. Thompson / David A. Thompson / 1991*										
369 3/8	57 1/8	55 7/8	46 1/8	50 1/8	10 2/8	11	7	7	0	362	56
	◆ *Coconino County / Carl M. Herrera / Carl M. Herrera / 1993*										
366 4/8	52 3/8	53 4/8	43 2/8	45 6/8	7 7/8	7 6/8	7	7	0	371	57
	◆ *Coconino County / Lloyd H. Farr / Lloyd H. Farr / 1994*										
365 2/8	50 4/8	53 6/8	39 6/8	43 2/8	10	9 6/8	7	7	0	375	58
	◆ *Navajo County / Joe B. Reynolds / Joe B. Reynolds / 1987*										
364 2/8	54	53 6/8	40 2/8	48	8 4/8	8 5/8	6	6	0	380	59
	◆ *Apache County / Jacob N. Allen / Jacob N. Allen / 1990*										
360 2/8	50 4/8	53 1/8	43 4/8	15 5/8	10 5/8	10 2/8	6	6	0	384	60
	◆ *Coconino County / Billie F. Bechtel / Billie F. Bechtel / 1984*										
398 3/8	60 3/8	65 4/8	50 5/8	52 6/8	8 5/8	8 3/8	7	8	6 6/8	*	*
	◆ *Navajo County / Marvin W. Wuertz / Marvin W. Wuertz / 1993*										
389 6/8	56 3/8	55 7/8	39 4/8	53	8 5/8	8 5/8	6	7	0	*	*
	◆ *Navajo County / Fred Fortier / Fred Fortier / 1985*										

Photograph Courtesy of David U. Inge

David U. Inge has taken two B&C bulls, one typical and one non- typical, on the Mescalero Apache Indian Reservation in south central New Mexico. David took this super 7x8 non-typical bull, scoring 392-4/8 points, during the 1989 season. One year later he scored again with a 7x7 typical bull that scores 381-6/8 points.

Photograph by Wm. H. Nesbitt

ARIZONA STATE RECORD
NON-TYPICAL AMERICAN ELK
SCORE: 445⅝
Locality: Apache Co.   Date: 1984
Hunter: Jerry J. Davis

ARIZONA

NON-TYPICAL AMERICAN ELK

Score	Length of Main Beam R	Length of Main Beam L	Inside Spread	Greatest Spread	Circumference at Smallest Place between First and Second Points R	Circumference at Smallest Place between First and Second Points L	Number of Points R	Number of Points L	Total of Lengths Abnormal Points	All-Time Rank	State Rank
♦ *Locality / Hunter / Owner / Date Killed*											
445 5/8	58	57 7/8	41 6/8	60 3/8	9 2/8	10	8	8	49 5/8	2	1
♦ *Apache County / Jerry J. Davis / Jerry J. Davis / 1984*											
423	53 4/8	52 3/8	40	57 4/8	8 2/8	8 6/8	8	10	47 4/8	5	2
♦ *Coconino County / James L. Ludvigson / James L. Ludvigson / 1985*											
422 3/8	51 6/8	52 2/8	40 3/8	45 4/8	10	9 6/8	8	8	44 6/8	6	3
♦ *Navajo County / John J. LoMonaco / John J. LoMonaco / 1992*											
417	57 5/8	56 5/8	48 4/8	50 6/8	10 6/8	9 6/8	7	6	20 6/8	8	4
♦ *Coconino County / Picked Up / Timothy A. Pender / 1993*											
408 5/8	57 1/8	58 1/8	41	47 5/8	9 5/8	11 1/8	8	8	38 7/8	12	5
♦ *Apache County / Herman C. Meyer / Herman C. Meyer / 1992*											
406 7/8	48 1/8	47 2/8	34 7/8	45 7/8	8 2/8	7 4/8	7	8	47	15	6
♦ *Apache County / Joe W. Carroll / Joe W. Carroll / 1982*											
403 3/8	49 5/8	58 3/8	38 2/8	49	9 1/8	9 6/8	8	8	23 3/8	19	7
♦ *Coconino County / Robert B. Krogh, Jr. / Robert B. Krogh, Jr. / 1983*											
395 3/8	51 5/8	50 7/8	40 4/8	48 3/8	8 7/8	9	7	7	12 3/8	39	8
♦ *Apache County / Mark W. White, Jr. / Mark W. White, Jr. / 1983*											
395 2/8	55 6/8	58 1/8	57	62 5/8	8 6/8	8 4/8	8	9	17 2/8	40	9
♦ *Coconino County / Edward Boutonnet / Edward Boutonnet / 1992*											
394 1/8	58	56 6/8	44 6/8	50 7/8	8 7/8	8	6	8	13 1/8	43	10
♦ *Apache County / Richard R. Childress / Richard R. Childress / 1991*											
393 6/8	54 5/8	55 6/8	46 6/8	57 2/8	7 5/8	7 4/8	7	8	32	44	11
♦ *Navajo County / Larry G. Van Hassle / Burke Hudnall / 1990*											
392 5/8	56 3/8	56 1/8	46 7/8	52 6/8	7 7/8	8	6	8	9 4/8	46	12
♦ *Coconino County / John L. Hontalas / John L. Hontalas / 1990*											
392	54 6/8	54	45 1/8	50	9 3/8	9 6/8	8	7	22 7/8	48	13
♦ *Mohave County / Alfred L. McMicking / Alfred L. McMicking / 1989*											
390 7/8	43 6/8	45 2/8	41	46 5/8	9 4/8	9 3/8	8	10	49 7/8	49	14
♦ *Apache County / Theodore E. Dugey, Jr. / Theodore E. Dugey, Jr. / 1978*											
385	57 2/8	57 3/8	36 7/8	45 7/8	10 4/8	10 5/8	7	6	13 1/8	57	15
♦ *Navajo County / David W. Baxter / David W. Baxter / 1991*											
385	55 5/8	55 4/8	42 1/8	62	9 1/8	9 1/8	8	7	30 7/8	57	15
♦ *Navajo County / Dennis K. Frandsen / Dennis K. Frandsen / 1993*											
412 5/8	51 5/8	51	43	50 5/8	9 3/8	9 3/8	9	8	22 3/8	*	*
♦ *Navajo County / John A. Gulius / John A. Gulius / 1990*											
408	53 5/8	53	40 6/8	50 6/8	9	9 1/8	7	8	30 4/8	*	*
♦ *Apache County / J.G. Brittingham & W. Dale / Jack G. Brittingham / 1987*											

Photograph Courtesy of Rocky Mountain Elk Foundation

COLORADO STATE RECORD
WORLD'S RECORD
TYPICAL AMERICAN ELK
SCORE: 442³/₈
Locality: Dark Canyon   Date: 1899
Hunter: John Plute
Owner: Ed Rozman

COLORADO
TYPICAL AMERICAN ELK

Score	Length of Main Beam R	L	Inside Spread	Greatest Spread	Circumference at Smallest Place between First and Second Points R	L	Number of Points R	L	Total of Lengths Abnormal Points	All-Time Rank	State Rank
♦ Locality / Hunter / Owner / Date Killed											
442 3/8	55 5/8	59 5/8	45 4/8	51 6/8	12 1/8	11 2/8	8	7	2 5/8	1	1
♦ Dark Canyon / John Plute / Ed Rozman / 1899											
407	56 7/8	56 6/8	43 4/8	53 4/8	9 4/8	8 4/8	8	7	0	13	2
♦ Summit County / Robert G. Young / Robert G. Young / 1967											
402 3/8	59 4/8	62 1/8	47 7/8	60 7/8	8 2/8	8 6/8	8	7	2 4/8	19	3
♦ San Miguel County / Lewis Fredrickson / Jay Scott / 1954											
400 4/8	59 4/8	61	48 4/8	61 1/8	8 2/8	8 5/8	8	7	2	26	4
♦ Routt County / Lewis Fredrickson / Lewis Fredrickson / 1953											
397 2/8	50 2/8	50 6/8	45 2/8	49 3/8	9 6/8	9 5/8	8	7	6	37	5
♦ Gunnison County / John R. Burritt / John R. Burritt / 1970											
392 4/8	51 3/8	51 1/8	42 3/8	58 5/8	7 7/8	7 7/8	7	7	10 5/8	63	6
♦ Buford / Picked Up / Robert T. Fulton / PR 1967											
392	54 6/8	56 6/8	45 2/8	51 4/8	10	10	6	6	0	66	7
♦ Jackson County / James A. Baller / North Park State Bank / 1969											
391 6/8	52 6/8	53 6/8	35 6/8	43 4/8	7 7/8	7 7/8	6	6	0	67	8
♦ Slater / W.J. Bracken / W.J. Bracken / 1963											
391 4/8	54 5/8	56 3/8	43 2/8	55 3/8	9 1/8	9	6	6	0	69	9
♦ Mt. Evans / Unknown / Frank Brady / 1874											
391 3/8	55 7/8	50 3/8	39 3/8	54 4/8	7 2/8	8 2/8	7	6	0	71	10
♦ Grand Lake / John Holzwarth / John Holzwarth / 1949											
390 2/8	51 1/8	52 1/8	49	63 3/8	9 2/8	8 7/8	7	6	2 2/8	76	11
♦ Las Animas County / Robert A. Schnee / Robert A. Schnee / 1993											
390	54 2/8	51 4/8	47 7/8	51 2/8	9 1/8	9 2/8	6	7	3 3/8	78	12
♦ Baca County / David B. Martin / David B. Martin / 1994											
388 6/8	50 6/8	47 2/8	45 6/8	49 2/8	10	9 4/8	7	6	0	90	13
♦ Larimer County / John Zimmerman / Ft. Collins Mus. / PR 1890											
386 2/8	52 4/8	54 1/8	48	50 1/8	8 7/8	9 1/8	6	6	0	120	14
♦ Delta County / Bert Johnson / Bert Johnson / 1974											
385 1/8	48 5/8	49 3/8	34 7/8	49 3/8	8 3/8	8 6/8	6	6	0	138	15
♦ Trappers Lake / Byron W. Kneff / Byron W. Kneff / 1954											
384 3/8	54 5/8	54 5/8	50 7/8	53 3/8	9 7/8	9 2/8	6	6	0	151	16
♦ Clear Creek County / John Wallace / John Wallace / 1973											
384	56 4/8	54	47	53 2/8	7 6/8	8 1/8	7	7	0	156	17
♦ Costilla County / William E. Carl / William E. Carl / 1967											

Score	Length of Main Beam		Inside Spread	Greatest Spread	Circumference at Smallest Place between First and Second Points		Number of Points		Total of Lengths Abnormal Points	All-Time Rank	State Rank
	R	L			R	L	R	L			
◆ *Locality / Hunter / Owner / Date Killed*											
383⁶⁄₈	54	51⁵⁄₈	46	57	8⁷⁄₈	9	6	6	0	161	18
◆ *Las Animas County / Michael W. Marbach / Michael W. Marbach / 1993*											
382⁴⁄₈	56⁶⁄₈	56⁷⁄₈	41⁶⁄₈	46³⁄₈	8⁷⁄₈	9²⁄₈	6	7	0	176	19
◆ *Summit County / Marshall Sherman / Marshall Sherman / 1966*											
382	53²⁄₈	51¹⁄₈	48	50⁶⁄₈	8⁷⁄₈	9¹⁄₈	6	6	0	190	20
◆ *Little Cimmaron / Newell Beauchamp / Bud Lovato / 1957*											
381³⁄₈	55⁴⁄₈	54⁵⁄₈	37⁴⁄₈	47⁵⁄₈	9⁶⁄₈	9¹⁄₈	7	7	2⁵⁄₈	203	21
◆ *Larimer County / Earl L. Erbes / Earl L. Erbes / 1972*											
380⁵⁄₈	50⁶⁄₈	54⁶⁄₈	47⁵⁄₈	54⁶⁄₈	9⁴⁄₈	9⁷⁄₈	6	6	0	216	22
◆ *Hayden / Mike Holliday / Mike Holliday / 1966*											
380⁵⁄₈	54²⁄₈	55	51³⁄₈	56²⁄₈	7⁷⁄₈	7⁴⁄₈	6	7	2²⁄₈	216	22
◆ *Chaffee County / Anton Purkat / Anton Purkat / 1972*											
380²⁄₈	53²⁄₈	55⁶⁄₈	55⁶⁄₈	57	9⁶⁄₈	9⁷⁄₈	7	7	0	224	24
◆ *Las Animas County / Picked Up / Crawford Ranch / 1987*											
378²⁄₈	51⁴⁄₈	52⁶⁄₈	50	58⁴⁄₈	9²⁄₈	10	6	7	4²⁄₈	272	25
◆ *White River / Art Wright / Art Wright / 1953*											
378	56¹⁄₈	56⁷⁄₈	44²⁄₈	48⁶⁄₈	7⁶⁄₈	7⁶⁄₈	7	6	9	276	26
◆ *Gunnison / Ed Lattimore, Jr. / Ed Lattimore, Jr. / 1966*											
377⁶⁄₈	51³⁄₈	52³⁄₈	45	49⁶⁄₈	8	8³⁄₈	7	7	0	279	27
◆ *Routt County / Tom Nidey / Tom Nidey / 1959*											
377⁴⁄₈	47⁵⁄₈	47²⁄₈	45	48⁶⁄₈	8⁴⁄₈	8⁵⁄₈	6	6	0	284	28
◆ *Gunnison County / Leo Welch / Leo Welch / 1972*											
376⁵⁄₈	58⁶⁄₈	56³⁄₈	48¹⁄₈	53	7⁶⁄₈	7⁶⁄₈	6	6	0	308	29
◆ *Granby / Melvin Van Lewen / Colo. Div. of Wildl. / 1961*											
376³⁄₈	48⁴⁄₈	49²⁄₈	40³⁄₈	51²⁄₈	8	8¹⁄₈	7	7	0	312	30
◆ *White River / Ron Vance / Ronald Crawford / 1957*											
376³⁄₈	49³⁄₈	49⁷⁄₈	41⁵⁄₈	55⁶⁄₈	7⁷⁄₈	7⁴⁄₈	6	6	0	312	30
◆ *Radium / Bill Mercer / Bill Mercer / 1964*											
376³⁄₈	55⁴⁄₈	55⁵⁄₈	39¹⁄₈	44⁵⁄₈	9	9	6	6	0	312	30
◆ *Gunnison County / Gerald J. Obertino / Gerald J. Obertino / 1986*											
376	60⁴⁄₈	59	44⁴⁄₈	50¹⁄₈	7⁵⁄₈	8	6	6	0	317	33
◆ *Almont / John Schwartz / John Schwartz / 1961*											
375⁶⁄₈	50³⁄₈	50⁶⁄₈	40⁴⁄₈	45⁷⁄₈	9⁴⁄₈	10⁴⁄₈	6	6	0	322	34
◆ *Crow Valley / Dale R. Leonard / Dale R. Leonard / 1961*											
375²⁄₈	55²⁄₈	52³⁄₈	47²⁄₈	51³⁄₈	8⁷⁄₈	8⁷⁄₈	8	8	2⁶⁄₈	342	35
◆ *Craig / Kenneth W. Cramer / Kenneth W. Cramer / 1960*											

COLORADO TYPICAL AMERICAN ELK *(continued)*

Score	Length of Main Beam R	L	Inside Spread	Greatest Spread	Circumference at Smallest Place between First and Second Points R	L	Number of Points R	L	Total of Lengths Abnormal Points	All-Time Rank	State Rank

♦ Locality / Hunter / Owner / Date Killed

Score	R	L	Inside Spread	Greatest Spread	R	L	R	L	Abnormal	All-Time	State
368 4/8	51 4/8	51 6/8	53	54 6/8	7 5/8	7 7/8	6	7	0	364	36

♦ *Rio Blanco County / P.R. Hays & J. Cook / Perry R. Hays / 1953*

| 364 6/8 | 54 2/8 | 56 | 40 4/8 | 45 1/8 | 9 | 8 6/8 | 6 | 6 | 0 | 377 | 37 |

♦ *Las Animas County / Ralph T. Geer / Ralph T. Geer / 1991*

| 364 4/8 | 53 2/8 | 53 1/8 | 42 2/8 | 45 2/8 | 8 3/8 | 8 7/8 | 6 | 6 | 0 | 378 | 38 |

♦ *Larimer County / Darrel D. Lemon / Darrel D. Lemon / 1993*

| 364 3/8 | 52 2/8 | 52 | 37 5/8 | 46 1/8 | 8 6/8 | 8 4/8 | 6 | 6 | 0 | 379 | 39 |

♦ *La Plata County / Carl L. Absher / Carl L. Absher / 1992*

| 414 6/8 | 55 3/8 | 58 3/8 | 53 3/8 | 56 4/8 | 13 5/8 | 13 | 9 | 7 | 9 5/8 | * | * |

♦ *Gunnison County / J.J. Carpenter / Hugh Carpenter / 1900*

| 391 1/8 | 57 5/8 | 57 3/8 | 42 4/8 | 49 1/8 | 10 3/8 | 10 3/8 | 6 | 7 | 0 | * | * |

♦ *Ouray County / Eugene D. Guilaroff / Eugene D. Guilaroff / 1973*

Photograph by J.T. Washburn

COLORADO STATE RECORD
NON-TYPICAL AMERICAN ELK
SCORE: 400
Locality: Routt Co.   Date: 1939
Hunter: William E. Goosman

COLORADO

NON-TYPICAL AMERICAN ELK

Score	Length of Main Beam		Inside Spread	Greatest Spread	Circumference at Smallest Place between First and Second Points		Number of Points		Total of Lengths Abnormal Points	All-Time Rank	State Rank
	R	L			R	L	R	L			
◆ Locality / Hunter / Owner / Date Killed											

| 400 | 55³⁄₈ | 53⁴⁄₈ | 42²⁄₈ | 47⁶⁄₈ | 9⁷⁄₈ | 9⁵⁄₈ | 6 | 7 | 13⁶⁄₈ | 34 | 1 |

◆ *Routt County / William E. Goosman / William E. Goosman / 1939*

IDAHO STATE RECORD
TYPICAL AMERICAN ELK
SCORE: 412⅝
Locality: Wieser River   Date: 1954
Hunter: Elmer Bacus

IDAHO

TYPICAL AMERICAN ELK

Score	Length of Main Beam R	Length of Main Beam L	Inside Spread	Greatest Spread	Circumference at Smallest Place between First and Second Points R	Circumference at Smallest Place between First and Second Points L	Number of Points R	Number of Points L	Total of Lengths Abnormal Points	All-Time Rank	State Rank
♦ *Locality / Hunter / Owner / Date Killed*											
412 5/8	51 6/8	51 1/8	42 5/8	47 4/8	10	9 1/8	9	8	2 2/8	11	1
♦ *Wieser River / Elmer Bacus / Elmer Bacus / 1954*											
400 4/8	59 1/8	60 1/8	42 6/8	49	9 3/8	10	7	7	0	26	2
♦ *Owyhee County / Cecil R. Coonts / Cecil R. Coonts / 1965*											
395	56 2/8	56 2/8	48 7/8	53 4/8	8 7/8	9	7	7	1 7/8	44	3
♦ *Salmon Natl. For. / Fred W. Thomson / Fred W. Thomson / 1964*											
394 4/8	53 4/8	53 2/8	46 4/8	54	8 7/8	8 7/8	6	6	0	47	4
♦ *Idaho County / L.M. White / L.M. White / 1977*											
393 5/8	56 2/8	52 4/8	42 5/8	49 7/8	9 1/8	9 4/8	7	7	0	55	5
♦ *Elmore County / Picked Up / Joe Adams / PR 1955*											
393 2/8	58 6/8	52 1/8	45 2/8	49	9 6/8	9 4/8	6	6	0	57	6
♦ *Winchester / Doyle Shriver / Doyle Shriver / 1954*											
390 6/8	59 6/8	58	42	46 2/8	8 7/8	9	7	7	0	72	7
♦ *Caribou County / Ken Homer / Ken Homer / 1963*											
389 3/8	56 5/8	60 5/8	43 7/8	57	8 3/8	8 2/8	6	6	0	85	8
♦ *Salmon River / Unknown / John M. Anderson / 1915*											
389 2/8	49 4/8	51 1/8	42 6/8	48 5/8	12 2/8	12 3/8	6	7	0	86	9
♦ *Nez Perce County / Picked Up / Michael Throckmorton / 1949*											
388	57 1/8	55 1/8	55	59	8 6/8	8 1/8	7	6	0	97	10
♦ *Medicine Lodge Creek / D.W. Marshall & E.J. Stacy / D.W. Marshall & E.J. Stacy / 1961*											
387 6/8	50 2/8	51 7/8	43 2/8	45 6/8	9 5/8	10 2/8	6	6	0	103	11
♦ *Fremont / Charles A. Preston / Charles A. Preston / 1963*											
386 4/8	49 2/8	50 3/8	39 6/8	46 4/8	8 6/8	9	7	7	0	117	12
♦ *Nez Perce County / H.H. Schnettler / H.H. Schnettler / 1957*											
386	53 7/8	55 4/8	51	57 7/8	9 6/8	9 6/8	6	6	0	125	13
♦ *Valley County / Denny Young / Kenny Poe / 1957*											
385 7/8	49 1/8	51 7/8	44 3/8	49 3/8	7 7/8	7 7/8	6	6	0	127	14
♦ *Shoshone County / Jerry Nearing / Jerry Nearing / 1976*											
385 5/8	53 2/8	53	40 3/8	47 4/8	8 4/8	8 1/8	6	6	0	130	15
♦ *Kootenai County / Arth Day / Arth Day / 1971*											
384 4/8	57	56 4/8	43 4/8	45	9 5/8	9 3/8	7	7	0	149	16
♦ *Bonneville County / David W. Anderson / David W. Anderson / 1967*											
384 4/8	53 2/8	53 7/8	43	46 7/8	8 5/8	8 2/8	7	7	0	149	16
♦ *Bonneville County / Keith W. Hadley / Keith W. Hadley / 1972*											

Score	Length of Main Beam		Inside Spread	Greatest Spread	Circumference at Smallest Place between First and Second Points		Number of Points		Total of Lengths Abnormal Points	All-Time Rank	State Rank
	R	L			R	L	R	L			
$383\frac{2}{8}$	$52\frac{2}{8}$	52	$41\frac{6}{8}$	$55\frac{2}{8}$	$9\frac{4}{8}$	$9\frac{2}{8}$	7	7	0	166	18
◆ *Nez Perce County / Thenton L. Todd / Thenton L. Todd / 1956*											
$382\frac{5}{8}$	$52\frac{3}{8}$	$52\frac{3}{8}$	$36\frac{5}{8}$	$45\frac{2}{8}$	$9\frac{2}{8}$	9	7	7	0	175	19
◆ *Kootenai County / Terry Cozad / Terry Cozad / 1968*											
$382\frac{2}{8}$	$54\frac{2}{8}$	$56\frac{6}{8}$	$44\frac{2}{8}$	49	9	$8\frac{4}{8}$	7	7	0	182	20
◆ *Clark County / John Larick, Jr. / John Larick, Jr. / 1963*											
381	48	$54\frac{4}{8}$	$40\frac{4}{8}$	47	$8\frac{5}{8}$	$8\frac{7}{8}$	7	8	0	211	21
◆ *Bonneville County / Mrs. E. LaRene Smith / Mrs. E. LaRene Smith / 1966*											
$379\frac{6}{8}$	52	$51\frac{6}{8}$	$36\frac{2}{8}$	$47\frac{5}{8}$	10	10	9	8	1	235	22
◆ *Adams County / William V. Baker / William V. Baker / 1976*											
$379\frac{5}{8}$	$53\frac{7}{8}$	$48\frac{2}{8}$	55	56	$8\frac{2}{8}$	$8\frac{4}{8}$	7	7	0	242	23
◆ *Valley County / Joe Gisler / Joe Gisler / 1961*											
379	$50\frac{4}{8}$	$51\frac{1}{8}$	$40\frac{6}{8}$	$44\frac{3}{8}$	9	$8\frac{6}{8}$	6	6	0	258	24
◆ *Big Creek / Picked Up / George Dovel / 1963*											
$378\frac{4}{8}$	$54\frac{3}{8}$	$55\frac{3}{8}$	$45\frac{2}{8}$	$48\frac{7}{8}$	$8\frac{6}{8}$	$8\frac{6}{8}$	6	6	0	266	25
◆ *Shoshone County / Edward L. Bradford / Edward L. Bradford / 1963*											
$378\frac{4}{8}$	$50\frac{1}{8}$	$50\frac{3}{8}$	$36\frac{2}{8}$	$44\frac{4}{8}$	$11\frac{5}{8}$	$11\frac{1}{8}$	8	7	0	266	25
◆ *Idaho County / Johnny Bliznak / Johnny Bliznak / 1990*											
$376\frac{5}{8}$	48	$50\frac{1}{8}$	$39\frac{3}{8}$	$50\frac{2}{8}$	$8\frac{5}{8}$	$8\frac{7}{8}$	7	7	0	308	27
◆ *Teton County / Edwin E. Schiess / Tim Schiess / 1966*											
$375\frac{6}{8}$	$52\frac{1}{8}$	$50\frac{4}{8}$	$37\frac{2}{8}$	$42\frac{2}{8}$	$8\frac{4}{8}$	$7\frac{7}{8}$	7	7	0	322	28
◆ *Shoshone County / Ralph H. Brandvold, Jr. / Ralph H. Brandvold, Jr. / 1983*											
375	$52\frac{6}{8}$	$52\frac{5}{8}$	$47\frac{4}{8}$	$54\frac{2}{8}$	$8\frac{6}{8}$	9	6	6	0	350	29
◆ *Fremont County / Eva Calonge / Eva Calonge / 1960*											
$366\frac{1}{8}$	$57\frac{3}{8}$	$57\frac{4}{8}$	$49\frac{1}{8}$	$54\frac{3}{8}$	$8\frac{6}{8}$	$9\frac{2}{8}$	6	7	0	372	30
◆ *Waverly Mts. / Wayne Lewis / Wayne Minkel / PR 1991*											
361	$50\frac{2}{8}$	$50\frac{4}{8}$	$38\frac{4}{8}$	$43\frac{3}{8}$	$8\frac{4}{8}$	$9\frac{4}{8}$	7	7	0	383	31
◆ *Valley County / Robert L. Dixon / Robert L. Dixon / 1963*											

Tom Wilkes (right) guided Butch Kuflak to this 389-5/8 point typical bull elk in 1990 in the Absaroka Wilderness Area of southwestern Montana. Butch received the first place award in the typical American elk category at B&C Club's 21st Big Game Awards Program held in Milwaukee, Wisconsin, in 1992.

Photograph by Wm. H. Nesbitt

IDAHO STATE RECORD
NON-TYPICAL AMERICAN ELK
SCORE: 403⅞
Locality: Shoshone Co.   Date: 1964
Hunter: Fred S. Scott
Owner: Mannie Moore

IDAHO

NON-TYPICAL AMERICAN ELK

Score	Length of Main Beam R	L	Inside Spread	Greatest Spread	Circumference at Smallest Place between First and Second Points R	L	Number of Points R	L	Total of Lengths Abnormal Points	All-Time Rank	State Rank

♦ Locality / Hunter / Owner / Date Killed

Score	Length of Main Beam R	L	Inside Spread	Greatest Spread	Circumference R	L	Number of Points R	L	Total Abnormal	All-Time Rank	State Rank
403 7/8	46 5/8	52	32 4/8	43 5/8	10 3/8	10 6/8	8	9	49 5/8	18	1

♦ *Shoshone County / Fred S. Scott / Mannie Moore / 1964*

| 402 4/8 | 53 1/8 | 49 4/8 | 47 2/8 | 52 2/8 | 8 4/8 | 8 5/8 | 7 | 11 | 28 2/8 | 25 | 2 |

♦ *Idaho / Unknown / William J. Barry / PR 1960*

| 393 3/8 | 50 2/8 | 48 4/8 | 41 2/8 | 70 1/8 | 9 5/8 | 10 1/8 | 8 | 7 | 106 5/8 | 45 | 3 |

♦ *Shoshone County / Hueh M. Kitzmiller / John M. Kitzmiller / 1974*

| 385 1/8 | 50 5/8 | 48 6/8 | 40 4/8 | 51 2/8 | 7 5/8 | 7 4/8 | 9 | 8 | 24 5/8 | 56 | 4 |

♦ *Latah County / James A. Carpenter / James A. Carpenter / 1985*

IOWA STATE RECORD (NEW)
TYPICAL AMERICAN ELK
SCORE: 387⅝

Locality: Cherokee Co.   Date: Prior to 1900
Hunter: C.A. Stiles
Owner: Jim Haas

IOWA

TYPICAL AMERICAN ELK

Score	Length of Main Beam		Inside Spread	Greatest Spread	Circumference at Smallest Place between First and Second Points		Number of Points		Total of Lengths Abnormal Points	All-Time Rank	State Rank
	R	L			R	L	R	L			
◆ Locality / Hunter / Owner / Date Killed											
387⅝	60²⁄₈	60	42⅞	51⅛	9	8⅞	7	7	0	105	1
◆ Cherokee County / C.A. Stiles / Jim Haas / PR 1900											

Photograph Courtesy of Jeff A. Newton

KANSAS STATE RECORD (NEW)
NON-TYPICAL AMERICAN ELK
SCORE: 402⅛
Locality: Morton Co.   Date: 1988
Hunter: Jeff A. Newton

KANSAS

NON-TYPICAL AMERICAN ELK

Score	Length of Main Beam		Inside Spread	Greatest Spread	Circumference at Smallest Place between First and Second Points		Number of Points		Total of Lengths Abnormal Points	All-Time Rank	State Rank
	R	L			R	L	R	L			
♦ Locality / Hunter / Owner / Date Killed											
402⅛	48⅝	49²⁄₈	41	53	11⅝	11⅞	7	8	19⅝	26	1
♦ Morton County / Jeff A. Newton / Jeff A. Newton / 1988											
398⁴⁄₈	52⅞	51⁴⁄₈	42⅜	46⅜	10⅛	10⅛	7	9	19⅜	36	2
♦ Morton County / Camron Paxton / Camron Paxton / 1987											

Photograph Courtesy of Rocky Mountain Elk Foundation

MONTANA STATE RECORD
TYPICAL AMERICAN ELK
SCORE: 419⁴⁄₈
Locality: Madison Co.   Date: 1958
Hunter: Fred C. Mercer

MONTANA

TYPICAL AMERICAN ELK

Score	Length of Main Beam R	L	Inside Spread	Greatest Spread	Circumference at Smallest Place between First and Second Points R	L	Number of Points R	L	Total of Lengths Abnormal Points	All-Time Rank	State Rank
419 4/8	59 7/8	60 1/8	53	55 3/8	9 2/8	9 3/8	7	7	0	6	1
♦ Madison County / Fred C. Mercer / Fred C. Mercer / 1958											
404 6/8	58 6/8	57	47 2/8	54	9 5/8	9 1/8	8	7	0	16	2
♦ Mineral County / Carl B. Snyder / Warren G. Stone / 1959											
403 2/8	54 4/8	55	61 1/8	64	9 6/8	10 3/8	7	7	0	17	3
♦ Montana / Robert Swan / B&C National Collection / 1912											
401 4/8	53 1/8	55 1/8	44 4/8	47 4/8	7 7/8	8 1/8	7	7	0	23	4
♦ Park County / Wayne A. Hertzler / Wayne A. Hertzler / 1977											
398 5/8	57 2/8	53 4/8	40 5/8	47 2/8	9	9 2/8	8	8	0	32	5
♦ Lewis & Clark County / Richard Mosher / J.A. Iverson / 1953											
397 6/8	53	53	44 2/8	48	8 7/8	9	8	7	0	36	6
♦ Cascade County / John W. Campbell / John W. Campbell / 1955											
395 4/8	56 2/8	51 2/8	43 6/8	46 1/8	10 2/8	9 5/8	6	6	0	41	7
♦ Silver Bow County / Wayne Estep / Wayne Estep / 1966											
394 6/8	54 2/8	60 7/8	47 2/8	51 5/8	8 2/8	8 4/8	6	6	0	46	8
♦ Jefferson County / John Willard / John Willard / 1953											
394 4/8	55	57 5/8	52 4/8	58 3/8	10	9 4/8	7	6	2 6/8	47	9
♦ Beaverhead County / Gwyn Brown / Gwyn Brown / 1944											
389 5/8	50 2/8	53	50 3/8	50 5/8	8	7 6/8	6	7	0	79	10
♦ Park County / Thomas B. Adams / Jack Adams / 1932											
389 5/8	55 1/8	54	45 7/8	50	7 7/8	8 1/8	7	7	0	79	10
♦ Park County / Butch Kuflak / Butch Kuflak / 1990											
389 4/8	55 4/8	56 2/8	45	52	10 5/8	10	6	6	0	82	12
♦ Helena / Picked Up / Robert L. Smith / 1964											
389 4/8	57 3/8	55 2/8	42	51 2/8	8	8	6	6	0	82	12
♦ Bitterroot Area / Unknown / John Le Blanc / 1965											
388	53 2/8	53 6/8	48 2/8	52 1/8	9	9 3/8	6	6	0	97	14
♦ Madison County / Terry Carlson / Christine Mullikin / 1961											
387 4/8	56 5/8	58 2/8	44 2/8	52 6/8	9	9	6	6	0	107	15
♦ Sage Creek / Joseph A. Vogel / Joseph A. Vogel / 1970											
387 3/8	52 2/8	52 3/8	47 3/8	50 5/8	8 1/8	8 1/8	6	6	0	109	16
♦ Park County / Lawrence P. Deering / Lawrence P. Deering / 1978											
387 1/8	54 6/8	58 1/8	46	49 4/8	9 5/8	9 5/8	7	8	8 5/8	110	17
♦ Meagher County / B. McLees & H. Zehntner / Bud McLees / 1971											

Score	Length of Main Beam R	L	Inside Spread	Greatest Spread	Circumference at Smallest Place between First and Second Points R	L	Number of Points R	L	Total of Lengths Abnormal Points	All-Time Rank	State Rank
$386\frac{7}{8}$	$48\frac{6}{8}$	$47\frac{2}{8}$	$41\frac{6}{8}$	$50\frac{4}{8}$	$9\frac{4}{8}$	$8\frac{5}{8}$	8	8	$4\frac{7}{8}$	112	18
◆ Powell County / Mildred Eder / Mildred Eder / 1969											
$386\frac{6}{8}$	$52\frac{2}{8}$	$51\frac{5}{8}$	$34\frac{4}{8}$	$47\frac{5}{8}$	$10\frac{3}{8}$	$10\frac{2}{8}$	7	6	$2\frac{2}{8}$	114	19
◆ Powell County / Unknown / Thomas W. Moen / 1960											
$386\frac{6}{8}$	$61\frac{6}{8}$	$61\frac{7}{8}$	$47\frac{4}{8}$	$51\frac{1}{8}$	$8\frac{7}{8}$	$9\frac{1}{8}$	6	6	0	114	19
◆ Flathead County / Floyd L. Jackson / Floyd L. Jackson / 1976											
$385\frac{3}{8}$	$57\frac{2}{8}$	$55\frac{7}{8}$	$42\frac{5}{8}$	$47\frac{5}{8}$	8	9	6	6	0	134	21
◆ Sanders County / George R. Johnson / George R. Johnson / 1977											
$385\frac{1}{8}$	$56\frac{7}{8}$	$56\frac{4}{8}$	$46\frac{5}{8}$	$52\frac{2}{8}$	$8\frac{3}{8}$	10	6	7	$7\frac{2}{8}$	138	22
◆ Bozeman / Robert B. McKnight / Robert B. McKnight / 1966											
385	$54\frac{7}{8}$	$53\frac{3}{8}$	$46\frac{6}{8}$	$49\frac{2}{8}$	8	$8\frac{3}{8}$	6	6	0	142	23
◆ Madison County / Boyd J. VanFleet / Boyd J. VanFleet / 1991											
$384\frac{3}{8}$	59	$58\frac{4}{8}$	$46\frac{3}{8}$	$50\frac{2}{8}$	$10\frac{5}{8}$	$9\frac{3}{8}$	6	6	0	151	24
◆ Beaverhead County / Phil Matovich / Phil Matovich / 1960											
384	$57\frac{7}{8}$	$56\frac{4}{8}$	44	$50\frac{4}{8}$	$9\frac{6}{8}$	$9\frac{1}{8}$	6	7	0	156	25
◆ Willow Creek / Mike Miles / Mike Miles / 1958											
384	$53\frac{2}{8}$	$51\frac{1}{8}$	$48\frac{3}{8}$	$58\frac{3}{8}$	$8\frac{5}{8}$	$8\frac{2}{8}$	6	7	$2\frac{5}{8}$	156	25
◆ Meagher County / Frank W. Fuller / Frank W. Fuller / 1963											
$382\frac{7}{8}$	$53\frac{4}{8}$	$51\frac{4}{8}$	$47\frac{4}{8}$	$54\frac{3}{8}$	$9\frac{7}{8}$	$10\frac{2}{8}$	7	8	$2\frac{7}{8}$	171	27
◆ Blacktail Creek / Floyd E. Winn / Floyd E. Winn / 1959											
$382\frac{4}{8}$	54	$55\frac{1}{8}$	$40\frac{6}{8}$	$47\frac{3}{8}$	$8\frac{4}{8}$	$9\frac{1}{8}$	7	7	0	176	28
◆ Cascade County / Robert J. Gliko / Robert J. Gliko / 1983											
$382\frac{2}{8}$	$55\frac{4}{8}$	55	$47\frac{4}{8}$	$51\frac{7}{8}$	$7\frac{4}{8}$	$7\frac{2}{8}$	6	6	0	182	29
◆ Gallatin County / Henry Lambert / Charles F. Miller / 1923											
$382\frac{1}{8}$	$57\frac{3}{8}$	$55\frac{7}{8}$	$44\frac{3}{8}$	$47\frac{4}{8}$	$8\frac{1}{8}$	$8\frac{2}{8}$	7	7	0	188	30
◆ Bob Marshall Wild. / Gene E. Trenary / Gene E. Trenary / 1958											
$382\frac{1}{8}$	$54\frac{3}{8}$	$54\frac{6}{8}$	$45\frac{7}{8}$	$50\frac{1}{8}$	8	$8\frac{2}{8}$	6	6	0	188	30
◆ Gallatin County / A. Francis Bailey / A. Francis Bailey / 1966											
382	$52\frac{2}{8}$	$51\frac{1}{8}$	$47\frac{2}{8}$	$57\frac{3}{8}$	$9\frac{2}{8}$	$8\frac{6}{8}$	8	7	0	190	32
◆ Missoula County / Fritz Frey / Clifford Frey / 1943											
$381\frac{7}{8}$	$59\frac{5}{8}$	58	$52\frac{1}{8}$	$56\frac{3}{8}$	$7\frac{6}{8}$	$7\frac{5}{8}$	7	8	0	192	33
◆ Gallatin County / H.K. Shields / H.K. Shields / 1958											
$381\frac{6}{8}$	$52\frac{2}{8}$	52	$49\frac{7}{8}$	$55\frac{1}{8}$	$10\frac{2}{8}$	$9\frac{3}{8}$	6	7	$3\frac{1}{8}$	193	34
◆ Beaverhead County / C.L. Jensen / C.L. Jensen / 1960											
$381\frac{6}{8}$	$50\frac{3}{8}$	$49\frac{7}{8}$	42	$44\frac{2}{8}$	$9\frac{1}{8}$	$8\frac{7}{8}$	8	7	3	193	34
◆ Madison County / Allan L. Mintken / Allan L. Mintken / 1986											

Score	Length of Main Beam R	L	Inside Spread	Greatest Spread	Circumference at Smallest Place between First and Second Points R	L	Number of Points R	L	Total of Lengths Abnormal Points	All-Time Rank	State Rank
381 5/8	56 2/8	56 2/8	41 5/8	49	10 4/8	10 1/8	6	6	0	198	36
◆ Granite County / Jeff Conn / Jeff Conn / 1971											
381 3/8	57 2/8	57 1/8	41 1/8	54 2/8	9 6/8	9 4/8	7	6	2	203	37
◆ Park County / Edward F. Skillman / Edward F. Skillman / 1968											
381 1/8	49 6/8	51 4/8	37 7/8	44 2/8	8 6/8	9	7	7	0	209	38
◆ Flathead County / Earl Weaver, Jr. / Earl Weaver, Jr. / 1962											
381	56 3/8	54 6/8	48 4/8	53 7/8	8 2/8	8 2/8	6	6	4 6/8	211	39
◆ Gallatin County / Jack Bauer / Jack Bauer / 1961											
381	51 2/8	50 5/8	43 6/8	47 3/8	8	7 5/8	7	7	0	211	39
◆ Big Horn County / Jerry Barnes / Jerry Barnes / 1962											
381	54	53 4/8	48 6/8	52 4/8	8	7 6/8	6	7	0	211	39
◆ Gallatin County / Gerald Schroeder / Gerald Schroeder / 1977											
380 6/8	51 7/8	51	43 6/8	47	10	9 7/8	7	7	0	215	42
◆ Park County / John Caputo / John Caputo / 1968											
380 2/8	56 1/8	57 2/8	49 4/8	54 2/8	8 1/8	8 6/8	7	7	0	224	43
◆ Madison County / Phil Hensel / Phil Hensel / 1959											
380 2/8	58 7/8	58 3/8	42 2/8	46 2/8	9 4/8	8 6/8	7	6	0	224	43
◆ Granite County / Richard Shoner / Richard Shoner / 1977											
380 1/8	59 1/8	58 2/8	50 5/8	52	7 6/8	7 3/8	6	6	0	229	45
◆ Beaverhead County / Edward Konda / Edward Konda / 1947											
379 6/8	58 3/8	58 4/8	45 2/8	51 4/8	9 2/8	9 6/8	6	6	0	235	46
◆ Ruby Mts. / Jack Ballard / Jack Ballard / 1960											
379 6/8	57 2/8	57 2/8	40 4/8	0	7 6/8	7 6/8	6	6	0	235	46
◆ Big Horn County / George F. Gamble / George F. Gamble / 1968											
379 6/8	54	54 6/8	45 6/8	49 5/8	7 7/8	8 1/8	6	6	0	235	46
◆ Daisy Pass / Larry R. Price / Larry R. Price / 1971											
379 4/8	51 7/8	52 3/8	39	45 2/8	9 7/8	9 7/8	6	6	0	244	49
◆ Madison County / LeRoy Schweitzer / LeRoy Schweitzer / 1964											
379 2/8	55 7/8	56 1/8	44 4/8	52 1/8	9	8 7/8	6	6	0	249	50
◆ Bozeman / K.L. Berry / K.L. Berry / 1959											
379 2/8	54 7/8	56 4/8	40 4/8	56 7/8	8 2/8	8 1/8	6	6	0	249	50
◆ Sanders County / Robert L. Coates / Robert L. Coates / 1974											
379	50 7/8	51	44 4/8	46 4/8	9 7/8	10 2/8	6	6	0	258	52
◆ Petroleum County / Lana J. Sluggett / Lana J. Sluggett / 1984											
378 6/8	55	54 4/8	45	48 3/8	8	7 4/8	6	6	0	263	53
◆ Gallatin County / Ted Shook / Ted Shook / 1966											

Score	Length of Main Beam		Inside Spread	Greatest Spread	Circumference at Smallest Place between First and Second Points		Number of Points		Total of Lengths Abnormal Points	All-Time Rank	State Rank
	R	L			R	L	R	L			

Locality / Hunter / Owner / Date Killed

378 4/8	58 3/8	56 3/8	43 6/8	48 1/8	8 4/8	8 3/8	6	6	0	266	54

♦ *Beaverhead County / Milton F. Steele / Milton F. Steele / 1963*

| 378 4/8 | 51 3/8 | 49 6/8 | 40 2/8 | 51 3/8 | 9 3/8 | 9 1/8 | 6 | 6 | 0 | 266 | 54 |

♦ *Park County / M.J. Young / M.J. Young / 1967*

| 378 | 49 3/8 | 50 2/8 | 39 5/8 | 46 3/8 | 8 1/8 | 8 6/8 | 7 | 7 | 2 3/8 | 276 | 56 |

♦ *Richard's Peak / Albert Sales / Richard Eastman / 1931*

| 377 6/8 | 56 6/8 | 55 6/8 | 41 6/8 | 53 | 8 2/8 | 8 2/8 | 7 | 10 | 14 2/8 | 279 | 57 |

♦ *Sanders County / Steve Barnes / Steve Barnes / 1973*

| 377 5/8 | 53 7/8 | 53 3/8 | 51 7/8 | 55 4/8 | 9 | 8 1/8 | 7 | 6 | 2 | 282 | 58 |

♦ *Beaverhead County / Edmund J. Giebel / Edmund J. Giebel / 1981*

| 377 4/8 | 54 3/8 | 51 5/8 | 45 5/8 | 52 6/8 | 8 6/8 | 8 6/8 | 7 | 7 | 1 1/8 | 284 | 59 |

♦ *Granite County / Tom Villeneue / Tom Villeneue / 1966*

| 377 3/8 | 60 | 58 | 41 7/8 | 46 | 8 5/8 | 8 4/8 | 6 | 6 | 0 | 288 | 60 |

♦ *Sanders County / Allen White / Allen White / 1968*

| 377 3/8 | 53 1/8 | 52 | 46 1/8 | 47 6/8 | 8 4/8 | 9 1/8 | 6 | 6 | 0 | 288 | 60 |

♦ *Missoula County / Tom Schenarts / Tom Schenarts / 1970*

| 377 3/8 | 49 3/8 | 49 7/8 | 40 3/8 | 44 7/8 | 11 2/8 | 10 2/8 | 6 | 6 | 0 | 288 | 60 |

♦ *Petroleum County / Jack Atcheson, Jr. / Jack Atcheson, Jr. / 1990*

| 377 2/8 | 53 5/8 | 53 6/8 | 49 2/8 | 53 4/8 | 8 2/8 | 8 2/8 | 6 | 7 | 0 | 292 | 63 |

♦ *Gallatin Range / E. Dehart, Sr., P. Van Beek, & H. Prestine / Earl Dehart, Sr. / 1960*

| 376 6/8 | 51 2/8 | 52 4/8 | 48 2/8 | 51 7/8 | 8 4/8 | 8 3/8 | 8 | 7 | 1 6/8 | 304 | 64 |

♦ *Lewis & Clark County / Cameron G. Mielke / Cameron G. Mielke / 1964*

| 375 7/8 | 54 6/8 | 54 4/8 | 43 5/8 | 52 6/8 | 8 4/8 | 8 5/8 | 8 | 8 | 0 | 320 | 65 |

♦ *Flathead County / Pat Roth / Pat Roth / 1966*

| 375 5/8 | 53 | 51 3/8 | 40 3/8 | 46 | 9 | 9 1/8 | 6 | 7 | 0 | 328 | 66 |

♦ *Madison River / Dale A. Hancock / Dale A. Hancock / 1967*

| 375 5/8 | 54 3/8 | 54 1/8 | 43 7/8 | 52 1/8 | 8 2/8 | 8 3/8 | 7 | 6 | 9 | 328 | 66 |

♦ *Sanders County / Tony B. Cox / Tony B. Cox / 1980*

| 375 4/8 | 57 6/8 | 55 2/8 | 48 4/8 | 54 2/8 | 8 7/8 | 8 1/8 | 6 | 6 | 0 | 331 | 68 |

♦ *Jefferson County / Ralph J. Huckaba / Ralph J. Huckaba / 1949*

| 375 4/8 | 47 6/8 | 52 6/8 | 34 1/8 | 53 5/8 | 7 6/8 | 8 1/8 | 8 | 6 | 7 5/8 | 331 | 68 |

♦ *Powell County / Allan F. Kruse / Allan F. Kruse / 1977*

| 375 3/8 | 52 | 52 | 43 6/8 | 48 2/8 | 9 2/8 | 10 1/8 | 7 | 6 | 2 3/8 | 335 | 70 |

♦ *Jefferson County / Mrs. Lou Sweet / Mrs. Lou Sweet / 1924*

| 375 3/8 | 52 6/8 | 54 6/8 | 44 5/8 | 47 6/8 | 9 | 8 3/8 | 7 | 7 | 0 | 335 | 70 |

♦ *Park County / Bruce Brown / Bruce Brown / 1967*

Score	Length of Main Beam R	Length of Main Beam L	Inside Spread	Greatest Spread	Circumference at Smallest Place between First and Second Points R	Circumference at Smallest Place between First and Second Points L	Number of Points R	Number of Points L	Total of Lengths Abnormal Points	All-Time Rank	State Rank
♦ *Locality / Hunter / Owner / Date Killed*											
375 3/8	49	50 6/8	39 7/8	42 2/8	7 5/8	7 5/8	6	6	0	335	70
♦ *Beaverhead County / Harold F. Krieger, Jr. / Harold F. Krieger, Jr. / 1970*											
375	57 3/8	54 4/8	41 2/8	45 2/8	9 3/8	9 5/8	7	7	0	350	73
♦ *Park County / Robert M. Brogan / Robert M. Brogan / 1972*											
375	59	58 6/8	42 2/8	46 7/8	9 7/8	9 2/8	6	6	0	350	73
♦ *Lewis & Clark County / James Bollinger / James Bollinger / 1982*											
373 2/8	52 3/8	51 6/8	44	48 1/8	9 2/8	9 5/8	6	7	0	358	75
♦ *Petroleum County / David W. Kuhns / David W. Kuhns / 1989*											
367 6/8	50 7/8	51	36 2/8	46 4/8	9 6/8	9 2/8	6	6	0	366	76
♦ *Teton County / Gene Ward / Gene Ward / 1994*											
367 5/8	50	52 1/8	37 6/8	44 5/8	8 2/8	8 3/8	7	8	5 1/8	367	77
♦ *Sweet Grass County / Marty T. Fleming / Marty T. Fleming / 1994*											

Photograph Courtesy of Rocky Mountain Elk Foundation

MONTANA STATE RECORD (NEW)
NON-TYPICAL AMERICAN ELK
SCORE: 423⁴⁄₈
Locality: Granite Co.   Date: 1971
Hunter: Lee F. Tracy
Loaned to B&C National Collection, Cody, Wyoming

MONTANA

NON-TYPICAL AMERICAN ELK

Score	Length of Main Beam R	L	Inside Spread	Greatest Spread	Circumference at Smallest Place between First and Second Points R	L	Number of Points R	L	Total of Lengths Abnormal Points	All-Time Rank	State Rank
◆ Locality / Hunter / Owner / Date Killed											
423⁴⁄₈	51⁴⁄₈	50⁶⁄₈	44⁷⁄₈	51³⁄₈	8⁴⁄₈	7⁷⁄₈	8	7	32³⁄₈	4	1
◆ Granite County / Lee F. Tracy / Lee F. Tracy / 1971											
408	51⁷⁄₈	50⁶⁄₈	39⁷⁄₈	48	7⁷⁄₈	8⁶⁄₈	7	9	14⁵⁄₈	13	2
◆ Sanders County / John Fitchett / John Fitchett / 1980											
407⁶⁄₈	54⁶⁄₈	54²⁄₈	46⁴⁄₈	51	9	8	8	8	29⁴⁄₈	14	3
◆ Granite County / Scott Hicks / Scott Hicks / 1971											
405⁴⁄₈	54³⁄₈	51⁷⁄₈	44	50⁵⁄₈	8⁶⁄₈	9	8	8	30²⁄₈	16	4
◆ Granite County / Arthur W. Lundgren / Grace Lundgren / 1946											
403²⁄₈	54⁵⁄₈	52⁴⁄₈	47⁴⁄₈	50³⁄₈	8⁶⁄₈	9²⁄₈	9	6	26⁶⁄₈	20	5
◆ Park County / Gary Beley / Gary Beley / 1964											
403	48²⁄₈	49	43⁶⁄₈	59³⁄₈	8	9	10	8	52⁴⁄₈	22	6
◆ Lincoln County / Delbert Bowe / Delbert Bowe / 1992											
402⁷⁄₈	48⁶⁄₈	50	39	47⁵⁄₈	8²⁄₈	8³⁄₈	8	9	19⁷⁄₈	24	7
◆ Powell County / Donald A. Roberson / Donald A. Roberson / 1987											
401⁷⁄₈	51⁶⁄₈	50	49²⁄₈	63⁴⁄₈	9⁴⁄₈	9⁴⁄₈	9	7	29⁵⁄₈	28	8
◆ Beaverhead County / Ben C. Holland / Ben C. Holland / 1953											
400⁶⁄₈	51²⁄₈	52	50³⁄₈	50³⁄₈	8⁵⁄₈	8³⁄₈	9	8	20³⁄₈	32	9
◆ Madison County / Arthur A. Cooper / Arthur A. Cooper / 1962											
398¹⁄₈	52²⁄₈	55	44²⁄₈	54²⁄₈	8⁵⁄₈	8³⁄₈	8	7	25⁵⁄₈	37	10
◆ Park County / Picked Up / O. Cline Stelzig / 1972											
397²⁄₈	53²⁄₈	51⁶⁄₈	45⁴⁄₈	52²⁄₈	9²⁄₈	8⁶⁄₈	8	8	11	38	11
◆ Powell County / Rex Sorenson / Univ. of Mont. Zool. Mus. / 1952											
388³⁄₈	50	51²⁄₈	41⁴⁄₈	48⁴⁄₈	9	8⁷⁄₈	7	8	9³⁄₈	51	12
◆ Glacier County / John D. Fitzgerald / John D. Fitzgerald / 1990											
386⁵⁄₈	51⁷⁄₈	50⁶⁄₈	45⁷⁄₈	60⁵⁄₈	8⁷⁄₈	8⁴⁄₈	8	7	15⁴⁄₈	53	13
◆ Beaverhead County / Unknown / William H. Flesch / PR 1962											
415⁶⁄₈	58²⁄₈	52³⁄₈	40²⁄₈	46¹⁄₈	10⁵⁄₈	10⁵⁄₈	8	7	31⁶⁄₈	*	*
◆ Madison County / Michael Gecho / Michael Gecho / 1958											

NEVADA STATE RECORD (NEW)
TYPICAL AMERICAN ELK
SCORE: 393 4/8
Locality: White Pine Co.   Date: 1993
Hunter: Paul Green

NEVADA

TYPICAL AMERICAN ELK

Score	Length of Main Beam		Inside Spread	Greatest Spread	Circumference at Smallest Place between First and Second Points		Number of Points		Total of Lengths Abnormal Points	All-Time Rank	State Rank
	R	L			R	L	R	L			

♦ *Locality / Hunter / Owner / Date Killed*

393 4/8 50 51 3/8 40 4/8 49 7/8 7 6/8 8 1/8 7 7 0 56 1
♦ *White Pine County / Paul Green / Paul Green / 1993*

381 3/8 53 4/8 53 7/8 43 7/8 48 3/8 9 5/8 8 5/8 6 6 0 203 2
♦ *White Pine County / Michael N. Kalafatic / Michael N. Kalafatic / 1985*

363 2/8 53 51 7/8 40 2/8 45 5/8 7 4/8 8 1/8 7 6 0 382 3
♦ *White Pine County / Richard P. Norrup / Richard P. Norrup / 1990*

Photograph Courtesy of Geoffrey H.S. House

NEVADA STATE RECORD (NEW)
NON-TYPICAL AMERICAN ELK
SCORE: 403⅞*
Locality: White Pine Co.   Date: 1994
Hunter: Geoffrey H.S. House

NEVADA

NON-TYPICAL AMERICAN ELK

Score	Length of Main Beam		Inside Spread	Greatest Spread	Circumference at Smallest Place between First and Second Points		Number of Points		Total of Lengths Abnormal Points	All-Time Rank	State Rank
	R	L			R	L	R	L			

♦ *Locality / Hunter / Owner / Date Killed*

| 403 7/8 | 51 4/8 | 47 2/8 | 43 1/8 | 51 1/8 | 9 2/8 | 9 | 9 | 7 | 30 | * | * |

♦ *White Pine County / Geoffrey H.S. House / Geoffrey H.S. House / 1994*

Photograph Courtesy of Don Schaufler

NEW NEXICO STATE RECORD
TYPICAL AMERICAN ELK
SCORE: 398
Locality: Mora Co.   Date: 1963
Hunter: Bernabe Alcon
Owner: Don Schaufler

NEW MEXICO

TYPICAL AMERICAN ELK

Score	Length of Main Beam R	Length of Main Beam L	Inside Spread	Greatest Spread	Circumference at Smallest Place between First and Second Points R	Circumference at Smallest Place between First and Second Points L	Number of Points R	Number of Points L	Total of Lengths Abnormal Points	All-Time Rank	State Rank
♦ *Locality / Hunter / Owner / Date Killed*											
398	50 5/8	50 7/8	39 4/8	42 7/8	10 5/8	11	7	7	0	33	1
♦ *Mora County / Bernabe Alcon / Don Schaufler / 1963*											
393 2/8	63 1/8	64 4/8	44 2/8	49 1/8	9 5/8	9 6/8	6	7	0	57	2
♦ *Socorro County / Floyd R. Owens / Floyd R. Owens / 1977*											
387	55	55 4/8	54 4/8	56 6/8	8 7/8	8 2/8	8	7	4 4/8	111	3
♦ *Chama / Herb Klein / Herb Klein / 1952*											
386 7/8	58 4/8	61 6/8	41 7/8	47 4/8	8 7/8	8 7/8	6	6	0	112	4
♦ *Otero County / Picked Up / William M. Wheless III / 1981*											
386 1/8	59 1/8	58	36 5/8	50 6/8	10 3/8	9 4/8	6	6	0	122	5
♦ *Mescalero Apache Res. / Larry W. Bailey, Sr. / Larry W. Bailey, Sr. / 1974*											
385 3/8	51 1/8	54 2/8	41 5/8	46 6/8	10 7/8	10 5/8	6	6	0	134	6
♦ *Otero County / Gregory C. Saunders / Gregory C. Saunders / 1985*											
384	52 5/8	53 6/8	41 1/8	47 6/8	11 4/8	11 1/8	7	7	2 1/8	156	7
♦ *Otero County / Robert McCasland / Robert McCasland / 1992*											
384	58 7/8	60	41 4/8	47	9 5/8	9 6/8	7	6	0	156	7
♦ *Otero County / George R. Sellers / George R. Sellers / 1992*											
382 2/8	50 5/8	49 1/8	50	55 7/8	8	7 5/8	7	6	0	182	9
♦ *Colfax County / Claude W. Hudson III / Claude W. Hudson III / 1994*											
381 6/8	54 3/8	52 5/8	38 4/8	51 3/8	9 2/8	10	7	7	0	193	10
♦ *Otero County / David U. Inge / David U. Inge / 1990*											
381 3/8	56 4/8	56 6/8	34 7/8	43 3/8	10 3/8	9 4/8	6	6	0	203	11
♦ *Catron County / Gary F. Jamieson / Gary F. Jamieson / 1993*											
381 2/8	55 1/8	55 1/8	50	50 4/8	9	9 1/8	7	8	0	207	12
♦ *Mora County / Andrew J. Ortega / Andrew J. Ortega / 1989*											
380 3/8	56 3/8	58	44 1/8	47 5/8	7 5/8	7 5/8	7	6	0	221	13
♦ *Catron County / Donald Parks, Jr. / Donald Parks, Jr. / 1988*											
379 6/8	58 2/8	58 4/8	46 6/8	51	8 6/8	8 6/8	7	7	0	235	14
♦ *Grant County / Tony R. Grijalva / Tony R. Grijalva / 1983*											
379 3/8	51 2/8	47	42 3/8	51 7/8	9 4/8	9 7/8	6	6	0	245	15
♦ *Otero County / Hubert R. Kennedy / Hubert R. Kennedy / 1985*											
379 3/8	52 4/8	53 6/8	40 1/8	43 2/8	11 1/8	12	6	6	0	245	15
♦ *Sierra County / James D. Wagner / James D. Wagner / 1986*											
376 1/8	58 3/8	56 4/8	42 1/8	48 3/8	8 4/8	8 2/8	6	6	0	316	17
♦ *Lincoln County / Jim Carter / Jim Carter / 1981*											

Score	Length of Main Beam		Inside Spread	Greatest Spread	Circumference at Smallest Place between First and Second Points		Number of Points		Total of Lengths Abnormal Points	All-Time Rank	State Rank
	R	L			R	L	R	L			
◆ *Locality / Hunter / Owner / Date Killed*											
375²⁄₈	55³⁄₈	55³⁄₈	41²⁄₈	46	8³⁄₈	8³⁄₈	6	6	0	342	18
◆ *Colfax County / Slim Pickens / Margaret M. Lindley / 1981*											
366⁶⁄₈	54⁴⁄₈	54²⁄₈	46⁶⁄₈	51¹⁄₈	8⁴⁄₈	8²⁄₈	6	6	0	370	19
◆ *Catron County / Brady J. Smith / Brady J. Smith / 1994*											
365⁵⁄₈	58²⁄₈	57¹⁄₈	43³⁄₈	43	10²⁄₈	10²⁄₈	8	7	0	373	20
◆ *Mescalero County / George Rose / George Rose / 1991*											
365¹⁄₈	51⁴⁄₈	51²⁄₈	38⁵⁄₈	41⁷⁄₈	10	10⁵⁄₈	7	7	0	376	21
◆ *Sandoval County / John C. McClendon / John C. McClendon / 1985*											
360²⁄₈	53⁶⁄₈	52⁴⁄₈	41⁶⁄₈	48	9⁶⁄₈	9	6	7	4⁴⁄₈	384	22
◆ *Catron County / Robert H. Pickett, Jr. / Robert H. Pickett, Jr. / 1987*											

Photograph Courtesy of Jack Atcheson, Jr.

The legendary Missouri Breaks in eastern Montana yielded this 377-3/8 point typical American elk to Jack Atcheson, Jr., during the 1990 hunting season. The odds of getting drawn in this limited entry area, which produces many outstanding bulls, are quite low.

Photograph by Mike Biggs

NEW MEXICO STATE RECORD (NEW)
NON-TYPICAL AMERICAN ELK
SCORE: 417⅞
Locality: Catron Co.   Date: 1992
Hunter: Martin D. Huggins

NEW MEXICO

NON-TYPICAL AMERICAN ELK

Score	Length of Main Beam R	Length of Main Beam L	Inside Spread	Greatest Spread	Circumference at Smallest Place between First and Second Points R	Circumference at Smallest Place between First and Second Points L	Number of Points R	Number of Points L	Total of Lengths Abnormal Points	All-Time Rank	State Rank
♦ *Locality / Hunter / Owner / Date Killed*											
417 6/8	58 1/8	52 1/8	47 4/8	53 4/8	9 3/8	9 2/8	7	9	26 4/8	7	1
♦ *Catron County / Martin D. Huggins / Martin D. Huggins / 1992*											
414	48 2/8	48 2/8	46 7/8	55 3/8	7 3/8	6 5/8	9	10	37 3/8	10	2
♦ *Taos County / Lou A. DePaolis / Lou A. DePaolis / 1974*											
410 1/8	46 3/8	47 1/8	50	57	9 6/8	9 3/8	11	10	123 4/8	11	3
♦ *Taos County / Picked Up / P.R. Ridilla & B. Adams / 1993*											
394 6/8	56	53 6/8	35 6/8	42	9	9 6/8	7	6	15 6/8	41	4
♦ *Otero County / Kelly R. Ginn / Kelly R. Ginn / 1991*											
392 4/8	46	47 5/8	41 6/8	48 6/8	12	12 1/8	7	8	28 4/8	47	5
♦ *Otero County / David U. Inge / David U. Inge / 1989*											
386 2/8	44 3/8	47 4/8	43 4/8	49 1/8	8 7/8	9	9	6	16	54	6
♦ *Socorro County / Richard P. Gould / Richard P. Gould / 1990*											
386 2/8	50	50 1/8	41 4/8	49 1/8	8 6/8	8 4/8	7	7	8	54	6
♦ *Otero County / William M. Pitcher / William M. Pitcher / 1992*											

Photograph by Mike Biggs

OREGON STATE RECORD (NEW)
TYPICAL AMERICAN ELK
SCORE: 418
Locality: Crook Co.   Date: 1942
Hunter: Hugh P. Evans
Owner: Joseph S. Jessel, Jr.

OREGON

TYPICAL AMERICAN ELK

Score	Length of Main Beam R	L	Inside Spread	Greatest Spread	Circumference at Smallest Place between First and Second Points R	L	Number of Points R	L	Total of Lengths Abnormal Points	All-Time Rank	State Rank
418	63²⁄₈	64²⁄₈	38²⁄₈	49⁷⁄₈	10¹⁄₈	9⁶⁄₈	7	7	0	8	1
◆ *Crook County / Hugh P. Evans / Joseph S. Jessel, Jr. / 1942*											
401³⁄₈	60⁴⁄₈	64⁵⁄₈	43⁷⁄₈	49²⁄₈	9³⁄₈	9	7	6	0	24	2
◆ *Grant County / James T. Sproul / James T. Sproul / 1972*											
400	56²⁄₈	57	49	52²⁄₈	9¹⁄₈	9¹⁄₈	7	7	0	29	3
◆ *Crook County / Picked Up / Randall L. Ryerse / 1984*											
395¹⁄₈	56⁴⁄₈	57²⁄₈	46⁵⁄₈	59¹⁄₈	10²⁄₈	9³⁄₈	7	8	3	43	4
◆ *Wallowa County / Lawton McDaniel / Lawton McDaniel / 1935*											
392³⁄₈	53⁴⁄₈	54⁴⁄₈	46³⁄₈	51²⁄₈	8³⁄₈	8⁶⁄₈	6	6	0	64	5
◆ *Umatilla County / Picked Up / Robert L. Brown / 1982*											
390²⁄₈	55	55⁴⁄₈	49²⁄₈	55⁴⁄₈	8⁶⁄₈	8⁶⁄₈	7	7	0	76	6
◆ *Hood River County / Bill Tensen / Bill Tensen / 1980*											
389	51	48³⁄₈	41⁶⁄₈	47	8²⁄₈	8²⁄₈	6	6	0	88	7
◆ *Meacham / H.M. Bailey / H.M. Bailey / 1963*											
387⁷⁄₈	55³⁄₈	57	37²⁄₈	50³⁄₈	10	9⁵⁄₈	7	6	1⁵⁄₈	100	8
◆ *Grant County / Arnold Troph / Arnold Troph / 1966*											
387⁴⁄₈	49¹⁄₈	49¹⁄₈	41⁷⁄₈	47³⁄₈	8⁷⁄₈	8⁷⁄₈	7	7	4³⁄₈	107	9
◆ *Grant County / Andy Chambers / Andy Chambers / 1959*											
385⁵⁄₈	52⁷⁄₈	54⁷⁄₈	46⁷⁄₈	49⁴⁄₈	9³⁄₈	9¹⁄₈	6	6	0	130	10
◆ *Wheeler County / Ronny E. Rhoden / Ronny E. Rhoden / 1986*											
382²⁄₈	55⁷⁄₈	53³⁄₈	39²⁄₈	50²⁄₈	9²⁄₈	9¹⁄₈	7	7	0	182	11
◆ *Grant County / Drake J. Davis / Drake J. Davis / 1981*											
380³⁄₈	62⁷⁄₈	63²⁄₈	47¹⁄₈	57⁵⁄₈	8⁶⁄₈	8⁶⁄₈	7	8	3⁶⁄₈	221	12
◆ *Harney County / Pat L. Wheeler / Pat L. Wheeler / 1967*											
377⁷⁄₈	52⁷⁄₈	53⁶⁄₈	47¹⁄₈	51⁴⁄₈	8⁴⁄₈	9⁴⁄₈	7	7	0	278	13
◆ *Baker County / Donald B. Martin / Donald B. Martin / 1961*											
376⁶⁄₈	59³⁄₈	59⁷⁄₈	45⁴⁄₈	48⁵⁄₈	10	9²⁄₈	8	7	2²⁄₈	304	14
◆ *Crook County / Picked Up / Larry E. Miller / 1983*											
375	57¹⁄₈	58¹⁄₈	42⁶⁄₈	48	9¹⁄₈	8⁶⁄₈	6	6	0	350	15
◆ *Wheeler County / William K. Bartlett / William K. Bartlett / 1986*											
372⁷⁄₈	50¹⁄₈	50⁶⁄₈	49⁵⁄₈	52	9⁴⁄₈	9	6	6	0	359	16
◆ *Grant County / Robert B. Abbott / Robert B. Abbott / 1989*											
370⁶⁄₈	56	55⁶⁄₈	47⁶⁄₈	51⁷⁄₈	8²⁄₈	8³⁄₈	7	6	3⁶⁄₈	361	17
◆ *Grant County / Lawrence E. Mayfield / Lawrence E. Mayfield / 1984*											

Photograph Courtesy of Todd Craig

SOUTH DAKOTA STATE RECORD
TYPICAL AMERICAN ELK
SCORE: 363⁶⁄₈
Locality: Custer Co.   Date: 1986
Hunter: Todd Craig

SOUTH DAKOTA

TYPICAL AMERICAN ELK

Score	Length of Main Beam R	L	Inside Spread	Greatest Spread	Circumference at Smallest Place between First and Second Points R	L	Number of Points R	L	Total of Lengths Abnormal Points	All-Time Rank	State Rank
◆ Locality / Hunter / Owner / Date Killed											
363⁶⁄₈	47⁴⁄₈	49¹⁄₈	40¹⁄₈	41⁵⁄₈	8³⁄₈	8³⁄₈	7	6	4⁷⁄₈	381	1
◆ Custer County / Todd Craig / Todd Craig / 1986											

Photograph Courtesy of Joe B. Finley

TEXAS STATE RECORD
TYPICAL AMERICAN ELK
SCORE: 375
Locality: Denton Co.   Date: 1934
Hunter: O.Z. Finley
Owner: Joe B. Finley, Jr.

TEXAS

TYPICAL AMERICAN ELK

Score	Length of Main Beam R	L	Inside Spread	Greatest Spread	Circumference at Smallest Place between First and Second Points R	L	Number of Points R	L	Total of Lengths Abnormal Points	All-Time Rank	State Rank
♦ Locality / Hunter / Owner / Date Killed											
375	57⅛	54	38	43	8	8	7	7	0	350	1
♦ Denton County / O.Z. Finley / Joe B. Finley, Jr. / 1934											

Photograph Courtesy of Edward C. Jessen

UTAH STATE RECORD (NEW)
TYPICAL AMERICAN ELK
SCORE: 386 $\frac{2}{8}$
Locality: Carbon Co.   Date: 1961
Hunter: Edward C. Jessen

UTAH

TYPICAL AMERICAN ELK

Score	Length of Main Beam R	L	Inside Spread	Greatest Spread	Circumference at Smallest Place between First and Second Points R	L	Number of Points R	L	Total of Lengths Abnormal Points	All-Time Rank	State Rank
386 2/8	56 3/8	57 4/8	46 6/8	49 3/8	9 3/8	8 6/8	6	6	0	120	1
♦ Carbon County / Edward C. Jessen / Edward C. Jessen / 1961											
385 4/8	56 2/8	57 3/8	37 4/8	46 5/8	8 2/8	8 2/8	6	6	0	133	2
♦ Emery County / Neville L. Wimmer / Russell N. Wimmer / 1939											
381 5/8	54 7/8	56 3/8	40 1/8	51 1/8	9 3/8	8	7	6	4 2/8	198	3
♦ Rich County / Walter R. Moore / Kirk W. Moore / 1935											
380 5/8	57 4/8	57 1/8	43 7/8	46 6/8	8 5/8	8 7/8	6	6	0	216	4
♦ Sevier County / Miles A. Anderson / Miles A. Anderson / 1970											
380 3/8	53 4/8	53 2/8	51 7/8	56 4/8	8 1/8	8 5/8	7	7	0	221	5
♦ Rich County / Fahy S. Robinson, Jr. / Fahy S. Robinson, Jr. / 1988											
374 4/8	53 2/8	54 2/8	40 2/8	46 3/8	7 7/8	8 2/8	6	6	0	356	6
♦ Garfield County / Brett R. Nybo / Brett R. Nybo / 1984											
373 3/8	52 5/8	51 7/8	49 3/8	49 7/8	8 4/8	7 5/8	7	7	1 1/8	357	7
♦ Sevier County / Picked Up / James R. Burr / 1989											
369 2/8	54 1/8	52 2/8	41 4/8	45	8 6/8	9 2/8	6	6	0	363	8
♦ Uintah County / Ronald J. Wopsock / Ronald J. Wopsock / 1990											
367 4/8	54 3/8	52 4/8	47 2/8	50 6/8	7 7/8	8	6	6	0	368	9
♦ Rich County / Gilbert T. Adams / Gilbert T. Adams / 1993											

Locality / Hunter / Owner / Date Killed

WASHINGTON STATE RECORD (NEW)
TYPICAL AMERICAN ELK
SCORE: 420⅘
Locality: Yakima Co.   Date: 1990
Hunter: Charles F. Gunnier

WASHINGTON
TYPICAL AMERICAN ELK

Score	Length of Main Beam R	L	Inside Spread	Greatest Spread	Circumference at Smallest Place between First and Second Points R	L	Number of Points R	L	Total of Lengths Abnormal Points	All-Time Rank	State Rank
♦ Locality / Hunter / Owner / Date Killed											
420 4/8	56 4/8	56 2/8	45 6/8	51 7/8	9	9 2/8	7	7	0	4	1
♦ Yakima County / Charles F. Gunnier / Charles F. Gunnier / 1990											
393 1/8	56 3/8	59 2/8	47 1/8	52 1/8	8 6/8	8 6/8	6	6	0	61	2
♦ Kittitas County / Paul Anderson / Paul Anderson / 1927											
381 2/8	57	55 4/8	44 2/8	53 4/8	9	8 6/8	6	6	0	207	3
♦ Kittitas County / Clinton W. Morrow / Clinton W. Morrow / 1957											
380 2/8	57 4/8	57 3/8	46 4/8	48 6/8	8 4/8	8 3/8	7	7	0	224	4
♦ Lewis County / Charles Rudolph / Charles Rudolph / 1973											
379 2/8	53 4/8	52 2/8	44	50 6/8	8	8 4/8	6	6	0	249	5
♦ Yakima County / Donald G. Stein / Donald G. Stein / 1985											
377	58 5/8	56 4/8	47 4/8	49 4/8	8 6/8	8 1/8	7	7	0	297	6
♦ Benton County / Daniel J. Bishop / Daniel J. Bishop / 1988											
375 4/8	55 1/8	54	42 4/8	47 6/8	9	9	6	6	0	331	7
♦ Skamania County / Kevin Schmid / Kevin Schmid / 1990											

WASHINGTON STATE RECORD (NEW)
NON-TYPICAL AMERICAN ELK
SCORE: 401⅝
Locality: Cowlitz Co.   Date: 1959
Hunter: Unknown
Owner: Steve Crossley

WASHINGTON

NON-TYPICAL AMERICAN ELK

Score	Length of Main Beam R	Length of Main Beam L	Inside Spread	Greatest Spread	Circumference at Smallest Place between First and Second Points R	Circumference at Smallest Place between First and Second Points L	Number of Points R	Number of Points L	Total of Lengths Abnormal Points	All-Time Rank	State Rank
♦ *Locality / Hunter / Owner / Date Killed*											
401 5/8	53 5/8	55 5/8	43 3/8	51 3/8	7 7/8	7 4/8	7	8	45 6/8	29	1
♦ *Cowlitz County / Unknown / Steve Crossley / 1959*											
398 5/8	52	52 3/8	43 5/8	49 2/8	9 1/8	9 5/8	7	7	27 2/8	35	2
♦ *Pierce County / Larry N. Mohler / Larry N. Mohler / 1991*											
420 4/8	56 4/8	57 7/8	45 1/8	53 4/8	10 5/8	10 3/8	8	9	37 5/8	*	*
♦ *Yakima County / Stan Orr / Cary Brune / 1933*											

Photograph Courtesy of Rocky Mountain Elk Foundation

WYOMING STATE RECORD
TYPICAL AMERICAN ELK
SCORE: 441⅝
Locality: Big Horn Mountains   Date: 1890
Hunter: Unknown
Owner: Jackson Hole Museum

WYOMING

TYPICAL AMERICAN ELK

Score	Length of Main Beam R	L	Inside Spread	Greatest Spread	Circumference at Smallest Place between First and Second Points R	L	Number of Points R	L	Total of Lengths Abnormal Points	All-Time Rank	State Rank
* Locality / Hunter / Owner / Date Killed												
441 6/8	61 6/8	61 2/8	47	50 2/8	10 2/8	9 7/8	8	7	0	2	1
* Big Horn Mts. / Unknown / Jackson Hole Museum / 1890												
418 7/8	58	55	43 1/8	54 3/8	10 5/8	11 3/8	6	7	3 6/8	7	2
* Wyoming / J.G. Millais / G. Kenneth Whitehead / 1886												
417 3/8	62	59 4/8	47 3/8	52 7/8	9 2/8	9 3/8	8	7	0	10	3
* Park County / Merwin D. Martin / Merwin D. Martin / 1991												
401 6/8	58 3/8	57 5/8	47 2/8	50 4/8	7 7/8	8	6	6	0	22	4
* Teton County / Douglas Spicer / Douglas Spicer / 1972												
400 2/8	56	55 2/8	46	53 7/8	8 2/8	8 4/8	7	7	0	28	5
* Jackson Hole / C. Atkins & O. Maynard / Thomas Myers / 1947												
397 7/8	52	55 1/8	52 1/8	62 4/8	8 1/8	7 6/8	7	7	0	35	6
* Sublette County / Ray Daugherty / Aldon L. Hale / 1950												
395 4/8	57 5/8	60 1/8	47	51 6/8	8 1/8	8 6/8	6	6	0	41	7
* Fremont County / Roger Linnell / Roger Linnell / 1955												
394 2/8	53 2/8	56 2/8	41 2/8	46	9 2/8	9 2/8	6	6	0	50	8
* Hoback Rim / Clyde Robbins / George Franz / 1940												
394 1/8	58	58 4/8	46 7/8	49 6/8	9 6/8	10 2/8	6	6	0	53	9
* Lincoln County / Roland Smith / Leon C. Smith / 1930												
393 2/8	53 5/8	51 6/8	46 2/8	49	10 2/8	10	6	6	0	57	10
* Big Horn County / Edwin Shaffer / Edwin Shaffer / 1946												
391 6/8	54 4/8	53	46	48 4/8	7 7/8	8 7/8	6	6	0	67	11
* Thoroughfare Creek / Thomas A. Yawkey / Thomas A. Yawkey / 1936												
391 4/8	52 2/8	52 7/8	51 2/8	53 2/8	8 5/8	9	7	6	0	69	12
* Big Horn Mts. / Robert K. Hamilton / Robert K. Hamilton / 1954												
390 3/8	57 1/8	54 1/8	40 1/8	48 6/8	9 2/8	9 1/8	7	7	0	75	13
* Hoback Canyon / Picked Up / Spanky Greenville / 1977												
389 4/8	53 7/8	54 7/8	46	52 6/8	8 7/8	8 7/8	6	6	0	82	14
* Big Horn County / Floyd A. Clark / Floyd A. Clark / 1976												
388 7/8	56	55 4/8	46 3/8	50 3/8	9 6/8	8 6/8	6	6	0	89	15
* Jackson Hole / Unknown / William Sonnenburg / PR 1912												
388	55 4/8	54 4/8	50 2/8	53 1/8	8 4/8	9	8	9	2 4/8	97	16
* Converse / Jerry F. Cook / J.F. Cook & Mrs. P. Muchmore / 1965												
387 7/8	54 4/8	55 5/8	44 5/8	50 7/8	9 6/8	9 5/8	7	6	1 2/8	100	17
* Kelly / Roger Penney / Bernard Bronk / 1963												

Score	Length of Main Beam R	Length of Main Beam L	Inside Spread	Greatest Spread	Circumference at Smallest Place between First and Second Points R	Circumference at Smallest Place between First and Second Points L	Number of Points R	Number of Points L	Total of Lengths Abnormal Points	All-Time Rank	State Rank
♦ *Locality / Hunter / Owner / Date Killed*											
387 7/8	52 1/8	53	44 5/8	50 2/8	7 7/8	8	6	6	0	100	17
♦ *Lincoln / Dexter R. Gardner / Dexter R. Gardner / 1967*											
387 6/8	57 6/8	56 4/8	51	54 6/8	8	7 7/8	7	6	0	103	19
♦ *Big Horn Mts. / Elgin T. Gates / Elgin T. Gates / 1954*											
386	52 4/8	53	48 2/8	51 4/8	8 4/8	8 4/8	6	7	0	125	20
♦ *Big Horn Mts. / Unknown / Fred Gray / 1966*											
385 3/8	55 4/8	55 2/8	47 3/8	54 3/8	10 1/8	10 5/8	6	6	0	134	21
♦ *Teton County / Gene J. Riordan / Timothy D. Riordan / 1960*											
385 1/8	46	48 2/8	44 3/8	54 1/8	7 6/8	8 2/8	6	6	0	138	22
♦ *Lincoln County / Ken Clark / Ken Clark / 1979*											
384 3/8	59 3/8	59 2/8	49 1/8	49 1/8	7 6/8	7 5/8	7	6	0	151	23
♦ *Jackson Hole / Francis X. Bouchard / Francis X. Bouchard / 1956*											
383 1/8	58 1/8	54 4/8	53 1/8	54	9	9 6/8	6	6	0	168	24
♦ *Snowy Range / Kermit Platt / Kermit Platt / 1961*											
382 6/8	56 1/8	54 5/8	41 5/8	47 5/8	9 7/8	10 2/8	7	6	8 3/8	173	25
♦ *Rattlesnake Mt. / Bob Edgar / Bob Edgar / 1966*											
382 4/8	49	48 5/8	36 6/8	46 3/8	8 5/8	8 6/8	6	6	0	176	26
♦ *Teton County / Randy Johnston / Randy Johnston / 1970*											
382 3/8	53 3/8	54	50 5/8	52 7/8	8 4/8	8 4/8	7	7	0	180	27
♦ *Sublette County / Frank Dew / Frank Dew / 1931*											
381 4/8	56 4/8	57 2/8	42 4/8	48 2/8	8 7/8	9 2/8	6	6	0	202	28
♦ *Fremont County / John S. Maxson / John S. Maxson / 1954*											
381 1/8	57 5/8	56 1/8	45 1/8	53	8	7 3/8	6	6	0	209	29
♦ *Laramie Peak / Lawrence Prager / Lawrence Prager / 1958*											
379 6/8	51 2/8	53 6/8	45 6/8	51 7/8	9 2/8	9 5/8	7	7	0	235	30
♦ *Park County / Timothy D. Metzler / Timothy D. Metzler / 1994*											
379 5/8	57	53 1/8	48 1/8	52 2/8	9 2/8	9 2/8	6	6	0	242	31
♦ *Big Horn Mts. / Unknown / L.M. Brownell / 1956*											
379 2/8	57 1/8	55 5/8	41 6/8	59 4/8	8 1/8	8	6	6	0	249	32
♦ *Freemont County / Larry C. Nicholas / Frank J. Vrablic / 1976*											
379	49	50 4/8	39	43 4/8	10 1/8	10 1/8	8	6	0	258	33
♦ *Teton Park / S.M. Vilven / S.M. Vilven / 1964*											
378 7/8	57 5/8	58 6/8	47 1/8	51 3/8	8 2/8	8 2/8	6	6	0	261	34
♦ *Carbon County / Donal F. Mueller / Donal F. Mueller / 1964*											
378 4/8	52 7/8	54 5/8	42 4/8	47 4/8	9 3/8	10	7	7	0	266	35
♦ *Park County / Kenneth Smith / Kenneth Smith / 1954*											

Score	Length of Main Beam		Inside Spread	Greatest Spread	Circumference at Smallest Place between First and Second Points		Number of Points		Total of Lengths Abnormal Points	All-Time Rank	State Rank
	R	L			R	L	R	L			
◆ *Locality / Hunter / Owner / Date Killed*											
377 4/8	52 2/8	54	41 4/8	47 2/8	8 6/8	8 3/8	6	7	0	284	36
◆ *Park County / Jon M. Mekeal / Jon M. Mekeal / 1984*											
377 3/8	59	55	39 3/8	47 4/8	9 7/8	9 1/8	6	6	0	288	37
◆ *Teton County / Walter V. Solinski / Walter V. Solinski / 1962*											
377 2/8	56	55 2/8	40 2/8	48 2/8	11 1/8	11	6	6	0	292	38
◆ *Park County / Mary J. Rickman / M.J. Rickman & E.R. Rickman, Jr. / 1965*											
377 1/8	53	51 6/8	45 4/8	52 2/8	9	8 5/8	6	8	4 7/8	296	39
◆ *Sublette County / Ted Dew / Ted Dew / 1928*											
376 7/8	55	55 6/8	38 2/8	43 6/8	9 5/8	10 2/8	7	6	1 7/8	301	40
◆ *Jackson Hole / H.M. Hanna / M.H. Haskell / PR 1890*											
376 7/8	56 4/8	57 2/8	52 7/8	58 6/8	7 3/8	7 1/8	6	6	0	301	40
◆ *Park County / Warren C. Cubbage / Warren C. Cubbage / 1957*											
376 6/8	56 2/8	54 4/8	44 6/8	52 5/8	9 4/8	9 3/8	7	7	9	304	42
◆ *Big Horn Mts. / Unknown / A.W. Hendershot / 1912*											
376 6/8	61	58 7/8	51	55 4/8	8 3/8	7 3/8	8	7	0	304	42
◆ *Teton County / Ward Keevert / Ward Keevert / 1968*											
376 4/8	55 1/8	53 4/8	49 6/8	53	8 2/8	8 5/8	8	7	0	310	44
◆ *Albany County / Jerry F. Cook / Jerry F. Cook / 1965*											
375 6/8	54 6/8	50 4/8	43	47 6/8	8 4/8	8 2/8	6	6	0	322	45
◆ *Big Horn Mts. / Robert F. Retzlaff / Robert F. Retzlaff / 1957*											
375 6/8	57 2/8	57 7/8	43	50 2/8	7 2/8	7 3/8	6	6	0	322	45
◆ *Buck Creek / Andrew W. Heard, Jr. / Andrew W. Heard, Jr. / 1958*											
375 6/8	55 1/8	54 4/8	39 4/8	46 6/8	8 7/8	8 2/8	6	6	0	322	45
◆ *North Fall Creek / Picked Up / Bob F. Penny / 1981*											
375 4/8	50	53 2/8	48 4/8	54 1/8	8 4/8	9 1/8	6	6	0	331	48
◆ *Fremont County / Edward J. Patik / Edward J. Patik / 1962*											
375 3/8	51 1/8	52	44 7/8	47 4/8	7 6/8	8 2/8	6	7	0	335	49
◆ *Teton County / Unknown / Nathan E. Hindman / PR 1950*											
375 3/8	58 7/8	56 6/8	43 1/8	48 4/8	8 3/8	9 1/8	6	7	0	335	49
◆ *Snake River / W.H. Robinson / W.H. Robinson / 1957*											
375 2/8	54 4/8	55 3/8	49	54 4/8	9 3/8	9 6/8	6	7	0	342	51
◆ *Jackson / Bill Blanchard / Bill Blanchard / 1954*											
375 2/8	51 4/8	53 1/8	36 2/8	45 1/8	7 7/8	7 4/8	7	7	0	342	51
◆ *Ten Sleep / Kenneth Hadland / Kenneth Hadland / 1959*											
375 2/8	53	52	41	49 6/8	10	10 4/8	7	8	0	342	51
◆ *Natrona County / Victor R. Jackson / Victor R. Jackson / 1976*											

Score	Length of Main Beam		Inside Spread	Greatest Spread	Circumference at Smallest Place between First and Second Points		Number of Points		Total of Lengths Abnormal Points	All-Time Rank	State Rank
	R	L			R	L	R	L			

◆ *Locality / Hunter / Owner / Date Killed*

375 2/8	56	55	38	48 4/8	8 4/8	8 4/8	6	6	0	342	51

◆ *Albany County / Don Stewart / Don Stewart / 1981*

368 2/8	50 5/8	50 4/8	42 4/8	48 6/8	8	9 1/8	6	6	0	365	55

◆ *Carbon County / Larry J. Thoney / Larry J. Thoney / 1978*

366 7/8	56 4/8	52	43 5/8	46 4/8	10 4/8	9 4/8	6	7	0	369	56

◆ *Fremont County / Sherwin L. Felter / Sherwin L. Felter / 1993*

410 6/8	55 2/8	55 4/8	42 6/8	59 4/8	9 7/8	9 7/8	6	6	0	*	*

◆ *Carbon County / Unknown / William H. Tott / 1945*

A very pleased Gilbert T. Adams poses with this very impressive typical American elk, scoring 367-4/8 points, that he took in 1990 while hunting with S. Kim Bonnett on the Deseret Ranch in Utah.

Photograph Courtesy of Trophy Show Productions

WYOMING STATE RECORD (NEW)
NON-TYPICAL AMERICAN ELK
SCORE: 415 $\frac{2}{8}$
Locality: Johnson Co.   Date: 1993
Hunter: Rod M. Odenbach

WYOMING

NON-TYPICAL AMERICAN ELK

Score	Length of Main Beam R	L	Inside Spread	Greatest Spread	Circumference at Smallest Place between First and Second Points R	L	Number of Points R	L	Total of Lengths Abnormal Points	All-Time Rank	State Rank
	♦ Locality / Hunter / Owner / Date Killed										
415²⁄₈	54	55	42⁶⁄₈	52	8⁷⁄₈	9⁴⁄₈	8	8	3	9	1
	♦ Johnson County / Rod M. Odenbach / Rod M. Odenbach / 1993										
403¹⁄₈	51⁷⁄₈	51⁷⁄₈	38⁷⁄₈	43¹⁄₈	8⁷⁄₈	9²⁄₈	7	9	15⁴⁄₈	21	2
	♦ Big Horn County / Unknown / Steve Crossley / PR 1985										
403	52⁵⁄₈	52³⁄₈	57¹⁄₈	62⁴⁄₈	8⁷⁄₈	8⁴⁄₈	7	8	20⁵⁄₈	22	3
	♦ Uinta County / Steven W. Condos / Norman Heater / 1967										
401⁴⁄₈	48	45¹⁄₈	39¹⁄₈	42⁶⁄₈	11⁵⁄₈	11	8	11	55³⁄₈	30	4
	♦ Teton County / Douglas G. DeVivo / Douglas G. DeVivo / 1992										
401¹⁄₈	51³⁄₈	51³⁄₈	47⁶⁄₈	53²⁄₈	9¹⁄₈	9⁴⁄₈	8	6	8¹⁄₈	31	5
	♦ Fremont County / Bud Cantleberry / Robert E. Cantleberry / 1948										
390⁷⁄₈	52⁶⁄₈	51⁴⁄₈	46	52²⁄₈	9⁷⁄₈	9²⁄₈	7	8	16⁵⁄₈	49	6
	♦ Sublette County / Dale A. Shaklee / Dale A. Shaklee / 1993										
388³⁄₈	53	50⁴⁄₈	53⁶⁄₈	57⁵⁄₈	10⁷⁄₈	11	6	7	34⁵⁄₈	51	7
	♦ Platte County / Gary A. Pagel / Gary A. Pagel / 1993										
436¹⁄₈	55⁵⁄₈	52²⁄₈	68⁷⁄₈	72²⁄₈	10¹⁄₈	11⁵⁄₈	9	10	35	*	*
	♦ Laramie County / Joseph C. Dereemer / Charles Bird / 1971										

Photograph by Wm. H. Nesbitt

ALBERTA PROVINCE RECORD
TYPICAL AMERICAN ELK
SCORE: 419⅝
Locality: Panther River   Date: 1977
Hunter: Clarence Brown

ALBERTA

TYPICAL AMERICAN ELK

Score	Length of Main Beam R	Length of Main Beam L	Inside Spread	Greatest Spread	Circumference at Smallest Place between First and Second Points R	Circumference at Smallest Place between First and Second Points L	Number of Points R	Number of Points L	Total of Lengths Abnormal Points	All-Time Rank	State Rank
♦ *Locality / Hunter / Owner / Date Killed*											
419 5/8	62 3/8	62 2/8	49 2/8	53 2/8	10 3/8	10 3/8	6	8	1 5/8	5	1
♦ *Panther River / Clarence Brown / Clarence Brown / 1977*											
418	54 1/8	50 4/8	44 2/8	52 6/8	8 4/8	8 4/8	6	6	0	8	2
♦ *Muddywater River / Bruce W. Hale / Bruce W. Hale / 1971*											
402 5/8	59 1/8	59 6/8	44 1/8	0	9 1/8	8 5/8	7	7	0	18	3
♦ *Red Deer River / Henry Folkman / Henry Folkman / 1946*											
400 7/8	59 3/8	59 3/8	47 5/8	0	8 4/8	8 2/8	7	7	0	25	4
♦ *Rock Lake / Ray Hindmarsh / Ray Hindmarsh / 1963*											
399 2/8	59 5/8	57 4/8	47 3/8	53 2/8	7 7/8	7 5/8	8	7	3 7/8	31	5
♦ *Ram River / Ralph A. Fry / Ralph A. Fry / 1952*											
398	50 3/8	53 5/8	46 6/8	49 4/8	8 4/8	8 4/8	6	6	0	33	6
♦ *Pincher Creek / Monty F. Adams / Pat Adams / 1977*											
396 1/8	51 5/8	50 2/8	49 7/8	0	7 4/8	7 4/8	7	8	0	40	7
♦ *Rock Lake / Harold R. Vaughn / Harold R. Vaughn / 1968*											
394 2/8	56 7/8	57 2/8	42 6/8	49 1/8	9 2/8	7 6/8	7	6	1 4/8	50	8
♦ *Panther River / Picked Up / George Browne / 1938*											
394 2/8	53 1/8	55 3/8	45 2/8	53	8 1/8	8 3/8	6	6	0	50	8
♦ *Elkwater / Roy Crawford / Roy Crawford / 1976*											
393 2/8	55 2/8	54 4/8	51 4/8	55 2/8	8 3/8	8 2/8	6	6	0	57	10
♦ *Watertown Natl. Park / Alan Foster / Alan Foster / 1952*											
392 5/8	58 7/8	58 4/8	48 5/8	52 5/8	8 7/8	9	7	7	0	62	11
♦ *Panther River / Bill Brooks / Bill Brooks / 1955*											
390 6/8	53 5/8	54 3/8	49 6/8	53	9 3/8	9 5/8	7	6	0	72	12
♦ *Clearwater River / Bob Dial / Bob Dial / 1955*											
388 2/8	59 1/8	59	54	57	7 5/8	7 6/8	6	6	0	92	13
♦ *Cutoff Creek / Joe A. Riveira / Joe A. Riveira / 1986*											
387 5/8	58 1/8	56	39 1/8	45 3/8	8 7/8	9 1/8	7	7	0	105	14
♦ *Yarrow Creek / D. Belyea / D. Belyea / 1970*											
386 5/8	59 3/8	60	52 1/8	55	9 6/8	9 1/8	7	7	0	116	15
♦ *Panther River / Leonard L. Hengen / Leonard L. Hengen / 1977*											
386 4/8	55 6/8	55 5/8	42	53 1/8	10	9 2/8	7	7	0	117	16
♦ *Smoky River / Stephen Trulik / Stephen Trulik / 1963*											
385 6/8	56 7/8	56 1/8	40 4/8	44 3/8	7 7/8	8	6	6	0	128	17
♦ *Big Smoky River / Fred T. Huntington, Jr. / Fred T. Huntington, Jr. / 1961*											

Score	Length of Main Beam		Inside Spread	Greatest Spread	Circumference at Smallest Place between First and Second Points		Number of Points		Total of Lengths Abnormal Points	All-Time Rank	State Rank
	R	L			R	L	R	L			

385 $\frac{1}{8}$ 51 52 $\frac{4}{8}$ 48 $\frac{4}{8}$ 54 $\frac{3}{8}$ 11 11 $\frac{4}{8}$ 8 6 8 $\frac{7}{8}$ 138 18
♦ *Grande Cache Lake / Kenneth A. Evans / Kenneth A. Evans / 1966*

384 $\frac{6}{8}$ 55 $\frac{3}{8}$ 54 $\frac{3}{8}$ 36 $\frac{4}{8}$ 39 $\frac{7}{8}$ 9 $\frac{2}{8}$ 9 6 6 0 143 19
♦ *Clearwater River / William Lenz / William Lenz / 1966*

384 $\frac{5}{8}$ 55 $\frac{3}{8}$ 54 $\frac{6}{8}$ 47 $\frac{1}{8}$ 54 8 $\frac{4}{8}$ 8 $\frac{7}{8}$ 6 6 0 147 20
♦ *Ram River / Joe Kramer / Joe Kramer / 1966*

383 $\frac{3}{8}$ 53 $\frac{5}{8}$ 55 50 $\frac{1}{8}$ 51 $\frac{2}{8}$ 8 $\frac{2}{8}$ 8 6 6 0 165 21
♦ *Maycroft / Steve Kubasek / Steve Kubasek / 1957*

383 52 $\frac{1}{8}$ 52 $\frac{3}{8}$ 51 $\frac{4}{8}$ 53 $\frac{1}{8}$ 9 $\frac{5}{8}$ 9 6 6 0 169 22
♦ *Panther River / Thomas Coupland / Echoglen Taxidermy / 1984*

382 $\frac{7}{8}$ 54 $\frac{3}{8}$ 52 $\frac{7}{8}$ 43 $\frac{5}{8}$ 47 $\frac{3}{8}$ 8 $\frac{6}{8}$ 8 $\frac{5}{8}$ 6 6 0 171 23
♦ *Castle River / Albert Truant / Albert Truant / 1970*

382 $\frac{4}{8}$ 49 $\frac{6}{8}$ 48 32 $\frac{7}{8}$ 40 $\frac{6}{8}$ 14 $\frac{4}{8}$ 13 9 7 16 $\frac{1}{8}$ 176 24
♦ *Elbow River / Harold F. Mailman / Harold F. Mailman / 1964*

381 $\frac{6}{8}$ 55 $\frac{2}{8}$ 57 $\frac{1}{8}$ 41 47 9 $\frac{6}{8}$ 9 $\frac{6}{8}$ 7 7 0 193 25
♦ *Red Deer River / Allan E. Brown / Allan E. Brown / 1980*

381 $\frac{6}{8}$ 56 $\frac{1}{8}$ 55 44 $\frac{4}{8}$ 19 9 $\frac{1}{8}$ 8 $\frac{5}{8}$ 7 7 0 193 25
♦ *Waterton River / Keith A. Keeler / Keith A. Keeler / 1989*

380 54 53 $\frac{5}{8}$ 48 $\frac{2}{8}$ 52 $\frac{3}{8}$ 8 $\frac{7}{8}$ 8 $\frac{4}{8}$ 7 7 0 230 27
♦ *Spring Creek / A.C. Bair / A.C. Bair / 1948*

379 $\frac{6}{8}$ 50 $\frac{2}{8}$ 51 $\frac{4}{8}$ 45 $\frac{4}{8}$ 52 $\frac{1}{8}$ 9 $\frac{4}{8}$ 9 $\frac{4}{8}$ 6 6 0 235 28
♦ *Rock Lake / Jim Soneff / Jim Soneff / 1961*

379 $\frac{1}{8}$ 56 57 $\frac{4}{8}$ 33 $\frac{7}{8}$ 47 8 $\frac{6}{8}$ 9 $\frac{1}{8}$ 6 6 0 256 29
♦ *Duvernay Bridge / Alec Mitchell / Alec Mitchell / 1917*

378 $\frac{7}{8}$ 56 $\frac{6}{8}$ 56 $\frac{1}{8}$ 46 $\frac{5}{8}$ 52 $\frac{2}{8}$ 8 $\frac{4}{8}$ 8 6 6 0 261 30
♦ *Wildhay River / Richard Clouthier / Richard Clouthier / 1973*

378 $\frac{5}{8}$ 52 55 $\frac{2}{8}$ 47 $\frac{7}{8}$ 51 $\frac{4}{8}$ 8 $\frac{7}{8}$ 8 $\frac{6}{8}$ 7 6 0 265 31
♦ *Dutch Creek / Harold King / Harold King / 1951*

377 54 $\frac{6}{8}$ 54 $\frac{1}{8}$ 47 $\frac{2}{8}$ 51 9 $\frac{2}{8}$ 8 $\frac{5}{8}$ 7 6 0 297 32
♦ *Brazeau River / Ted Loblaw / Ted Loblaw / 1960*

377 49 $\frac{4}{8}$ 48 $\frac{1}{8}$ 39 48 $\frac{3}{8}$ 7 $\frac{1}{8}$ 7 $\frac{4}{8}$ 7 7 0 297 32
♦ *Clearwater River / Don H. Grimes / Don H. Grimes / 1985*

376 $\frac{4}{8}$ 56 $\frac{5}{8}$ 57 39 $\frac{4}{8}$ 48 9 $\frac{3}{8}$ 9 $\frac{5}{8}$ 7 7 0 310 34
♦ *Highwood River / L. Edwards / L. Edwards / 1956*

376 $\frac{3}{8}$ 54 $\frac{2}{8}$ 55 $\frac{5}{8}$ 43 $\frac{3}{8}$ 50 9 9 $\frac{1}{8}$ 6 6 0 312 35
♦ *Rocky Mt. House / George P. Ebl / George P. Ebl / 1966*

ALBERTA TYPICAL AMERICAN ELK *(continued)*

Score	Length of Main Beam R	Length of Main Beam L	Inside Spread	Greatest Spread	Circumference at Smallest Place between First and Second Points R	Circumference at Smallest Place between First and Second Points L	Number of Points R	Number of Points L	Total of Lengths Abnormal Points	All-Time Rank	State Rank
♦ *Locality / Hunter / Owner / Date Killed*											
376	55	54 1/8	42	50 2/8	9 3/8	9 1/8	6	6	0	317	36
♦ *Dormer River / D.C. Thomas / D.C. Thomas / 1978*											
365 3/8	56 7/8	55 5/8	43 6/8	49 4/8	8 6/8	7 4/8	7	8	6 3/8	374	37
♦ *Barrier Mt. / James A. Bauer / James A. Bauer / 1985*											

Photograph Courtesy of Robert H. Jochim

ALBERTA PROVINCE RECORD
NON-TYPICAL AMERICAN ELK
SCORE: 402 2/8*
Locality: Dogrib Creek   Date: 1984
Hunter: Robert H. Jochim

ALBERTA
NON-TYPICAL AMERICAN ELK

Score	Length of Main Beam		Inside Spread	Greatest Spread	Circumference at Smallest Place between First and Second Points		Number of Points		Total of Lengths Abnormal Points	All-Time Rank	State Rank
	R	L			R	L	R	L			

♦ *Locality / Hunter / Owner / Date Killed*

| 402 2/8 | 55 6/8 | 55 7/8 | 50 1/8 | 53 2/8 | 9 7/8 | 10 1/8 | 7 | 7 | 24 3/8 | * | * |

♦ *Dogrib Creek / Robert H. Jochim / Robert H. Jochim / 1984*

BRITISH COLUMBIA PROVINCE RECORD
TYPICAL AMERICAN ELK
SCORE: 401⅞
Locality: Kootenay Lake   Date: Picked Up 1986
Owner: Rick D. Armstrong

BRITISH COLUMBIA

TYPICAL AMERICAN ELK

Score	Length of Main Beam R	Length of Main Beam L	Inside Spread	Greatest Spread	Circumference at Smallest Place between First and Second Points R	Circumference at Smallest Place between First and Second Points L	Number of Points R	Number of Points L	Total of Lengths Abnormal Points	All-Time Rank	State Rank
♦ *Locality / Hunter / Owner / Date Killed*											
401 7/8	55 3/8	54 4/8	45 3/8	50 6/8	9 6/8	9 4/8	6	6	0	20	1
♦ *Kootenay Lake / Picked Up / Rick D. Armstrong / 1986*											
388 2/8	56 1/8	54 7/8	40	50 7/8	9 2/8	9 7/8	7	6	4 6/8	92	2
♦ *Sentinel Mt. / Martin Braun / Martin Braun / 1986*											
388 1/8	56 3/8	56 4/8	46 4/8	48 4/8	8 3/8	8 4/8	8	7	3 5/8	96	3
♦ *Slocan River / Trevor W. Stetsko / Trevor W. Stetsko / 1991*											
378 1/8	52 4/8	53 2/8	39 7/8	45 1/8	7 1/8	6 7/8	7	8	0	274	4
♦ *Langill Lake / Gary D. Fodor / Gary D. Fodor / 1989*											

BRITISH COLUMBIA PROVINCE RECORD (NEW)
NON-TYPICAL AMERICAN ELK
SCORE: 430 6/8

Locality: Fraser River   Date: 1980
Hunter: Ben Young
Owner: John Young

BRITISH COLUMBIA
NON-TYPICAL AMERICAN ELK

Score	Length of Main Beam		Inside Spread	Greatest Spread	Circumference at Smallest Place between First and Second Points		Number of Points		Total of Lengths Abnormal Points	All-Time Rank	State Rank
	R	L			R	L	R	L			

◆ *Locality / Hunter / Owner / Date Killed*

430⁶⁄₈	46⁵⁄₈	51⁵⁄₈	45³⁄₈	50⁶⁄₈	8⁶⁄₈	9⁴⁄₈	10	8	71¹⁄₈	3	1

◆ *Fraser River / Ben Young / John Young / 1980*

400⁴⁄₈	54⁷⁄₈	54⁶⁄₈	40⁵⁄₈	57¹⁄₈	7⁴⁄₈	7²⁄₈	10	8	47³⁄₈	33	2

◆ *Whipsaw Creek / Harold Margerison / Harold Margerison / 1960*

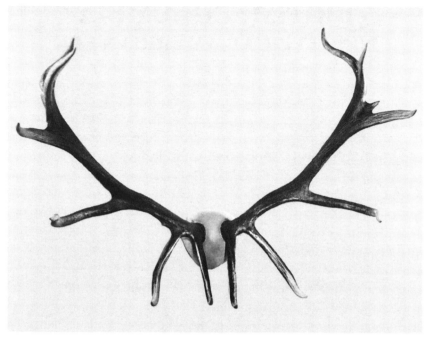

Photograph by Wm. H. Nesbitt

MANITOBA PROVINCE RECORD
TYPICAL AMERICAN ELK
SCORE: 406 7/8
Locality: Duck Mountain   Date: 1980
Hunter: Herb Andres
Owner: Larry L. Huffman

MANITOBA

TYPICAL AMERICAN ELK

Score	Length of Main Beam R	Length of Main Beam L	Inside Spread	Greatest Spread	Circumference at Smallest Place between First and Second Points R	Circumference at Smallest Place between First and Second Points L	Number of Points R	Number of Points L	Total of Lengths Abnormal Points	All-Time Rank	State Rank
♦ *Locality / Hunter / Owner / Date Killed*											
406 7/8	52 7/8	52 6/8	49 3/8	57 6/8	8 6/8	9 2/8	6	7	3 6/8	14	1
♦ *Duck Mt. / Herb Andres / Larry L. Huffman / 1980*											
396 2/8	48	50 4/8	32 4/8	44 4/8	10	9 4/8	7	7	0	39	2
♦ *Duck Mt. / Paul Kirkowich / Paul Kirkowich / 1960*											
394 4/8	55 2/8	54 6/8	37	46	9 2/8	10	6	6	0	47	3
♦ *Duck Mt. / Melvin J. Podaima / Melvin J. Podaima / 1991*											
380	51 5/8	51 6/8	41 6/8	45 3/8	7 6/8	8 3/8	6	6	0	230	4
♦ *Duck Mt. / G.N. Burton / G.N. Burton / 1965*											
379 2/8	53 2/8	53 4/8	41 4/8	46 4/8	8 5/8	8 7/8	6	6	0	249	5
♦ *Whirlpool River / Rudy R. Usick / Rudy R. Usick / 1989*											
378 6/8	54 6/8	52 7/8	44 2/8	48 7/8	9 7/8	9 6/8	6	5	0	263	6
♦ *Otter Lake / Walter Giesbrecht / Walter Giesbrecht / 1989*											
378 2/8	43 4/8	47 3/8	40	47 6/8	9 6/8	9 6/8	9	8	14 2/8	272	7
♦ *Duck Mt. / John D. Harbarenko / John D. Harbarenko / 1973*											
375 6/8	49 3/8	49 6/8	38	52 6/8	9 6/8	9 4/8	6	6	0	322	8
♦ *Glenboro / Peter Sawatzky / Peter Sawatzky / 1992*											

Photograph by Wm. H. Nesbitt

MANITOBA PROVINCE RECORD
WORLD'S RECORD
NON-TYPICAL AMERICAN ELK
SCORE: 447⅛
Locality: Gilbert Plains   Date: 1961
Hunter: James R. Berry
Owner: Bob Howard

MANITOBA
NON-TYPICAL AMERICAN ELK

Score	Length of Main Beam R	L	Inside Spread	Greatest Spread	Circumference at Smallest Place between First and Second Points R	L	Number of Points R	L	Total of Lengths Abnormal Points	All-Time Rank	State Rank

♦ *Locality / Hunter / Owner / Date Killed*

447⅛	54⅛	52⅝	39⅞	52⅞	11	10²⁄₈	9	9	37²⁄₈	1	1

♦ *Gilbert Plains / James R. Berry / Bob Howard / 1961*

405³⁄₈	59⁴⁄₈	58⅛	40²⁄₈	43⁶⁄₈	8⁴⁄₈	8²⁄₈	7	8	10³⁄₈	17	2

♦ *Vermilion River / Ernie M. Bernat / Ernie M. Bernat / 1986*

402	51⅞	46³⁄₈	38³⁄₈	48⅝	8⁶⁄₈	8²⁄₈	8	9	29⅛	27	3

♦ *Lundar / Picked Up / Fred Thorkelson / 1980*

394³⁄₈	40²⁄₈	39²⁄₈	34³⁄₈	50	10²⁄₈	10	14	11	57⁴⁄₈	42	4

♦ *Carberry / Brent Maxwell / Brent Maxwell / 1991*

SASKATCHEWAN FOURTH PLACE
TYPICAL AMERICAN ELK
SCORE: 377⅝
Locality: Mistatim   Date: 1984
Hunter: Peter Hrbachek

SASKATCHEWAN
TYPICAL AMERICAN ELK

Score	Length of Main Beam R	L	Inside Spread	Greatest Spread	Circumference at Smallest Place between First and Second Points R	L	Number of Points R	L	Total of Lengths Abnormal Points	All-Time Rank	State Rank
389$\frac{5}{8}$	56$\frac{5}{8}$	52$\frac{5}{8}$	52$\frac{5}{8}$	0	9$\frac{2}{8}$	9$\frac{2}{8}$	7	7	0	79	1
♦ Ft. A La Corne / Jim Crozier / Jim Crozier / 1955											
389$\frac{2}{8}$	49$\frac{7}{8}$	48$\frac{1}{8}$	40	0	10$\frac{7}{8}$	10$\frac{3}{8}$	6	6	0	86	2
♦ Saskatchewan / Unknown / B.P.O. Elks Lodge / PR 1956											
386$\frac{1}{8}$	57$\frac{5}{8}$	57$\frac{1}{8}$	48$\frac{5}{8}$	57$\frac{1}{8}$	7$\frac{7}{8}$	8$\frac{5}{8}$	6	6	0	122	3
♦ Forest Gate Store / Edwin L. Roberts / Edwin L. Roberts / 1962											
377$\frac{6}{8}$	53$\frac{3}{8}$	53$\frac{4}{8}$	41$\frac{6}{8}$	53$\frac{3}{8}$	9	9$\frac{5}{8}$	9	9	8$\frac{6}{8}$	279	4
♦ Mistatim / Peter Hrbachek / Peter Hrbachek / 1984											
376$\frac{7}{8}$	46$\frac{5}{8}$	45$\frac{6}{8}$	42$\frac{5}{8}$	46$\frac{4}{8}$	10	9$\frac{5}{8}$	7	6	5$\frac{3}{8}$	301	5
♦ Flotten Lake / Garry G. Ronald / Garry G. Ronald / 1987											
375$\frac{1}{8}$	52	53$\frac{4}{8}$	39$\frac{3}{8}$	46$\frac{5}{8}$	9	10	6	6	0	348	6
♦ Prince Albert / Unknown / Lucky Lake Sask. Elks / 1926											

TOP 10 ROOSEVELT'S ELK LISTINGS INDEX

Tabulations of Recorded Roosevelt's Elk

The trophy data shown on the following pages are taken from score charts in the records archives of the Boone and Crockett Club. A comparison of the rankings of this book with those of the first edition of *Records of North American Elk and Mule Deer* will reveal some significant differences. This is primarily due to the addition of trophies from the 21st (1989-1991) and the 22nd (1992-1994) Awards Programs.

Roosevelt's elk, named after Theodore Roosevelt, the great conservationist who founded the Boone and Crockett Club, are larger bodied than American elk but have smaller racks. They occur in the coastal Pacific states, with geographic boundaries described for entry (See the 10th edition of the all-time records book for a boundary description).

The scores and ranks shown are final, except the trophies shown with an asterisk (*). The asterisk identifies entry scores subject to final certification by an Awards Panel of Judges. The asterisk can be removed (except in the case of a potential World's Record) by the submission of two additional, independent scorings by Official Measurers of the Boone and Crockett Club. The Records Committee of the Club will review the three scorings available (original plus two additional) and determine which, if any, will be accepted in lieu of a Judges' Panel measurement. When the score has been accepted as final by the Records Committee, the asterisk will be removed in future editions of this book and the all-time records book, *Records of North American Big Game*. In the case of a potential World's Record, the trophy must come before a Judges' Panel at the end of an entry period. Only a Judges' Panel can certify a World's Record and finalize its score. Asterisked trophies are unranked at the end of their category.

Photograph Courtesy of Leo Prshora

CALIFORNIA STATE RECORD
ROOSEVELT'S ELK
SCORE: 332 ⅜
Locality: Humboldt Co.   Date: Picked Up 1955
Owner: Leo Prshora

CALIFORNIA
ROOSEVELT'S ELK

Score	Length of Main Beam		Inside Spread	Greatest Spread	Circumference at Smallest Place between First and Second Points		Number of Points		Total of Lengths Abnormal Points	All-Time Rank	State Rank
	R	L			R	L	R	L			
◆ Locality / Hunter / Owner / Date Killed											

$332\frac{2}{8}$ $51\frac{6}{8}$ $51\frac{4}{8}$ $41\frac{2}{8}$ $46\frac{2}{8}$ $8\frac{6}{8}$ $9\frac{1}{8}$ 8 6 0 36 1
◆ *Humboldt County / Picked Up / Leo Prshora / 1955*

$318\frac{5}{8}$ 48 $49\frac{2}{8}$ 40 $43\frac{1}{8}$ $8\frac{2}{8}$ 8 7 6 0 61 2
◆ *Del Norte County / Richard K. Armas / Richard K. Armas / 1988*

$306\frac{4}{8}$ 47 $47\frac{5}{8}$ $43\frac{5}{8}$ $45\frac{5}{8}$ $7\frac{5}{8}$ $7\frac{6}{8}$ 6 6 0 83 3
◆ *Humboldt County / Michael L. Johnson / Michael L. Johnson / 1976*

$298\frac{2}{8}$ $47\frac{6}{8}$ $47\frac{2}{8}$ $40\frac{5}{8}$ $43\frac{3}{8}$ 9 9 6 6 0 106 4
◆ *Humboldt County / Eugene M. Boyd IV / Eugene M. Boyd IV / 1988*

Photograph by Wm. H. Nesbitt

OREGON STATE RECORD
ROOSEVELT'S ELK
SCORE: 384⅜
Locality: Clatsop Co.   Date: 1949
Hunter: Robert Sharp

OREGON
ROOSEVELT'S ELK

Score	Length of Main Beam R	L	Inside Spread	Greatest Spread	Circumference at Smallest Place between First and Second Points R	L	Number of Points R	L	Total of Lengths Abnormal Points	All-Time Rank	State Rank
◆ Locality / Hunter / Owner / Date Killed											
384 3/8	48 4/8	49	41 1/8	49 1/8	8 7/8	9 4/8	9	8	0	2	1
◆ Clatsop County / Robert Sharp / Robert Sharp / 1949											
378 5/8	53 2/8	51 3/8	37	41 3/8	8 7/8	8 5/8	7	9	0	4	2
◆ Clatsop County / Fred M. Williamson / Loaned to B&C Natl. Coll. / 1947											
367 5/8	50 3/8	53	37 4/8	42	9	8 5/8	7	7	0	7	3
◆ Clatsop County / Pravomil Raichl / Pravomil Raichl / 1959											
366 5/8	43	45 5/8	35 4/8	48 3/8	9 6/8	9 5/8	7	8	0	9	4
◆ Columbia County / Floyd M. Lindberg / Floyd M. Lindberg / 1962											
362 6/8	45 7/8	45 5/8	37 4/8	43 4/8	9 4/8	9 1/8	7	7	0	10	5
◆ Lincoln County / James H. Flescher / James H. Flescher / 1955											
358 6/8	51 4/8	51 4/8	42 2/8	51 4/8	9 6/8	10 2/8	7	7	0	11	6
◆ Clatsop County / Donald A. Schoenborn / Eric Schoenborn / 1939											
358 5/8	55 4/8	53 4/8	42	45 1/8	9 5/8	8 7/8	8	8	3 6/8	12	7
◆ Tillamook County / Albert Hoffarber / Ray Hoffarber / 1940											
353 4/8	52	53 3/8	38 4/8	44	8 5/8	9 1/8	6	7	0	13	8
◆ Washington County / Kenneth R. Adamson / Kenneth R. Adamson / 1985											
350 3/8	47 6/8	47 4/8	35 7/8	46 2/8	11 1/8	11 7/8	7	7	1 1/8	15	9
◆ Coos County / E.V. Schmidt / Steve Crossley / 1948											
347 6/8	41 3/8	42 3/8	46 2/8	48 4/8	8 2/8	8	7	7	0	16	10
◆ Tillamook County / Bud Davis / Herb W. Davis / 1957											
347	47 2/8	46 4/8	44 2/8	50 2/8	9 1/8	9 1/8	8	7	0	17	11
◆ Columbia County / Al Glenn / Al Glenn / 1955											
345 6/8	51 5/8	51 3/8	40 5/8	44	11 1/8	11 1/8	6	7	14 3/8	18	12
◆ Columbia County / Unknown / Harold E. Stepp / 1962											
341 2/8	45 1/8	42 4/8	44 6/8	57 2/8	9 6/8	9 3/8	7	8	0	21	13
◆ Josephine County / Robert Veatch / Cass E. Raymond / PR 1890											
341	45 1/8	45 2/8	33 5/8	39 1/8	10 3/8	10	8	8	0	22	14
◆ Columbia County / Derl Roberts / Derl Roberts / 1965											
340 4/8	46 1/8	45	36	43	9 3/8	9	6	8	1 2/8	24	15
◆ Columbia County / Bud Holmes / James C. Oroth / 1962											
340 2/8	49	46 4/8	43 5/8	49 6/8	9 5/8	9 5/8	7	8	8 5/8	25	16
◆ Clatsop County / Fain J. Little / Fain J. Little / 1945											
338	43 4/8	44 1/8	41 1/8	47 3/8	9 7/8	9 1/8	7	7	0	27	17
◆ Tillamook County / Tony W. Hancock / Tony W. Hancock / 1985											

Score	Length of Main Beam R	L	Inside Spread	Greatest Spread	Circumference at Smallest Place between First and Second Points R	L	Number of Points R	L	Total of Lengths Abnormal Points	All-Time Rank	State Rank
	♦ Locality / Hunter / Owner / Date Killed										
336⁶⁄₈	50⁴⁄₈	47⁶⁄₈	39	43	8	8⁶⁄₈	6	7	0	31	18
	♦ Tillamook County / Gary L. Cox / Gary L. Cox / 1965										
336⁴⁄₈	46⁶⁄₈	46⁶⁄₈	40³⁄₈	43²⁄₈	8⁷⁄₈	9¹⁄₈	7	6	0	32	19
	♦ Oregon Coast Range / Unknown / Richard Leach / PR 1981										
335¹⁄₈	51²⁄₈	51⁷⁄₈	42¹⁄₈	46⁵⁄₈	10¹⁄₈	10³⁄₈	7	7	0	34	20
	♦ Clatsop County / Picked Up / Andy Mendenhall, Jr. / 1978										
332	49	48⁴⁄₈	45	47²⁄₈	8¹⁄₈	8⁵⁄₈	7	6	0	37	21
	♦ Tillamook County / Robert B. Thornton / Robert B. Thornton / 1964										
329⁵⁄₈	48⁷⁄₈	50¹⁄₈	39³⁄₈	45¹⁄₈	8⁵⁄₈	8²⁄₈	6	6	0	39	22
	♦ Tillamook County / Gary H. Purdy / Gary H. Purdy / 1969										
327³⁄₈	48⁵⁄₈	50⁵⁄₈	42³⁄₈	50¹⁄₈	8³⁄₈	8¹⁄₈	8	7	9⁴⁄₈	42	23
	♦ Tillamook County / Picked Up / Dave Griffith / 1958										
327²⁄₈	50⁵⁄₈	50	40⁵⁄₈	44	8⁷⁄₈	9¹⁄₈	7	6	1⁵⁄₈	43	24
	♦ Clatsop County / Billy L. Jasper / Billy L. Jasper / 1946										
325³⁄₈	50	49	43⁶⁄₈	47⁶⁄₈	9	9⁶⁄₈	8	7	2	47	25
	♦ Columbia County / Edgar J. Rea / Edgar J. Rea / 1973										
323	45⁵⁄₈	47	37⁷⁄₈	40⁶⁄₈	7²⁄₈	7¹⁄₈	7	7	0	51	26
	♦ Clatsop County / Clarence V. Jurhs / Clarence V. Jurhs / 1958										
322³⁄₈	47⁶⁄₈	44⁵⁄₈	38¹⁄₈	47¹⁄₈	8⁷⁄₈	9²⁄₈	8	7	16²⁄₈	52	27
	♦ Columbia County / William E. Curtis / Duane M. Bernard / 1952										
322²⁄₈	44⁶⁄₈	45²⁄₈	41³⁄₈	42¹⁄₈	8⁵⁄₈	9¹⁄₈	7	7	0	53	28
	♦ Lincoln County / James R. Goodwin / James R. Goodwin / 1960										
322¹⁄₈	43²⁄₈	41	41²⁄₈	42⁷⁄₈	10³⁄₈	10³⁄₈	7	7	2	54	29
	♦ Clatsop County / Reed Holding / Reed Holding / 1939										
322¹⁄₈	45⁵⁄₈	45³⁄₈	42²⁄₈	45	11⁴⁄₈	11	6	6	0	54	29
	♦ Polk County / R.L. Stamps / R.L. Stamps / 1985										
320⁴⁄₈	47¹⁄₈	51¹⁄₈	32⁵⁄₈	43⁶⁄₈	8⁶⁄₈	8⁶⁄₈	7	6	0	56	31
	♦ Tillamook County / Stanley E. Kephart / Stanley E. Kephart / 1964										
320²⁄₈	43¹⁄₈	43⁵⁄₈	47¹⁄₈	50	8⁵⁄₈	8⁴⁄₈	7	7	0	57	32
	♦ Columbia County / Harry R. Olsen / Harry R. Olsen / 1961										
320¹⁄₈	43²⁄₈	48⁶⁄₈	42²⁄₈	44⁴⁄₈	10⁶⁄₈	10⁶⁄₈	5	7	0	59	33
	♦ Clatsop County / Jack O. Bay / Jack O. Bay / 1963										
319⁵⁄₈	49⁴⁄₈	47⁶⁄₈	39⁷⁄₈	43	6⁷⁄₈	6⁶⁄₈	6	7	0	60	34
	♦ Clatsop County / Picked Up / John T. Mee / 1969										
317²⁄₈	41³⁄₈	41⁵⁄₈	37⁶⁄₈	45	9	8⁷⁄₈	6	7	0	63	35
	♦ Columbia County / Max Oblack / Max Oblack / 1967										

Score	Length of Main Beam R	L	Inside Spread	Greatest Spread	Circumference at Smallest Place between First and Second Points R	L	Number of Points R	L	Total of Lengths Abnormal Points	All-Time Rank	State Rank
					◆ Locality / Hunter / Owner / Date Killed						
316⁶/₈	51³/₈	49	39	42⁷/₈	8⁶/₈	9⁷/₈	6	7	0	64	36
	◆ Columbia County / Harry R. Olsen / Harry R. Olsen / 1969										
316⁵/₈	45⁴/₈	45⁴/₈	41⁵/₈	46	8⁶/₈	8⁶/₈	6	6	0	65	37
	◆ Lincoln County / Verlin H. Rhoades / Verlin H. Rhoades / 1944										
315⁴/₈	48²/₈	47⁷/₈	42	46	9⁴/₈	9	6	6	0	68	38
	◆ Columbia County / William E. Curtis / Duane M. Bernard / 1965										
314⁶/₈	46⁶/₈	46⁶/₈	42²/₈	43	8	8⁵/₈	7	8	0	69	39
	◆ Columbia County / Picked Up / Harold E. Stepp / 1962										
314⁴/₈	52¹/₈	49²/₈	36³/₈	40⁶/₈	9⁵/₈	9³/₈	6	6	0	70	40
	◆ Coos County / Robert D. Dunson / Robert D. Dunson / 1982										
314³/₈	45⁷/₈	46¹/₈	42³/₈	45	8⁴/₈	8	7	7	0	71	41
	◆ Clatsop County / Robert L. Brown / Robert L. Brown / 1966										
310⁴/₈	44³/₈	44	33⁵/₈	42⁶/₈	9⁵/₈	9⁶/₈	7	7	0	75	42
	◆ Clatsop County / Elman Peterson, Jr. / Elman Peterson, Jr. / 1968										
310²/₈	44¹/₈	44⁶/₈	43²/₈	46	8³/₈	9³/₈	8	5	0	76	43
	◆ Clatsop County / Donald R. Chisholm / D.R. Chisholm & A. Holdridge / 1957										
309⁶/₈	43¹/₈	48¹/₈	31⁶/₈	37¹/₈	9²/₈	9⁴/₈	7	7	0	78	44
	◆ Clatsop County / Terry E. Andrews / Terry E. Andrews / 1984										
309¹/₈	47³/₈	43⁷/₈	37⁷/₈	40	9²/₈	8⁷/₈	6	6	0	79	45
	◆ Clatsop County / Valentine T. Mueller / John A. Mueller / 1938										
308³/₈	48	48	41⁵/₈	45²/₈	9⁷/₈	9²/₈	6	7	0	80	46
	◆ Coos County / Dean Dunson / Dean Dunson / 1986										
307⁴/₈	46¹/₈	45⁶/₈	40⁶/₈	43¹/₈	7⁷/₈	7⁷/₈	7	7	0	81	47
	◆ Tillamook County / John A. Wehinger / John A. Wehinger / 1964										
306⁶/₈	50²/₈	50⁴/₈	38⁶/₈	43¹/₈	7⁶/₈	8	6	6	0	82	48
	◆ Polk County / James E. Wallen / James E. Wallen / 1980										
306	40⁴/₈	39³/₈	40⁴/₈	43¹/₈	9¹/₈	9⁴/₈	7	7	0	84	49
	◆ Washington County / Michael R. Jamieson / Michael R. Jamieson / 1982										
304⁶/₈	49	41¹/₈	39¹/₈	44	9⁷/₈	9³/₈	6	7	3⁵/₈	85	50
	◆ Clatsop County / William D. Mellinger / William D. Mellinger / 1958										
304¹/₈	39⁶/₈	38¹/₈	31¹/₈	35⁴/₈	8	7⁶/₈	8	8	0	87	51
	◆ Yamhill County / Kevin E. Mishler / Kevin E. Mishler / 1989										
302⁶/₈	49	49¹/₈	38⁴/₈	41⁷/₈	7⁷/₈	7⁷/₈	6	6	0	90	52
	◆ Columbia County / Picked Up / Rick A. Hood / 1991										
302⁵/₈	41	39⁶/₈	44	44¹/₈	9⁷/₈	9⁵/₈	9	6	2⁴/₈	93	53
	◆ Lincoln County / Michael Kosydar / Michael Kosydar / 1985										

Score	Length of Main Beam R	L	Inside Spread	Greatest Spread	Circumference at Smallest Place between First and Second Points R	L	Number of Points R	L	Total of Lengths Abnormal Points	All-Time Rank	State Rank
301 6/8	43	43 7/8	36 2/8	41 5/8	8 6/8	9 4/8	8	8	0	95	54
♦ Clatsop County / Pravomil Raichl / Pravomil Raichl / 1963											
300 2/8	43	40 6/8	37 4/8	41 2/8	9	8 4/8	6	6	0	98	55
♦ Columbia County / Harry R. Olsen / Harry R. Olsen / 1963											
299 6/8	48 7/8	49 1/8	37 2/8	41	8 2/8	7 7/8	6	6	0	99	56
♦ Lincoln County / Jullian Smallwood / Gerald Smallwood / 1945											
299 4/8	42 2/8	40 7/8	39	43 2/8	8 2/8	7 7/8	7	7	0	101	57
♦ Lincoln County / Gene Nyhus / Gene Nyhus / 1950											
299 2/8	42 4/8	41 6/8	46 4/8	48 6/8	7 2/8	7 5/8	7	6	0	102	58
♦ Columbia County / Charles H. Atkins / Charles H. Atkins / 1964											
298 5/8	43 4/8	50 6/8	39 6/8	48 1/8	8 4/8	8	8	8	18 2/8	104	59
♦ Clatsop County / Harold O. Hundere / Harold O. Hundere / 1943											
298 2/8	47	44 3/8	37 4/8	40	7 6/8	7 4/8	8	6	0	106	60
♦ Columbia County / Nicholas A. Berg / Nicholas A. Berg / 1963											
298 2/8	42 5/8	43 1/8	40 6/8	43	8 4/8	8 7/8	7	6	0	106	60
♦ Polk County / R.L. Stamps / R.L. Stamps / 1981											
296	46	46 6/8	36 6/8	42 3/8	7 7/8	7 7/8	7	7	0	114	62
♦ Yamhill County / Steven E. Anderson / Steven E. Anderson / 1983											
295 4/8	39 7/8	41 6/8	41	49 6/8	8 2/8	8	6	6	0	116	63
♦ Columbia County / Reed Holding / Reed Holding / 1950											
294 7/8	45 4/8	45 4/8	34 6/8	39 3/8	7 7/8	8 1/8	6	6	0	117	64
♦ Clatsop County / Picked Up / Robert L. Brown / 1965											
294 5/8	46 5/8	46 1/8	43 1/8	46 2/8	9	8 3/8	6	6	0	118	65
♦ Clatsop County / Nolen R. Schoenborn / Nolen R. Schoenborn / 1944											
293 7/8	43 5/8	43 6/8	36 7/8	42 2/8	7 6/8	7 5/8	6	6	0	119	66
♦ Tillamook County / Steven F. Kellow / Steven F. Kellow / 1979											
291 4/8	38 2/8	38 7/8	33 7/8	36 2/8	8 2/8	8 1/8	8	7	0	121	67
♦ Tillamook County / Picked Up / Tim J. Christensen / 1975											
291 3/8	43 5/8	43 5/8	35 1/8	38 5/8	6 6/8	7	6	6	0	122	68
♦ Clatsop County / Picked Up / Robert L. Brown / 1979											
290 7/8	45 6/8	44 1/8	37 4/8	40 1/8	9	9 3/8	6	6	0	124	69
♦ Coos County / Gerald W. Hurst / Gerald W. Hurst / 1979											
283 4/8	42 7/8	44 1/8	35 2/8	42 5/8	6 7/8	6 7/8	7	6	0	127	70
♦ Columbia County / Thomas E. Eilertsen / Thomas E. Eilertsen / 1968											
279 7/8	47 1/8	45	39 3/8	40	8 3/8	8 2/8	6	5	0	129	71
♦ Tillamook County / Denis Schmitz / Denis Schmitz / 1987											

Score	Length of Main Beam R L	Inside Spread	Greatest Spread	Circumference at Smallest Place between First and Second Points R L		Number of Points R L		Total of Lengths Abnormal Points	All-Time Rank	State Rank
	◆ *Locality / Hunter / Owner / Date Killed*									
279⁶⁄₈	42⁴⁄₈ 42⁶⁄₈	40	42⁶⁄₈	8⁶⁄₈	8⁷⁄₈	6	6	1³⁄₈	130	72
	◆ *Tillamook County / Karl F. Hale / Karl F. Hale / 1985*									
340²⁄₈	46⁵⁄₈ 46	38⁴⁄₈	45²⁄₈	7²⁄₈	7⁷⁄₈	8	7	0	*	*
	◆ *Columbia County / Harry R. Olsen / Harry R. Olsen / 1970*									

Photograph by Wm. H. Nesbitt

**WASHINGTON STATE RECORD
ROOSEVELT'S ELK
SCORE: 380⅝**
Locality: Jefferson Co.   Date: 1983
Hunter: Sam Argo

WASHINGTON

ROOSEVELT'S ELK

Score	Length of Main Beam R	Length of Main Beam L	Inside Spread	Greatest Spread	Circumference at Smallest Place between First and Second Points R	Circumference at Smallest Place between First and Second Points L	Number of Points R	Number of Points L	Total of Lengths Abnormal Points	All-Time Rank	State Rank
♦ *Locality / Hunter / Owner / Date Killed*											
380 6/8	52 3/8	52 6/8	45 1/8	55 3/8	8 3/8	8 1/8	8	8	0	3	1
♦ *Jefferson County / Sam Argo / Sam Argo / 1983*											
376 3/8	53 2/8	52 3/8	41 5/8	48 5/8	10 1/8	10 3/8	8	7	0	5	2
♦ *Clallam County / Picked Up / Roy C. Ewen / 1912*											
367	51 6/8	51 4/8	43 2/8	50 2/8	9 6/8	9 6/8	6	6	0	8	3
♦ *Mason County / Unknown / George B. Putnam / 1900*											
344 2/8	49 2/8	47 5/8	40	45 4/8	8 4/8	8 5/8	7	7	0	19	4
♦ *Jefferson County / Carroll E. Koenke / Carroll E. Koenke / 1966*											
342 1/8	52	50 4/8	34 5/8	0	9 5/8	10 3/8	6	7	0	20	5
♦ *Jefferson County / Ralph Warren / Ralph Warren / 1972*											
341	47	47	38 7/8	48 3/8	8 7/8	9 3/8	8	7	0	22	6
♦ *Lewis County / Keith A. Heldreth / Keith A. Heldreth / 1988*											
337 1/8	49 5/8	52	30 2/8	41 5/8	9 1/8	8 4/8	7	6	0	29	7
♦ *Wahkiakum County / E.L. McKie & T. Faubian / E.L. McKie / 1962*											
337 1/8	46	44 4/8	37 6/8	47	8 7/8	8 7/8	7	7	0	29	7
♦ *Jefferson County / Dave D. Godfrey / Dave D. Godfrey / 1966*											
336 2/8	46	48 3/8	40	46 6/8	8 3/8	9 1/8	7	7	0	33	9
♦ *Clallam County / Howard M. Cameron / Lawrence C. Cameron / 1936*											
334 4/8	52	52 1/8	43 1/8	50 2/8	9 4/8	9 6/8	7	7	0	35	10
♦ *Clallam County / Albert Clevenger / Albert Clevenger / 1931*											
327 4/8	47 4/8	46	44 4/8	44 4/8	10 3/8	11	6	6	0	41	11
♦ *Clallam County / Daniel D. Hinchen / Daniel D. Hinchen / 1976*											
326 4/8	54 1/8	54 2/8	40	51 2/8	7 5/8	7 7/8	7	7	0	44	12
♦ *Pacific County / Donald Beasley / Donald Beasley / 1963*											
326 1/8	49 6/8	49 2/8	33 6/8	38 5/8	8 1/8	8 1/8	7	7	0	45	13
♦ *Wahkiakum County / Otis E. Wright / Otis E. Wright / 1966*											
325 5/8	47 3/8	47 6/8	43 2/8	49 1/8	7 2/8	8	7	8	0	46	14
♦ *Wahkiakum County / Robert B. Seaberg / Robert B. Seaberg / 1958*											
324 2/8	40 6/8	44 2/8	43 6/8	45 5/8	7 7/8	7 6/8	7	7	0	49	15
♦ *Jefferson County / Newton P. Morris / Newton P. Morris / 1975*											
323 4/8	44	43 4/8	44	48 1/8	8 1/8	7 3/8	7	7	0	50	16
♦ *Jefferson County / Larry W. Haddock / Larry W. Haddock / 1988*											
320 2/8	49 6/8	48 2/8	42 4/8	44 4/8	8 4/8	8 1/8	6	6	0	57	17
♦ *Mason County / Tony J. Bogachus / Tony J. Bogachus / 1955*											

Score	Length of Main Beam R	Length of Main Beam L	Inside Spread	Greatest Spread	Circumference at Smallest Place between First and Second Points R	Circumference at Smallest Place between First and Second Points L	Number of Points R	Number of Points L	Total of Lengths Abnormal Points	All-Time Rank	State Rank
♦ *Locality / Hunter / Owner / Date Killed*											
316 5/8	41 6/8	41 5/8	38 3/8	42 7/8	9 1/8	8 6/8	6	6	0	65	18
♦ *Clallam County / Daniel M. Hilt / Daniel M. Hilt / 1982*											
316	47 3/8	46 5/8	43 1/8	50	10 3/8	10 1/8	6	6	0	67	19
♦ *Jefferson County / Hans Norbisrath / Hans Norbisrath / 1966*											
312 7/8	43 5/8	45 1/8	43 4/8	44 1/8	8	7 5/8	7	8	1 7/8	72	20
♦ *Clallam County / Donald W. Coman / Donald W. Coman / 1981*											
311 2/8	47 6/8	40 3/8	41 2/8	43 4/8	8 6/8	8 6/8	7	7	0	73	21
♦ *Jefferson County / Walter L. Campbell / Walter L. Campbell / 1987*											
310 5/8	43 4/8	44 6/8	38 2/8	45 6/8	7 7/8	7 3/8	7	7	0	74	22
♦ *Clallam County / Daniel M. Hilt / Daniel M. Hilt / 1958*											
310 1/8	44 5/8	44 4/8	34	39	10 2/8	9 3/8	7	7	4	77	23
♦ *Jefferson County / Howard L. Hill / Michael R. Raffaell / 1969*											
304 3/8	46 2/8	46 3/8	47 1/8	47 5/8	10	9 5/8	6	6	0	86	24
♦ *Grays Harbor County / Richard B. Grinols / Richard B. Grinols / 1992*											
303	47 4/8	47 6/8	42 2/8	44 4/8	9	8 6/8	7	5	0	89	25
♦ *Jefferson County / C.F. & C.H. Bernhardt / C.F. & C.H. Bernhardt / 1972*											
302 6/8	50	50	36 7/8	40 7/8	7 3/8	7 7/8	6	6	0	90	26
♦ *Jefferson County / Gary Talley / Gary Talley / 1981*											
302 6/8	45 6/8	44 3/8	37 2/8	41 1/8	8 6/8	9	6	6	0	90	26
♦ *Grays Harbor County / Donald M. Vestal / Dean Vestal / 1981*											
302 1/8	41 3/8	41 2/8	37 5/8	4 2/8	8 2/8	8 4/8	6	6	0	94	28
♦ *Wahkiakum County / Kyle J. Parker / Kyle J. Parker / 1990*											
301 1/8	46 5/8	44	34 2/8	40 1/8	8 5/8	8 2/8	7	7	0	96	29
♦ *Jefferson County / C.F. & C.H. Bernhardt / C.F. & C.H. Bernhardt / 1973*											
299 5/8	41 1/8	42 1/8	33 6/8	42	9 1/8	9 5/8	7	6	0	100	30
♦ *Grays Harbor County / Robert Lentz / Robert Lentz / 1948*											
298 6/8	41 2/8	40 7/8	38 6/8	39 4/8	8 1/8	7 7/8	6	6	0	103	31
♦ *Jefferson County / Douglas A. Smith / Douglas A. Smith / 1989*											
297 6/8	46	45 7/8	42 7/8	43 7/8	7 3/8	7 3/8	6	6	0	109	32
♦ *Clallam County / Arnold J. LaGambina / Arnold J. LaGambina / 1988*											
297 1/8	47 2/8	45 6/8	36 7/8	42 1/8	9	9	7	7	4 2/8	110	33
♦ *Clallam County / Ronald W. Sanchez / Ronald W. Sanchez / 1988*											
296 6/8	43 1/8	42 4/8	34 7/8	38	9 3/8	9 2/8	6	6	0	111	34
♦ *Clallam County / Randy F. Mesenbrink / Randy F. Mesenbrink / 1977*											
296 6/8	46 6/8	48 6/8	47 6/8	48 7/8	8 4/8	8 5/8	5	7	1 4/8	111	34
♦ *Clallam County / Aubrey F. Taylor / Aubrey F. Taylor / 1984*											

Score	Length of Main Beam R	L	Inside Spread	Greatest Spread	Circumference at Smallest Place between First and Second Points R	L	Number of Points R	L	Total of Lengths Abnormal Points	All-Time Rank	State Rank
	◆ *Locality / Hunter / Owner / Date Killed*										
296⅛	39	39⅜	35²⁄₈	43⅜	8²⁄₈	7⅞	7	7	0	113	36
	◆ *Jefferson County / Max E. Graves / Max E. Graves / 1970*										
295⅞	44⅜	44⅛	41⅝	42⅞	8⅜	7⅝	7	7	0	115	37
	◆ *Jefferson County / Newton P. Morris / Newton P. Morris / 1970*										
293⅛	42	42⅛	41⅜	41⁶⁄₈	8²⁄₈	8⅞	6	6	0	120	38
	◆ *Jefferson County / William H. Boatman / William H. Boatman / 1951*										
291⅛	41⁶⁄₈	40⁴⁄₈	43⁶⁄₈	44⅞	6⅞	6⁶⁄₈	6	6	0	123	39
	◆ *Jefferson County / George R. Bernethy / George R. Bernethy / 1956*										
290⅞	44⅛	44⅜	42⅝	44⅝	7⅞	8⁶⁄₈	6	6	1⅝	124	40
	◆ *Jefferson County / William A. Harrison / William A. Harrison / 1984*										
288⅜	48²⁄₈	47⅜	36⅜	41⅝	8⅛	7⁶⁄₈	6	6	0	126	41
	◆ *Clallam County / Charles Spaulding / Charles Spaulding / 1993*										
283⅛	37⅝	37²⁄₈	30⅞	36	9⅛	9²⁄₈	7	7	0	128	42
	◆ *Clallam County / Jesse Elder / Jesse Elder / 1968*										
373⅜	57⁴⁄₈	55⅞	44⅛	53²⁄₈	7²⁄₈	7⅞	7	7	0	*	*
	◆ *Wahkiakum County / William Williams / William Williams / 1968*										
371²⁄₈	47⅜	51⁶⁄₈	35⅞	44⁴⁄₈	10⁶⁄₈	10⁴⁄₈	7	7	0	*	*
	◆ *Clallam County / Joe Pavel / Joe Pavel / 1942*										
342⅞	47²⁄₈	49⁶⁄₈	43⅛	50	8²⁄₈	7⅝	8	7	0	*	*
	◆ *Clallam County / C.F. & C.H. Bernhardt / C.F. & C.H. Bernhardt / 1979*										
312⅛	48⅝	46⅝	34⅜	39⁶⁄₈	8⅝	8²⁄₈	6	7	0	*	*
	◆ *Clallam County / Michael L. Fisher / Michael L. Fisher / 1993*										

BRITISH COLUMBIA PROVINCE RECORD
WORLD'S RECORD
ROOSEVELT'S ELK
SCORE: 388⅜
Locality: Tsitika River   Date: 1989
Hunter: Wayne Coe

BRITISH COLUMBIA
ROOSEVELT'S ELK

Score	Length of Main Beam		Inside Spread	Greatest Spread	Circumference at Smallest Place between First and Second Points		Number of Points		Total of Lengths Abnormal Points	All-Time Rank	State Rank
	R	L			R	L	R	L			
♦ Locality / Hunter / Owner / Date Killed											
388³⁄₈	44²⁄₈	46⁷⁄₈	36¹⁄₈	46⁴⁄₈	11²⁄₈	11²⁄₈	11	8	1⁵⁄₈	1	1
♦ Tsitika River / Wayne Coe / Wayne Coe / 1989											
367⁶⁄₈	47⁴⁄₈	47⁶⁄₈	42⁷⁄₈	45	9⁵⁄₈	10	8	7	3²⁄₈	6	2
♦ Woss Lake / Johnny Bliznak / Johnny Bliznak / 1992											
351⁵⁄₈	45	45⁵⁄₈	40²⁄₈	45⁵⁄₈	9¹⁄₈	9⁷⁄₈	8	9	4⁶⁄₈	14	3
♦ Menzies Bay / Gordon J. Birgbauer, Jr. / Gordon J. Birgbauer, Jr. / 1991											
339⁶⁄₈	45⁵⁄₈	45⁴⁄₈	42⁶⁄₈	46⁶⁄₈	8³⁄₈	8	8	7	0	26	4
♦ Gold River / William H. Taylor / William H. Taylor / 1987											
337⁴⁄₈	52³⁄₈	50³⁄₈	34³⁄₈	45⁵⁄₈	9	9	9	9	18³⁄₈	28	5
♦ Greenstone Creek / Gerald L. Warnock / Gerald L. Warnock / 1989											
330	51	50¹⁄₈	38⁴⁄₈	45	8⁷⁄₈	9	6	6	0	38	6
♦ Nanaimo Lakes / Picked Up / Eric D. Martin / 1988											
328⁷⁄₈	46⁴⁄₈	46⁴⁄₈	38⁴⁄₈	44	8⁷⁄₈	8⁵⁄₈	7	7	0	40	7
♦ Vancouver Island / Wayne H. Zaccarelli / Wayne H. Zaccarelli / 1981											
324⁷⁄₈	50¹⁄₈	47⁴⁄₈	36⁵⁄₈	41¹⁄₈	8⁷⁄₈	8⁶⁄₈	7	7	0	48	8
♦ Ucona River / Norman W. Dougan / Norman W. Dougan / 1986											
318³⁄₈	41³⁄₈	41⁵⁄₈	36²⁄₈	42⁴⁄₈	9	8⁶⁄₈	8	7	0	62	9
♦ Grilise Creek / Jack Foord / Jack Foord / 1984											
303⁶⁄₈	42²⁄₈	45⁷⁄₈	36⁴⁄₈	46¹⁄₈	9³⁄₈	9⁴⁄₈	7	7	0	88	10
♦ Gold River / Abe Dougan / Abe Dougan / 1988											
300⁷⁄₈	44	43⁵⁄₈	41	44⁶⁄₈	9³⁄₈	9⁵⁄₈	7	6	2⁴⁄₈	97	11
♦ Vancouver Island / William C. Holcombe / William C. Holcombe / 1989											
298³⁄₈	43⁵⁄₈	44¹⁄₈	38³⁄₈	41	8	8¹⁄₈	6	6	0	105	12
♦ White River / Harvey J. King / Harvey J. King / 1987											
373³⁄₈	50⁴⁄₈	50	34³⁄₈	44¹⁄₈	8⁷⁄₈	9²⁄₈	6	8	0	*	*
♦ Memekay River / Shane Jamieson / Shane Jamieson / 1987											
370⁷⁄₈	50⁶⁄₈	49	35¹⁄₈	48¹⁄₈	8⁴⁄₈	8³⁄₈	9	9	0	*	*
♦ Ucona River / David R. Summers / David R. Summers / 1978											
364⁶⁄₈	54	54³⁄₈	40¹⁄₈	0	9²⁄₈	8⁵⁄₈	7	9	1²⁄₈	*	*
♦ Vancouver Island / Lawrence A. Ondzik / Alf Spineto / 1981											
356²⁄₈	46	46⁴⁄₈	39⁷⁄₈	49²⁄₈	11²⁄₈	9⁵⁄₈	8	7	0	*	*
♦ White River / George Korhonen / George Korhonen / 1982											
344⁴⁄₈	52	50²⁄₈	41²⁄₈	48	10	10	6	6	0	*	*
♦ Kelsey Bay / David Webber / David Webber / 1981											

Score	Length of Main Beam		Inside Spread	Greatest Spread	Circumference at Smallest Place between First and Second Points		Number of Points		Total of Lengths Abnormal Points	All-Time Rank	State Rank
	R	L			R	L	R	L			

♦ *Locality / Hunter / Owner / Date Killed*

342 4/8	43 5/8	47 4/8	44 7/8	49 4/8	8 7/8	9 7/8	7	7	0	*	*

♦ *Nimpkish Valley / Larry X. Hodgson / Larry X. Hodgson / 1992*

341 2/8	46 1/8	47 7/8	40 7/8	49	9	9 2/8	7	7	0	*	*

♦ *Moakwa Creek / Harry Whitehead / Harry Whitehead / 1982*

312 4/8	45 7/8	44 2/8	39 4/8	44 3/8	8 2/8	8 3/8	6	6	0	*	*

♦ *Nimpish River / Noel J. Poux / Noel J. Poux / 1993*

306 7/8	46 3/8	45 1/8	37 4/8	41 3/8	7 6/8	8 3/8	7	7	0	*	*

♦ *Memekay River / Harold Ratushniak / Harold Ratushniak / 1993*

Photograph Courtesy of Gordon J. Birgbauer, Jr.

Gordon J. Birgbauer, Jr., with the Roosevelt's elk bull he took on Vancouver Island, British Columbia, in 1991 and for which he received the second place award at the 22nd Awards Program in Milwaukee, Wisconsin, in 1992. Gordon's bull scores 351-5/8 points.

TOP 10 MULE DEER LISTINGS INDEX

Tabulations of Recorded Mule Deer

The trophy data shown on the following pages are taken from score charts in the records archives of the Boone and Crockett Club. A comparison of the rankings of this book with those of the first edition of *Records of North American Elk and Mule Deer* will reveal many significant differences. This is primarily due to the addition of numerous trophies from the 21st (1989-1991) and the 22nd (1992-1994) Awards Programs, including seven new state/provincial records.

Mule deer are the western counterpart of the common whitetail deer. They are easily identified by their large ears (like a mule's) and Y-fork antlers from other deer, making a geographic boundary for records keeping unnecessary. Geographic boundaries are described for the smaller antlered Columbia and Sitka blacktail deer, to prevent entry of common mule deer into either of these categories.

The scores and ranks shown are final, except for trophies shown with an asterisk (*). The asterisk identifies entry scores subject to final certification by an Awards Panel of Judges. The asterisk can be removed (except in the case of a potential World's Record) by the submission of two additional, independent scorings by Official Measurers of the Boone and Crockett Club. The Records Committee of the Club will review the three scorings available (original plus two additional) and determine which, if any, will be accepted in lieu of the Judges' Panel measurement. When the score has been accepted as final by the Records Committee, the asterisk will be removed in future editions of this book and the all-time records book, *Records of North American Big Game*. In the case of a potential World's Record, the trophy must come before a Judges' Panel at the end of an entry period. Only a Judges' Panel can certify a World's Record and finalize its score. Asterisked trophies are unranked at the end of their category.

ARIZONA STATE RECORD
TYPICAL MULE DEER
SCORE: 209⅝
Locality: Coconino Co.   Date: Prior to 1985
Hunter: Unknown
Owner: John C. McClendon

ARIZONA

TYPICAL MULE DEER

Score	Length of Main Beam R	L	Inside Spread	Greatest Spread	Circumference at Smallest Place between Burr and First Point R	L	Number of Points R	L	Total of Lengths Abnormal Points	All-Time Rank	State Rank
$209\frac{5}{8}$	$27\frac{5}{8}$	$26\frac{5}{8}$	$30\frac{6}{8}$	$35\frac{3}{8}$	$4\frac{7}{8}$	$5\frac{2}{8}$	6	8	10	17	1

◆ *Coconino County / Unknown / John C. McClendon / PR 1985*

$208\frac{6}{8}$	$27\frac{6}{8}$	$26\frac{7}{8}$	$26\frac{2}{8}$	30	$5\frac{1}{8}$	5	6	5	$3\frac{4}{8}$	26	2

◆ *North Kaibab / Horace T. Fowler / Horace T. Fowler / 1938*

$206\frac{5}{8}$	$27\frac{4}{8}$	$28\frac{3}{8}$	$28\frac{7}{8}$	$35\frac{2}{8}$	$4\frac{6}{8}$	$4\frac{6}{8}$	6	5	8	45	3

◆ *Coconino County / Lamell Ellsworth / Lamell Ellsworth / 1971*

$206\frac{3}{8}$	$27\frac{1}{8}$	$26\frac{5}{8}$	$24\frac{3}{8}$	$35\frac{6}{8}$	$5\frac{1}{8}$	$5\frac{1}{8}$	6	7	$6\frac{4}{8}$	46	4

◆ *Coconino County / Robert C. Kaufman / Robert C. Kaufman / 1978*

$203\frac{7}{8}$	$25\frac{6}{8}$	$28\frac{4}{8}$	$18\frac{7}{8}$	$21\frac{5}{8}$	$6\frac{2}{8}$	$5\frac{5}{8}$	5	5	0	77	5

◆ *Apache County / Picked Up / Mike A. Searles / 1994*

$203\frac{4}{8}$	$25\frac{7}{8}$	$29\frac{5}{8}$	$27\frac{6}{8}$	36	$5\frac{4}{8}$	$5\frac{2}{8}$	5	5	0	84	6

◆ *Kaibab Forest / Herb Graham / Herb Graham / 1939*

$203\frac{1}{8}$	$26\frac{2}{8}$	$26\frac{6}{8}$	$27\frac{1}{8}$	31	$5\frac{6}{8}$	$5\frac{6}{8}$	5	5	$7\frac{5}{8}$	94	7

◆ *North Kaibab / Monico Marquez / Monico Marquez / 1957*

$202\frac{3}{8}$	$27\frac{1}{8}$	26	$21\frac{4}{8}$	$25\frac{1}{8}$	$5\frac{6}{8}$	6	5	6	$2\frac{5}{8}$	111	8

◆ *Coconino County / Steve B. Parizek / Steve B. Parizek / 1993*

202	$27\frac{1}{8}$	$26\frac{1}{8}$	$26\frac{6}{8}$	$34\frac{4}{8}$	$5\frac{4}{8}$	$5\frac{4}{8}$	5	5	0	119	9

◆ *Coconino County / Donald Vanderwall / Donald Vanderwall / 1992*

$200\frac{5}{8}$	$25\frac{7}{8}$	25	$27\frac{5}{8}$	32	$5\frac{3}{8}$	5	5	5	0	173	10

◆ *Yavapai County / Joseph C. Pecha / Joseph C. Pecha / 1983*

$200\frac{1}{8}$	$24\frac{4}{8}$	$25\frac{4}{8}$	26	$35\frac{5}{8}$	$5\frac{2}{8}$	$5\frac{3}{8}$	7	6	$8\frac{5}{8}$	199	11

◆ *Mohave County / Jay M. Ogden / Jay M. Ogden / 1990*

200	$29\frac{6}{8}$	$29\frac{7}{8}$	$24\frac{4}{8}$	$29\frac{5}{8}$	$5\frac{3}{8}$	$5\frac{2}{8}$	6	6	7	203	12

◆ *Mouqi / Tom Corey / Tom Corey / 1964*

$199\frac{7}{8}$	$25\frac{7}{8}$	$27\frac{2}{8}$	$25\frac{7}{8}$	$29\frac{7}{8}$	$4\frac{7}{8}$	5	7	6	$5\frac{4}{8}$	211	13

◆ *Coconino County / John L. Johnson / John L. Johnson / 1972*

$199\frac{2}{8}$	$26\frac{1}{8}$	$25\frac{1}{8}$	$24\frac{1}{8}$	$28\frac{7}{8}$	$5\frac{6}{8}$	$5\frac{5}{8}$	6	6	$4\frac{5}{8}$	232	14

◆ *Hidden Canyon / Milton Wyman / Milton Wyman / 1972*

$199\frac{2}{8}$	$28\frac{6}{8}$	$30\frac{4}{8}$	$25\frac{6}{8}$	$34\frac{6}{8}$	$5\frac{7}{8}$	$5\frac{4}{8}$	9	6	$17\frac{6}{8}$	232	14

◆ *Coconino County / John R. Fogle / John R. Fogle / 1992*

199	$24\frac{2}{8}$	$24\frac{2}{8}$	21	$29\frac{2}{8}$	5	$5\frac{2}{8}$	5	6	$1\frac{4}{8}$	248	16

◆ *Mohave County / William M. Berger, Jr. / William M. Berger, Jr. / 1973*

$198\frac{4}{8}$	28	$26\frac{1}{8}$	$28\frac{2}{8}$	$31\frac{3}{8}$	5	5	5	6	1	262	17

◆ *Kaibab Forest / W.O. Hart / W.O. Hart / 1946*

Score	Length of Main Beam		Inside Spread	Greatest Spread	Circumference at Smallest Place between Burr and First Point		Number of Points		Total of Lengths Abnormal Points	All-Time Rank	State Rank
	R	L			R	L	R	L			
	Locality / Hunter / Owner / Date Killed										

198 4/8	27	26 2/8	28 6/8	34	5	5	5	5	0	262	17
◆ *North Kaibab / Simon C. Krevitsky / Simon C. Krevitsky / 1963*											
198 3/8	25	25 5/8	26	28 6/8	6	5 7/8	6	6	5 4/8	271	19
◆ *Mt. Trumbull / E.O. Brown / E.O. Brown / 1960*											
198 2/8	24 4/8	25	25 3/8	30 1/8	5 1/8	4 7/8	5	5	0	274	20
◆ *Coconino County / Dale C. Morse / Dale C. Morse / 1977*											
197 7/8	25 2/8	25 1/8	24 5/8	30	4 6/8	4 7/8	5	6	1 4/8	295	21
◆ *Kaibab Forest / Eoans Pababla / Eoans Pababla / 1957*											
196 7/8	24	24 5/8	26 4/8	34 1/8	5 1/8	5 2/8	5	6	1 2/8	357	22
◆ *North Kaibab / Alex J. Haas / Alex J. Haas / 1961*											
196 6/8	24	24 1/8	23 6/8	32 2/8	5 7/8	6 1/8	5	6	1 4/8	362	23
◆ *Coconino County / James D. Wagner / James D. Wagner / 1986*											
196	27 5/8	26 6/8	23 3/8	32 7/8	5 3/8	5 2/8	7	6	7 3/8	414	24
◆ *Kaibab Forest / Graves Peeler / John E. Conner Museum / PR 1930*											
196	27 2/8	26	21 6/8	0	5 3/8	5 3/8	5	7	0	414	24
◆ *North Kaibab / John D. McNeley / John D. McNeley / 1948*											
196	23 6/8	24 1/8	22 4/8	26 1/8	5	5 1/8	5	5	0	414	24
◆ *Kaibab Forest / Elgin T. Gates / Elgin T. Gates / 1958*											
195 3/8	28 7/8	28 4/8	25 5/8	28 3/8	5 2/8	5 2/8	5	7	2 6/8	464	27
◆ *Mohave County / Bob B. Coker / Bob B. Coker / 1972*											
195 3/8	28 4/8	27 3/8	28 6/8	31	6	5 5/8	7	5	3 1/8	464	27
◆ *Apache County / William D. Beck / William D. Beck / 1991*											
195 1/8	26 5/8	26 1/8	24 7/8	31 7/8	4 7/8	5 1/8	6	7	5 6/8	482	29
◆ *Coconino County / Gary R. Clark / Gary R. Clark / 1972*											
191 4/8	26 3/8	26 1/8	25 4/8	31 1/8	5 2/8	5	6	7	6	528	30
◆ *Coconino County / Steven G. Mallory / Steven G. Mallory / 1988*											
189 3/8	25	27 6/8	27 1/8	31 4/8	5 1/8	6 2/8	5	6	3 2/8	556	31
◆ *Coconino County / Frederick T. Lau / Frederick T. Lau / 1988*											

Jay M. Ogden was hunting in Whitmore Canyon, Arizona, southwest of Mt. Logan, when he connected with this typical mulie buck with an outside spread of 35-5/8 points. In spite of 8-5/8 inches of abnormal points, this buck scores 200-1/8 points.

Photograph by N.A. Winter

ARIZONA STATE RECORD
NON-TYPICAL MULE DEER
SCORE: 324⅛
Locality: North Kaibab   Date: 1943
Hunter: William L. Murphy
Owner: Michael R. Karam

ARIZONA
NON-TYPICAL MULE DEER

Score	Length of Main Beam R	L	Inside Spread	Greatest Spread	Circumference at Smallest Place between Burr and First Point R	L	Number of Points R	L	Total of Lengths Abnormal Points	All-Time Rank	State Rank
	◆ Locality / Hunter / Owner / Date Killed										
324 1/8	25 5/8	25 1/8	32 7/8	43 3/8	6 5/8	6 5/8	16	17	115 2/8	4	1
◆ North Kaibab / William L. Murphy / Michael R. Karam / 1943											
311 6/8	26 7/8	24 7/8	24 1/8	32 5/8	6 1/8	6 5/8	22	21	105 1/8	8	2
◆ Kaibab / Vernor Wilson / Don Schaufler / 1941											
294 1/8	27 1/8	26 1/8	24 3/8	36	5 7/8	5 5/8	14	16	86 2/8	21	3
◆ Coconino County / Philip K. Coffeen / William A. Coffeen / 1939											
282 3/8	22 5/8	21 3/8	22 1/8	40 2/8	4 5/8	5 1/8	18	15	103 6/8	36	4
◆ North Kaibab / Robert C. Rantz / Robert C. Rantz / 1969											
280 2/8	29	31 2/8	29 4/8	43 1/8	5 1/8	5 4/8	11	16	76	39	5
◆ Coconino County / Unknown / Marlen D. Murphy / 1941											
279 6/8	26 6/8	24 2/8	17 3/8	37 6/8	6 4/8	5 4/8	18	10	89 5/8	41	6
◆ Kaibab Forest / M. Powell & D. Auld, Jr. / Milroy Powell / 1950											
274 3/8	27 2/8	26 6/8	25 5/8	35 7/8	5 6/8	5 3/8	11	10	55 5/8	56	7
◆ Kaibab Forest / Unknown / Don Schaufler / PR 1950											
270 3/8	24	25	27 4/8	39 3/8	5 6/8	6	10	10	69 3/8	73	8
◆ Kaibab Forest / Dean Naylor / D.B. Sanford / 1948											
270 2/8	29 2/8	32 1/8	28	42 3/8	4 6/8	4 6/8	12	13	60	74	9
◆ North Kaibab / Thomas M. Knoles, Jr. / Thomas M. Knoles, Jr. / 1944											
268 6/8	28 3/8	28 4/8	24 6/8	37	5 5/8	5 5/8	12	13	58 2/8	76	10
◆ Kaibab Forest / Milroy Powell / Milroy Powell / 1952											
266 2/8	27	28 3/8	24 1/8	38 1/8	6 1/8	5 5/8	15	9	75 1/8	90	11
◆ Mohave County / Carl A. Luedeman / Carl A. Luedeman / 1993											
264 1/8	22 2/8	22	20 2/8	34 2/8	4 5/8	4 5/8	13	14	84 7/8	104	12
◆ Coconino County / Gilbert T. Adams, Jr. / Gilbert T. Adams, Jr. / 1989											
263	26 3/8	27 5/8	25 4/8	33 4/8	5	5	12	12	79	109	13
◆ Kaibab Forest / Unknown / Bob Housholder / 1940											
262 4/8	28 2/8	29	28	41 2/8	5 4/8	5 4/8	14	12	71 6/8	111	14
◆ Kaibab Forest / Jack Verner / Jack Verner / 1947											
261	25 2/8	26 2/8	25 5/8	0	5	5 1/8	12	12	0	123	15
◆ Kaibab Forest / Unknown / Larry Arndt / 1930											
260 4/8	25 5/8	27	26 6/8	41 5/8	5 7/8	5 7/8	13	14	81 6/8	126	16
◆ Kaibab Forest / David Bevly / David Bevly / 1949											
260	27 2/8	25 6/8	32 6/8	34 6/8	5 6/8	6 2/8	13	11	64 2/8	130	17
◆ Mohave County / John W. Sokatch / John W. Sokatch / 1978											

Score	Length of Main Beam R	L	Inside Spread	Greatest Spread	Circumference at Smallest Place between Burr and First Point R	L	Number of Points R	L	Total of Lengths Abnormal Points	All-Time Rank	State Rank

◆ Locality / Hunter / Owner / Date Killed

Score	R	L	Inside	Greatest	R	L	R	L	Abn	AT	St
258 7/8	28 5/8	27 7/8	28 2/8	35 4/8	4 6/8	4 7/8	13	13	49 7/8	140	18

◆ North Kaibab / Marvin Fridenmaker / Marvin Fridenmaker / 1968

258	26 5/8	29	27 6/8	34 3/8	5 4/8	5 3/8	14	16	47	150	19

◆ Coconino County / William T. Parsons / William T. Parsons / 1967

257 7/8	27 6/8	26 5/8	27 4/8	35 4/8	6 1/8	6 4/8	10	12	44 7/8	152	20

◆ Apache County / Lamell Ellsworth / Lamell Ellsworth / 1992

257 5/8	27 2/8	29	28 7/8	39	5 5/8	5 5/8	15	14	60	155	21

◆ Kaibab Forest / Graves Peeler / John E. Connor Museum / 1946

257 5/8	25 7/8	26 5/8	25 1/8	39 5/8	5 6/8	5 5/8	12	11	54 2/8	155	21

◆ Kaibab Forest / Graves Peeler / John E. Connor Museum / 1947

257 5/8	24 2/8	26 7/8	20 6/8	34	5 3/8	5 4/8	11	13	59 7/8	155	21

◆ Hell's Hole / D.L. DeMente / D.L. DeMente / 1965

256 2/8	27 4/8	28 2/8	26 6/8	32 4/8	4 7/8	5 1/8	10	8	55 4/8	174	24

◆ Mt. Trumbull / Ervin M. Schmutz / Ervin M. Schmutz / 1965

255 4/8	23 3/8	23 5/8	25 5/8	37	5 6/8	5 7/8	12	12	56 5/8	182	25

◆ Coconino County / Glenn A. Hunt / Glenn A. Hunt / 1985

253 6/8	25	26 1/8	25 6/8	39 5/8	6 1/8	6 1/8	9	12	54 2/8	192	26

◆ Mohave County / Manuel Machado / Manuel Machado / 1973

252 5/8	26 7/8	28 7/8	29 1/8	36	5 3/8	5 5/8	15	13	60 6/8	204	27

◆ Kaibab Forest / Graves Peeler / Graves Peeler / PR 1951

250	25	27 1/8	21 4/8	32 5/8	6 5/8	6 4/8	14	14	61	234	28

◆ Mohave County / Douglas C. Mallory / Douglas C. Mallory / 1980

249 6/8	23 3/8	21 6/8	23 3/8	42	6 2/8	5 7/8	12	12	77 5/8	235	29

◆ Mt. Dellenbaugh / Ted Riggs / Don Schaufler / 1965

249 1/8	25 4/8	26	25 1/8	32 4/8	5 1/8	5 1/8	8	11	36 2/8	243	30

◆ Kaibab / Robert G. McDonald / Robert G. McDonald / 1969

248 4/8	25 4/8	25 1/8	26	31 6/8	5 6/8	5 5/8	13	11	45	249	31

◆ Kaibab Forest / H.W. Meisch / H.W. Meisch / 1942

248 3/8	26 3/8	26 6/8	23 4/8	41 2/8	5 4/8	5 2/8	10	16	62 3/8	250	32

◆ Kaibab Forest / O.M. Corbett / O.M. Corbett / 1953

248 2/8	25	25 3/8	26 7/8	38 6/8	6 6/8	7	12	12	57 3/8	253	33

◆ Kaibab Forest / Graves Peeler / Graves Peeler / PR 1951

247 5/8	25 2/8	25 4/8	22 2/8	28 4/8	6 1/8	6	12	16	63 7/8	265	34

◆ Mohave County / Brad L. Johnson / Brad L. Johnson / 1986

246 3/8	24 7/8	24 6/8	25 1/8	30 1/8	5 2/8	5 2/8	11	14	49 6/8	289	35

◆ Kaibab Forest / Elgin T. Gates / Elgin T. Gates / 1960

Score	Length of Main Beam R	L	Inside Spread	Greatest Spread	Circumference at Smallest Place between Burr and First Point R	L	Number of Points R	L	Total of Lengths Abnormal Points	All-Time Rank	State Rank
	◆ *Locality / Hunter / Owner / Date Killed*										
246	27 1/8	26 5/8	31 6/8	37 3/8	5 5/8	5 5/8	8	8	36 7/8	294	36
	◆ *Mohave County / Bernard E. Anderson / Bernard E. Anderson / 1969*										
245	24 6/8	22 5/8	18 5/8	33 3/8	6 5/8	7	12	14	55 1/8	305	37
	◆ *Mt. Trumbull / Tony Stromei / Tony Stromei / 1960*										
244 4/8	24 6/8	26 6/8	26	32 2/8	5	4 6/8	11	11	56	315	38
	◆ *Kaibab Forest / C.M. Randal, Jr. / C.M. Randal, Jr. / 1953*										
244 2/8	24 4/8	26 2/8	28 4/8	38 1/8	5 6/8	5 5/8	9	8	38 4/8	316	39
	◆ *Kaibab Forest / Ray Ramsey / Ray Ramsey / 1952*										
243 6/8	26 5/8	25 2/8	29 7/8	40 7/8	4 7/8	4 7/8	9	13	56 1/8	331	40
	◆ *Apache County / Jay M. Ogden / Jay M. Ogden / 1991*										
240 7/8	27 4/8	28 2/8	22	29 2/8	5 7/8	6	7	12	24 5/8	380	41
	◆ *Coconino County / Robert B. Metzgus / Robert B. Metzgus / 1993*										
240 5/8	26 4/8	27 6/8	23 2/8	32 7/8	6	5 7/8	10	13	43 7/8	384	42
	◆ *Kaibab Forest / Bert E. George / Bert E. George / 1949*										
240 4/8	22	22 3/8	17 4/8	22 6/8	4 5/8	4 4/8	13	11	71 4/8	386	43
	◆ *Coconino County / Craig R. Dunlap / Craig R. Dunlap / 1993*										
240 2/8	27 3/8	27 1/8	21 7/8	35 3/8	5 2/8	5 2/8	9	11	43 1/8	393	44
	◆ *Mt. Dellenbaugh / Edwin R. Riggs / Edwin R. Riggs / 1964*										
238 4/8	27	27 1/8	28 7/8	29 6/8	6 1/8	5 4/8	17	13	65 3/8	401	45
	◆ *Pima County / Richard M. Cordora / Richard M. Cordora / 1989*										
238 4/8	26 2/8	25 6/8	23 7/8	33	5 1/8	5 2/8	11	13	50 5/8	401	45
	◆ *Coconino County / Gilbert T. Adams / Gilbert T. Adams / 1992*										
237 6/8	25 3/8	25 2/8	25	31 4/8	4 5/8	4 5/8	9	11	44 2/8	404	47
	◆ *Coconino County / Ronald J. Wolosyn / Ronald J. Wolosyn / 1992*										

CALIFORNIA STATE RECORD
TYPICAL MULE DEER
SCORE: 195⅞
Locality: Lassen Co.   Date: 1943
Hunter: Sulo E. Lakso
Owner: Tracey A. Jenkins

154

CALIFORNIA

TYPICAL MULE DEER

Score	Length of Main Beam R	Length of Main Beam L	Inside Spread	Greatest Spread	Circumference at Smallest Place between Burr and First Point R	Circumference at Smallest Place between Burr and First Point L	Number of Points R	Number of Points L	Total of Lengths Abnormal Points	All-Time Rank	State Rank
♦ *Locality / Hunter / Owner / Date Killed*											
195 7/8	27 6/8	25 7/8	26 4/8	31 1/8	4 6/8	4 6/8	5	7	4 7/8	424	1
♦ *Lassen County / Sulo E. Lakso / Tracy A. Jenkins / 1943*											

CALIFORNIA STATE RECORD
NON-TYPICAL MULE DEER
SCORE: 319 4/8
Locality: Mariposa Co.   Date: 1972
Hunter: Harold R. Laird
Owner: Don Schaufler

CALIFORNIA

NON-TYPICAL MULE DEER

Score	Length of Main Beam		Inside Spread	Greatest Spread	Circumference at Smallest Place between Burr and First Point		Number of Points		Total of Lengths Abnormal Points	All-Time Rank	State Rank
	R	L			R	L	R	L			
◆ Locality / Hunter / Owner / Date Killed											
319 4/8	24 2/8	24	23 5/8	35 6/8	7 7/8	7 1/8	27	23	132 3/8	7	1
◆ Mariposa County / Harold R. Laird / Don Schaufler / 1972											
305 6/8	23 7/8	24 1/8	21 3/8	35 2/8	6 1/8	6 4/8	17	17	102 5/8	11	2
◆ Shasta County / Artie McGram / Artie McGram / 1987											
267 4/8	24	25 3/8	18 2/8	37 4/8	6 2/8	7 2/8	16	15	87 2/8	85	3
◆ Mariposa County / Ray Douglas / John Douglas / 1948											
246 6/8	23 4/8	21	26 3/8	36 3/8	6 2/8	6 4/8	13	14	67 4/8	285	4
◆ Modoc County / Bill Foster / Foster's Bighorn Rest. / 1930											
240 4/8	26 4/8	27	21 4/8	33	6 2/8	5 6/8	10	9	51	386	5
◆ Modoc County / Niilo Niemi / Niilo Niemi / 1968											

COLORADO STATE RECORD
WORLD'S RECORD
TYPICAL MULE DEER
SCORE: 226⁴⁄₈
Locality: Dolores Co.   Date: 1972
Hunter: Doug Burris, Jr.

COLORADO
TYPICAL MULE DEER

Score	Length of Main Beam R	L	Inside Spread	Greatest Spread	Circumference at Smallest Place between Burr and First Point R	L	Number of Points R	L	Total of Lengths Abnormal Points	All-Time Rank	State Rank
226 4/8	30 1/8	28 6/8	30 7/8	33 2/8	5 2/8	5 3/8	6	5	2 5/8	1	1
◆ Dolores County / Doug Burris, Jr. / Doug Burris, Jr. / 1972											
214 3/8	27 5/8	27 4/8	31 3/8	35	4 7/8	4 7/8	5	5	0	5	2
◆ Gypsum Creek / Paul A. Muehlbauer / Paul A. Muehlbauer / 1967											
212	29	27	21 4/8	25 6/8	5 4/8	5 4/8	5	5	0	9	3
◆ Grand County / Wesley B. Brock / Wesley B. Brock / 1963											
210 2/8	29 1/8	29 2/8	27	31 4/8	5 2/8	5 2/8	6	5	3	14	4
◆ Southern Ute Res. / Jack D. Johnston / Jack D. Johnston / 1963											
210 2/8	27 7/8	27 4/8	31 4/8	34	5 1/8	5	5	6	3 7/8	14	4
◆ Delta County / Tom Donaldson / Tom Donaldson / 1972											
209 5/8	29 7/8	29 2/8	29 2/8	35 6/8	5	5 2/8	5	7	8 1/8	17	6
◆ Montrose County / Mike Thomas / Mike Thomas / 1974											
209 2/8	27 6/8	27 1/8	27 4/8	32 4/8	5 6/8	5 6/8	5	5	0	22	7
◆ Amherst Mt. / Herbert Graham / Mrs. W.J. Graham / 1963											
209	24 4/8	25 4/8	24 1/8	27 7/8	6 1/8	6 2/8	5	7	2 5/8	24	8
◆ Saquache County / William B. Pennington / William B. Pennington / 1967											
208 6/8	24 4/8	24 6/8	17 4/8	25 6/8	5 3/8	5 3/8	6	6	3 2/8	26	9
◆ Garfield County / George Shearer / Richard L. Baker / 1952											
208 5/8	26 7/8	27 1/8	27 2/8	32 7/8	5	5	5	5	0	29	10
◆ Mesa County / Robert L. Zaina / Robert L. Zaina / 1960											
207 3/8	28 1/8	29 4/8	28 7/8	34	5 6/8	5 5/8	9	7	18 2/8	34	11
◆ Mesa County / Wally Bruegman / Wally Bruegman / 1972											
207 2/8	28 5/8	27 1/8	28 1/8	36 6/8	6 5/8	6 4/8	6	6	2 5/8	35	12
◆ Montrose County / Bill Crouch / Don Schaufler / 1974											
207 1/8	26 6/8	26 2/8	24 1/8	28 7/8	5 6/8	5 4/8	6	5	2 4/8	36	13
◆ Golden / Harold B. Moser / Harold B. Moser / 1967											
207	28	28 2/8	29	32	6	6	6	5	3	37	14
◆ Montrose / Warren S. Bachhofer / Warren S. Bachhofer / 1966											
206 7/8	26 1/8	25 7/8	21 3/8	24 6/8	4 6/8	4 7/8	5	5	0	41	15
◆ Montrose County / W.L. Boynton / W.L. Boynton / 1973											
206 6/8	27	27 4/8	29 4/8	36 7/8	6 2/8	6 1/8	5	8	9 4/8	43	16
◆ Pagosa Springs / Richard V. Price / Richard V. Price / 1962											
206 6/8	26 3/8	25 6/8	28 2/8	31 4/8	5 1/8	4 7/8	6	5	1 5/8	43	16
◆ Pagosa Springs / Henry Trujillo, Jr. / Henry Trujillo, Jr. / 1963											

Score	Length of Main Beam R	L	Inside Spread	Greatest Spread	Circumference at Smallest Place between Burr and First Point R	L	Number of Points R	L	Total of Lengths Abnormal Points	All-Time Rank	State Rank
206 3/8	27 2/8	27 7/8	28 1/8	32 4/8	5 1/8	5	5	4	0	46	18
◆ *Eagle County / Harold Taylor / Fred Palmer / 1960*											
206 2/8	28 6/8	28 6/8	22 4/8	26 4/8	6	6	9	7	6 6/8	49	19
◆ *Montrose County / Patrick E. Courtin, Jr. / Patrick E. Courtin, Jr. / 1972*											
206 2/8	26 5/8	27 5/8	23 4/8	25 7/8	5 5/8	5 7/8	5	5	0	49	19
◆ *Mesa County / Picked Up / James S. Bennett / 1974*											
206	24	22 1/8	25	34 1/8	6	6 1/8	5	5	0	54	21
◆ *Eagle / Harold L. Loesch / Harold L. Loesch / 1967*											
205 6/8	24 3/8	24 3/8	23 4/8	26 3/8	5 4/8	5 4/8	5	5	0	55	22
◆ *Eagle County / Mark A. McCormick / Mark A. McCormick / 1981*											
205 4/8	29 1/8	28 4/8	27 5/8	31 6/8	5 1/8	5 2/8	6	6	3 5/8	57	23
◆ *Carbondale / Richard Cobb / Richard Cobb / 1962*											
205 4/8	25 3/8	27 3/8	22 7/8	26	5 4/8	5 4/8	6	5	1 1/8	57	23
◆ *Kremmling / Larry Bell / Larry Bell / 1962*											
205 2/8	27 5/8	28	30 1/8	31 6/8	4 4/8	4 7/8	5	5	0	63	25
◆ *Montrose County / Joe M. Gardner / Z. Gardner Holland / 1954*											
204 7/8	27 2/8	27	23 5/8	30 4/8	5 5/8	5 4/8	6	5	1	66	26
◆ *Delta County / Frank Peterson / Frank Peterson / 1956*											
204 7/8	26 4/8	26 1/8	26 3/8	29 6/8	5 2/8	5 2/8	5	5	0	66	26
◆ *Southern Ute Res. / Nolan Martins / Nolan Martins / 1967*											
204 5/8	25 5/8	24 3/8	19 4/8	29	5 5/8	5 4/8	7	5	3 5/8	68	28
◆ *Eagle County / Robert V. Doerr / Robert V. Doerr / 1982*											
204 3/8	26 1/8	26 4/8	20 5/8	26 5/8	5 6/8	5 5/8	5	5	0	69	29
◆ *Grand Junction / Charles M. Bentley / Charles M. Bentley / 1962*											
204 1/8	27 5/8	26 1/8	25 1/8	29	5	5	5	5	0	72	30
◆ *Hinsdale County / Norman E. Ebbley / Jim Temple / 1961*											
204	27	27 3/8	24	33 2/8	5 4/8	5 3/8	5	5	0	76	31
◆ *Pitkin County / Jens O. Solberg / Jens O. Solberg / 1950*											
203 7/8	24 5/8	26	24 4/8	28 4/8	5 7/8	5 6/8	6	6	3 3/8	77	32
◆ *North Park / Edison A. Pillmore / Mrs. E.A. Pillmore / 1949*											
203 7/8	26 3/8	27 5/8	26 3/8	38 6/8	5 2/8	5 3/8	6	6	4 6/8	77	32
◆ *Mesa Creek / Ed Craig / Jerome Craig / 1951*											
203 5/8	28 3/8	27 3/8	24 4/8	30 4/8	5 7/8	5 6/8	6	5	1 5/8	81	34
◆ *La Plata County / B.E. Gressett / B.E. Gressett / 1950*											
203 5/8	24 5/8	25 5/8	25 6/8	32 3/8	4 5/8	4 6/8	5	5	0	81	34
◆ *Mesa County / William P. Burger / William P. Burger / 1957*											

Score	Length of Main Beam R	L	Inside Spread	Greatest Spread	Circumference at Smallest Place between Burr and First Point R	L	Number of Points R	L	Total of Lengths Abnormal Points	All-Time Rank	State Rank
\multicolumn{13}{l}{♦ *Locality / Hunter / Owner / Date Killed*}											
203 4/8	27 5/8	28 3/8	25	28 2/8	4 5/8	4 6/8	5	7	3	84	36
\multicolumn{13}{l}{♦ *Garfield County / John T. Sewell / John T. Sewell / 1985*}											
203 2/8	25 7/8	28	22 4/8	25	4 4/8	4 4/8	6	5	2 7/8	89	37
\multicolumn{13}{l}{♦ *White River / Ron Vance / Ronald Crawford / 1943*}											
203 2/8	28	28 4/8	29 6/8	34	5 2/8	5 2/8	5	5	0	89	37
\multicolumn{13}{l}{♦ *De Beque / Francis A. Moore / Francis A. Moore / 1962*}											
203 2/8	27 1/8	26 6/8	22 2/8	30 3/8	4 7/8	4 6/8	5	5	2 4/8	89	37
\multicolumn{13}{l}{♦ *Collbran / Joe R. Colingo / Joe R. Colingo / 1973*}											
203 1/8	22 5/8	22 7/8	27 6/8	34 2/8	5 3/8	6 3/8	6	6	6 6/8	94	40
\multicolumn{13}{l}{♦ *Hayden / M.W. Giboney / M.W. Giboney / 1959*}											
203	25	23 5/8	24	31 3/8	5 2/8	5 2/8	5	5	0	96	41
\multicolumn{13}{l}{♦ *Mesa County / James K. Scott / James K. Scott / 1966*}											
203	26 3/8	25 5/8	27 1/8	31	5 4/8	5 6/8	9	8	15 7/8	96	41
\multicolumn{13}{l}{♦ *Montrose County / Earl L. Markley / Earl L. Markley / 1968*}											
202 6/8	25 3/8	24 7/8	19 2/8	23 2/8	6 6/8	6 7/8	5	5	0	102	43
\multicolumn{13}{l}{♦ *Ouray County / Jewel E. Schottel / Jewel E. Schottel / 1966*}											
202 5/8	26 3/8	25 5/8	21 5/8	26	5 1/8	5	5	5	0	104	44
\multicolumn{13}{l}{♦ *Ouray County / Louis V. Schlosser / Louis V. Schlosser / 1965*}											
202 4/8	30 4/8	30	21 2/8	28 4/8	6	5 7/8	6	4	5 6/8	106	45
\multicolumn{13}{l}{♦ *Collbran / Jack Thompson / Jack Thompson / 1968*}											
202 4/8	26 7/8	24 7/8	21 6/8	28 1/8	5 1/8	5	4	6	2 2/8	106	45
\multicolumn{13}{l}{♦ *Garfield County / James S. Harden / James S. Harden / 1982*}											
202 3/8	25 6/8	26 1/8	23 5/8	30 1/8	5 3/8	5 3/8	7	6	3 6/8	111	47
\multicolumn{13}{l}{♦ *Boulder County / Bob Wallace / Bob Wallace / 1963*}											
202 2/8	25 6/8	26	26 5/8	33 4/8	5 1/8	5	5	7	3 2/8	116	48
\multicolumn{13}{l}{♦ *Pagosa Springs / Allen R. Arnwine / Allen R. Arnwine / 1960*}											
202 2/8	30 2/8	29 6/8	20 6/8	30 4/8	4 7/8	4 7/8	4	5	2 6/8	116	48
\multicolumn{13}{l}{♦ *Archuleta County / Duane Yearwood / Duane Yearwood / 1973*}											
202	26 4/8	25 4/8	29 4/8	36	5 1/8	5 3/8	5	6	3 2/8	119	50
\multicolumn{13}{l}{♦ *Gunnison Natl. For. / James M. Newsom / James M. Newsom / 1963*}											
202	27 4/8	27 1/8	24 2/8	29 2/8	5 2/8	5 1/8	5	6	4 4/8	119	50
\multicolumn{13}{l}{♦ *Montrose County / Kenneth Klees / Kenneth Klees / 1966*}											
201 7/8	26 5/8	27 2/8	26 3/8	28 6/8	4 6/8	4 5/8	6	5	1 1/8	129	52
\multicolumn{13}{l}{♦ *Dolores County / Leonard J. Ashcraft / Leonard J. Ashcraft / 1958*}											
201 5/8	26 2/8	26 4/8	23 3/8	31 5/8	5 1/8	5	5	5	0	135	53
\multicolumn{13}{l}{♦ *Gunnison County / Robert D. Rader / Robert D. Rader / 1966*}											

Score	Length of Main Beam		Inside Spread	Greatest Spread	Circumference at Smallest Place between Burr and First Point		Number of Points		Total of Lengths Abnormal Points	All-Time Rank	State Rank
	R	L			R	L	R	L			
201 5/8	26 6/8	25 6/8	28 4/8	35 4/8	5 2/8	5	6	6	5 7/8	135	53
◆ Eagle County / Richard C. Bergquist / Richard C. Bergquist / 1981											
201 4/8	27	26	26	33 2/8	5	5	5	5	0	138	55
◆ Garfield County / Unknown / Ronald E. McKinney / 1954											
201 4/8	23	24	20	26 2/8	5 4/8	5 2/8	6	6	2	138	55
◆ Moffat County / Carl E. Jacobson / Carl E. Jacobson / 1967											
201 3/8	25 4/8	26 1/8	30 1/8	37 6/8	6 1/8	6	5	5	0	144	57
◆ Archuleta County / Joe Moore / Joe Moore / 1962											
201 3/8	25 5/8	26 4/8	25 3/8	30 6/8	5 4/8	5 4/8	5	5	0	144	57
◆ Grand Junction / William C. Byrd / William C. Byrd / 1967											
201 3/8	25 6/8	24 6/8	23 1/8	28	5 4/8	5 4/8	5	5	0	144	57
◆ Montrose County / Grant Morlang / Grant Morlang / 1972											
201 2/8	28	29	28	38	5	4 6/8	6	6	6 2/8	152	60
◆ Bayfield / D. Rockwell / D. Rockwell / 1956											
201 1/8	26 2/8	26 2/8	25 3/8	32 3/8	5	4 7/8	5	5	0 4/8	155	61
◆ Cameo / Thomas C. Krauss / Thomas C. Krauss / 1962											
201 1/8	26 4/8	27 2/8	26 6/8	34	6 3/8	6 5/8	5	7	2 5/8	155	61
◆ Bayfield / Les Patrick / Les Patrick / 1966											
201	29	26 2/8	22 6/8	31 5/8	6 1/8	6 1/8	6	8	14 6/8	159	63
◆ Grand Junction / Ernest Mancuso / Ernest Mancuso / 1954											
201	25	25 1/8	24 4/8	32 2/8	4 7/8	5	5	5	0	159	63
◆ Dolores County / Mark Loverin / Mark Loverin / 1978											
201	26 2/8	26 2/8	23 6/8	26 6/8	5 1/8	5 1/8	5	5	0	159	63
◆ La Plata County / Larry Pennington / Larry Pennington / 1978											
200 7/8	28	28 4/8	25 4/8	33	5 2/8	5 2/8	6	6	10 5/8	164	66
◆ Collbran / Homer O. Hartley / Homer O. Hartley / 1962											
200 6/8	27 1/8	25 2/8	22 4/8	25 4/8	5 7/8	5 6/8	5	5	0	166	67
◆ Eagle County / John Robertson / John Robertson / 1958											
200 6/8	27	27 3/8	26	31 1/8	5	5 1/8	5	5	0	166	67
◆ Southern Ute Res. / Jerry E. Morgan / Jerry E. Morgan / 1965											
200 6/8	26	26 6/8	23 4/8	30 2/8	5 6/8	5 4/8	6	7	7 6/8	166	67
◆ Delta / Emil Warber, Jr. / Emil Warber, Jr. / 1966											
200 6/8	28 4/8	28 5/8	23	27 2/8	5 2/8	5	8	5	12 6/8	166	67
◆ Gunnison County / James B. Holbrooks / James B. Holbrooks / 1977											
200 5/8	27	25 2/8	26 5/8	31 2/8	5	5 1/8	5	5	0	173	71
◆ La Plata County / Unknown / Ronald F. Lax / 1979											

Score	Length of Main Beam		Inside Spread	Greatest Spread	Circumference at Smallest Place between Burr and First Point		Number of Points		Total of Lengths Abnormal Points	All-Time Rank	State Rank
	R	L			R	L	R	L			
◆ Locality / Hunter / Owner / Date Killed											
200 4/8	25	25 4/8	25	31 1/8	4 6/8	5	5	5	0	177	72
◆ Eagle County / Jack Stevens / Jack Stevens / 1975											
200 4/8	24	24 6/8	23 3/8	29 1/8	4 6/8	5	5	6	1 3/8	177	72
◆ Dolores County / James L. Horneck / James L. Horneck / 1988											
200 3/8	27 4/8	27 4/8	26 1/8	31 4/8	5 4/8	5 3/8	7	7	7	186	74
◆ Uncompahgre Natl. For. / Richard M. Holbrook / Richard M. Holbrook / 1972											
200 3/8	26 7/8	29 1/8	24 4/8	30 1/8	5 1/8	5 1/8	5	7	3 3/8	186	74
◆ Gypsum / Gene D. Lintz / Gene D. Lintz / 1974											
200 2/8	26 4/8	26	27	34	5 6/8	5 6/8	5	6	1 6/8	190	76
◆ Mesa County / Mitchell J. Sacco / Mitchell J. Sacco / 1966											
200 2/8	29 7/8	28 3/8	23 6/8	29	4 7/8	4 6/8	5	5	0	190	76
◆ Southern Ute Res. / Arthur Burch / Steven Burch / 1966											
200 2/8	27 4/8	27	26 7/8	34 1/8	5	4 7/8	6	5	2 5/8	190	76
◆ Ouray County / Joseph T. Hollingshead / Joseph T. Hollingshead / 1967											
200 2/8	25 7/8	24 1/8	19 6/8	25 5/8	4 6/8	4 5/8	5	5	0	190	76
◆ Montrose County / Nelson Harding / Nelson Harding / 1985											
200 1/8	27 2/8	28 6/8	25 7/8	31 3/8	4 6/8	4 6/8	5	5	0	199	80
◆ Mesa County / John M. Domingos / John M. Domingos / 1965											
200	26 2/8	27	27	30 5/8	5 5/8	5 5/8	5	6	1 4/8	203	81
◆ Summit County / Picked Up / Bill Knorr / 1959											
200	24 2/8	25 4/8	25 2/8	30	4 7/8	4 6/8	5	5	0	203	81
◆ Piedra River / Glenn A. Smith / Glenn A. Smith / 1960											
200	27	27 4/8	28 5/8	33 1/8	6 1/8	6 1/8	5	5	0	203	81
◆ Silt / George McCoy / George McCoy / 1961											
200	27 4/8	28 7/8	29 3/8	32 5/8	6 3/8	6 3/8	6	5	1 1/8	203	81
◆ Garfield County / Picked Up / John F. Frost / 1963											
200	28	27 5/8	21 6/8	26	5 7/8	6	6	5	6 4/8	203	81
◆ Park County / Jim Fitzgerald / Rob Firth / 1971											
200	27 1/8	26	24 4/8	30	4 7/8	4 7/8	5	5	0	203	81
◆ Eagle County / Dale R. Leonard / David P. Moore / 1976											
199 7/8	22 6/8	23 2/8	22 6/8	30 2/8	5 1/8	5 1/8	7	6	4 7/8	211	87
◆ Jackson County / G.B. Berger, Jr. / Denver Mus. Natl. Hist. / 1934											
199 7/8	24 4/8	25 3/8	26 1/8	28 7/8	5 6/8	5 6/8	5	5	0	211	87
◆ Disappointment Creek / Clifford Le Neve / Clifford Le Neve / 1954											
199 7/8	24 1/8	24 7/8	23 1/8	28 5/8	5	5 1/8	5	5	0	211	87
◆ Uncompahgre Natl. For. / H.E. Gerhart / H.E. Gerhart / 1963											

Score	Length of Main Beam R	L	Inside Spread	Greatest Spread	Circumference at Smallest Place between Burr and First Point R	L	Number of Points R	L	Total of Lengths Abnormal Points	All-Time Rank	State Rank
	◆ *Locality / Hunter / Owner / Date Killed*										
199⁷⁄₈	26⁴⁄₈	26⁴⁄₈	24⁴⁄₈	31²⁄₈	4⁷⁄₈	4⁷⁄₈	6	6	2⁷⁄₈	211	87
	◆ *Eagle County / George S. Burton / Betty Burton / 1967*										
199⁶⁄₈	29⁷⁄₈	29	21⁵⁄₈	32⁶⁄₈	5²⁄₈	5²⁄₈	6	8	14³⁄₈	217	91
	◆ *Montrose County / James O. McCleary / John E. McCleary / 1951*										
199⁴⁄₈	28²⁄₈	27³⁄₈	28	37¹⁄₈	6¹⁄₈	6²⁄₈	7	8	20⁴⁄₈	222	92
	◆ *Pagosa Springs / Perry Dixon / Perry Dixon / 1957*										
199⁴⁄₈	25	25⁴⁄₈	26	31²⁄₈	4⁶⁄₈	5	5	5	0	222	92
	◆ *Dolores County / Kenneth L. Peters / Kenneth L. Peters / 1976*										
199³⁄₈	27³⁄₈	26	25¹⁄₈	27⁷⁄₈	5⁴⁄₈	6	4	4	0	228	94
	◆ *Silt / V.M. Spiller / V.M. Spiller / 1961*										
199²⁄₈	27⁴⁄₈	26¹⁄₈	26⁴⁄₈	28⁴⁄₈	5¹⁄₈	5¹⁄₈	5	5	0	232	95
	◆ *Eagle County / Howard Stoker / Howard Stoker / 1965*										
199²⁄₈	26⁶⁄₈	26⁴⁄₈	25⁵⁄₈	32²⁄₈	5³⁄₈	5³⁄₈	7	5	4⁵⁄₈	232	95
	◆ *Eagle County / Anthony W. DeToy / Anthony W. DeToy / 1978*										
199²⁄₈	25²⁄₈	25¹⁄₈	25¹⁄₈	30¹⁄₈	5²⁄₈	5²⁄₈	7	6	7⁵⁄₈	232	95
	◆ *Garfield County / Gary W. Hartley / Gary W. Hartley / 1978*										
198⁷⁄₈	26⁴⁄₈	24²⁄₈	19³⁄₈	24⁷⁄₈	5⁷⁄₈	5⁷⁄₈	7	5	2⁴⁄₈	253	98
	◆ *Burns / Charles D. Rush / Charles D. Rush / 1967*										
198⁵⁄₈	26²⁄₈	27²⁄₈	24⁵⁄₈	32⁴⁄₈	5	5	6	7	5⁴⁄₈	257	99
	◆ *Carbondale / Ralph Clock / Ralph Clock / 1961*										
198⁴⁄₈	29	27²⁄₈	32⁷⁄₈	37⁶⁄₈	5⁵⁄₈	5⁴⁄₈	6	9	18⁶⁄₈	262	100
	◆ *Del Norte / Esequiel Trujillo / Esequiel Trujillo / 1947*										
198⁴⁄₈	26	25⁴⁄₈	21⁴⁄₈	26⁴⁄₈	5³⁄₈	5²⁄₈	5	4	2²⁄₈	262	100
	◆ *Routt County / Lloyd D. Kindsfater / Lloyd D. Kindsfater / 1966*										
198⁴⁄₈	29	28⁷⁄₈	22⁴⁄₈	26¹⁄₈	5¹⁄₈	5¹⁄₈	4	5	0	262	100
	◆ *Dark Canyon / O.P. McGuire / O.P. McGuire / 1966*										
198⁴⁄₈	29⁵⁄₈	30	28⁴⁄₈	32³⁄₈	4⁶⁄₈	4⁵⁄₈	6	7	11²⁄₈	262	100
	◆ *La Plata County / Pauline J. Bostic / Pauline J. Bostic / 1971*										
198³⁄₈	26⁶⁄₈	26⁵⁄₈	28	35²⁄₈	5²⁄₈	5²⁄₈	6	6	2⁵⁄₈	271	104
	◆ *Moffat County / Lucille Gooch / George Gooch / 1951*										
198²⁄₈	26⁴⁄₈	27⁴⁄₈	26⁴⁄₈	32⁴⁄₈	4⁷⁄₈	4⁷⁄₈	6	8	6	274	105
	◆ *Summit County / Picked Up / Louis Ceriani / PR 1965*										
198²⁄₈	26²⁄₈	26	26⁶⁄₈	31	5²⁄₈	5⁴⁄₈	5	5	0	274	105
	◆ *Gunnison County / Bobby J. Watson / Bobby J. Watson / 1975*										
198¹⁄₈	25³⁄₈	26¹⁄₈	23⁷⁄₈	34	5⁶⁄₈	5⁷⁄₈	5	6	3⁶⁄₈	280	107
	◆ *Bayfield / C. Ben Boyd / C. Ben Boyd / 1967*										

COLORADO TYPICAL MULE DEER *(continued)*

Score	Length of Main Beam R	Length of Main Beam L	Inside Spread	Greatest Spread	Circumference at Smallest Place between Burr and First Point R	Circumference at Smallest Place between Burr and First Point L	Number of Points R	Number of Points L	Total of Lengths Abnormal Points	All-Time Rank	State Rank
♦ *Locality / Hunter / Owner / Date Killed*											
198 1/8	25 1/8	26 1/8	25 7/8	29 6/8	5 4/8	5 4/8	5	6	1	280	107
♦ *Routt County / William E. Goswick / William E. Goswick / 1968*											
198 1/8	27 4/8	27 2/8	23 2/8	27 4/8	5	5	7	6	10 3/8	280	107
♦ *Montrose County / Robert A. Klatt / Robert A. Klatt / 1975*											
198 1/8	26 6/8	27 5/8	24 5/8	28 1/8	5 1/8	5 1/8	6	8	4 2/8	280	107
♦ *Colorado / Unknown / Richard A. Heitman / PR 1989*											
198	25 2/8	25 5/8	22 4/8	30	6 1/8	6	8	5	11	287	111
♦ *Garfield County / Leroy Failor / Leroy Failor / 1944*											
198	23 7/8	25 4/8	27 1/8	29 1/8	4 7/8	4 7/8	7	7	0	287	111
♦ *Gunnison County / E.D. Palmer / E.D. Palmer / 1962*											
198	24	24 7/8	22 4/8	29 2/8	6 1/8	5 6/8	7	6	7 4/8	287	111
♦ *Eagle County / Larry Schlasinger / Larry Schlasinger / 1978*											
198	27	26 1/8	28 6/8	37 4/8	4 6/8	5 3/8	4	5	0	287	111
♦ *Hinsdale County / Alan L. VanDenBerg / Alan L. VanDenBerg / 1978*											
197 7/8	27 7/8	27	26 2/8	29	5 2/8	5	5	8	4 3/8	295	115
♦ *Chaffee County / Marguerite Hill / Marguerite Hill / 1956*											
197 7/8	27 6/8	27 7/8	28 5/8	32 2/8	5 1/8	5 3/8	5	5	0	295	115
♦ *San Miguel County / Everett Stutler / Everett Stutler / 1965*											
197 7/8	26 1/8	27 4/8	24 1/8	29 6/8	4 7/8	5	5	5	0	295	115
♦ *Rio Blanco County / Gary L. Bicknell / Gary L. Bicknell / 1967*											
197 7/8	28 6/8	28 6/8	25 6/8	30 4/8	5	5	6	5	3 5/8	295	115
♦ *Eagle County / Lee Frudden / Lee Frudden / 1978*											
197 5/8	27	26 6/8	22 7/8	28 3/8	5 7/8	5 5/8	6	6	6 6/8	308	119
♦ *San Miguel County / Virgil L. Burbridge / Jerry D. Burbridge / 1964*											
197 5/8	23 5/8	29 5/8	21 3/8	26 5/8	5	5	5	5	0	308	119
♦ *Eagle County / Joseph Sokel, Jr. / Steve J. Sokel / 1965*											
197 4/8	24	26	21 2/8	27 5/8	5 4/8	5 6/8	5	5	0	317	121
♦ *Moffat County / Russ H. Winslow / Russ H. Winslow / 1967*											
197 4/8	24 6/8	27	23 4/8	0	6	5 7/8	8	9	13 6/8	317	121
♦ *Routt County / William E. Goswick / William E. Goswick / 1969*											
197 4/8	22 1/8	24	24	28 4/8	5 6/8	5 5/8	6	5	4 2/8	317	121
♦ *Gunnison County / Thomas Gray, Jr. / Thomas Gray, Jr. / 1980*											
197 3/8	26 7/8	26 5/8	24 5/8	26 7/8	5	5	5	6	1	324	124
♦ *White River Natl. For. / Picked Up / Jack Thompson / PR 1957*											
197 3/8	27 1/8	27 4/8	24 2/8	34 4/8	5	5	5	7	9 3/8	324	124
♦ *Montrose / H.R. Clark / H.R. Clark / 1961*											

Score	Length of Main Beam R	L	Inside Spread	Greatest Spread	Circumference at Smallest Place between Burr and First Point R	L	Number of Points R	L	Total of Lengths Abnormal Points	All-Time Rank	State Rank
197 3/8	26 6/8	26	25 4/8	31 2/8	5 2/8	5 2/8	5	6	1 1/8	324	124
◆ *Pagosa Springs / John D. Guess / John D. Guess / 1966*											
197 3/8	26	26 2/8	23 2/8	28	5 6/8	5 5/8	6	6	6 5/8	324	124
◆ *Gunnison County / Mark L. Hanna / Mark L. Hanna / 1980*											
197 2/8	26 1/8	26 4/8	23 6/8	27 4/8	5 4/8	5 5/8	6	7	5 6/8	333	128
◆ *Custer County / Jerome L. DeGree / Jerome L. DeGree / 1972*											
197 2/8	24 5/8	23 4/8	24 2/8	28 1/8	5 3/8	5 3/8	5	5	0	333	128
◆ *Elbert County / Francis Wilson / Francis Wilson / 1993*											
197 1/8	27 1/8	26 7/8	29 7/8	34	6 1/8	6 4/8	5	5	0	342	130
◆ *Gunnison County / Ted Wolcott, Jr. / Ted Wolcott, Jr. / 1961*											
197 1/8	27	28	30	33 7/8	5 3/8	5 3/8	7	6	8 5/8	342	130
◆ *Delta County / B. Allan Jones / B. Allan Jones / 1977*											
197 1/8	28 1/8	27 3/8	22 7/8	29 1/8	5	5	5	6	2	342	130
◆ *Mesa County / Willis A. Kinsey / Willis A. Kinsey / 1978*											
197	27 4/8	26 3/8	29 3/8	34	5 4/8	5 6/8	5	5	0	347	133
◆ *Jackson County / Alvin Bush / Jerry Haldeman / 1961*											
197	24 2/8	25 4/8	25 2/8	30 6/8	5 5/8	5 6/8	5	5	0	347	133
◆ *Grand County / Woodrow W. Dixon / Woodrow W. Dixon / 1962*											
197	26 6/8	26	28 4/8	35	5 3/8	5 3/8	6	5	5 2/8	347	133
◆ *Archuleta County / Hugh W. Gardner / Hugh W. Gardner / 1971*											
196 6/8	25 1/8	25 4/8	24 4/8	28 5/8	5 2/8	5 5/8	5	5	0	362	136
◆ *Delta / Howard G. Reed / Howard G. Reed / 1968*											
196 6/8	24 2/8	23 4/8	23 1/8	31 2/8	6 3/8	6 2/8	5	6	2 1/8	362	136
◆ *De Beque / Walter C. Friauf / Walter C. Friauf / 1970*											
196 6/8	26 1/8	26	22 2/8	28 3/8	5	5	5	5	0	362	136
◆ *San Juan Natl. For. / Wilford E. Seymour, Jr. / Wilford E. Seymour, Jr. / 1974*											
196 5/8	26	26 6/8	24 1/8	32 1/8	4 4/8	4 6/8	5	5	0	369	139
◆ *Slater / W.J. Bracken / W.J. Bracken / 1959*											
196 5/8	26 2/8	26 7/8	23 3/8	31	6 5/8	5 3/8	8	8	18 2/8	369	139
◆ *Moffat County / Tran Canton / Tran Canton / 1960*											
196 5/8	27 6/8	24 2/8	22 5/8	25 2/8	5 4/8	5 4/8	5	5	0	369	139
◆ *Grand Mesa / Marvin L. Shepard / Marvin L. Shepard / 1960*											
196 5/8	26 5/8	26 4/8	27 2/8	33 5/8	4 7/8	4 7/8	6	6	3	369	139
◆ *Mesa County / Bill Styers / Bill Styers / 1964*											
196 5/8	24 7/8	25	23 5/8	26 3/8	4 4/8	4 5/8	5	5	0	369	139
◆ *Maybell / James W. Johnson / James W. Johnson / 1968*											

Score	Length of Main Beam R	Length of Main Beam L	Inside Spread	Greatest Spread	Circumference at Smallest Place between Burr and First Point R	L	Number of Points R	L	Total of Lengths Abnormal Points	All-Time Rank	State Rank

♦ Locality / Hunter / Owner / Date Killed

Score	R	L	Inside	Greatest	R	L	R	L	Abnormal	All-Time	State
196 4/8	23 2/8	22 6/8	19 6/8	26	5 1/8	5	5	5	0	379	144

♦ Garfield County / Elmer Nelson / Elmer Nelson / 1962

| 196 4/8 | 22 1/8 | 22 2/8 | 23 5/8 | 32 | 5 3/8 | 5 4/8 | 5 | 6 | 3 2/8 | 379 | 144 |

♦ Summit County / Steve Orecchio / Steve Orecchio / 1967

| 196 4/8 | 25 3/8 | 24 5/8 | 23 | 29 7/8 | 5 5/8 | 5 7/8 | 5 | 5 | 0 | 379 | 144 |

♦ Southern Ute Res. / William C. Forsyth / William C. Forsyth / 1974

| 196 3/8 | 26 4/8 | 26 | 24 4/8 | 29 3/8 | 5 2/8 | 5 3/8 | 6 | 5 | 1 3/8 | 391 | 147 |

♦ Durango / Ronald Chitwood / Ronald Chitwood / 1964

| 196 3/8 | 28 1/8 | 28 1/8 | 26 1/8 | 29 5/8 | 4 7/8 | 5 | 5 | 4 | 0 | 391 | 147 |

♦ Uncompahgre Plateau / Earl L. Markley / Earl L. Markley / 1969

| 196 2/8 | 27 2/8 | 27 3/8 | 20 6/8 | 31 4/8 | 5 6/8 | 5 2/8 | 5 | 8 | 8 | 396 | 149 |

♦ Meeker / Mike Murphy / Mike Murphy / 1971

| 196 2/8 | 25 4/8 | 25 4/8 | 25 5/8 | 31 4/8 | 5 | 5 1/8 | 5 | 5 | 0 | 396 | 149 |

♦ Meeker / Max R. Zoeller / Max R. Zoeller / 1972

| 196 1/8 | 25 2/8 | 25 | 23 5/8 | 29 2/8 | 5 4/8 | 5 3/8 | 4 | 4 | 0 | 409 | 151 |

♦ Uncompahgre Natl. For. / Harry L. Whitlock / Harry L. Whitlock / 1968

| 196 1/8 | 25 5/8 | 25 3/8 | 25 5/8 | 28 4/8 | 4 6/8 | 4 7/8 | 5 | 5 | 0 | 409 | 151 |

♦ Eagle County / Jeffery D. Harrison / Jeffery D. Harrison / 1981

| 196 | 27 6/8 | 27 4/8 | 27 2/8 | 33 4/8 | 5 6/8 | 5 6/8 | 5 | 5 | 0 | 414 | 153 |

♦ Huerfano County / Frank C. Hibben / Frank C. Hibben / 1963

| 195 7/8 | 26 6/8 | 26 7/8 | 26 5/8 | 26 7/8 | 5 4/8 | 5 4/8 | 6 | 6 | 11 4/8 | 424 | 154 |

♦ Southern Ute Res. / Richard Schmidt / Southern Ute Tribe / 1960

| 195 7/8 | 27 4/8 | 26 5/8 | 24 7/8 | 27 2/8 | 5 5/8 | 5 5/8 | 5 | 5 | 0 | 424 | 154 |

♦ San Miguel County / Jerry E. Albin / Jerry E. Albin / 1972

| 195 6/8 | 25 3/8 | 25 2/8 | 23 4/8 | 31 | 5 1/8 | 5 | 5 | 5 | 0 | 433 | 156 |

♦ Jefferson County / Lloyd O. Rauchfuss / Lloyd O. Rauchfuss / 1947

| 195 6/8 | 27 | 23 7/8 | 24 2/8 | 29 2/8 | 5 2/8 | 5 1/8 | 5 | 6 | 1 4/8 | 433 | 156 |

♦ Huerfano County / Mike Disert / Janet D. Wasson / 1954

| 195 6/8 | 25 2/8 | 26 4/8 | 24 6/8 | 30 7/8 | 4 6/8 | 4 6/8 | 5 | 5 | 0 | 433 | 156 |

♦ Gunnison / Randall R. Kieft / Randall R. Kieft / 1967

| 195 6/8 | 24 6/8 | 25 2/8 | 22 6/8 | 29 6/8 | 5 | 5 | 5 | 7 | 3 2/8 | 433 | 156 |

♦ Montrose County / Larry D. Bitta / Larry D. Bitta / 1969

| 195 6/8 | 22 7/8 | 24 6/8 | 23 5/8 | 29 6/8 | 5 3/8 | 5 2/8 | 5 | 6 | 1 5/8 | 433 | 156 |

♦ Gunnison County / George L. Hoffman, Jr. / George L. Hoffman, Jr. / 1972

| 195 6/8 | 25 6/8 | 25 3/8 | 24 1/8 | 28 4/8 | 6 2/8 | 6 2/8 | 6 | 6 | 2 3/8 | 433 | 156 |

♦ Eagle County / James B. Mesecke / James B. Mesecke / 1985

Score	Length of Main Beam R	L	Inside Spread	Greatest Spread	Circumference at Smallest Place between Burr and First Point R	L	Number of Points R	L	Total of Lengths Abnormal Points	All-Time Rank	State Rank
195 5/8	25 1/8	25 4/8	21 3/8	27 2/8	4 6/8	4 4/8	5	4	0	446	162
♦ Pitkin County / William F. Kirby / William F. Kirby / 1966											
195 5/8	27 5/8	25 3/8	20 5/8	24 6/8	4 7/8	4 6/8	5	5	0	446	162
♦ Delta County / Royce J. Carville / Royce J. Carville / 1974											
195 5/8	25 3/8	25 4/8	21 3/8	28	5 2/8	5	5	6	1 4/8	446	162
♦ Grand County / C. Jay Stout / C. Jay Stout / 1981											
195 5/8	26 5/8	27	24 3/8	32 2/8	5 2/8	5 2/8	9	5	19	446	162
♦ Archuleta County / Matthew J. Arkins / Matthew J. Arkins / 1986											
195 5/8	25 3/8	25 3/8	26 3/8	30 4/8	5 3/8	5 5/8	5	5	0	446	162
♦ Huerfano County / Hub R. Grounds / Hub R. Grounds / 1989											
195 5/8	25 6/8	25 7/8	26 2/8	31	5 4/8	5 2/8	5	5	0	446	162
♦ Mesa County / John F. Stewart / John F. Stewart / 1989											
195 4/8	24 2/8	24 7/8	24 2/8	33 4/8	5 2/8	5 2/8	7	6	9 4/8	456	168
♦ Garfield County / Billy R. Babb / Billy R. Babb / 1969											
195 4/8	24 2/8	25	20 4/8	24 1/8	5 6/8	5 7/8	5	5	0	456	168
♦ Montrose / Tony L. Hill / Tony L. Hill / 1969											
195 3/8	26 4/8	25 7/8	26 3/8	29 6/8	5 2/8	5 1/8	6	5	9 6/8	464	170
♦ Moffat County / Frank J. Kubin / Frank J. Kubin / 1978											
195 2/8	29 1/8	27 7/8	25 7/8	31 7/8	5 3/8	5 4/8	7	6	4 7/8	472	171
♦ Gunnison County / Herman F. Tomky / Russell J. Tomky / 1937											
195 2/8	24 4/8	24 3/8	24 6/8	32	4 5/8	4 6/8	5	6	5 2/8	472	171
♦ Moffat County / Orville R. Meineke / Craig Sports / 1964											
195 2/8	26 4/8	27 1/8	27	35	5 5/8	5 7/8	7	7	6 2/8	472	171
♦ Montrose County / Edward A. Ipser / Edward A. Ipser / 1965											
195 2/8	26 4/8	27	25 7/8	32 3/8	5 1/8	5 1/8	7	6	10 5/8	472	171
♦ Marble / David R. Allen / David R. Allen / 1968											
195 1/8	26 3/8	26 1/8	24 1/8	27 2/8	6	5 7/8	6	5	3 2/8	482	175
♦ Montrose County / Eldon L. Webb / Eldon L. Webb / 1965											
195	26	25 5/8	23 4/8	26 1/8	4 5/8	5	5	5	0	491	176
♦ Larimer County / Michael D. Blehm / Michael D. Blehm / 1972											
195	24 6/8	24 7/8	22 4/8	26 2/8	5	5 1/8	5	5	0	491	176
♦ Rio Blanco County / Gene Lawrence / Gene Lawrence / 1977											
194 4/8	25 6/8	25 2/8	23 2/8	30 7/8	5	5 1/8	5	5	0	506	178
♦ Eagle County / William E. Pipes III / William E. Pipes III / 1984											
193 6/8	27 6/8	27 2/8	29 4/8	37	5 5/8	5 3/8	4	6	3 2/8	510	179
♦ Cimmaron / Reynolds L. Vanstrom / Reynolds L. Vanstrom / 1960											

Score	Length of Main Beam R L	Inside Spread	Greatest Spread	Circumference at Smallest Place between Burr and First Point R	L	Number of Points R	L	Total of Lengths Abnormal Points	All-Time Rank	State Rank
				◆ Locality / Hunter / Owner / Date Killed						
193²⁄₈	26 26⁷⁄₈	25²⁄₈	27¹⁄₈	6	6¹⁄₈	5	6	1⁶⁄₈	514	180
	◆ Gunnison County / Bill Morrow / Nancy Morrow / 1960									
192⁷⁄₈	25¹⁄₈ 26	20³⁄₈	24	4⁶⁄₈	4⁶⁄₈	5	5	0	516	181
	◆ Colorado / Unknown / Dana J. Hollinger / 1953									
192⁶⁄₈	26 25⁶⁄₈	21²⁄₈	28¹⁄₈	5⁴⁄₈	5⁵⁄₈	6	5	2²⁄₈	517	182
	◆ Gunnison County / Stephen A. Mahurin / Stephen A. Mahurin / 1968									
192⁵⁄₈	27¹⁄₈ 25¹⁄₈	30⁴⁄₈	35⁴⁄₈	5³⁄₈	5⁴⁄₈	6	8	9⁵⁄₈	518	183
	◆ Delta / Alvin T. Stivers / Alvin T. Stivers / 1965									
192	26⁴⁄₈ 25⁷⁄₈	27⁷⁄₈	33	5³⁄₈	5³⁄₈	5	5	0	524	184
	◆ Delta County / James W. Arellano / James W. Arellano / 1977									
192	23³⁄₈ 24⁶⁄₈	22⁴⁄₈	33	5	5	5	5	0	524	184
	◆ Larimer County / Picked Up / John R. Steffes, Sr. / PR 1990									
191¹⁄₈	23³⁄₈ 25¹⁄₈	24³⁄₈	27³⁄₈	4³⁄₈	4⁴⁄₈	5	5	0	532	186
	◆ Grand County / Zane Palmer / Zane Palmer / 1981									
190⁶⁄₈	26 25¹⁄₈	25²⁄₈	31	4⁶⁄₈	4⁶⁄₈	5	5	0	537	187
	◆ Jackson County / Guy Ambergey / Guy Ambergey / 1969									
190⁵⁄₈	24¹⁄₈ 24⁶⁄₈	22⁴⁄₈	30	6²⁄₈	5⁶⁄₈	6	5	3³⁄₈	539	188
	◆ Douglas County / Harold A. Weippert / Harold A. Weippert / 1990									
190⁵⁄₈	25⁶⁄₈ 26¹⁄₈	22⁵⁄₈	26²⁄₈	5	4⁶⁄₈	5	5	0	539	188
	◆ Las Animas County / Mark W. Streissguth / Mark W. Streissguth / 1994									
190⁴⁄₈	26 25⁴⁄₈	21⁶⁄₈	29⁵⁄₈	5¹⁄₈	5¹⁄₈	6	5	1⁴⁄₈	541	190
	◆ Garfield County / Donald M. Alburtus / Dennis J. DaSilva / 1963									
190⁴⁄₈	25¹⁄₈ 25⁴⁄₈	26⁴⁄₈	32⁴⁄₈	5	4⁶⁄₈	5	5	0	541	190
	◆ Archuleta County / James M. Russell III / James M. Russell III / 1985									
190³⁄₈	24⁷⁄₈ 25³⁄₈	26	28⁶⁄₈	4⁴⁄₈	4⁴⁄₈	5	5	0	543	192
	◆ Mesa / Robert W. Hill / Robert W. Hill / 1963									
189¹⁄₈	25 28⁴⁄₈	21	31²⁄₈	5	5²⁄₈	7	7	6⁷⁄₈	560	193
	◆ La Plata County / James L. Leyshon / James L. Leyshon / 1986									
188³⁄₈	21¹⁄₈ 21⁶⁄₈	18⁶⁄₈	27⁶⁄₈	4³⁄₈	4³⁄₈	5	6	1³⁄₈	569	194
	◆ Larimer County / Fred W. Loy / Fred W. Loy / 1965									
188	27³⁄₈ 26⁵⁄₈	22²⁄₈	26⁷⁄₈	4⁴⁄₈	3⁷⁄₈	5	5	5⁴⁄₈	576	195
	◆ San Miguel County / Roy Guinn / Elizabeth G. Wilson / 1965									
188	26²⁄₈ 26⁴⁄₈	21¹⁄₈	26⁶⁄₈	5⁶⁄₈	5⁴⁄₈	7	5	4⁵⁄₈	576	195
	◆ Kit Carson County / Thomas Aasbo / Thomas Aasbo / 1990									
187⁷⁄₈	26⁶⁄₈ 25²⁄₈	26⁵⁄₈	28⁵⁄₈	4⁷⁄₈	4³⁄₈	5	4	0	579	197
	◆ Routt County / Thomas N. Garvin / Thomas N. Garvin / 1986									

Score	Length of Main Beam R	Length of Main Beam L	Inside Spread	Greatest Spread	Circumference at Smallest Place between Burr and First Point R	Circumference at Smallest Place between Burr and First Point L	Number of Points R	Number of Points L	Total of Lengths Abnormal Points	All-Time Rank	State Rank
♦ *Locality / Hunter / Owner / Date Killed*											
187 7/8	24 7/8	25 7/8	27 2/8	30 5/8	4 5/8	4 6/8	5	5	0	579	197
♦ *Pitkin County / Kenneth N. Tucker / Kenneth N. Tucker / 1990*											
187 2/8	26 3/8	25 5/8	23 1/8	28 2/8	4 6/8	4 7/8	7	7	6 3/8	587	199
♦ *Garfield County / Picked Up / Jack Thompson / 1982*											
187 2/8	25 3/8	26 2/8	27 4/8	30 5/8	5	5	7	6	6	587	199
♦ *White River Natl. For. / Picked Up / Jack Thompson / PR 1987*											
187	24 4/8	25	28 1/8	30 2/8	5	5 1/8	5	5	0	590	201
♦ *Moffat County / Warren C. Nuzum / Warren C. Nuzum / 1987*											
186 7/8	24	24 6/8	23	28 4/8	4 5/8	4 6/8	6	5	1 3/8	593	202
♦ *Garfield County / Gary L. Hecht / Gary L. Hecht / 1986*											
186 6/8	23 6/8	23 6/8	24	30 5/8	5 4/8	5 3/8	5	5	0	596	203
♦ *Routt County / Willie Jones / Willie Jones / 1976*											
186 5/8	25	23 2/8	26	32 1/8	4 6/8	4 7/8	5	6	1 5/8	598	204
♦ *Fremont County / Donald B. Anderson, Jr. / Donald B. Anderson, Jr. / 1986*											
186 1/8	27	27 1/8	23 7/8	27 4/8	4 5/8	4 6/8	5	5	0	603	205
♦ *Garfield County / Picked Up / Jack Thompson / 1984*											
186	24 4/8	26	21	27	5 7/8	5 4/8	4	4	0	606	206
♦ *Pitkin County / Anthony E. Urwick / Anthony E. Urwick / 1982*											
185 7/8	24 7/8	26 6/8	24 1/8	26 7/8	5 1/8	5 1/8	6	6	10 4/8	609	207
♦ *Routt County / LeRoy S. Nelson / LeRoy S. Nelson / 1967*											
185 6/8	26	26 3/8	23 6/8	27 2/8	4 6/8	4 6/8	5	5	0	612	208
♦ *White River Natl. For. / Picked Up / Jack Thompson / PR 1987*											
185 5/8	25 6/8	24 5/8	23 6/8	27 1/8	5 1/8	5	5	7	4 5/8	613	209
♦ *Garfield County / Picked Up / Jack Thompson / 1982*											
185 3/8	25 3/8	25 3/8	23 5/8	31	4 6/8	4 4/8	5	5	0	618	210
♦ *Delta County / Mark S. Petrucci / Mark S. Petrucci / 1989*											
182 6/8	25	24 4/8	24 6/8	27 4/8	5 1/8	5 1/8	8	6	10	623	211
♦ *Las Animas County / Donald P. Travis / Donald P. Travis / 1992*											
181 5/8	25 1/8	23 4/8	25 1/8	31 2/8	5 2/8	4 6/8	5	4	0	627	212
♦ *Delta County / Vernon D. Holleman / Vernon D. Holleman / 1962*											
181	23 5/8	27 4/8	19 6/8	33	5	5	7	7	10 6/8	631	213
♦ *Pitkin County / James H. Calyer / James H. Calyer / 1992*											
181	24 2/8	23 4/8	20 4/8	29 6/8	4 6/8	5	5	6	3 6/8	631	213
♦ *Rio Blanco County / R. Charles Prosek / R. Charles Prosek / 1993*											
180 1/8	24 2/8	26	20 6/8	23 6/8	4 5/8	4 6/8	5	6	3 5/8	634	215
♦ *Delta County / John R. Arellano / John R. Arellano / 1989*											

COLORADO TYPICAL MULE DEER *(continued)*

Score	Length of Main Beam		Inside Spread	Greatest Spread	Circumference at Smallest Place between Burr and First Point		Number of Points		Total of Lengths Abnormal Points	All-Time Rank	State Rank
	R	L			R	L	R	L			
◆ *Locality / Hunter / Owner / Date Killed*											
180	22	22²⁄₈	20	26	5⁶⁄₈	5⁴⁄₈	5	5	0	635	216
◆ *Mesa County / Charles T. Joranco / Charles T. Joranco / 1970*											

Photograph by Doug Holleman

**COLORADO STATE RECORD
NON-TYPICAL MULE DEER
SCORE: 306⅖**
Locality: Norwood   Date: 1954
Hunter: Steve H. Herndon
Owner: Vernon D. & Dan F. Holleman

COLORADO

NON-TYPICAL MULE DEER

Score	Length of Main Beam R	L	Inside Spread	Greatest Spread	Circumference at Smallest Place between Burr and First Point R	L	Number of Points R	L	Total of Lengths Abnormal Points	All-Time Rank	State Rank
	♦ Locality / Hunter / Owner / Date Killed										
306²⁄₈	28⁶⁄₈	27⁴⁄₈	22⁶⁄₈	38⁵⁄₈	5⁶⁄₈	5⁴⁄₈	14	23	86⁴⁄₈	9	1
	♦ Norwood / Steve H. Herndon / V.D. & D.F. Holleman / 1954										
303⁶⁄₈	26⁴⁄₈	26⁷⁄₈	24³⁄₈	32³⁄₈	5²⁄₈	5	13	11	85⁷⁄₈	12	2
	♦ Eagle County / James Austill / Don Schaufler / 1962										
302⁴⁄₈	25¹⁄₈	26²⁄₈	25²⁄₈	41	5⁷⁄₈	6³⁄₈	18	14	84⁴⁄₈	13	3
	♦ Paonia / Louis H. Huntington, Jr. / Louis H. Huntington, Jr. / 1965										
300	27	25⁶⁄₈	23¹⁄₈	41	5³⁄₈	5³⁄₈	14	12	80⁵⁄₈	16	4
	♦ Mesa County / George Blackmon, Jr. / Don Schaufler / 1961										
299⁵⁄₈	26⁶⁄₈	28¹⁄₈	29¹⁄₈	41¹⁄₈	6²⁄₈	5²⁄₈	19	17	113⁴⁄₈	17	5
	♦ Elk Creek / Andrew Daum / Unknown / 1886										
296²⁄₈	30¹⁄₈	30²⁄₈	26⁵⁄₈	37	5⁷⁄₈	5⁷⁄₈	12	14	83¹⁄₈	20	6
	♦ Mesa County / Unknown / Don Schaufler / PR 1981										
286³⁄₈	29⁴⁄₈	29⁶⁄₈	35⁴⁄₈	37³⁄₈	5¹⁄₈	5¹⁄₈	13	13	61¹⁄₈	26	7
	♦ Eagle County / Albert L. Mulnix / Don Schaufler / 1928										
278⁷⁄₈	24⁴⁄₈	26	18	29¹⁄₈	4⁷⁄₈	5¹⁄₈	8	11	75¹⁄₈	43	8
	♦ Montrose County / Keith Thaute / Keith Thaute / 1961										
278⁷⁄₈	26⁷⁄₈	30	24⁶⁄₈	42¹⁄₈	6²⁄₈	6³⁄₈	12	12	78⁵⁄₈	43	8
	♦ Eagle County / Dale L. Becker / Dale L. Becker / 1978										
277¹⁄₈	25²⁄₈	24⁷⁄₈	25³⁄₈	41¹⁄₈	5²⁄₈	5⁵⁄₈	12	10	63⁵⁄₈	47	10
	♦ Colorado / Indian / Charles McAden / 1930										
276⁴⁄₈	26⁵⁄₈	25	23	44¹⁄₈	4⁷⁄₈	5	11	12	78	49	11
	♦ Glenwood Springs / Larry Prehm / Spanky Greenville / 1967										
274⁵⁄₈	25¹⁄₈	26	24²⁄₈	41	5²⁄₈	5⁶⁄₈	11	13	60⁷⁄₈	55	12
	♦ Pueblo County / Picked Up / Butler Ranch / 1988										
273⁶⁄₈	23²⁄₈	24²⁄₈	23³⁄₈	40¹⁄₈	5⁴⁄₈	5⁶⁄₈	15	15	73³⁄₈	62	13
	♦ Hayden / Roy I. Roney / Colo. Div. of Wildl. / 1930										
272⁵⁄₈	29	28	21⁵⁄₈	27⁶⁄₈	5³⁄₈	5²⁄₈	16	14	62	67	14
	♦ Glenwood Springs / William L. Kurtz / William L. Kurtz / 1967										
272⁴⁄₈	28³⁄₈	27²⁄₈	21²⁄₈	31⁶⁄₈	6³⁄₈	6²⁄₈	19	17	59²⁄₈	68	15
	♦ Eagle County / Eddie Stephenson, Jr. / Eddie Stephenson, Jr. / 1978										
268³⁄₈	25⁴⁄₈	27⁵⁄₈	23	34⁴⁄₈	6¹⁄₈	6	17	11	64⁷⁄₈	80	16
	♦ Delta County / Shirley Smith / Shirley Smith / 1962										
267¹⁄₈	23⁷⁄₈	25³⁄₈	24²⁄₈	32	5²⁄₈	5⁴⁄₈	15	11	67³⁄₈	86	17
	♦ Eagle County / Josef Langegger / Josef Langegger / 1969										

Score	Length of Main Beam R	L	Inside Spread	Greatest Spread	Circumference at Smallest Place between Burr and First Point R	L	Number of Points R	L	Total of Lengths Abnormal Points	All-Time Rank	State Rank
264 3/8	26	27 5/8	21 4/8	32 5/8	5 4/8	5 3/8	13	10	57 3/8	102	18
♦ Gunnison County / Gordon E. Blay / Gorden E. Blay / 1975											
263 4/8	26 5/8	26 4/8	23 6/8	39 2/8	5	5	12	12	58 4/8	107	19
♦ Montrose / Robert L. Price / Robert L. Price / 1963											
262 3/8	30 7/8	29 3/8	29 4/8	0	5 3/8	5 6/8	10	11	51 5/8	112	20
♦ Brush Creek / Pete Taullie / Pete Taullie / 1967											
261 1/8	23	23 1/8	21 3/8	37 4/8	5 4/8	5 2/8	12	13	62 4/8	122	21
♦ Rio Blanco County / L.C. Denny, Jr. / L.C. Denny, Jr.. / 1961											
259 6/8	24 2/8	25 4/8	21 3/8	36 7/8	5 3/8	5 3/8	13	13	78 5/8	135	22
♦ Routt County / R.V. Rhoads / Cecil R. Weston / 1949											
258 3/8	27	28 4/8	25 1/8	38 6/8	5 1/8	5 1/8	11	10	54	146	23
♦ Monte Vista / Geis Nettlebeck / Phil Skinner / 1956											
257 5/8	25 3/8	25 2/8	24	37 5/8	4 7/8	5 1/8	12	13	56 7/8	155	24
♦ Rio Blanco County / Rachael Palmer / Rachael Palmer / 1970											
257 3/8	24 6/8	26 3/8	23 1/8	38 4/8	4 6/8	4 7/8	12	8	60 4/8	163	25
♦ New Castle / Unknown / A.E. Hudson / 1952											
255 2/8	28	27 3/8	28 2/8	39 6/8	5 7/8	5 5/8	14	12	41 4/8	183	26
♦ Garfield County / Louis Lindauer / Louis Lindauer / 1932											
255 1/8	25	25 7/8	26 5/8	46 3/8	4 7/8	5	7	9	47 4/8	185	27
♦ Eagle County / Dennis Martinson / Dennis Martinson / 1980											
255	21 5/8	22 4/8	19 7/8	29 3/8	5 5/8	5 4/8	9	9	56 7/8	187	28
♦ Dunkley Flat / Richard A. Gorden / Richard A. Gorden / 1966											
254 2/8	30	28 6/8	23 4/8	0	6 2/8	6 4/8	7	8	0	191	29
♦ Columbine / M.A. Story / M.A. Story / 1955											
253 4/8	24 6/8	25 1/8	25 6/8	39 6/8	5 2/8	5 1/8	11	10	47 5/8	193	30
♦ Silt / George McCoy / George McCoy / 1961											
253 3/8	25 3/8	23 4/8	26 1/8	43 4/8	5 4/8	5 4/8	13	17	61 2/8	195	31
♦ Meeker / George R. Howey / Robert L. Howey / 1917											
253 3/8	27 6/8	26 6/8	21	0	5 2/8	5 3/8	11	13	0	195	31
♦ Georgetown / George Lappin / Doug Grubbe / 1947											
253	25 5/8	25 4/8	25 2/8	41 3/8	5 6/8	6	11	11	52 2/8	201	33
♦ Paonia / F.F. Parham / F.F. Parham / 1961											
252 2/8	30	30	26 6/8	39	6	5 4/8	15	14	47	206	34
♦ Garfield County / B.J. Slack / B.J. Slack / 1973											
252	24 7/8	23	24 5/8	31	5	5	9	13	69 7/8	209	35
♦ Eagle County / Richard G. Lundock / Richard G. Lundock / 1945											

Score	Length of Main Beam R	Length of Main Beam L	Inside Spread	Greatest Spread	Circumference at Smallest Place between Burr and First Point R	Circumference at Smallest Place between Burr and First Point L	Number of Points R	Number of Points L	Total of Lengths Abnormal Points	All-Time Rank	State Rank
	♦ *Locality / Hunter / Owner / Date Killed*										
251 5/8	27 4/8	25 2/8	23 6/8	29 5/8	5 2/8	5 2/8	9	14	46 3/8	214	36
	♦ *Gunnison County / John M. Ringler / John M. Ringler / 1956*										
251 5/8	24 1/8	26 1/8	21	38 4/8	5 1/8	5 4/8	10	14	52 7/8	214	36
	♦ *Roan Creek / Anthony Morabito / Anthony Morabito / 1965*										
251 1/8	27 5/8	25 6/8	25 7/8	40 7/8	5 3/8	5 2/8	10	9	46	218	38
	♦ *Meeker / Henry Zietz, Jr. / Henry Zietz, Jr. / 1955*										
250 6/8	29	29 1/8	35 1/8	43 5/8	5 4/8	5 3/8	11	13	52 3/8	222	39
	♦ *Pagosa Springs / Thomas Jarrett / Thomas Jarrett / 1962*										
250 3/8	29	28 4/8	27 4/8	41 4/8	5 1/8	4 6/8	10	12	39 5/8	229	40
	♦ *Moffat County / Unknown / Carrol Grounds / 1960*										
250 3/8	26 2/8	24 7/8	25 4/8	36 6/8	5	5	10	10	50 5/8	229	40
	♦ *Cedaredge / F.K. Plante / F.K. Plante / 1963*										
250 1/8	26	26	24	34 4/8	5 4/8	5 6/8	15	11	56 1/8	232	42
	♦ *Montezuma County / Jack E. Reed / Jack E. Reed / 1981*										
249 3/8	25	24 2/8	19 6/8	35 2/8	5 4/8	5 3/8	12	9	47 7/8	237	43
	♦ *Routt County / Howard Stoker / Howard Stoker / 1958*										
249 2/8	23 5/8	23 4/8	20 7/8	35 1/8	5	4 5/8	12	10	55 3/8	240	44
	♦ *Mesa County / Gene Cavanagh / Gene Cavanagh / 1967*										
249	25 1/8	23 4/8	23 1/8	43 4/8	5 1/8	5	14	10	69 1/8	244	45
	♦ *Minturn / John F. Baldauf / L.F. Nowotny / 1941*										
249	26 7/8	26 7/8	26 7/8	35 4/8	5 1/8	5 1/8	8	10	39 5/8	244	45
	♦ *New Castle / William Wiedenfeld / William Wiedenfeld / 1969*										
248 3/8	24 4/8	25 1/8	25 1/8	35 4/8	5 5/8	5 3/8	10	12	46 2/8	250	47
	♦ *Mesa County / Edwin Baal / Edwin Baal / 1988*										
248 3/8	29 2/8	27 6/8	27 2/8	33 3/8	6 1/8	6 2/8	10	9	31 7/8	250	47
	♦ *Costilla County / Ronald E. Lewis / Ronald E. Lewis / 1988*										
248 1/8	25 7/8	24 7/8	22 6/8	31 5/8	5	5 1/8	11	10	36 3/8	254	49
	♦ *Rio Blanco County / Claude E. Shults / Claude E. Shults / 1956*										
248 1/8	25 4/8	25	23	34 6/8	5 2/8	5	15	18	66 5/8	254	49
	♦ *San Juan Natl. For. / Leland R. Tate / Leland R. Tate / 1973*										
248	25 5/8	26 4/8	24 7/8	29 6/8	5 2/8	5	11	10	50 1/8	256	51
	♦ *Columbine / Bobby McLaughlin / Bobby McLaughlin / 1962*										
247 7/8	26	25 3/8	25	38	5 6/8	6	16	11	66 5/8	259	52
	♦ *Norwood / Walter L. Reisbeck / Walter L. Reisbeck / 1951*										
247 5/8	26	24 1/8	26 5/8	36 2/8	7 3/8	7 5/8	16	20	69 3/8	265	53
	♦ *Hinsdale County / Fred Jardine / Fred Jardine / 1966*										

Score	Length of Main Beam R	L	Inside Spread	Greatest Spread	Circumference at Smallest Place between Burr and First Point R	L	Number of Points R	L	Total of Lengths Abnormal Points	All-Time Rank	State Rank
					Locality / Hunter / Owner / Date Killed						
247 4/8	28 3/8	28 5/8	28 3/8	35 5/8	5 1/8	5	9	10	40 7/8	268	54
	♦ *Archuleta County / Vince Plaskett / Vince Plaskett / 1970*										
247 3/8	28 6/8	28 1/8	25 2/8	33 4/8	5	5	10	9	38 7/8	271	55
	♦ *Eagle County / Earl M. Johnson / Earl M. Johnson / 1966*										
247 1/8	28 3/8	27 7/8	25	32 7/8	6 1/8	6	10	15	41 5/8	276	56
	♦ *San Miguel County / W.F. Grice / W.F. Grice / 1978*										
247	23 4/8	24 2/8	21 1/8	30 4/8	4 7/8	4 7/8	11	8	50 3/8	280	57
	♦ *Montrose County / Thomas M. Bost / Thomas M. Bost / 1967*										
246 7/8	23 5/8	23	26 4/8	38	5 1/8	5 1/8	11	10	56	282	58
	♦ *Craig / Fred E. Trouth / Fred E. Trouth / 1960*										
246 6/8	24 2/8	23 3/8	25 1/8	43	5 2/8	5 2/8	13	11	57	285	59
	♦ *Eagle County / William M. Nickels / William M. Nickels / 1963*										
246 3/8	25 2/8	25	26	33	5 4/8	5 2/8	9	11	56 1/8	289	60
	♦ *Glenwood Springs / Grady P. Lester / Grady P. Lester / 1959*										
246 2/8	28 1/8	26 6/8	28 2/8	35 4/8	5 1/8	4 6/8	8	9	41 1/8	291	61
	♦ *Eagle County / Charles H. Thornberg / Charles H. Thornberg / 1949*										
246 1/8	26 6/8	25 4/8	25 4/8	37 1/8	5 3/8	5 4/8	12	10	32 3/8	293	62
	♦ *Mesa County / Joseph J. Pitcherella / Joseph J. Pitcherella / 1972*										
246	23 5/8	26 1/8	24 1/8	32 4/8	6 3/8	5 6/8	14	13	57 3/8	294	63
	♦ *Mesa County / Harry A. Gay / Harry A. Gay / 1962*										
245 5/8	27 5/8	28	23 3/8	35 2/8	5 1/8	5 2/8	13	11	65	299	64
	♦ *Rio Blanco County / Charlie Grove / Dorothy Shults / 1934*										
245 5/8	27 2/8	28 2/8	23 2/8	30 2/8	5 3/8	5 4/8	9	8	41 5/8	299	64
	♦ *Eagle County / James Caraccioli / James Caraccioli / 1978*										
245 3/8	28 2/8	24	31 6/8	40	5 1/8	5 1/8	10	7	52 5/8	301	66
	♦ *Saquache County / Walter A. Larsen / Walter A. Larsen / 1962*										
244 7/8	28 3/8	28 5/8	25	31 4/8	5 5/8	6 4/8	9	11	29 5/8	308	67
	♦ *Eagle / Robert Rambo / Robert Rambo / 1963*										
244 5/8	25 5/8	25 4/8	20 3/8	32 2/8	5 1/8	5 1/8	13	10	54	310	68
	♦ *Delta County / Neil A. Briscoe, Jr. / Neil A. Briscoe, Jr. / 1969*										
244 2/8	28 4/8	28 7/8	30 1/8	41	5 2/8	5 4/8	9	8	36 3/8	316	69
	♦ *Oak Creek / Scott C. Hinkle / Scott C. Hinkle / 1961*										
244 2/8	27 3/8	29 2/8	29 6/8	35 4/8	5 2/8	5 5/8	9	9	38 4/8	316	69
	♦ *Montrose County / Jim Herndon / Mrs. Jim Herndon / 1974*										
244 2/8	23 1/8	25	23 6/8	34 1/8	5 2/8	5 3/8	12	11	49 6/8	316	69
	♦ *Mesa County / Thomas S. Hundley / Thomas S. Hundley / 1986*										

Score	Length of Main Beam R	L	Inside Spread	Greatest Spread	Circumference at Smallest Place between Burr and First Point R	L	Number of Points R	L	Total of Lengths Abnormal Points	All-Time Rank	State Rank
	◆ Locality / Hunter / Owner / Date Killed										
244 1/8	24 2/8	25 1/8	27	37 4/8	5 1/8	5 1/8	14	9	49 2/8	323	72
	◆ Mesa County / Edward B. Walsh / Mrs. Edward B. Walsh / 1960										
244 1/8	25 1/8	22 6/8	23 2/8	33 4/8	5 2/8	5 3/8	12	13	51 7/8	323	72
	◆ Grand County / Kenneth H. Newbury / Kenneth H. Newbury / 1966										
243 6/8	26	24 5/8	22 4/8	39 4/8	6 2/8	6 4/8	10	12	62	331	74
	◆ San Miguel County / Ben Crandell / Ben Crandell / 1939										
243 4/8	23 6/8	22 7/8	21	40 5/8	5 4/8	5 5/8	10	13	56	336	75
	◆ Clear Creek County / Louis I. Kingsley / Louis I. Kingsley / 1981										
243 2/8	28 4/8	28 1/8	25 5/8	37 3/8	4 6/8	4 7/8	10	10	44 1/8	338	76
	◆ Colorado / Unknown / Brad A. Bauer / 1954										
243 1/8	29 2/8	28 2/8	28 6/8	43 6/8	4 6/8	5 2/8	8	9	30 3/8	339	77
	◆ Harrison Gulch / George R. Mattern / George R. Mattern / 1958										
242 4/8	27 4/8	27 5/8	25 4/8	29 1/8	6 1/8	5 6/8	9	8	24	350	78
	◆ Hinsdale County / Picked Up / Rick House / 1991										
242 2/8	23 2/8	23	20 2/8	36 2/8	5 3/8	5 6/8	12	17	71 2/8	353	79
	◆ Middle Park / Picked Up / Karl H. Knorr / PR 1961										
242 2/8	25 4/8	25 3/8	23 2/8	32 3/8	5	4 7/8	9	12	46	353	79
	◆ Rabbit Ears Pass / Douglas Valentine / Douglas Valentine / 1964										
242 1/8	26	25 4/8	28	32 4/8	5 2/8	5 2/8	12	10	50 1/8	356	81
	◆ Hinsdale County / Bill Crose / Bill Crose / 1973										
242	22 6/8	23 5/8	18 6/8	32 4/8	5 4/8	5 7/8	12	14	49 4/8	359	82
	◆ Garfield County / Daniel J. Stanek / Daniel J. Stanek / 1981										
241 7/8	26 4/8	26 2/8	30 6/8	36 4/8	4 5/8	4 6/8	10	9	48 5/8	362	83
	◆ La Plata County / Randall N. Bostick / Randall N. Bostick / 1984										
241 4/8	25 1/8	25 7/8	23 3/8	32 3/8	4 4/8	4 4/8	10	9	40 5/8	369	84
	◆ Summit County / Robert R. Ross / Robert R. Ross / 1974										
241 4/8	27 2/8	27	22 5/8	30 1/8	5 3/8	5 3/8	17	12	51 3/8	369	84
	◆ Douglas County / Donald E. Ditmars / Donald E. Ditmars / 1994										
241 2/8	26 6/8	25 1/8	18 5/8	27 4/8	5	5	10	11	51 4/8	376	86
	◆ Oak Creek / Richard J. Peltier / Richard J. Peltier / 1967										
240 7/8	27	27 2/8	25 2/8	30 3/8	5 2/8	5 1/8	6	6	39 1/8	380	87
	◆ New Castle / Harold F. Auld / Harold F. Auld / 1960										
240 6/8	27	25 6/8	27 1/8	39	5 7/8	5 1/8	10	8	33	383	88
	◆ Eagle County / Steve B. Humann / Steve B. Humann / 1982										
240 4/8	23 6/8	22	22 6/8	34 1/8	5 1/8	5 4/8	10	11	48 6/8	386	89
	◆ Eagle County / James P. Hale / James P. Hale / 1979										

Score	Length of Main Beam		Inside Spread	Greatest Spread	Circumference at Smallest Place between Burr and First Point		Number of Points		Total of Lengths Abnormal Points	All-Time Rank	State Rank
	R	L			R	L	R	L			
◆ *Locality / Hunter / Owner / Date Killed*											
240 4/8	23	24 4/8	21 5/8	37 1/8	5 2/8	5 2/8	15	14	53 1/8	386	89
◆ *Garfield County / James E. Powell, Jr. / James E. Powell, Jr. / 1983*											
240	25 7/8	24 4/8	23 2/8	34 2/8	5 4/8	5 6/8	12	10	51 2/8	396	91
◆ *Grand Valley / Ed Peters, Jr. / Ed Peters, Jr. / 1962*											
240	26 1/8	28 5/8	27 1/8	40 3/8	4 6/8	4 7/8	9	8	38 7/8	396	91
◆ *San Juan Wild. / Tommie Cornelius / Tommie Cornelius / 1967*											
232 3/8	27 2/8	26 5/8	22 2/8	26	5 3/8	5 5/8	14	9	27 1/8	412	93
◆ *Colorado / Unknown / Melvin A. Mitchell, Jr. / PR 1900*											
232	23 1/8	24	18 3/8	34 3/8	5 3/8	5 3/8	10	17	36 7/8	413	94
◆ *Grand County / William L. Henry / William L. Henry / 1986*											
297 5/8	26 1/8	26 3/8	26 5/8	34 7/8	6 4/8	6 6/8	17	15	90 4/8	*	*
◆ *Larimer County / Jack Autrey / Warren C. Autrey / 1941*											
277	25 7/8	24 2/8	23 6/8	32	5 5/8	5 7/8	11	15	73	*	*
◆ *Delta County / Robert G. Wilson / Robert G. Wilson / 1989*											
266 4/8	26 4/8	25 4/8	22 7/8	41 7/8	5 5/8	5 6/8	15	13	62 7/8	*	*
◆ *Ouray County / Eugene D. Guilaroff / Eugene D. Guilaroff / 1971*											

James L. Horneck connected with this trophy typical mule deer buck, scoring 200-4/8 points, in Dolores County, Colorado, during the 1988 archery season. Trophies in velvet are not eligible for entry into B&C unless the velvet is removed before scoring.

Photograph by Arlene Hanson

IDAHO STATE RECORD
TYPICAL MULE DEER
SCORE: 215⅝
Locality: Franklin Co.   Date: 1961
Hunter: Ray Talbot
Loaned to the B&C National Collection

IDAHO

TYPICAL MULE DEER

Score	Length of Main Beam R	Length of Main Beam L	Inside Spread	Greatest Spread	Circumference at Smallest Place between Burr and First Point R	L	Number of Points R	L	Total of Lengths Abnormal Points	All-Time Rank	State Rank
$215\frac{5}{8}$	$27\frac{3}{8}$	$27\frac{1}{8}$	$28\frac{5}{8}$	$30\frac{4}{8}$	$5\frac{4}{8}$	$5\frac{4}{8}$	5	6	$1\frac{6}{8}$	3	1
$212\frac{6}{8}$	$26\frac{6}{8}$	$26\frac{7}{8}$	$25\frac{4}{8}$	$32\frac{2}{8}$	$5\frac{2}{8}$	$5\frac{2}{8}$	5	5	0	6	2
$212\frac{1}{8}$	$28\frac{1}{8}$	$28\frac{5}{8}$	$24\frac{5}{8}$	$28\frac{4}{8}$	$5\frac{1}{8}$	5	5	5	0	7	3
$211\frac{7}{8}$	$30\frac{3}{8}$	$30\frac{1}{8}$	$25\frac{3}{8}$	$27\frac{4}{8}$	5	5	5	6	$2\frac{6}{8}$	10	4
$210\frac{3}{8}$	28	$27\frac{6}{8}$	$23\frac{1}{8}$	$29\frac{3}{8}$	$4\frac{5}{8}$	$4\frac{6}{8}$	6	6	$4\frac{2}{8}$	13	5
209	$26\frac{7}{8}$	27	$24\frac{2}{8}$	$28\frac{6}{8}$	$5\frac{6}{8}$	$5\frac{6}{8}$	5	5	0	24	6
208	$26\frac{6}{8}$	$26\frac{6}{8}$	$31\frac{6}{8}$	34	$5\frac{3}{8}$	$5\frac{1}{8}$	6	5	$2\frac{6}{8}$	30	7
$207\frac{6}{8}$	$25\frac{5}{8}$	26	$23\frac{2}{8}$	$27\frac{6}{8}$	$4\frac{7}{8}$	$5\frac{1}{8}$	5	6	$2\frac{6}{8}$	32	8
$206\frac{7}{8}$	29	$29\frac{2}{8}$	$29\frac{7}{8}$	$34\frac{7}{8}$	$5\frac{3}{8}$	$5\frac{3}{8}$	6	5	$2\frac{3}{8}$	41	9
$206\frac{1}{8}$	$24\frac{7}{8}$	$25\frac{1}{8}$	$25\frac{2}{8}$	$29\frac{6}{8}$	$5\frac{1}{8}$	$5\frac{1}{8}$	5	5	0	52	10
$203\frac{4}{8}$	28	$26\frac{5}{8}$	$30\frac{5}{8}$	0	$5\frac{4}{8}$	$5\frac{2}{8}$	6	5	$1\frac{6}{8}$	84	11
$202\frac{7}{8}$	$24\frac{2}{8}$	$26\frac{3}{8}$	$26\frac{3}{8}$	$29\frac{1}{8}$	6	$5\frac{7}{8}$	5	5	0	98	12
$202\frac{7}{8}$	$26\frac{5}{8}$	26	$23\frac{7}{8}$	$30\frac{7}{8}$	$4\frac{7}{8}$	$4\frac{7}{8}$	6	7	$5\frac{6}{8}$	98	12
$202\frac{5}{8}$	$27\frac{1}{8}$	$26\frac{1}{8}$	$25\frac{1}{8}$	$30\frac{1}{8}$	5	$5\frac{1}{8}$	5	5	0	104	14
$202\frac{4}{8}$	$26\frac{1}{8}$	$26\frac{2}{8}$	$28\frac{2}{8}$	35	$4\frac{7}{8}$	$4\frac{7}{8}$	5	6	$1\frac{2}{8}$	106	15
202	28	27	26	26	$5\frac{3}{8}$	$5\frac{6}{8}$	9	6	$11\frac{2}{8}$	119	16
202	$26\frac{1}{8}$	$26\frac{4}{8}$	$21\frac{4}{8}$	$24\frac{5}{8}$	5	$4\frac{7}{8}$	5	5	0	119	16

♦ Locality / Hunter / Owner / Date Killed

♦ Franklin County / Ray Talbot / Loaned to B&C Natl. Coll. / 1961

♦ Gem County / Kirk Payne / Kirk Payne / 1967

♦ Idaho County / Urban H. Riener / Masters Trophy Coll. / 1979

♦ Adams County / Boyd W. Dennis / Boyd W. Dennis / 1970

♦ Madison County / Todd L. Landon / Todd L. Landon / 1986

♦ Boise County / Charles Root / Soron Root / 1970

♦ Franklin County / Herb Voyler, Jr. / Herb Voyler, Jr. / 1972

♦ Gem County / Thomas A. Sutton / Thomas A. Sutton / 1991

♦ Washington County / E. Jack Raby / E. Jack Raby / 1968

♦ Idaho County / William B. Joyner / William B. Joyner / 1965

♦ Adams County / Roy Eastlick / Roy Eastlick / 1975

♦ Adams County / James S. Denney / James S. Denney / 1939

♦ Idaho County / Myron L. Gilbert / Myron L. Gilbert / 1975

♦ Adams County / David J. Couch / David J. Couch / 1970

♦ Bear Lake County / Alan R. Crane / Alan R. Crane / 1962

♦ Bear Lake County / David L. Williams / Raymond L. Williams / 1949

♦ Idaho County / John H. Davis / John H. Davis / 1981

Score	Length of Main Beam R	L	Inside Spread	Greatest Spread	Circumference at Smallest Place between Burr and First Point R	L	Number of Points R	L	Total of Lengths Abnormal Points	All-Time Rank	State Rank
	♦ *Locality / Hunter / Owner / Date Killed*										
201 4/8	27 1/8	26 2/8	22 6/8	28 6/8	5 1/8	5 2/8	5	5	0	138	18
	♦ *Adams County / Gary D. Lewis / Gary D. Lewis / 1990*										
201 3/8	27 6/8	27 6/8	26 4/8	36 5/8	5 4/8	5 4/8	7	7	12 5/8	144	19
	♦ *Blaine County / Brent Jones / Brent Jones / 1965*										
201 3/8	28 3/8	29 7/8	34 2/8	37 4/8	5 3/8	5 6/8	4	5	0	144	19
	♦ *Butte County / John A. Little / John A. Little / 1981*										
201	26 6/8	26 1/8	24 5/8	29 4/8	5 1/8	5 2/8	7	5	2 3/8	159	21
	♦ *Idaho / Unknown / Rick Stover / PR 1990*										
200 6/8	25 2/8	25 2/8	26 7/8	30 5/8	5 3/8	5 2/8	5	7	3 2/8	166	22
	♦ *Boise County / Delbert W. Crawford / Delbert W. Crawford / 1969*										
200 4/8	26 7/8	28 6/8	27 6/8	34 6/8	5 1/8	5 1/8	5	6	0	177	23
	♦ *Bear Lake County / Frank Bidart / Frank Bidart / 1965*										
200 4/8	27	25 6/8	23 6/8	30 4/8	5 1/8	5	7	6	8 6/8	177	23
	♦ *Bear Lake County / Lee Bridges / Lee Bridges / 1966*										
200 4/8	26 4/8	26 6/8	23	25 6/8	5 3/8	5 3/8	5	5	0	177	23
	♦ *Caribou County / Herb Voyler, Jr. / Herb Voyler, Jr. / 1972*										
200 4/8	27 2/8	26	30 5/8	39	5 4/8	5 3/8	6	5	1 6/8	177	23
	♦ *Adams County / Roy Eastlick / Roy Eastlick / 1974*										
200 2/8	23 6/8	24 5/8	19 3/8	23 3/8	5	4 7/8	5	6	1 3/8	190	27
	♦ *Bonneville County / Richard A. Kelley / Richard A. Kelley / 1990*										
200 2/8	26 3/8	27 1/8	19	24 2/8	4 6/8	4 6/8	5	5	0	190	27
	♦ *Boise County / Richard L. Jakomeit / Richard L. Jakomeit / 1992*										
199 4/8	26 2/8	28 4/8	28 7/8	30	4 6/8	4 7/8	7	7	6 6/8	222	29
	♦ *Salmon River / C.A. Schwope / C.A. Schwope / 1959*										
199 4/8	24 2/8	24 2/8	21 2/8	27	5 5/8	5 5/8	5	5	0	222	29
	♦ *Bonneville County / Leonard J. Vella / Leonard J. Vella / 1972*										
199 1/8	27	28 3/8	27 6/8	30 1/8	5 3/8	5 3/8	5	8	7 5/8	243	31
	♦ *Bonneville County / Scott B. Huntsman / Scott B. Huntsman / 1992*										
199	24 7/8	23 6/8	23 3/8	29 5/8	4 7/8	4 6/8	6	5	2 1/8	248	32
	♦ *Power County / Jim A. Rose / Jim A. Rose / 1977*										
198 5/8	24 4/8	24 7/8	24 1/8	30 4/8	5 3/8	5 5/8	6	6	0	257	33
	♦ *Swan Valley / Harry G. Brinkley, Jr. / Harry G. Brinkley, Jr. / 1966*										
198 5/8	25	24 7/8	23 5/8	27 5/8	4 7/8	4 7/8	5	5	0	257	33
	♦ *Elmore County / William Hartwig / William Hartwig / 1984*										
198 3/8	25	25 4/8	19 5/8	25 5/8	4 5/8	4 5/8	5	5	0	271	35
	♦ *Bonneville County / Tony Dawson / Tony Dawson / 1973*										

Score	Length of Main Beam R	L	Inside Spread	Greatest Spread	Circumference at Smallest Place between Burr and First Point R	L	Number of Points R	L	Total of Lengths Abnormal Points	All-Time Rank	State Rank
♦ Locality / Hunter / Owner / Date Killed											
198²⁄₈	28²⁄₈	28³⁄₈	27	32³⁄₈	5⁴⁄₈	5³⁄₈	5	7	5⁴⁄₈	274	36
♦ Bonneville County / Thomas N. Thiel / Thomas N. Thiel / 1987											
198¹⁄₈	25³⁄₈	26	25²⁄₈	32⁶⁄₈	5⁴⁄₈	5⁴⁄₈	5	4	4⁷⁄₈	280	37
♦ Irwin / Chet Warwick / Chet Warwick / 1959											
198	25	25	22⁴⁄₈	30²⁄₈	5⁶⁄₈	5⁶⁄₈	5	5	0	287	38
♦ Montpelier / Charles R. Mann / Charles R. Mann / 1973											
197⁷⁄₈	28³⁄₈	28²⁄₈	25⁷⁄₈	30⁴⁄₈	5⁶⁄₈	5⁵⁄₈	7	6	11⁶⁄₈	295	39
♦ Blaine County / James D. Scarrow / James D. Scarrow / 1983											
197⁶⁄₈	24³⁄₈	26⁴⁄₈	27³⁄₈	29¹⁄₈	5	5¹⁄₈	5	5	0	302	40
♦ Bonneville County / Preston L. Winchell / Preston L. Winchell / 1974											
197⁵⁄₈	24³⁄₈	24¹⁄₈	24⁷⁄₈	29³⁄₈	4⁷⁄₈	5	5	5	0	308	41
♦ Ashton / Earl Johnson / O.M. Corbett / 1959											
197⁴⁄₈	27²⁄₈	27¹⁄₈	23⁶⁄₈	30²⁄₈	4³⁄₈	4³⁄₈	4	5	0	317	42
♦ Bonneville County / LaDon Harriell / LaDon Harriell / 1982											
197³⁄₈	26⁵⁄₈	27⁵⁄₈	26³⁄₈	31¹⁄₈	4⁶⁄₈	4⁷⁄₈	6	6	4⁴⁄₈	324	43
♦ Fremont County / Stanley A. Gilgen / Stanley A. Gilgen / 1964											
197²⁄₈	26⁵⁄₈	25⁷⁄₈	26⁴⁄₈	30⁵⁄₈	5²⁄₈	5³⁄₈	5	6	4²⁄₈	333	44
♦ Blaine County / Bart Hofmann / Bart Hofmann / 1980											
197	24⁷⁄₈	25⁷⁄₈	22	29	5³⁄₈	5³⁄₈	5	5	0	347	45
♦ Franklin County / Robert C. Porter / Robert C. Porter / 1972											
197	25²⁄₈	24¹⁄₈	25	27⁵⁄₈	4⁷⁄₈	4⁶⁄₈	5	5	0	347	45
♦ Camas County / Bret C. Silver / Bret C. Silver / 1980											
196⁷⁄₈	24⁵⁄₈	24⁴⁄₈	22⁵⁄₈	27²⁄₈	5⁶⁄₈	5⁵⁄₈	5	5	0	357	47
♦ Boise County / Andrew T. Rogers / Andrew T. Rogers / 1967											
196⁶⁄₈	24⁴⁄₈	23⁶⁄₈	24⁴⁄₈	30⁷⁄₈	5³⁄₈	5²⁄₈	7	5	6²⁄₈	362	48
♦ Bear Lake County / Nels H. Pehrson / Ralph V. Pehrson / 1936											
196⁶⁄₈	23³⁄₈	24¹⁄₈	22⁴⁄₈	30⁵⁄₈	5¹⁄₈	5²⁄₈	5	5	0	362	48
♦ Bonneville County / William G. Pine / William G. Pine / 1969											
196⁵⁄₈	22	22⁶⁄₈	21⁵⁄₈	29⁶⁄₈	5	5¹⁄₈	7	6	3²⁄₈	369	50
♦ Lemhi County / Hubert M. Livingston / Hubert M. Livingston / 1967											
196⁴⁄₈	24⁷⁄₈	26²⁄₈	27⁵⁄₈	31⁷⁄₈	5⁴⁄₈	5⁴⁄₈	4	7	3	379	51
♦ Bonneville County / Michael Pinkham / Michael Pinkham / 1985											
196²⁄₈	25⁴⁄₈	25⁶⁄₈	22⁴⁄₈	31²⁄₈	5²⁄₈	5³⁄₈	6	6	5	396	52
♦ Bingham County / Thomas D. Robison / Thomas D. Robison / 1972											
196¹⁄₈	26	27⁷⁄₈	24⁴⁄₈	29⁵⁄₈	5⁷⁄₈	5⁶⁄₈	5	7	4⁵⁄₈	409	53
♦ Boise County / H.L. Rice / H.L. Rice / 1966											

Score	Length of Main Beam R	L	Inside Spread	Greatest Spread	Circumference at Smallest Place between Burr and First Point R	L	Number of Points R	L	Total of Lengths Abnormal Points	All-Time Rank	State Rank
	♦ Locality / Hunter / Owner / Date Killed										
196	25⁴⁄₈	28	23	26	5⁵⁄₈	5⁶⁄₈	5	6	2	414	54
	♦ Franklin County / Larry W. Cross / Larry W. Cross / 1974										
195⁷⁄₈	26²⁄₈	25⁷⁄₈	26²⁄₈	31⁴⁄₈	5⁶⁄₈	5⁵⁄₈	7	7	8¹⁄₈	424	55
	♦ Bannock County / William J. Barry / William J. Barry / 1956										
195⁷⁄₈	27	28⁴⁄₈	28⁴⁄₈	33	5³⁄₈	5⁴⁄₈	7	7	4⁷⁄₈	424	55
	♦ Franklin County / Melvin S. Thomson / Melvin S. Thomson / 1987										
195⁶⁄₈	27³⁄₈	28²⁄₈	26³⁄₈	30⁷⁄₈	5⁴⁄₈	5⁵⁄₈	7	6	4⁷⁄₈	433	57
	♦ Custer County / Sylvester Potaman / W. Douglas Lightfoot / 1900										
195⁶⁄₈	24⁵⁄₈	26¹⁄₈	24	27⁴⁄₈	5¹⁄₈	5¹⁄₈	5	5	0	433	57
	♦ Caribou County / John B. Kochever / John B. Kochever / 1986										
195⁶⁄₈	27²⁄₈	27¹⁄₈	23²⁄₈	25⁶⁄₈	5⁴⁄₈	5¹⁄₈	5	5	0	433	57
	♦ Caribou County / Robin W. Bechtel / Robin W. Bechtel / 1989										
195⁴⁄₈	26	26¹⁄₈	25⁴⁄₈	27⁶⁄₈	5	5	5	6	1⁴⁄₈	456	60
	♦ Bear Lake County / Joseph R. Given / Joseph R. Given / 1985										
195²⁄₈	24⁴⁄₈	24⁴⁄₈	23⁴⁄₈	30²⁄₈	5³⁄₈	5²⁄₈	5	5	0	472	61
	♦ Twin Falls County / Alvin Tollini / Alvin Tollini / 1990										
195²⁄₈	26⁴⁄₈	28¹⁄₈	25¹⁄₈	30³⁄₈	4⁶⁄₈	4⁶⁄₈	7	6	8¹⁄₈	472	61
	♦ Nez Perce County / Patrick G. Sinclair / Patrick G. Sinclair / 1991										
195¹⁄₈	25	25⁶⁄₈	22⁴⁄₈	28⁴⁄₈	5	4⁷⁄₈	5	8	5¹⁄₈	482	63
	♦ Idaho County / Gary BeVan / Gary BeVan / 1970										
195	24⁶⁄₈	24	28	30³⁄₈	5	5¹⁄₈	5	5	0	491	64
	♦ Blaine County / Donald G. Sams / Donald G. Sams / 1992										
193²⁄₈	23⁶⁄₈	24	22²⁄₈	29	5²⁄₈	5⁴⁄₈	6	6	2⁶⁄₈	514	65
	♦ Franklin County / L. Munk & T. Braegger / Larry Munk / 1990										
192⁴⁄₈	24⁴⁄₈	25	20¹⁄₈	26	5	5	5	6	3¹⁄₈	520	66
	♦ Bear Lake County / Lee Bridges / Lee Bridges / 1967										
192¹⁄₈	25⁴⁄₈	25²⁄₈	23³⁄₈	30⁵⁄₈	4⁷⁄₈	4⁷⁄₈	7	8	10⁴⁄₈	523	67
	♦ Bonneville County / Glen M. Brown / Glen M. Brown / 1949										
190⁷⁄₈	27⁴⁄₈	27⁷⁄₈	27	32¹⁄₈	4⁵⁄₈	5	6	6	3⁵⁄₈	536	68
	♦ Elmore County / Michael H. Felton / Michael H. Felton / 1980										
190³⁄₈	26	27⁵⁄₈	20¹⁄₈	27³⁄₈	4⁵⁄₈	4⁵⁄₈	5	5	0	543	69
	♦ Lemhi County / Mac A. Hughes / Brad Sweeney / 1978										
189⁵⁄₈	24²⁄₈	23⁵⁄₈	22⁷⁄₈	30⁷⁄₈	5⁵⁄₈	5⁵⁄₈	5	7	2²⁄₈	552	70
	♦ Bingham County / Clinton G. Jensen II / Clinton G. Jensen II / 1992										
189³⁄₈	24⁷⁄₈	25²⁄₈	25²⁄₈	34¹⁄₈	5¹⁄₈	5⁴⁄₈	5	6	1¹⁄₈	556	71
	♦ Caribou County / Robert E. Anderson / Robert E. Anderson / 1990										

Score	Length of Main Beam R	L	Inside Spread	Greatest Spread	Circumference at Smallest Place between Burr and First Point R	L	Number of Points R	L	Total of Lengths Abnormal Points	All-Time Rank	State Rank
	◆ Locality / Hunter / Owner / Date Killed										
188 4/8	24 7/8	26	26 1/8	29 2/8	5 1/8	5 2/8	5	5	0	567	72
	◆ Bannock County / Richard L. Lockyer / Richard L. Lockyer / 1961										
188 3/8	26 2/8	24 4/8	22 7/8	30 5/8	4 5/8	4 5/8	7	6	4 6/8	569	73
	◆ Camas County / Jeff J. Cornilles / Jeff J. Cornilles / 1991										
187 5/8	25 2/8	22 6/8	19 1/8	22 4/8	4 7/8	4 7/8	5	5	0	582	74
	◆ Cassia County / Richard M. Gleason / Richard M. Gleason / 1990										
187	25 2/8	24 6/8	26 3/8	32	4 6/8	4 7/8	5	5	0	590	75
	◆ Bonneville County / Rockie L. Walker / Rockie L. Walker / 1986										
186 7/8	24 6/8	22 3/8	19 7/8	28 6/8	4 5/8	4 5/8	5	5	0	593	76
	◆ Idaho County / Tom M. Schachten / Tom M. Schachten / 1987										
185 5/8	26 2/8	26 2/8	20 7/8	27 7/8	5 5/8	5 5/8	5	8	4	613	77
	◆ Franklin County / R. Ashley Lyman III / R. Ashley Lyman III / 1964										
185 5/8	26 5/8	25 7/8	17 5/8	23 2/8	5 2/8	5 1/8	6	5	3 2/8	613	77
	◆ Caribou County / Ralph E. Peldo / Ralph E. Peldo / 1988										
185 4/8	24	24 6/8	20 6/8	27 2/8	5 1/8	5 1/8	5	5	0	616	79
	◆ Franklin County / K. Bruce Kidman / K. Bruce Kidman / 1988										
182 4/8	26 1/8	25 6/8	26 2/8	31 2/8	4 5/8	4 5/8	6	7	8 1/8	624	80
	◆ Caribou County / Charlie Bridges / Lee Bridges / 1976										
182 2/8	24	24 4/8	21 4/8	25 4/8	4 7/8	4 6/8	5	5	0	625	81
	◆ Cassia County / Harvey Knoll / Harvey Knoll / 1986										
181 4/8	21 7/8	22 2/8	20 2/8	27 2/8	4 5/8	4 4/8	5	7	4 4/8	629	82
	◆ Cassia County / Michael Bridges / Michael Bridges / 1979										
213 4/8	26 7/8	26 6/8	25 2/8	31 4/8	5 2/8	5 2/8	5	5	0	*	*
	◆ Bonneville County / Ike Ellis / Raymond R. Cross / 1986										
205 2/8	26	27 2/8	24 3/8	28 1/8	5 1/8	5 1/8	5	6	1 1/8	*	*
	◆ Fremont County / Michael W.G. Neff / Michael W.G. Neff / 1990										
203 5/8	28 5/8	28 7/8	27 1/8	33 3/8	5 2/8	5 3/8	7	5	4 6/8	*	*
	◆ Caribou County / William E. Van Antwerp / William E. Van Antwerp / 1992										

Photograph by Mike Biggs

IDAHO STATE RECORD (NEW)
NON-TYPICAL MULE DEER
SCORE: 320⁴⁄₈
Locality: Madison Co.   Date: 1960
Hunter: Grover Browning
Owner: Bob Howard

IDAHO
NON-TYPICAL MULE DEER

Score	Length of Main Beam R	Length of Main Beam L	Inside Spread	Greatest Spread	Circumference at Smallest Place between Burr and First Point R	Circumference at Smallest Place between Burr and First Point L	Number of Points R	Number of Points L	Total of Lengths Abnormal Points	All-Time Rank	State Rank
320 4/8	23 5/8	24 7/8	25	30 4/8	6	6 2/8	17	20	127 3/8	6	1
♦ Madison County / Grover Browning / Bob Howard / 1960											
300 7/8	24	22 6/8	29 4/8	33 7/8	5 5/8	5 3/8	17	16	108 3/8	15	2
♦ Bonneville County / Brett J. Sauer / Don Schaufler / 1985											
288 2/8	25	25 7/8	26	41	6	6	16	13	95 1/8	25	3
♦ Hailey / Robby Miller / Don Schaufler / 1969											
285 7/8	27 1/8	27 6/8	26 7/8	38 4/8	6	6 1/8	19	16	86 4/8	30	4
♦ Adams County / Picked Up / Raymond R. Cross / PR 1968											
280 4/8	27	26 6/8	23 4/8	34 6/8	6	6	15	14	65 2/8	38	5
♦ Gem County / Ronald S. Holbrook / Ronald S. Holbrook / 1982											
279 5/8	21 7/8	22 5/8	30 4/8	39	6 3/8	6 2/8	18	17	104 4/8	42	6
♦ Cuprum / Ed Martin / Ed Martin / 1966											
278 3/8	27 2/8	28	26	34 7/8	5 2/8	5 3/8	11	13	63 5/8	45	7
♦ Soda Springs / Jack White / Don Schaufler / 1957											
274 2/8	22 3/8	25	23 2/8	26 1/8	6 6/8	6 1/8	13	13	89 4/8	57	8
♦ Sublett / Mrs. Jack Keen / Mr. & Mrs. Jack Keen / 1957											
274 2/8	24 4/8	25 7/8	24 5/8	34 6/8	5 6/8	5 3/8	14	13	68 3/8	57	8
♦ Fremont County / David L. Maurer / David L. Maurer / 1979											
274 1/8	21 7/8	23 6/8	22 2/8	32 4/8	4 7/8	5	11	11	70 7/8	59	10
♦ North Fork / James D. Edwards / Idaho Fish & Game Dept. / 1967											
272 7/8	24 1/8	26 2/8	27 1/8	31 6/8	5 4/8	5 5/8	15	16	66 1/8	66	11
♦ Caribou County / Picked Up / Don Schaufler / 1948											
269 4/8	28 3/8	28 7/8	25 7/8	41 6/8	5 5/8	6	14	13	65 5/8	75	12
♦ Owyhee County / Frank Cogdill / Raymond R. Cross / 1939											
267 5/8	23 2/8	23 3/8	23 5/8	40 2/8	4 7/8	4 6/8	18	16	99	83	13
♦ Idaho County / Alan B. Hermann / Alan B. Hermann / 1991											
265	24	24 2/8	19 4/8	35 1/8	4 7/8	5	13	15	67 6/8	100	14
♦ Custer County / John L. Simmons / John L. Simmons / 1986											
264 5/8	26	26 5/8	22 4/8	35 4/8	5 4/8	5 6/8	18	13	65 7/8	101	15
♦ Bannock County / Jarel Neeser / Jarel Neeser / 1974											
263 1/8	27 4/8	26 1/8	26 4/8	42	6 2/8	6 1/8	20	13	73 1/8	108	16
♦ Bigwood River / Robert C. Young / Robert C. Young / 1956											
262 1/8	25 6/8	24 4/8	23 3/8	32 7/8	5 6/8	5 3/8	15	13	75 6/8	114	17
♦ Franklin County / Lester Lowe / Dana J. Hollinger / 1933											

Score	Length of Main Beam R	L	Inside Spread	Greatest Spread	Circumference at Smallest Place between Burr and First Point R	L	Number of Points R	L	Total of Lengths Abnormal Points	All-Time Rank	State Rank
◆ *Locality / Hunter / Owner / Date Killed*											
261 3/8	25 4/8	24	27 2/8	0	5 2/8	5	10	10	0	120	18
◆ *Blaine County / Roger A. Crowder / Roger A. Crowder / 1957*											
260 6/8	26 5/8	26 3/8	22 3/8	36 4/8	4 7/8	4 7/8	10	13	63 1/8	124	19
◆ *Ada County / Howard R. Cromwell / Raymond R. Cross / 1975*											
260 2/8	23 1/8	24 3/8	25 4/8	36 1/8	5 7/8	6	15	17	68 7/8	127	20
◆ *Boise / George M. Tweedy / George M. Tweedy / 1946*											
260	22 7/8	25	20	35 5/8	5	5	12	12	61 6/8	130	21
◆ *Caribou County / Arthur H. Summers / Arthur H. Summers / 1966*											
259 7/8	25 1/8	25 2/8	22 2/8	39 2/8	5	5	8	10	50 1/8	132	22
◆ *Caribou County / Jerry Hunt / Jerry Hunt / 1966*											
259 6/8	25 7/8	24 7/8	29	37 4/8	6 3/8	5 7/8	15	14	66 3/8	135	23
◆ *Gooding County / Charles Hollingsworth / Charles Hollingsworth / 1970*											
259 4/8	24 3/8	24	25 3/8	41 6/8	5	5 2/8	13	15	66 7/8	138	24
◆ *Boise County / LeRoy Massey / LeRoy Massey / 1959*											
258 6/8	27 5/8	27 6/8	24 5/8	31 4/8	5	5	15	10	49 7/8	141	25
◆ *Valley County / Larry Dwonch / Larry Dwonch / 1972*											
258 1/8	27 3/8	26 4/8	23 6/8	40 3/8	5 1/8	5 1/8	13	14	70 1/8	148	26
◆ *Atlanta / Kenneth E. Potts / Kenneth E. Potts / 1968*											
257 4/8	25 3/8	26	27 2/8	35	5 4/8	5 4/8	9	14	69	159	27
◆ *Blaine County / Philip T. Homer / Philip T. Homer / 1983*											
257	29 1/8	27 7/8	26 2/8	40 2/8	4 6/8	4 6/8	10	10	48 4/8	165	28
◆ *Madison County / Grover Browning / Dana J. Hollinger / 1959*											
256 7/8	23 7/8	22 4/8	21 4/8	34 1/8	4 1/8	4 6/8	12	13	71 5/8	167	29
◆ *Elmore County / Paul Vetter / Paul Vetter / 1972*											
256 1/8	22 7/8	22 4/8	20 1/8	30 5/8	4 5/8	5	14	12	70 2/8	175	30
◆ *Irwin / Hale K. Charlton / Hale K. Charlton / 1966*											
256	26 7/8	26 5/8	22 6/8	35 2/8	9 4/8	6 5/8	16	9	62 6/8	178	31
◆ *Gem County / Jay P. Baker / Jay P. Baker / 1981*											
255 1/8	25 6/8	26 6/8	29 4/8	37	5 6/8	5 4/8	10	11	48 5/8	185	32
◆ *Hells Canyon / Basil C. Bradbury / Basil C. Bradbury / 1955*											
255	26 6/8	25 4/8	23 4/8	32	4 6/8	4 6/8	8	8	46	187	33
◆ *Adams County / Fred Bain / Raymond R. Cross / 1974*											
253 2/8	24 3/8	25 2/8	20 5/8	35 6/8	5 2/8	5 5/8	15	17	72 1/8	199	34
◆ *Salmon / Ben H. Quick / Ben H. Quick / 1960*											
252 6/8	25 6/8	24 6/8	25 6/8	32 5/8	5 5/8	5 5/8	10	14	47 2/8	203	35
◆ *Fremont County / Trevor D. Larson / Trevor D. Larson / 1990*											

IDAHO NON-TYPICAL MULE DEER *(continued)*

Score	Length of Main Beam R	Length of Main Beam L	Inside Spread	Greatest Spread	Circumference at Smallest Place between Burr and First Point R	Circumference at Smallest Place between Burr and First Point L	Number of Points R	Number of Points L	Total of Lengths Abnormal Points	All-Time Rank	State Rank
	♦ *Locality / Hunter / Owner / Date Killed*										
252 5/8	20 5/8	21 7/8	18 3/8	40 3/8	4 5/8	4 6/8	12	13	69 2/8	204	36
	♦ *Valley County / Picked Up / Raymond R. Cross / PR 1989*										
251 6/8	24	25 4/8	20	38 1/8	5 1/8	5	13	14	57	212	37
	♦ *Gem County / A.K. England / Roscoe E. Ferris / 1969*										
251	25 1/8	26 1/8	26 1/8	40	5 1/8	5 1/8	13	14	54 3/8	220	38
	♦ *Adams County / Clark Childers / Clark Childers / 1955*										
250 6/8	26 4/8	27 4/8	28 3/8	40 6/8	5 1/8	5 2/8	11	11	54 6/8	222	39
	♦ *Idaho / Unknown / Dana J. Hollinger / PR 1970*										
250 4/8	29 7/8	26 7/8	22 4/8	31 5/8	6 2/8	8	7	13	42 2/8	225	40
	♦ *Kunard Valley / Ralph D. Hogan / Ralph D. Hogan / 1966*										
250 4/8	29	26 7/8	30 2/8	43 3/8	5 4/8	5 6/8	10	13	44 2/8	225	40
	♦ *Shoshone County / Ron L. Purnell / Ron L. Purnell / 1987*										
249 3/8	27	27 4/8	27 5/8	35 5/8	6 1/8	6 2/8	7	11	48 1/8	237	42
	♦ *Adams County / Howard E. Paradis / Howard E. Paradis / 1966*										
249 3/8	25	24 6/8	22 6/8	35 6/8	5 4/8	5 4/8	18	16	55 1/8	237	42
	♦ *Owyhee County / Tom Tomlinson / Raymond R. Cross / 1968*										
248 5/8	26 6/8	25 6/8	33 6/8	45 4/8	6 2/8	5 2/8	14	10	51 1/8	248	44
	♦ *Franklin County / Joan Butterworth / Quinten Butterworth / 1961*										
247 6/8	24 7/8	23 5/8	22 2/8	34 4/8	5	5 1/8	11	16	69 6/8	263	45
	♦ *Shoshone County / Gary J. Finney / Gary J. Finney / 1983*										
247 3/8	22 5/8	22 6/8	22 5/8	33 1/8	4 4/8	4 4/8	11	9	52 6/8	271	46
	♦ *Fremont County / Donald R. Craig / Donald R. Craig / 1982*										
247 2/8	24 3/8	24 1/8	24 7/8	39 7/8	5 3/8	5 5/8	13	10	52 3/8	274	47
	♦ *Owyhee County / Elwin J. Saxton / Raymond R. Cross / 1975*										
247 1/8	26 2/8	25	27 2/8	37	4 6/8	4 5/8	12	9	35 7/8	276	48
	♦ *Whitebird / Harold Gustin / Wayne Demaray / 1965*										
246 7/8	27 2/8	21 3/8	29 2/8	40 4/8	5 2/8	5 4/8	14	14	65 1/8	282	49
	♦ *Needle Peak / Michael G. Cameron / Michael G. Cameron / 1966*										
245 1/8	24	23 2/8	20 2/8	37 5/8	5 3/8	5 4/8	12	9	47 5/8	304	50
	♦ *Power County / Mark B. Cooper / Mark B. Cooper / 1984*										
245	25 6/8	25 5/8	29 6/8	31 6/8	5 5/8	5 4/8	17	15	45 4/8	305	51
	♦ *Bonner County / Dick Sherwood / Dick Sherwood / 1963*										
243 1/8	25 4/8	23 4/8	25 1/8	37 3/8	5 4/8	5 7/8	8	11	38 6/8	339	52
	♦ *Fremont County / Larry D. Hawker / Larry D. Hawker / 1970*										
242 7/8	22 4/8	23 7/8	26 4/8	39 6/8	5 4/8	5 3/8	10	12	49 6/8	345	53
	♦ *Gem County / Roland Bright / Roland Bright / 1965*										

Score	Length of Main Beam R	L	Inside Spread	Greatest Spread	Circumference at Smallest Place between Burr and First Point R	L	Number of Points R	L	Total of Lengths Abnormal Points	All-Time Rank	State Rank
242 7/8	26 4/8	26 2/8	22 3/8	35 2/8	5 5/8	5 7/8	11	16	42 6/8	345	53
◆ *Gem County / Cary G. Cada / Raymond R. Cross / 1975*											
242 5/8	25	26 3/8	18 3/8	25 4/8	6	5 6/8	11	10	44	348	55
◆ *Baison / Daniel E. Osborne / Daniel E. Osborne / 1959*											
242 4/8	27 2/8	25 3/8	29 4/8	37	5	5	10	11	62	350	56
◆ *Blaine County / Roger A. Crowder / Roger A. Crowder / 1957*											
242 1/8	28	27 6/8	22 1/8	32 4/8	6 1/8	6 1/8	9	11	36 6/8	356	57
◆ *Bear Lake County / Robert N. Gale / Robert N. Gale / 1970*											
241 5/8	27 1/8	27	23 4/8	35 4/8	5 3/8	5 3/8	13	10	51 5/8	367	58
◆ *Adam County / Joseph N. Ruscigno / Joseph N. Ruscigno / 1960*											
241 3/8	22 3/8	23 7/8	20 4/8	36	5 1/8	5 2/8	10	12	51 7/8	372	59
◆ *Adams County / Peter Renberg / Peter Renberg / 1963*											
241 3/8	26 6/8	24 7/8	24 3/8	35 4/8	5	5 1/8	12	13	43 4/8	372	59
◆ *Salmon River / Richard Shilling / Richard Shilling / 1965*											
240 1/8	23 4/8	23 1/8	23 2/8	36 7/8	5 6/8	5 5/8	12	12	43 1/8	394	61
◆ *Elmore County / Phillip K. Messer / Phillip K. Messer / 1971*											
237 3/8	27 2/8	23 7/8	20 2/8	35 6/8	4 6/8	5 4/8	8	13	59 1/8	406	62
◆ *Hawley Creek / Clifford Nealis / Clifford Nealis / 1960*											
237 3/8	23 6/8	23 2/8	23 3/8	37	5 5/8	5 7/8	11	12	52 4/8	406	62
◆ *Bonneville County / Bert L. Freed / Bert L. Freed / 1987*											
234 2/8	29	28 4/8	28 2/8	36	6 3/8	6 4/8	9	13	33 6/8	409	64
◆ *Boise County / Lowell B. Nosker / Lowell B. Nosker / 1946*											
232 7/8	28 3/8	27 4/8	23 3/8	32 5/8	5 3/8	5 2/8	9	11	26 2/8	410	65
◆ *Caribou County / Michael H. Ferrera / Michael H. Ferrera / 1992*											
231 7/8	24 6/8	24 6/8	23 5/8	40 3/8	5 6/8	5 4/8	9	10	36 4/8	414	66
◆ *Bear Lake County / George L. Clifford / George L. Clifford / 1966*											
231	23 7/8	26	19 3/8	33	5 7/8	5 4/8	7	13	42 7/8	416	67
◆ *Teton County / Unknown / Dana J. Hollinger / 1979*											
228 7/8	27 1/8	26 5/8	24	44 6/8	5 2/8	5 4/8	8	12	36 7/8	419	68
◆ *Franklin County / Michael H. Vroman / Michael H. Vroman / 1986*											
227 1/8	27 5/8	26	22 4/8	33	4 7/8	4 6/8	8	7	44 5/8	423	69
◆ *Nez Perce County / Richard S. Lowe / Richard S. Lowe / 1986*											
252 7/8	22 4/8	18 6/8	19 1/8	36 1/8	5 4/8	5 4/8	11	22	82 6/8	*	*
◆ *Boise County / Dennis D. Snider / Dennis D. Snider / 1983*											

Delta County, Colorado, produced this handsome typical mule deer buck, scoring 185-3/8 points, for Mark S. Petrucci in 1989.

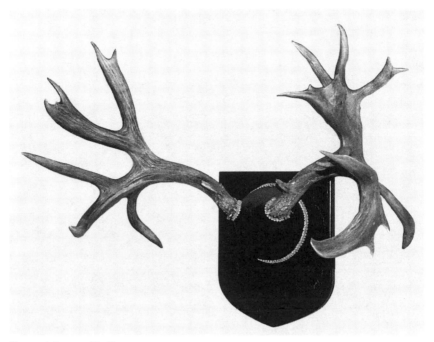

IOWA STATE RECORD (NEW)
NON-TYPICAL MULE DEER
SCORE: 246
Locality: Cherokee Co.   Date: Prior to 1900
Hunter: C.A. Stiles
Owner: Jim Haas

IOWA
NON-TYPICAL MULE DEER

Score	Length of Main Beam R L	Inside Spread	Greatest Spread	Circumference at Smallest Place between Burr and First Point R L	Number of Points R L	Total of Lengths Abnormal Points	All-Time Rank	State Rank
◆ Locality / Hunter / Owner / Date Killed								
246	26⅞ 25⅜	26⅘	32⅝	5 4⅝	9 13	55⅝	294	1
◆ Cherokee County / C.A. Stiles / Jim Haas / PR 1900								

Photograph Courtesy of Marvin W. Dechant

KANSAS STATE RECORD (NEW)
TYPICAL MULE DEER
SCORE: 188⅝
Locality: Lane Co.   Date: 1986
Hunter: Marvin W. Dechant

KANSAS

TYPICAL MULE DEER

Score	Length of Main Beam R	Length of Main Beam L	Inside Spread	Greatest Spread	Circumference at Smallest Place between Burr and First Point R	Circumference at Smallest Place between Burr and First Point L	Number of Points R	Number of Points L	Total of Lengths Abnormal Points	All-Time Rank	State Rank
♦ Locality / Hunter / Owner / Date Killed												

188⅝	25	24⅜	22⅞	32	5⅛	6	6	7	7⅜	562	1
♦ *Lane County / Marvin W. Dechant / Marvin W. Dechant / 1986*												

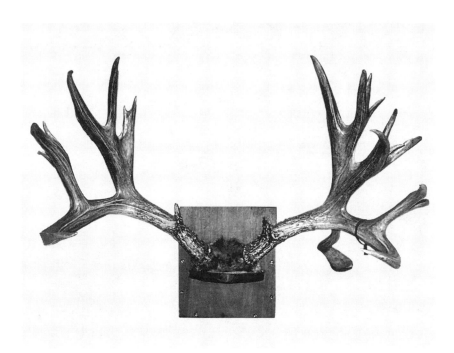

KANSAS STATE RECORD
NON-TYPICAL MULE DEER
SCORE: 260 6/8
Locality: Rooks Co.   Date: 1965
Hunter: Lee Odle

KANSAS
NON-TYPICAL MULE DEER

Score	Length of Main Beam		Inside Spread	Greatest Spread	Circumference at Smallest Place between Burr and First Point		Number of Points		Total of Lengths Abnormal Points	All-Time Rank	State Rank
	R	L			R	L	R	L			
♦ *Locality / Hunter / Owner / Date Killed*											
260⁶⁄₈	29⁴⁄₈	27⁷⁄₈	28⁶⁄₈	36⁷⁄₈	5⁴⁄₈	5⁷⁄₈	10	14	58⁴⁄₈	124	1
♦ *Rooks County / Lee Odle / Lee Odle / 1965*											
225¹⁄₈	25¹⁄₈	24²⁄₈	21⁴⁄₈	29¹⁄₈	4⁶⁄₈	5¹⁄₈	9	12	39⁷⁄₈	424	2
♦ *Smith County / Richard L. Quinn / Richard L. Quinn / 1989*											

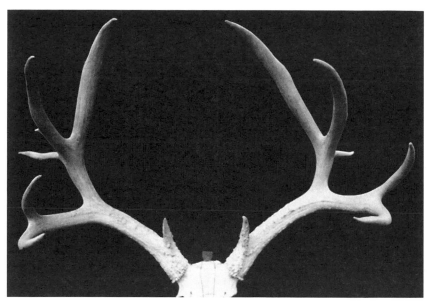

Photograph Courtesy of William E. Hubbard

MONTANA STATE RECORD
TYPICAL MULE DEER
SCORE: 202
Locality: Lincoln Co.   Date: 1963
Hunter: William E. Hubbard

MONTANA

TYPICAL MULE DEER

Score	Length of Main Beam R	Length of Main Beam L	Inside Spread	Greatest Spread	Circumference at Smallest Place between Burr and First Point R	Circumference at Smallest Place between Burr and First Point L	Number of Points R	Number of Points L	Total of Lengths Abnormal Points	All-Time Rank	State Rank
♦ *Locality / Hunter / Owner / Date Killed*											
202	26 7/8	27 2/8	27 6/8	33 2/8	6 3/8	6 3/8	6	6	7	119	1
♦ *Lincoln County / William E. Hubbard / William E. Hubbard / 1963*											
201 4/8	28 1/8	28 3/8	22 7/8	27 1/8	5 6/8	5 4/8	5	7	2 3/8	138	2
♦ *Ravalli County / Sherman L. Williams / Sherman L. Williams / 1973*											
200 4/8	27 3/8	27 4/8	31	33 4/8	5 5/8	5 4/8	5	5	0	177	3
♦ *Madison County / Glenn S. Shelton / Glenn S. Shelton / 1976*											
199 7/8	25 3/8	24 5/8	25 1/8	29 1/8	5 4/8	5 4/8	5	5	0	211	4
♦ *Stillwater County / Basil C. Bradbury / Basil C. Bradbury / 1965*											
197 6/8	27 4/8	26 2/8	24 4/8	28 6/8	4 6/8	4 6/8	5	5	0	302	5
♦ *Jefferson County / James W. Rowe / James W. Rowe / 1964*											
197 2/8	24 4/8	24 4/8	23 2/8	27 2/8	4 6/8	4 6/8	5	6	1 2/8	333	6
♦ *Flathead County / James E. Betters / James E. Betters / 1986*											
196 7/8	25 6/8	24	21 5/8	29 4/8	5 2/8	5 4/8	5	5	0	357	7
♦ *Lincoln County / Dennis J. Hauke / Dennis J. Hauke / 1973*											
196 4/8	24 5/8	25 5/8	25 1/8	33 2/8	5 2/8	5 1/8	7	5	2 1/8	379	8
♦ *Flathead River / Stanley Rauscher / Stanley Rauscher / 1959*											
196 4/8	23 5/8	23 5/8	23	27	5 2/8	5 2/8	5	5	0	379	8
♦ *Powell County / Raymond A. Fitzgerald / Raymond A. Fitzgerald / 1983*											
196 3/8	24 6/8	25 1/8	24 4/8	26 4/8	5 3/8	5 3/8	6	5	1 1/8	391	10
♦ *Powell County / Stanley F. Malcolm / Stanley F. Malcolm / 1958*											
196 2/8	27 4/8	27 1/8	25 1/8	29 7/8	4 5/8	5 1/8	7	5	3 3/8	396	11
♦ *Lincoln County / Tommy Boothman / Tommy Boothman / 1960*											
196 2/8	25 6/8	25 4/8	23 6/8	29 1/8	5 3/8	5 4/8	5	6	2 2/8	396	11
♦ *Ravalli County / Gary Godfrey / Calvin D. Kluth / 1965*											
196	25	24 4/8	24	28 3/8	5 3/8	5	5	5	0	414	13
♦ *Corwin Springs / Donald Strazzabosco / Donald Strazzabosco / 1966*											
195 5/8	26 5/8	27 1/8	26 1/8	29 5/8	4 7/8	4 6/8	5	5	0	446	14
♦ *Ravalli County / William H. Cowan / William H. Cowan / 1959*											
195 4/8	25 2/8	27 1/8	22 7/8	29 6/8	5 6/8	5 4/8	6	6	6 7/8	456	15
♦ *Flathead County / Sharon M. Gaughan / B&C National Collection / 1980*											
195 4/8	26 3/8	26 5/8	25 2/8	28	5 6/8	5 5/8	5	5	0	456	15
♦ *Sanders County / William B. Hart / William B. Hart / 1984*											
195	27 1/8	27 4/8	21 4/8	25	5 1/8	4 4/8	5	5	0	491	17
♦ *Powder River County / Roy Dahlby / Michael R. Dahlby / 1963*											

Score	Length of Main Beam R	Length of Main Beam L	Inside Spread	Greatest Spread	Circumference at Smallest Place between Burr and First Point R	Circumference at Smallest Place between Burr and First Point L	Number of Points R	Number of Points L	Total of Lengths Abnormal Points	All-Time Rank	State Rank
♦ *Locality / Hunter / Owner / Date Killed*											
195	27 1/8	26 1/8	22 4/8	27 4/8	5 6/8	5 6/8	5	5	0	491	17
♦ *Sun River / Dick Lyman / Dick Lyman / 1966*											
189 3/8	26	24	25 4/8	30	5 3/8	5 3/8	7	5	2 3/8	556	19
♦ *Custer County / Hugh R. Neumann / Hugh R. Neumann / 1969*											
187 5/8	25 6/8	26 1/8	24 1/8	26 3/8	5 4/8	5	5	5	0	582	20
♦ *Flathead County / Jeffrey A. Bechtel / Jeffrey A. Bechtel / 1983*											
187 5/8	25 1/8	24 2/8	19 1/8	25 6/8	4 6/8	4 6/8	6	5	1 4/8	582	20
♦ *Rosebud County / Patrick J. Gilligan / Patrick J. Gilligan / 1992*											
186 5/8	24 7/8	25 1/8	23 1/8	29 2/8	5 2/8	5 3/8	5	6	4	598	22
♦ *Sanders County / Michael D. Turner / Michael D. Turner / 1992*											
186	22 7/8	22 1/8	20 6/8	28 3/8	5 3/8	4 7/8	8	7	8 2/8	606	23
♦ *Gallatin County / Charles C. Swinehart / Charles C. Swinehart / 1991*											
180 2/8	23 4/8	24 5/8	24	25 6/8	4 6/8	4 5/8	5	5	0	633	24
♦ *Teton County / Ralph C. Bledsoe, Jr. / Ralph C. Bledsoe, Jr. / 1992*											

Hub Grounds, who has assisted many other hunters in collecting a B&C trophy, poses here with his own typical mulie buck that he took in Huerfano County, Colorado, in 1989. It scores 195-5/8 points.

Photograph Courtesy of Peter Zemljak

MONTANA STATE RECORD
NON-TYPICAL MULE DEER
SCORE: 275 7/8
Locality: Highland Mountains   Date: 1962
Hunter: Peter Zemljak, Sr.
Owner: Peter Zemljak

MONTANA
NON-TYPICAL MULE DEER

Score	Length of Main Beam R L		Inside Spread	Greatest Spread	Circumference at Smallest Place between Burr and First Point R L		Number of Points R L		Total of Lengths Abnormal Points	All-Time Rank	State Rank
275⅞	29²⁄₈	25⁴⁄₈	34³⁄₈	41⁵⁄₈	5⁵⁄₈	5⁶⁄₈	16	13	92³⁄₈	50	1
♦ Highland Mts. / Peter Zemljak, Sr. / Peter Zemljak / 1962											
275⅛	23⁶⁄₈	22⁴⁄₈	20⁵⁄₈	43⁴⁄₈	5⅞	6	14	15	82²⁄₈	53	2
♦ Ruby Mts. / Peter Zemljak / Peter Zemljak / 1960											
273	22⅛	24	24	34⅛	5⅞	5⁶⁄₈	10	13	77⁶⁄₈	65	3
♦ Madison County / Ray Ypma / Ray Ypma / 1946											
270⁵⁄₈	23⁶⁄₈	24²⁄₈	21⅛	38³⁄₈	4³⁄₈	4³⁄₈	10	12	73⁴⁄₈	72	4
♦ Big Horn County / R. Turnsback & J.V. Elsen / William Erdmann / 1961											
268⁴⁄₈	21³⁄₈	23⁶⁄₈	17⁴⁄₈	32²⁄₈	6⁵⁄₈	6⁵⁄₈	17	16	86	79	5
♦ Cascade County / Unknown / Kent Austin / PR 1980											
268⅛	29⁶⁄₈	27⅞	26²⁄₈	31⁴⁄₈	5³⁄₈	5²⁄₈	10	10	54⁵⁄₈	81	6
♦ Gallatin County / Michael O. Wold / Michael O. Wold / 1992											
266²⁄₈	24⁴⁄₈	24⅞	21	37⁶⁄₈	5³⁄₈	5⁴⁄₈	12	18	83⁴⁄₈	90	7
♦ Park County / Benton R. Venable / Benton R. Venable / 1945											
265⅞	25⁵⁄₈	26⁴⁄₈	27⁶⁄₈	39⅛	5⁴⁄₈	5⁶⁄₈	8	12	54⁵⁄₈	94	8
♦ Sidney / Buster Dodson / F.P. Murray / 1954											
265⅞	23⁵⁄₈	24⅛	22⅞	31⅞	5⁵⁄₈	5⁶⁄₈	20	15	80⁶⁄₈	94	8
♦ Powder River County / Michael A. Siewert / Michael A. Siewert / 1987											
262⁵⁄₈	26²⁄₈	24	23⅞	31⅞	4⁶⁄₈	4⁶⁄₈	14	13	83²⁄₈	110	10
♦ Dawson County / Johnny Scheitlin / Bob Scheitlin / 1949											
262⅛	26⁵⁄₈	26²⁄₈	29³⁄₈	36⅞	5²⁄₈	4⅞	17	12	64⁴⁄₈	114	11
♦ Montana / Unknown / Nick M. Messmer / PR 1943											
261⁶⁄₈	24⁴⁄₈	23³⁄₈	20⁵⁄₈	32²⁄₈	5⁴⁄₈	5⁴⁄₈	16	14	70⁵⁄₈	118	12
♦ Gallatin County / Clifford R. Plum / Clifford R. Plum / 1932											
252²⁄₈	23⁴⁄₈	22	14⁵⁄₈	33³⁄₈	5⁶⁄₈	5⁶⁄₈	16	15	80⅛	206	13
♦ Glacier County / Bob Scriver / Philip Schlegel / 1934											
250³⁄₈	26⁵⁄₈	26²⁄₈	28⅛	33³⁄₈	4⁶⁄₈	5	10	12	62⁴⁄₈	229	14
♦ Petroleum County / Lawrence T. Keenan / Lawrence T. Keenan / 1979											
247³⁄₈	27⁵⁄₈	28⁴⁄₈	33⁶⁄₈	41	6⅛	6⁴⁄₈	11	12	47⅞	271	15
♦ Missoula County / Harold Wample / Ralph Raymond / 1949											
247⅛	30⁴⁄₈	30³⁄₈	28³⁄₈	36⁵⁄₈	6⅛	6²⁄₈	11	11	38²⁄₈	276	16
♦ Drummond / Tom Brosovich / Tom Brosovich / 1957											
246²⁄₈	23⁴⁄₈	24⅛	26⁴⁄₈	35⅛	5⅛	5⅛	12	11	57⁵⁄₈	291	17
♦ Ravalli County / Lloyd G. Hunter / Lloyd G. Hunter / 1963											

Score	Length of Main Beam R	Length of Main Beam L	Inside Spread	Greatest Spread	Circumference at Smallest Place between Burr and First Point R	Circumference at Smallest Place between Burr and First Point L	Number of Points R	Number of Points L	Total of Lengths Abnormal Points	All-Time Rank	State Rank
♦ *Locality / Hunter / Owner / Date Killed*											
244 5/8	25 1/8	25 3/8	22 1/8	29 5/8	5 1/8	5 2/8	9	10	42 4/8	310	18
♦ *Park County / Unknown / Don Schaufler / PR 1968*											
242 5/8	27 3/8	26 7/8	25 5/8	43 2/8	5 7/8	5 6/8	12	9	47 2/8	348	19
♦ *Sanders County / Robert D. Frisk / Robert D. Frisk / 1974*											
241 7/8	21	18	14 7/8	29 2/8	4 3/8	5 3/8	12	15	75 6/8	362	20
♦ *Sanders County / Buzz Faro / Buzz Faro / 1963*											
241	26 2/8	27 3/8	26 3/8	0	4 6/8	4 6/8	11	11	53 1/8	379	21
♦ *Lewis & Clark County / Mike Filcher / Mike Filcher / 1972*											
240 3/8	22 3/8	24 5/8	21 2/8	25 6/8	5 5/8	5 7/8	13	12	56 5/8	392	22
♦ *Missoula County / Richard A. Gendrow / Richard A. Gendrow / 1973*											
239 4/8	25 1/8	25 5/8	19 2/8	30 1/8	5 3/8	5 2/8	14	13	50 4/8	400	23
♦ *Pondera County / Dan Mougeot / Dan Mougeot / 1961*											
229	23 2/8	21 7/8	19 2/8	30 4/8	4 7/8	5	9	11	46 6/8	418	24
♦ *Ravalli County / James Milleson / James Milleson / 1984*											
228 3/8	25 3/8	24 7/8	24 4/8	31	5 4/8	5 5/8	8	9	28 5/8	422	25
♦ *Yellowstone County / Paul P. Reichert / Paul P. Reichert / 1951*											

Herald A. Friedenberger and the non-typical mule deer buck he took in 1988 near Summit Lake, British Columbia. It has 15 and 13 measurable points on the right and left antlers, respectively, and scores a whopping 256-1/8 points.

Photograph Courtesy of Terry L. Sandstrom

NEBRASKA STATE RECORD
TYPICAL MULE DEER
SCORE: 196 2/8
Locality: Dawes Co.   Date: 1968
Hunter: Terry L. Sandstrom

NEBRASKA
TYPICAL MULE DEER

Score	Length of Main Beam R	L	Inside Spread	Greatest Spread	Circumference at Smallest Place between Burr and First Point R	L	Number of Points R	L	Total of Lengths Abnormal Points	All-Time Rank	State Rank
◆ Locality / Hunter / Owner / Date Killed											
196²⁄₈	26	26⁴⁄₈	26	28	5⁴⁄₈	5⁴⁄₈	5	5	0	396	1
◆ Dawes County / Terry L. Sandstrom / Terry L. Sandstrom / 1968											
195³⁄₈	26³⁄₈	26	26¹⁄₈	28⁷⁄₈	4⁶⁄₈	4⁶⁄₈	5	5	0	464	2
◆ Frontier County / Brent S. Klein / Brent S. Klein / 1984											
189⁵⁄₈	26⁵⁄₈	27²⁄₈	20⁷⁄₈	24⁶⁄₈	4⁷⁄₈	5	5	7	6²⁄₈	552	3
◆ Lincoln County / Michael L. Seaman / Michael L. Seaman / 1992											
185	24⁴⁄₈	25⁶⁄₈	27⁵⁄₈	30³⁄₈	4⁴⁄₈	4⁵⁄₈	6	6	5	620	4
◆ Grant County / Michael L. Dietrich / Michael L. Dietrich / 1991											

Photograph Courtesy of Art Thomsen

NEBRASKA STATE RECORD
NON-TYPICAL MULE DEER
SCORE: 256⅞
Locality: Chadron   Date: 1960
Hunter: Art Thomsen

NEBRASKA
NON-TYPICAL MULE DEER

Score	Length of Main Beam R	L	Inside Spread	Greatest Spread	Circumference at Smallest Place between Burr and First Point R	L	Number of Points R	L	Total of Lengths Abnormal Points	All-Time Rank	State Rank
	◆ Locality / Hunter / Owner / Date Killed										
256⅞	26⅝	27²⁄₈	22⁶⁄₈	28⅛	5⅜	5⁶⁄₈	20	14	60⅞	167	1
	◆ Chadron / Art Thomsen / Art Thomsen / 1960										
249⁶⁄₈	24⅞	25²⁄₈	22	35	5	4⅞	10	14	57	235	2
	◆ Red Willow County / Delman H. Tuller / Delman H. Tuller / 1965										
228⅝	20⅞	21⁴⁄₈	24⅛	31⅛	4⁴⁄₈	4⁴⁄₈	11	11	63⅜	421	3
	◆ Dundy County / Dennis D. Holliday / Dennis D. Holliday / 1993										

NEVADA STATE RECORD
TYPICAL MULE DEER
SCORE: 205 4/8
Locality: Lincoln Co.   Date: 1983
Hunter: Erich P. Burkhard

NEVADA
TYPICAL MULE DEER

Score	Length of Main Beam R	L	Inside Spread	Greatest Spread	Circumference at Smallest Place between Burr and First Point R	L	Number of Points R	L	Total of Lengths Abnormal Points	All-Time Rank	State Rank
205 4/8	26 4/8	26 4/8	25 2/8	35 4/8	5 1/8	4 6/8	6	5	1 4/8	57	1

♦ Lincoln County / Erich P. Burkhard / Erich P. Burkhard / 1983

203 4/8	27 2/8	24	24 2/8	27 4/8	5 4/8	5 3/8	5	5	0	84	2

♦ Elko County / C.H. Wahl / C.H. Wahl / 1953

202	27 4/8	27 3/8	25 6/8	28 7/8	5 2/8	5 2/8	5	5	0	119	3

♦ Elko County / Arlo M. Hummell / Arlo M. Hummell / 1989

201 6/8	26	26 3/8	27 1/8	33 2/8	5 2/8	5 2/8	6	5	1 1/8	132	4

♦ Washoe County / Gordon Frazier / Ron W. Biggs / 1991

200 7/8	30 4/8	25 7/8	28 3/8	36	4 6/8	4 4/8	5	5	0	164	5

♦ Elko County / Harry Irland / Mrs. Harry Irland / 1919

200 1/8	24 7/8	23 6/8	28 3/8	33 2/8	5 5/8	5 6/8	5	5	0	199	6

♦ Ruby Mt. / Earl Frantzen / Earl Frantzen / 1941

199 5/8	25 4/8	24 2/8	21 7/8	27 4/8	6 1/8	6	5	5	0	220	7

♦ Humboldt County / Robert L. Swinney / Robert L. Swinney / 1982

199 2/8	25 2/8	25 2/8	25	27	5 2/8	5 4/8	5	5	0	232	8

♦ Washoe County / Joseph N. Ruscigno / Joseph N. Ruscigno / 1955

197 5/8	25 4/8	26 5/8	29 4/8	34 5/8	5 5/8	5 5/8	5	5	0	308	9

♦ Elko County / Manfred E. Koska / Manfred E. Koska / 1966

197 2/8	23	24	25	30 4/8	4 6/8	4 4/8	7	5	7 6/8	333	10

♦ Elko County / John C. Burman / John C. Burman / 1980

196	26 4/8	28 2/8	29 1/8	33	5 2/8	5 3/8	5	5	0	414	11

♦ Elko County / Johnny W. Filippini / Johnny W. Filippini / 1991

195 1/8	25	25 2/8	22 1/8	25 6/8	5 1/8	5 1/8	5	5	0	482	12

♦ Elko County / Donald G. Heidtman / Donald G. Heidtman / 1954

195	27	25 6/8	28 1/8	32 6/8	5 5/8	5 7/8	6	6	4 4/8	491	13

♦ Elko County / Steve Beneto, Sr. / Steve Beneto, Sr. / 1966

193 6/8	26	26 6/8	27 1/8	31 4/8	4 2/8	4 1/8	6	5	1	510	14

♦ Lander County / Picked Up / John W. Filippini / 1992

193 3/8	26 7/8	27 2/8	23 3/8	33 1/8	4 7/8	4 7/8	5	5	0	513	15

♦ Washoe County / Barbara M. Conley / Barbara M. Conley / 1987

191 1/8	26 4/8	26 3/8	26 1/8	28 3/8	4 5/8	4 4/8	5	5	0	532	16

♦ Washoe County / Jay Walker / Jay Walker / 1967

189 7/8	27 2/8	26	26 1/8	28 3/8	5 2/8	5 2/8	5	5	0	550	17

♦ Humboldt County / Manuel Santos, Jr. / Manuel Santos, Jr. / 1993

Score	Length of Main Beam R	L	Inside Spread	Greatest Spread	Circumference at Smallest Place between Burr and First Point R	L	Number of Points R	L	Total of Lengths Abnormal Points	All-Time Rank	State Rank
	♦ *Locality / Hunter / Owner / Date Killed*										
$188\frac{5}{8}$	$26\frac{4}{8}$	$26\frac{2}{8}$	$23\frac{5}{8}$	$29\frac{4}{8}$	5	$5\frac{2}{8}$	8	5	8	562	18
	♦ *Washoe County / Christine L. Matley / Christine L. Matley / 1986*										
$188\frac{5}{8}$	26	$25\frac{6}{8}$	$23\frac{1}{8}$	29	$4\frac{5}{8}$	$4\frac{4}{8}$	5	5	$1\frac{6}{8}$	562	18
	♦ *Washoe County / Darin D. Clements / Darin D. Clements / 1989*										
$188\frac{4}{8}$	$24\frac{6}{8}$	$24\frac{5}{8}$	$24\frac{7}{8}$	$27\frac{6}{8}$	$4\frac{7}{8}$	5	5	6	$1\frac{2}{8}$	567	20
	♦ *Elko County / Alan S. Boyack / Alan S. Boyack / 1991*										
$187\frac{4}{8}$	$23\frac{3}{8}$	$23\frac{1}{8}$	$23\frac{3}{8}$	$29\frac{4}{8}$	5	$5\frac{1}{8}$	5	7	$3\frac{3}{8}$	585	21
	♦ *White Pine County / David R. Harrow / David R. Harrow / 1991*										
$187\frac{3}{8}$	$23\frac{6}{8}$	$23\frac{4}{8}$	$22\frac{7}{8}$	$26\frac{7}{8}$	$6\frac{2}{8}$	$6\frac{3}{8}$	5	5	0	586	22
	♦ *Washoe County / Sandra D. Cooper / Sandra D. Cooper / 1991*										
$204\frac{6}{8}$	$26\frac{2}{8}$	$26\frac{2}{8}$	$24\frac{6}{8}$	$32\frac{7}{8}$	$4\frac{7}{8}$	$4\frac{6}{8}$	5	5	0	*	*
	♦ *Elko County / Donnie L. Thompson / Donnie L. Thompson / 1982*										

John B. Kochever caught up with this once-in-a-lifetime typical mule deer buck at 100 yards near Grey's Lake, Caribou County, Idaho, in 1986. It scores 195-6/8 points.

NEVADA STATE RECORD (NEW)
NON-TYPICAL MULE DEER
SCORE: 325⅝
Locality: Nye Co.   Date: 1955
Hunter: Clifton Fauria
Owner: Don Schaufler

NEVADA

NON-TYPICAL MULE DEER

Score	Length of Main Beam R	Length of Main Beam L	Inside Spread	Greatest Spread	Circumference at Smallest Place between Burr and First Point R	Circumference at Smallest Place between Burr and First Point L	Number of Points R	Number of Points L	Total of Lengths Abnormal Points	All-Time Rank	State Rank
♦ *Locality / Hunter / Owner / Date Killed*											
325 6/8	24 5/8	23 5/8	21 6/8	37 6/8	4 6/8	4 7/8	21	21	133 6/8	3	1
♦ *Nye County / Clifton Fauria / Don Schaufler / 1955*											
299 1/8	27 7/8	28 3/8	24 4/8	40	5 6/8	5 4/8	13	16	86 7/8	18	2
♦ *Eureka County / Dan Avery, Jr. / Don Schaufler / 1968*											
286 1/8	24 4/8	25	26 4/8	38 2/8	5	5	12	13	85 3/8	27	3
♦ *Elko County / Joseph W. Dooley / Raymond R. Cross / 1954*											
264	25 5/8	26 1/8	22 7/8	40 2/8	6 2/8	5 7/8	14	13	46 5/8	105	4
♦ *Elko County / Jim Stichter / Jim Stichter / 1965*											
258 5/8	25 3/8	25 4/8	21	35 7/8	5 2/8	5 3/8	12	10	56 7/8	144	5
♦ *Elko County / Edward J. Giauque / Edward J. Giauque / 1960*											
253	26 1/8	25 1/8	23 2/8	37 2/8	5	5 1/8	10	13	48 4/8	201	6
♦ *Elko County / Joseph Souza / Joseph Souza / 1953*											
247 2/8	18 1/8	23 4/8	19 2/8	32 5/8	5	4 7/8	8	11	69	274	7
♦ *Elko County / Picked Up / Ron Druck / 1980*											
247	29 7/8	28 6/8	24 5/8	42 3/8	6	5 4/8	14	16	43 7/8	280	8
♦ *Elko County / Walter B. Hester / Walter B. Hester / 1957*											
243	25 6/8	27 2/8	29	37 2/8	5 3/8	5 3/8	11	10	45 4/8	342	9
♦ *Elko County / Paul Giuliani / Paul Giuliani / 1971*											
240 5/8	22	23 2/8	21	28 5/8	4 7/8	4 7/8	10	9	46 3/8	384	10
♦ *Elko County / George M. Boman / George M. Boman / 1956*											

Photograph Courtesy of John D. Morgan

NEW MEXICO STATE RECORD
TYPICAL MULE DEER
SCORE: 211 7/8
Locality: Chama   Date: 1965
Hunter: Joseph A. Garcia
Owner: Masters Trophy Collection

NEW MEXICO
TYPICAL MULE DEER

Score	Length of Main Beam R	L	Inside Spread	Greatest Spread	Circumference at Smallest Place between Burr and First Point R	L	Number of Points R	L	Total of Lengths Abnormal Points	All-Time Rank	State Rank
$211\frac{7}{8}$	$28\frac{6}{8}$	28	$27\frac{6}{8}$	$34\frac{4}{8}$	$6\frac{5}{8}$	$6\frac{5}{8}$	5	6	$1\frac{7}{8}$	10	1
◆ Chama / Joseph A. Garcia / Masters Trophy Coll. / 1965											
$209\frac{5}{8}$	$27\frac{4}{8}$	$27\frac{7}{8}$	$28\frac{7}{8}$	$32\frac{1}{8}$	$5\frac{5}{8}$	$5\frac{5}{8}$	5	7	$2\frac{2}{8}$	17	2
◆ Rio Arriba County / Kelly Baird / Kelly Baird / 1984											
$208\frac{6}{8}$	26	$27\frac{3}{8}$	$26\frac{4}{8}$	28	$5\frac{2}{8}$	$5\frac{2}{8}$	4	5	0	26	3
◆ Rio Arriba County / James R. Odiorne, Jr. / James R. Odiorne, Jr. / 1978											
$206\frac{3}{8}$	$27\frac{4}{8}$	$26\frac{3}{8}$	$26\frac{7}{8}$	$30\frac{6}{8}$	$5\frac{2}{8}$	$5\frac{3}{8}$	5	5	0	46	4
◆ Rio Arriba County / Jim Roddie / Jim Roddie / 1971											
$206\frac{2}{8}$	26	$27\frac{4}{8}$	$26\frac{4}{8}$	$29\frac{4}{8}$	$5\frac{5}{8}$	$5\frac{5}{8}$	6	5	$1\frac{6}{8}$	49	5
◆ Rio Arriba County / Harley Hinds / Oran M. Roberts / 1963											
$205\frac{4}{8}$	$26\frac{2}{8}$	$25\frac{1}{8}$	$23\frac{5}{8}$	$29\frac{6}{8}$	$5\frac{4}{8}$	$5\frac{3}{8}$	6	7	$5\frac{3}{8}$	57	6
◆ Rio Arriba County / Picked Up / Eudane Vicenti / 1993											
$204\frac{1}{8}$	$28\frac{6}{8}$	$30\frac{4}{8}$	$24\frac{1}{8}$	$31\frac{1}{8}$	$4\frac{5}{8}$	$4\frac{7}{8}$	6	5	$7\frac{6}{8}$	72	7
◆ Jicarilla Apache Res. / Juan Monarco / Juan Monarco / 1960											
$204\frac{1}{8}$	$27\frac{2}{8}$	27	$25\frac{7}{8}$	$29\frac{3}{8}$	$5\frac{2}{8}$	$5\frac{2}{8}$	6	5	$2\frac{2}{8}$	72	7
◆ Rio Arriba County / Waymon Burkhalter / Waymon Burkhalter / 1992											
$203\frac{7}{8}$	$29\frac{3}{8}$	$29\frac{4}{8}$	$25\frac{5}{8}$	$28\frac{5}{8}$	$5\frac{6}{8}$	$5\frac{5}{8}$	5	5	0	77	9
◆ Jicarilla Apache Res. / Dick Wright / Dick Wright / 1966											
$203\frac{4}{8}$	27	$28\frac{1}{8}$	$24\frac{4}{8}$	$26\frac{7}{8}$	$5\frac{4}{8}$	$5\frac{4}{8}$	5	6	1	84	10
◆ Rio Arriba County / Arnold Wendt / John W. Hughes / 1965											
$202\frac{7}{8}$	$27\frac{5}{8}$	$27\frac{4}{8}$	$26\frac{6}{8}$	0	6	$5\frac{7}{8}$	5	7	0	98	11
◆ Jicarilla Apache Res. / Anthony Julian / Anthony Julian / 1961											
$202\frac{6}{8}$	$28\frac{2}{8}$	$29\frac{2}{8}$	$25\frac{4}{8}$	$27\frac{6}{8}$	$5\frac{3}{8}$	$5\frac{2}{8}$	5	5	0	102	12
◆ Rio Arriba County / James F. Leveritt, Jr. / James F. Leveritt, Jr. / 1980											
$202\frac{4}{8}$	$27\frac{4}{8}$	$27\frac{6}{8}$	27	$28\frac{6}{8}$	$5\frac{3}{8}$	$5\frac{2}{8}$	6	6	$4\frac{2}{8}$	106	13
◆ Rio Arriba County / Gerald J. Weber / Gerald J. Weber / 1970											
$202\frac{3}{8}$	$29\frac{5}{8}$	$28\frac{4}{8}$	$30\frac{3}{8}$	$30\frac{3}{8}$	$5\frac{1}{8}$	$5\frac{1}{8}$	5	6	$2\frac{6}{8}$	111	14
◆ Jicarilla Apache Res. / Theodore Serafin / Theodore Serafin / 1959											
$201\frac{4}{8}$	$26\frac{6}{8}$	$24\frac{7}{8}$	$28\frac{4}{8}$	$30\frac{4}{8}$	$6\frac{3}{8}$	6	5	5	0	138	15
◆ Chama / James W. Smith II / James W. Smith II / 1969											
$201\frac{3}{8}$	$26\frac{3}{8}$	$26\frac{3}{8}$	$25\frac{4}{8}$	$27\frac{4}{8}$	$5\frac{5}{8}$	$5\frac{5}{8}$	6	5	$2\frac{3}{8}$	144	16
◆ Rio Arriba County / Donald W. Johnson / Donald W. Johnson / 1970											
$201\frac{2}{8}$	$26\frac{6}{8}$	$27\frac{6}{8}$	$26\frac{6}{8}$	31	6	6	5	6	$2\frac{2}{8}$	152	17
◆ Jicarilla Apache Res. / Anthony Julian / Anthony Julian / 1961											

Score	Length of Main Beam		Inside Spread	Greatest Spread	Circumference at Smallest Place between Burr and First Point		Number of Points		Total of Lengths Abnormal Points	All-Time Rank	State Rank
	R	L			R	L	R	L			
	Locality / Hunter / Owner / Date Killed										
201 2/8	28 4/8	28 3/8	24	29 6/8	5 1/8	5 3/8	5	5	0	152	17
♦ *Chama / Emitt W. Mundy / Emitt W. Mundy / 1961*											
201 1/8	25 6/8	26 1/8	26 4/8	31 1/8	5	5 4/8	5	6	1 6/8	155	19
♦ *Jicarilla Apache Res. / Arnold Cassador / Arnold Cassador / 1967*											
200 4/8	26 7/8	27	24	28 6/8	5	5	5	5	0	177	20
♦ *Rio Arriba County / Jay Walker / Jay Walker / 1993*											
199 3/8	25 5/8	26 3/8	26 4/8	28 2/8	4 5/8	4 3/8	5	4	1 6/8	228	21
♦ *San Miguel County / Frank Mata / Robert Cordova / 1965*											
199 3/8	27	27 6/8	23 7/8	27 6/8	5 4/8	5 4/8	4	4	0	228	21
♦ *Rio Arriba County / John A. Farrell / John A. Farrell / 1966*											
199 3/8	26 7/8	25 7/8	24 4/8	27 1/8	5 6/8	5 5/8	5	6	2 5/8	228	21
♦ *Rio Arriba County / Johnny L. Montgomery / Johnny L. Montgomery / 1967*											
199 1/8	28 3/8	27 2/8	27 6/8	31	6	5 6/8	8	6	8 1/8	243	24
♦ *Jicarilla Apache Res. / David L. Chandler / David L. Chandler / 1961*											
198 7/8	26 5/8	27 1/8	26 5/8	30 4/8	5 7/8	6	5	7	4 6/8	253	25
♦ *Jicarilla Apache Res. / Anthony Julian / Jicarilla Apache Res. / 1961*											
198 6/8	32 7/8	32 4/8	25 3/8	35 1/8	6 3/8	7	7	6	15 5/8	255	26
♦ *Dulce / Picked Up / Everett M. Vigil / 1967*											
198 5/8	26	25 3/8	28	31 6/8	5 4/8	5 7/8	5	7	4 1/8	257	27
♦ *Rio Arriba County / Stanley Davis / Stanley Davis / 1965*											
198 4/8	26 4/8	27 6/8	29 2/8	31 6/8	6 1/8	5 6/8	5	6	1 4/8	262	28
♦ *San Juan County / Dan R. Anderson / Dan R. Anderson / 1964*											
198 2/8	27 2/8	27 4/8	24 7/8	32 3/8	5 7/8	5 7/8	5	6	2 5/8	274	29
♦ *Rio Arriba County / Charles Tapia / Charles Tapia / 1991*											
197 4/8	26	26 2/8	23 2/8	26 2/8	5 2/8	5 1/8	5	6	1	317	30
♦ *Rio Arriba County / Jerry Longenbaugh / Jerry Longenbaugh / 1969*											
197 3/8	25 5/8	27 1/8	26 1/8	28 4/8	5 3/8	5 4/8	5	5	0	324	31
♦ *Apache Mesa / Tom Martine / Tom Martine / 1970*											
197	26 4/8	26 4/8	27 5/8	32	5 2/8	5 4/8	5	5	0	347	32
♦ *Rio Arriba County / Ross Lopez / Ross Lopez / 1964*											
196 2/8	26 1/8	23 7/8	23 4/8	28 2/8	6	5 7/8	5	6	2 6/8	396	33
♦ *Chama / Laura Wilson / Laura Wilson / 1967*											
196 2/8	27	27 1/8	24 7/8	30 2/8	5 4/8	5 4/8	7	9	12 5/8	396	33
♦ *Rio Arriba County / B.D. Shipwash / B.D. Shipwash / 1969*											
196 1/8	27 2/8	27 7/8	27	33 1/8	5 1/8	5 1/8	6	9	9 1/8	409	35
♦ *Chama / Jerry Washburn / Jerry Washburn / 1960*											

Score	Length of Main Beam R	Length of Main Beam L	Inside Spread	Greatest Spread	Circumference at Smallest Place between Burr and First Point R	Circumference at Smallest Place between Burr and First Point L	Number of Points R	Number of Points L	Total of Lengths Abnormal Points	All-Time Rank	State Rank
	♦ *Locality / Hunter / Owner / Date Killed*										
196 1/8	26 3/8	27 3/8	22 3/8	27 1/8	6	6 1/8	7	6	5 6/8	409	35
	♦ *Jicarilla Apache Res. / Tim Vicenti / Tim Vicenti / 1960*										
196	29 4/8	29 2/8	25 2/8	28 7/8	5	5	5	5	0	414	37
	♦ *Jicarilla Apache Res. / Collins F. Kellogg / Collins F. Kellogg / 1973*										
195 7/8	28	28	26 1/8	32 3/8	5 4/8	5 5/8	5	4	7 2/8	424	38
	♦ *Rio Arriba County / Arlene Perea / Arlene Perea / 1991*										
195 5/8	30 5/8	29	26 4/8	31 2/8	6 2/8	6 2/8	6	8	7 3/8	446	39
	♦ *Jicarilla Apache Res. / Eldrid Vigil / Eldrid Vigil / 1962*										
195 4/8	26 3/8	25 1/8	26 2/8	31 1/8	5 3/8	5 2/8	5	5	0	456	40
	♦ *Raton / Unknown / John H. Steinle III / 1963*										
195 3/8	25 4/8	24 2/8	24 5/8	30 5/8	5	5	5	4	0	464	41
	♦ *Rio Arriba County / Robert W. Highfill / Robert W. Highfill / 1964*										
195 1/8	25 4/8	24 2/8	24 1/8	27 4/8	5 5/8	5 6/8	5	5	0	482	42
	♦ *Rio Arriba County / Eddie W. Brieno, Jr. / Eddie W. Brieno, Jr. / 1965*										
195 1/8	25 5/8	26 1/8	26 1/8	34 1/8	5 3/8	5 2/8	6	6	5	482	42
	♦ *Rio Arriba County / David Shadrick / David Shadrick / 1988*										
195	25 1/8	25 1/8	25	28 3/8	4 4/8	4 7/8	5	5	0	491	44
	♦ *Rio Arriba County / Pat Wilson / John Lind, Jr. / 1967*										
194	25 1/8	25 4/8	27 4/8	30 1/8	5 4/8	5 4/8	5	5	0	508	45
	♦ *Rio Arriba County / C.J. McElroy / C.J. McElroy / 1970*										
192 4/8	28 2/8	26 3/8	27	29	6 1/8	6 2/8	5	5	0	520	46
	♦ *Rio Arriba County / Charles Tapia / Charles Tapia / 1993*										
191 3/8	25 5/8	25 2/8	24 7/8	31 5/8	4 7/8	4 7/8	5	6	1 2/8	529	47
	♦ *Grant County / Robin W. Bechtel / Robin W. Bechtel / 1988*										
191 3/8	27 2/8	26 6/8	25 5/8	28 4/8	5 5/8	5 5/8	5	5	0	529	47
	♦ *Rio Arriba County / Michael B. O'Banion / Michael B. O'Banion / 1993*										
188 5/8	24 4/8	23 7/8	24 4/8	30 2/8	5 2/8	5 2/8	5	6	1 7/8	562	49
	♦ *Rio Arriba County / George R. Payne / George R. Payne / 1973*										
181 3/8	25 6/8	24 6/8	24 7/8	27 1/8	5 6/8	5 3/8	5	5	0	630	50
	♦ *Rio Arriba County / John C. Simmons / John C. Simmons / 1991*										

Photograph Courtesy of Don Schaufler

NEW MEXICO STATE RECORD
NON-TYPICAL MULE DEER
SCORE: 306 2/8
Locality: Chama   Date: 1963
Hunter: Joseph A. Garcia
Owner: Don Schaufler

NEW MEXICO

NON-TYPICAL MULE DEER

Score	Length of Main Beam R	L	Inside Spread	Greatest Spread	Circumference at Smallest Place between Burr and First Point R	L	Number of Points R	L	Total of Lengths Abnormal Points	All-Time Rank	State Rank
$306^2/_8$	29	$28^5/_8$	$28^7/_8$	$40^6/_8$	$5^4/_8$	$5^5/_8$	18	18	$103^3/_8$	9	1

♦ *Chama / Joseph A. Garcia / Don Schaufler / 1963*

| $288^6/_8$ | $30^4/_8$ | $31^6/_8$ | $26^5/_8$ | $49^2/_8$ | $6^5/_8$ | $6^3/_8$ | 12 | 10 | $51^3/_8$ | 24 | 2 |

♦ *Chama / Frank B. Maestas / W.H. Mundy, Jr. / 1962*

| $267^5/_8$ | $26^4/_8$ | $25^7/_8$ | $26^3/_8$ | $29^6/_8$ | $4^7/_8$ | $4^6/_8$ | 13 | 18 | $58^2/_8$ | 83 | 3 |

♦ *Jicarilla Apache Res. / Byrd L. Minter, Jr. / Byrd L. Minter, Jr. / 1961*

| $265^5/_8$ | $24^7/_8$ | $26^7/_8$ | $27^2/_8$ | $36^1/_8$ | $6^7/_8$ | $6^5/_8$ | 16 | 14 | 67 | 97 | 4 |

♦ *Chama / Stephanie D. Tartaglia / Stephanie D. Tartaglia / 1966*

| $262^3/_8$ | $30^2/_8$ | $27^6/_8$ | $28^2/_8$ | 39 | $6^2/_8$ | $6^4/_8$ | 10 | 15 | $51^1/_8$ | 112 | 5 |

♦ *Tierra Amarilla / Pat Lovato, Jr. / Pat Lovato, Jr. / 1966*

| $259^7/_8$ | $28^4/_8$ | $27^4/_8$ | $29^4/_8$ | $38^1/_8$ | $5^7/_8$ | $5^5/_8$ | 12 | 15 | $53^3/_8$ | 132 | 6 |

♦ *Catron County / Jeff K. Gunnell / Jeff K. Gunnell / 1981*

| 258 | $20^4/_8$ | $22^1/_8$ | $19^3/_8$ | $32^3/_8$ | $4^2/_8$ | $4^5/_8$ | 13 | 13 | $89^1/_8$ | 150 | 7 |

♦ *Cimarron / Ralph L. Smith / Don Schaufler / 1957*

| $257^7/_8$ | $27^1/_8$ | 26 | $26^7/_8$ | $41^6/_8$ | $5^7/_8$ | $5^6/_8$ | 14 | 14 | 69 | 152 | 8 |

♦ *Jicarilla Apache Res. / Henry Callado / Henry Callado / 1961*

| $256^5/_8$ | $25^7/_8$ | $27^2/_8$ | $25^6/_8$ | $35^4/_8$ | $5^3/_8$ | $5^3/_8$ | 14 | 13 | $57^1/_8$ | 171 | 9 |

♦ *Jicarilla Apache Res. / Picked Up / S.L. Canterbury III / 1967*

| $255^2/_8$ | 26 | $26^5/_8$ | $25^1/_8$ | 33 | $4^7/_8$ | $4^5/_8$ | 9 | 9 | $42^1/_8$ | 183 | 10 |

♦ *Rio Arriba County / Gene Garcia / Gene Garcia / 1964*

| 249 | $27^7/_8$ | $29^7/_8$ | $25^6/_8$ | 36 | $5^3/_8$ | $5^1/_8$ | 11 | 8 | 47 | 244 | 11 |

♦ *Jemez Mts. / Max S. Jenson / Max S. Jenson / 1962*

| $245^6/_8$ | $27^1/_8$ | $28^2/_8$ | $24^4/_8$ | $34^4/_8$ | $5^6/_8$ | $5^7/_8$ | 11 | 9 | 30 | 298 | 12 |

♦ *Rio Arriba County / Kenneth W. Lee / Kenneth W. Lee / 1971*

| $245^2/_8$ | $26^5/_8$ | $27^4/_8$ | $21^2/_8$ | $29^7/_8$ | $5^6/_8$ | $5^6/_8$ | 10 | 10 | $45^6/_8$ | 302 | 13 |

♦ *Jicarilla Apache Res. / Arthur Wanoskea / Arthur Wanoskea / 1960*

| $243^4/_8$ | $22^2/_8$ | $18^4/_8$ | $23^5/_8$ | $32^6/_8$ | $4^6/_8$ | $4^5/_8$ | 14 | 11 | $70^6/_8$ | 336 | 14 |

♦ *Cibola County / Fred R. Valdez, Jr. / Don Schaufler / 1986*

| $242^2/_8$ | 24 | $25^2/_8$ | 21 | $27^2/_8$ | 6 | 6 | 9 | 11 | $45^4/_8$ | 353 | 15 |

♦ *Rio Arriba County / Elvon DeVaney / Shannon DeVaney / 1971*

| $241^4/_8$ | $26^4/_8$ | 27 | 27 | 31 | 5 | $5^3/_8$ | 8 | 7 | 26 | 369 | 16 |

♦ *Socorro County / James T. Everheart / James T. Everheart / 1973*

| $240^7/_8$ | $27^7/_8$ | $27^5/_8$ | 29 | $36^4/_8$ | $5^3/_8$ | $5^1/_8$ | 7 | 9 | 29 | 380 | 17 |

♦ *Rio Arriba County / Douglas Bryant / Douglas Bryant / 1988*

Score	Length of Main Beam		Inside Spread	Greatest Spread	Circumference at Smallest Place between Burr and First Point		Number of Points		Total of Lengths Abnormal Points	All-Time Rank	State Rank
	R	L			R	L	R	L			
◆ *Locality / Hunter / Owner / Date Killed*											
231⅞	25⅝	30⅜	25⅜	37⅛	5	4⅞	11	9	36⅛	414	18
◆ *Rio Arriba County / Dan F. Holleman / Vernon D. Holleman / 1966*											

Photograph Courtesy of Mike B. O'Banion

The Jicarilla Apache Indian Reservation is world famous for the trophy mule deer it produces year after year. Michael J. O'Banion took this very symmetrical typical mule deer buck, scoring 191-3/8 points, there in 1993.

Photograph Courtesy of Roy Mitten, Jr.

NORTH DAKOTA STATE RECORD (TIE)
TYPICAL MULE DEER
SCORE: 196 4/8
Locality: McKenzie Co.   Date: 1937
Hunter: Roy Mitten, Sr.
Owner: Roy Mitten, Jr.

NORTH DAKOTA
TYPICAL MULE DEER

Score	Length of Main Beam R	L	Inside Spread	Greatest Spread	Circumference at Smallest Place between Burr and First Point R	L	Number of Points R	L	Total of Lengths Abnormal Points	All-Time Rank	State Rank
◆ *Locality / Hunter / Owner / Date Killed*											
196 4/8	25	24 5/8	28 4/8	32 3/8	4 4/8	4 4/8	6	5	2 2/8	379	1
◆ *McKenzie County / Roy Mitten, Sr. / Roy Mitten, Jr. / 1937*											
196 4/8	26 3/8	27 5/8	27 5/8	36 2/8	5	4 7/8	5	6	5 1/8	379	1
◆ *Missouri River / Unknown / Robert L. Klisares / PR 1958*											

Photograph Courtesy of Stan J. Neitling, Jr.

OREGON STATE RECORD
TYPICAL MULE DEER
SCORE: 209 4/8
Locality: Wallowa Co.   Date: 1920
Hunter: John C. Evans
Owner: Stan J. Neitling, Jr.

OREGON

TYPICAL MULE DEER

Score	Length of Main Beam R	L	Inside Spread	Greatest Spread	Circumference at Smallest Place between Burr and First Point R	L	Number of Points R	L	Total of Lengths Abnormal Points	All-Time Rank	State Rank
					Locality / Hunter / Owner / Date Killed						
209 4/8	28 7/8	29 6/8	28	30 1/8	5 7/8	5 7/8	6	8	8 4/8	20	1
	Wallowa County / John C. Evans / Stan J. Neitling, Jr. / 1920										
205 3/8	26 6/8	27	26 7/8	29 1/8	5 3/8	5 3/8	5	5	0	62	2
	Starkey / H.M. Bailey / H.M. Bailey / 1963										
202 3/8	26 3/8	25 5/8	24 5/8	30 7/8	5 6/8	5 6/8	8	7	11 4/8	111	3
	Baker County / Brett N. Hayes / Brett N. Hayes / 1982										
201 7/8	27	26	26 5/8	30 6/8	5 1/8	5 1/8	5	5	0	129	4
	Union County / Brian M. Erwin / Brian M. Erwin / 1991										
201 5/8	26 2/8	27 3/8	24 3/8	29 3/8	5 4/8	5 4/8	5	5	0	135	5
	Baker County / Terry Williams / Terry Williams / 1988										
201 4/8	26 3/8	25 3/8	24 2/8	28 7/8	5 3/8	5 2/8	5	5	0	138	6
	Malheur County / David L. Bauer / David L. Bauer / 1971										
200 6/8	26 2/8	28	25 6/8	29 7/8	5 4/8	5 4/8	5	5	0	166	7
	Malheur County / Raymond Duncan / Raymond Duncan / 1949										
199 6/8	25 1/8	25 3/8	25	31 2/8	5 1/8	5 1/8	5	5	0	217	8
	Grant County / Steve M. Stevenson / Steve M. Stevenson / 1982										
198 1/8	26 5/8	25 5/8	28	30 4/8	4 6/8	4 7/8	5	5	0	280	9
	Wallowa County / Dan L. Gober / Dan L. Gober / 1980										
197 2/8	29 4/8	30 2/8	28 6/8	33 3/8	5 4/8	5 5/8	7	6	4	333	10
	Harney County / Guy E. Osborne / Guy E. Osborne / 1963										
197 1/8	26 5/8	27 6/8	26 3/8	35 3/8	5 2/8	5 1/8	5	5	10	342	11
	Ashwood / Harvey Rhoads / Harvey Rhoads / 1962										
197	25 7/8	26	22 3/8	28 7/8	5 5/8	5 3/8	7	7	7 5/8	347	12
	Grant County / Bruce J. Brothers / Bruce J. Brothers / 1993										
196 6/8	25 4/8	24 4/8	26 1/8	27 1/8	5 1/8	4 6/8	5	5	0	362	13
	Clackamas County / Picked Up / Curt M. Funk / 1983										
196 4/8	25 7/8	26 6/8	25 1/8	30 6/8	5 2/8	5 4/8	7	5	4 3/8	379	14
	Wasco County / Steven W. Forman / Steven W. Forman / 1986										
196 2/8	27 1/8	27 5/8	26	28 1/8	5 2/8	5	5	5	0	396	15
	Baker County / Vivian M. Zikmund / Vivian M. Zikmund / 1986										
195 6/8	27 4/8	29	26 2/8	28 5/8	5 5/8	5 4/8	7	9	9	433	16
	Keating / Al Delepierre / Francis A. Delepierre / 1966										
195 6/8	28 7/8	28 4/8	28 4/8	31 7/8	5 1/8	5 3/8	5	5	0	433	16
	Grant County / Larry Parlette / Larry Parlette / 1967										

Score	Length of Main Beam R	Length of Main Beam L	Inside Spread	Greatest Spread	Circumference at Smallest Place between Burr and First Point R	Circumference at Smallest Place between Burr and First Point L	Number of Points R	Number of Points L	Total of Lengths Abnormal Points	All-Time Rank	State Rank
♦ *Locality / Hunter / Owner / Date Killed*											
195 6/8	26	28	33	33 7/8	5 5/8	5 4/8	5	5	0	433	16
♦ *Grant County / Gordon E. Mitchell / Gordon E. Mitchell / 1982*											
195 3/8	25	25 2/8	25 1/8	27 3/8	4 4/8	4 4/8	6	5	2	464	19
♦ *Wallowa County / Michael R. Shirley / Michael R. Shirley / 1986*											
194 2/8	26	24 4/8	27 4/8	30 6/8	4 6/8	4 7/8	5	5	0	507	20
♦ *Grant County / Richard W. Erickson / Richard W. Erickson / 1994*											
191 2/8	24 5/8	24 6/8	26	28 5/8	4 6/8	4 4/8	5	5	0	531	21
♦ *Morrow County / Russell D. Britt / Russell D. Britt / 1990*											
186 6/8	24	22 7/8	18 2/8	25 4/8	5 5/8	5 2/8	6	6	3 2/8	596	22
♦ *Grant County / Leslie M. Brady / Leslie M. Brady / 1986*											

Bruce J. Brothers (right) poses here with Grant County, Oregon, rancher Steve Holmes and the 197 point typical mulie he took on Steve's ranch in 1993, proving that good hunter-landowner relationships can pay big dividends. Many of the finest big-game hunting opportunities occur on private property in North America.

**OREGON SECOND PLACE
NON-TYPICAL MULE DEER
SCORE: 297⅞**
Locality: Malheur Co.   Date: 1971
Hunter: Bradley Barclay

OREGON

NON-TYPICAL MULE DEER

Score	Length of Main Beam R	Length of Main Beam L	Inside Spread	Greatest Spread	Circumference at Smallest Place between Burr and First Point R	Circumference at Smallest Place between Burr and First Point L	Number of Points R	Number of Points L	Total of Lengths Abnormal Points	All-Time Rank	State Rank
♦ *Locality / Hunter / Owner / Date Killed*											
321 1/8	28 1/8	25 4/8	26 5/8	34 2/8	6 7/8	6 7/8	17	25	114 6/8	5	1
♦ *Umatilla County / Albert C. Peterson / Don Schaufler / 1925*											
297 7/8	29 1/8	27 5/8	35 4/8	39 6/8	5 4/8	5 3/8	20	18	99 2/8	19	2
♦ *Malheur County / Bradley Barclay / Bradley Barclay / 1971*											
277 1/8	26 1/8	24 6/8	24 3/8	38 7/8	5 6/8	5 5/8	13	13	74 2/8	47	3
♦ *Bly / Alice C. O'Brien / Don Schaufler / 1949*											
273 6/8	26	26 4/8	26 1/8	41 7/8	5	5	15	18	91 1/8	62	4
♦ *Klamath County / J.J. McDaniels / J.J. McDaniels / 1952*											
270 6/8	28 6/8	28 2/8	27 6/8	37 3/8	5 7/8	5 7/8	15	15	71	71	5
♦ *Crook County / C.F. Cheney / C.F. Cheney / 1962*											
268 5/8	24 2/8	22 7/8	27	38 7/8	6	6 3/8	14	15	113 3/8	77	6
♦ *Grant County / Lige Davis / Coy Johnston / 1941*											
266	25 3/8	24 2/8	27 7/8	35 3/8	5 6/8	5 5/8	16	20	73 7/8	93	7
♦ *Grant County / Harold T. Oathes / Harold T. Oathes / 1965*											
262	24 2/8	24 6/8	16 5/8	34 4/8	4 6/8	4 7/8	14	16	87 7/8	116	8
♦ *John Day River / Glen E. Park / Glen E. Park / 1962*											
256 4/8	28 3/8	28 4/8	22	32 5/8	5 1/8	5 1/8	10	9	48 6/8	172	9
♦ *Baker County / Thomas M. Rousseau / Thomas M. Rousseau / 1988*											
249 2/8	26 1/8	28 4/8	29 1/8	37 5/8	5 6/8	6 1/8	14	10	52 4/8	240	10
♦ *Klamath County / Fred Teeny / Rick Teeny / 1947*											
247 4/8	25 2/8	24 7/8	24 3/8	36 6/8	6 2/8	5 6/8	12	16	71 7/8	268	11
♦ *Bend / L.M. Martinson / L.M. Martinson / 1949*											
243 7/8	23 3/8	23 4/8	21 3/8	39 3/8	4 3/8	4 4/8	11	10	58	328	12
♦ *Malheur County / Larry L. Herron / Larry L. Herron / 1983*											
243	25 7/8	25 6/8	20	0	5 2/8	5	15	12	0	342	13
♦ *Crook County / Wes Mitts / Wes Mitts / 1936*											
242	26 2/8	26 6/8	28 1/8	35	5 4/8	5 4/8	10	8	31 2/8	359	14
♦ *Klamath County / Corinne Fields / Corinne Fields / 1946*											
241 7/8	24 5/8	24 2/8	25	0	5 2/8	5 2/8	11	19	0	362	15
♦ *Jefferson County / Spencer L. Darrar / Spencer L. Darrar / 1953*											
240 1/8	24 2/8	24	19 6/8	36 6/8	5 6/8	5 7/8	13	12	61 7/8	394	16
♦ *Harney County / R.G. Creager / R.G. Creager / 1957*											
268 4/8	25 6/8	23	22 7/8	37 3/8	5 4/8	5 6/8	17	14	89 7/8	*	*
♦ *Deschutes County / Devon Talley / Devon Talley / 1983*											

SOUTH DAKOTA STATE RECORD (NEW)
TYPICAL MULE DEER
SCORE: 190⁶/₈
Locality: Fall River Co.   Date: 1953
Hunter: Art Thomsen

SOUTH DAKOTA
TYPICAL MULE DEER

Score	Length of Main Beam		Inside Spread	Greatest Spread	Circumference at Smallest Place between Burr and First Point		Number of Points		Total of Lengths Abnormal Points	All-Time Rank	State Rank
	R	L			R	L	R	L			
◆ *Locality / Hunter / Owner / Date Killed*											
190⁶⁄₈	27	26⅛	20⁴⁄₈	25⁴⁄₈	5²⁄₈	5²⁄₈	5	5	0	537	1
◆ *Fall River County / Art Thomsen / Art Thomsen / 1953*											
185⁴⁄₈	24²⁄₈	24²⁄₈	23⁶⁄₈	28⅛	4⅞	4⅞	6	6	3⁶⁄₈	616	2
◆ *Brule County / Kenny E. Yeaton / Kenny E. Yeaton / 1985*											

SOUTH DAKOTA STATE RECORD
NON-TYPICAL MULE DEER
SCORE: 266⅝
Locality: Philip   Date: 1959
Hunter: Clifford Ramsey

SOUTH DAKOTA
NON-TYPICAL MULE DEER

Score	Length of Main Beam R L	Inside Spread	Greatest Spread	Circumference at Smallest Place between Burr and First Point R	L	Number of Points R	L	Total of Lengths Abnormal Points	All-Time Rank	State Rank
	◆ Locality / Hunter / Owner / Date Killed									
266⅝	25⅝ 25²⁄₈	20⁰⁄₈	28⅝	5	5	13	11	85⅞	89	1
	◆ Philip / Clifford Ramsey / Clifford Ramsey / 1959									
246⁶⁄₈	24⁶⁄₈ 24⅞	22⅛	34⅜	4⅝	4⁶⁄₈	10	14	54⅝	285	2
	◆ Lawrence County / Unknown / Old Style Saloon / 1945									

235

UTAH STATE RECORD
TYPICAL MULE DEER
SCORE: 212⅛
Locality: San Juan Co.   Date: 1973
Hunter: V.R. Rayburn

UTAH
TYPICAL MULE DEER

Score	Length of Main Beam R	L	Inside Spread	Greatest Spread	Circumference at Smallest Place between Burr and First Point R	L	Number of Points R	L	Total of Lengths Abnormal Points	All-Time Rank	State Rank
$212\frac{1}{8}$	$26\frac{3}{8}$	$26\frac{6}{8}$	$26\frac{4}{8}$	$30\frac{4}{8}$	$6\frac{1}{8}$	$6\frac{1}{8}$	8	6	$6\frac{5}{8}$	7	1
	\u2666 San Juan County / V.R. Rayburn / V.R. Rayburn / 1973										
210	$26\frac{2}{8}$	$26\frac{4}{8}$	$25\frac{4}{8}$	$31\frac{6}{8}$	$5\frac{2}{8}$	$5\frac{1}{8}$	6	6	$3\frac{6}{8}$	16	2
	\u2666 Manti-Lasal Mts. / William Norton / William Norton / 1970										
$209\frac{2}{8}$	28	$29\frac{4}{8}$	$28\frac{4}{8}$	$34\frac{4}{8}$	$4\frac{7}{8}$	$4\frac{6}{8}$	5	5	0	22	3
	\u2666 Rich County / Dee Hildt / Dee Hildt / 1968										
208	29	$26\frac{4}{8}$	$34\frac{3}{8}$	$35\frac{1}{8}$	5	$5\frac{1}{8}$	5	5	0	30	4
	\u2666 Utah County / Ned H. Losser / Ned H. Losser / 1972										
$207\frac{4}{8}$	$27\frac{4}{8}$	26	24	$32\frac{2}{8}$	$4\frac{7}{8}$	$4\frac{7}{8}$	5	5	0	33	5
	\u2666 Washington County / John K. Frei / Don Schaufler / 1987										
207	$28\frac{3}{8}$	$29\frac{3}{8}$	27	$34\frac{2}{8}$	$5\frac{5}{8}$	$5\frac{4}{8}$	5	7	9	37	6
	\u2666 Kane County / Picked Up / John K. Springer / 1986										
$206\frac{1}{8}$	$26\frac{3}{8}$	$26\frac{3}{8}$	$26\frac{7}{8}$	$34\frac{2}{8}$	6	6	5	8	$8\frac{6}{8}$	52	7
	\u2666 Peterson / Picked Up / Paul Crittenden / PR 1965										
$205\frac{6}{8}$	$26\frac{6}{8}$	$27\frac{6}{8}$	$25\frac{2}{8}$	$37\frac{2}{8}$	$5\frac{4}{8}$	$5\frac{2}{8}$	5	7	$8\frac{2}{8}$	55	8
	\u2666 Kanab / Loyd A. Folkstad / Loyd A. Folkstad / 1968										
$205\frac{1}{8}$	$26\frac{3}{8}$	$25\frac{6}{8}$	$25\frac{5}{8}$	$30\frac{2}{8}$	$4\frac{4}{8}$	$4\frac{4}{8}$	5	5	0	65	9
	\u2666 Morgan County / Gale Allen / Gale Allen / 1946										
$204\frac{2}{8}$	26	$26\frac{2}{8}$	$22\frac{2}{8}$	$30\frac{2}{8}$	$5\frac{4}{8}$	$5\frac{4}{8}$	5	5	0	71	10
	\u2666 Garfield County / James D. Perkins / James D. Perkins / 1969										
$204\frac{1}{8}$	$24\frac{6}{8}$	26	$27\frac{6}{8}$	$34\frac{5}{8}$	$4\frac{7}{8}$	$4\frac{7}{8}$	6	5	$1\frac{1}{8}$	72	11
	\u2666 Morgan County / Kenneth R. Dickamore / Kenneth R. Dickamore / 1967										
$203\frac{5}{8}$	$28\frac{6}{8}$	$30\frac{2}{8}$	$30\frac{1}{8}$	$34\frac{3}{8}$	5	5	5	5	$7\frac{2}{8}$	81	12
	\u2666 Grand County / Glen Dumas / S. Kim Bonnett / PR 1960										
$203\frac{2}{8}$	$25\frac{6}{8}$	$26\frac{6}{8}$	$23\frac{3}{8}$	$27\frac{3}{8}$	$4\frac{6}{8}$	$4\frac{7}{8}$	6	5	$1\frac{7}{8}$	89	13
	\u2666 Garfield County / James D. Perkins / Mrs. James D. Perkins / 1965										
$202\frac{2}{8}$	$27\frac{2}{8}$	$28\frac{1}{8}$	$31\frac{3}{8}$	$42\frac{4}{8}$	$5\frac{2}{8}$	$5\frac{2}{8}$	10	7	$12\frac{7}{8}$	116	14
	\u2666 Carbon County / Robert R. Henderson / Robert R. Henderson / 1965										
$201\frac{7}{8}$	$27\frac{2}{8}$	$27\frac{3}{8}$	$27\frac{3}{8}$	35	$6\frac{1}{8}$	$5\frac{6}{8}$	6	6	$9\frac{2}{8}$	129	15
	\u2666 Daggett County / Earl Eldredge / Phil Brotherson / 1940										
$201\frac{3}{8}$	$30\frac{1}{8}$	$28\frac{2}{8}$	$28\frac{7}{8}$	$32\frac{4}{8}$	$4\frac{5}{8}$	$4\frac{6}{8}$	5	5	0	144	16
	\u2666 Wasatch County / Paul Probst / Paul Probst / 1971										
$201\frac{1}{8}$	$29\frac{1}{8}$	$29\frac{2}{8}$	31	$43\frac{4}{8}$	$5\frac{2}{8}$	$5\frac{3}{8}$	7	8	$11\frac{3}{8}$	155	17
	\u2666 Sanpete County / Roger M. Allred / Roger M. Allred / 1958										

Score	Length of Main Beam R	L	Inside Spread	Greatest Spread	Circumference at Smallest Place between Burr and First Point R	L	Number of Points R	L	Total of Lengths Abnormal Points	All-Time Rank	State Rank
201	$28\frac{2}{8}$	$28\frac{6}{8}$	$28\frac{6}{8}$	40	5	$5\frac{2}{8}$	6	4	$3\frac{2}{8}$	159	18

♦ *Summit County / Clinton A. Larson / Clinton A. Larson / 1949*

| | $26\frac{7}{8}$ | $26\frac{3}{8}$ | 23 | 28 | $4\frac{6}{8}$ | $4\frac{7}{8}$ | 5 | 5 | 0 | 166 | 19 |
| 200$\frac{6}{8}$ | | | | | | | | | | | |

♦ *Provo Canyon / Karl D. Zaugg / Karl D. Zaugg / 1948*

| $200\frac{5}{8}$ | 27 | $26\frac{4}{8}$ | $26\frac{4}{8}$ | $35\frac{2}{8}$ | $4\frac{6}{8}$ | 5 | 7 | 9 | $12\frac{7}{8}$ | 173 | 20 |

♦ *Ogden / Carl F. Worden / Carl F. Worden / 1948*

| $200\frac{4}{8}$ | $28\frac{5}{8}$ | $27\frac{5}{8}$ | $28\frac{2}{8}$ | $31\frac{4}{8}$ | $4\frac{7}{8}$ | $4\frac{6}{8}$ | 4 | 5 | 0 | 177 | 21 |

♦ *Utah County / Elroy A. Loveridge / Elroy A. Loveridge / 1965*

| $200\frac{3}{8}$ | $25\frac{7}{8}$ | $25\frac{7}{8}$ | $20\frac{1}{8}$ | 26 | $5\frac{2}{8}$ | $5\frac{1}{8}$ | 5 | 6 | 2 | 186 | 22 |

♦ *Duchesne County / William E. Lewis / William E. Lewis / PR 1980*

| $200\frac{2}{8}$ | $25\frac{2}{8}$ | $27\frac{2}{8}$ | $25\frac{2}{8}$ | $35\frac{3}{8}$ | $4\frac{7}{8}$ | 5 | 6 | 5 | $3\frac{2}{8}$ | 190 | 23 |

♦ *Sevier County / Mayben J. Crane / Mayben J. Crane / 1987*

| $199\frac{6}{8}$ | $26\frac{6}{8}$ | $25\frac{4}{8}$ | $24\frac{5}{8}$ | 31 | $5\frac{3}{8}$ | 5 | 6 | 5 | $2\frac{3}{8}$ | 217 | 24 |

♦ *Kane County / Gilbert T. Adams, Jr. / Gilbert T. Adams, Jr. / 1993*

| $199\frac{4}{8}$ | $25\frac{5}{8}$ | $26\frac{4}{8}$ | $23\frac{6}{8}$ | $27\frac{4}{8}$ | $4\frac{7}{8}$ | 5 | 5 | 6 | $2\frac{4}{8}$ | 222 | 25 |

♦ *Sanpete County / Kevin P. Price / Kevin P. Price / 1973*

| $199\frac{2}{8}$ | $27\frac{5}{8}$ | 28 | $25\frac{4}{8}$ | $30\frac{4}{8}$ | $5\frac{2}{8}$ | $5\frac{2}{8}$ | 5 | 5 | 0 | 232 | 26 |

♦ *Strawberry / Steve Payne / Steve Payne / 1962*

| $199\frac{2}{8}$ | $26\frac{4}{8}$ | $26\frac{2}{8}$ | $27\frac{4}{8}$ | $30\frac{4}{8}$ | $5\frac{6}{8}$ | $5\frac{5}{8}$ | 5 | 5 | 0 | 232 | 26 |

♦ *Grand County / Picked Up / Jon P. Leatham / 1976*

| $199\frac{1}{8}$ | 25 | $24\frac{3}{8}$ | $24\frac{3}{8}$ | $30\frac{2}{8}$ | $5\frac{6}{8}$ | $5\frac{5}{8}$ | 6 | 5 | $4\frac{2}{8}$ | 243 | 28 |

♦ *San Juan County / Phyllis O. Crookston / Phyllis O. Crookston / 1971*

| $199\frac{1}{8}$ | $25\frac{4}{8}$ | $25\frac{3}{8}$ | $23\frac{3}{8}$ | $27\frac{2}{8}$ | $5\frac{6}{8}$ | 6 | 5 | 5 | 0 | 243 | 28 |

♦ *Morgan County / H. Ritman Jons / H. Ritman Jons / 1987*

| 199 | $26\frac{6}{8}$ | $27\frac{1}{8}$ | $26\frac{2}{8}$ | $30\frac{5}{8}$ | $4\frac{7}{8}$ | $5\frac{1}{8}$ | 5 | 5 | 0 | 248 | 30 |

♦ *Echo / Wilford Zaugg / Wilford Zaugg / 1958*

| 199 | $28\frac{4}{8}$ | $27\frac{7}{8}$ | $24\frac{1}{8}$ | 29 | $5\frac{1}{8}$ | $5\frac{2}{8}$ | 4 | 5 | $1\frac{5}{8}$ | 248 | 30 |

♦ *San Juan County / Bradley J. Young / Bradley J. Young / 1991*

| $198\frac{4}{8}$ | $25\frac{5}{8}$ | $25\frac{6}{8}$ | $20\frac{4}{8}$ | $25\frac{2}{8}$ | 5 | 5 | 5 | 5 | 0 | 262 | 32 |

♦ *Tabiona / Picked Up / H.A. Zumbrock / 1957*

| 198 | $25\frac{1}{8}$ | $25\frac{2}{8}$ | $22\frac{4}{8}$ | $25\frac{3}{8}$ | $5\frac{1}{8}$ | 5 | 4 | 4 | 0 | 287 | 33 |

♦ *Davis County / Carl D. Craig / Jay D. Craig / 1939*

| 198 | $25\frac{4}{8}$ | $24\frac{6}{8}$ | $25\frac{1}{8}$ | $30\frac{4}{8}$ | $5\frac{4}{8}$ | $5\frac{3}{8}$ | 6 | 5 | $1\frac{1}{8}$ | 287 | 33 |

♦ *Smithfield Canyon / Stanley Richardson / Stanley Richardson / 1961*

| $197\frac{6}{8}$ | $25\frac{4}{8}$ | $25\frac{7}{8}$ | $23\frac{6}{8}$ | 33 | $5\frac{2}{8}$ | $5\frac{2}{8}$ | 6 | 5 | $2\frac{2}{8}$ | 302 | 35 |

♦ *Elk Ridge / Bill King / Joseph Fitting / 1956*

Score	Length of Main Beam R	L	Inside Spread	Greatest Spread	Circumference at Smallest Place between Burr and First Point R	L	Number of Points R	L	Total of Lengths Abnormal Points	All-Time Rank	State Rank
197 5/8	25 1/8	25	27 5/8	36 4/8	5 1/8	5 3/8	8	6	6	308	36

♦ *Summit County / Wendell M. Smith / Nathan H. Smith / 1954*

197 5/8	26 7/8	27 3/8	26	32 5/8	5	4 7/8	6	5	4 3/8	308	36

♦ *Uintah County / Robert C. Chapoose, Jr. / Robert C. Chapoose, Jr. / 1987*

197 3/8	26 7/8	25	22 3/8	26 2/8	5 4/8	5 3/8	5	5	0	324	38

♦ *Currant Creek / Morris Kidd / Morris Kidd / 1960*

197 3/8	28 7/8	28 6/8	23 4/8	27 5/8	5 3/8	5 4/8	7	6	7 5/8	324	38

♦ *Garfield County / James R. McCourt / James R. McCourt / 1985*

197 2/8	26 2/8	26 1/8	21 2/8	28 4/8	4 3/8	4 4/8	5	5	0	333	40

♦ *Weber County / Abe B. Murdock / Abe B. Murdock / 1972*

197 1/8	25 1/8	24 3/8	25 5/8	30 2/8	4 2/8	4 3/8	5	5	0	342	41

♦ *Morgan County / Gayle Allen / Gayle Allen / 1948*

197	25 3/8	27	22 3/8	25 6/8	5	4 7/8	5	6	1 1/8	347	42

♦ *Utah County / L. Doug Carlton / L. Doug Carlton / 1982*

196 5/8	25 6/8	25 5/8	24 2/8	30 4/8	5	4 7/8	7	6	4 3/8	369	43

♦ *Summit County / Jerry L. Henriod / Jerry L. Henriod / 1967*

196 4/8	24 2/8	25 1/8	21	26 7/8	6 1/8	6 1/8	5	5	0	379	44

♦ *Vernal / Selby G. Tanner / Selby G. Tanner / 1966*

196 4/8	26 2/8	26 1/8	25 2/8	30 7/8	5 2/8	5 6/8	6	5	1 4/8	379	44

♦ *Morgan County / Elwood Williams / Elwood Williams / 1968*

196 3/8	28 3/8	28 4/8	23 5/8	27 4/8	5 3/8	5 4/8	7	5	3 6/8	391	46

♦ *Beaver County / Dawson Barnes / Dawson Barnes / 1992*

196 2/8	22 5/8	22 5/8	21 6/8	35	5 3/8	5 3/8	6	7	5	396	47

♦ *Millard County / Burnell Washburn / Burnell Washburn / 1967*

196 2/8	25 6/8	26	28 4/8	33 2/8	5 4/8	5 3/8	6	4	1 6/8	396	47

♦ *San Juan County / John Rowley / John Rowley / 1989*

195 7/8	28 5/8	28	26 5/8	32 6/8	5 5/8	5 5/8	7	8	22 6/8	424	49

♦ *Cache County / Richard E. Reeder / Richard E. Reeder / 1968*

195 5/8	26 1/8	26 1/8	24	30 5/8	5	5	6	5	1 1/8	446	50

♦ *Washington County / Scott M. Bulloch / Scott M. Bulloch / 1985*

195 4/8	25 1/8	25 4/8	22 6/8	30	5 2/8	5 2/8	5	5	0	456	51

♦ *Grover / Vicki Davis / R.J. Davis / 1959*

195 3/8	25	25 5/8	25 5/8	29 3/8	5 3/8	5 2/8	5	5	0	464	52

♦ *Garfield County / John E. Braithwaite / John E. Braithwaite / 1987*

195 2/8	25	26 4/8	24 4/8	31	5 7/8	5 5/8	5	5	0	472	53

♦ *Davis County / Mitchell L. Cochran / Mitchell L. Cochran / 1972*

Score	Length of Main Beam R	L	Inside Spread	Greatest Spread	Circumference at Smallest Place between Burr and First Point R	L	Number of Points R	L	Total of Lengths Abnormal Points	All-Time Rank	State Rank
									Locality / Hunter / Owner / Date Killed		
195 1/8	24 4/8	24 3/8	22 2/8	25 3/8	5 6/8	5 5/8	6	5	1 3/8	482	54
	Utah / Unknown / Jarvie Taxidermy / 1959										
195 1/8	27 3/8	28 2/8	27 1/8	31 2/8	5 5/8	5 5/8	5	5	0	482	54
	Kane County / Cecil Hunt / Cecil Hunt / 1987										
195	25 2/8	25 1/8	22 2/8	31 1/8	4 6/8	4 5/8	5	5	0	491	56
	Beaver County / Unknown / Mark R. Dotson / 1969										
195	27 1/8	26 5/8	27 1/8	31 1/8	5 3/8	5 2/8	5	7	6 7/8	491	56
	Carbon County / Thomas E. Wilson / Thomas E. Wilson / 1988										
194 6/8	25 4/8	24 6/8	23 1/8	31 3/8	4 3/8	4 3/8	6	5	1 5/8	501	58
	Utah / Unknown / Jarvie Taxidermy / 1947										
194 6/8	28	27 5/8	26 7/8	30 4/8	4 5/8	4 7/8	6	8	15 7/8	501	58
	Grand County / Richard V. Beesley / Richard V. Beesley / 1986										
194 5/8	28 3/8	28 3/8	26 6/8	38 3/8	5 5/8	5 5/8	6	7	20 1/8	503	60
	Duchesne County / Kate Hamilton / Raymond R. Cross / 1948										
194 5/8	25 7/8	25 4/8	25 1/8	30 4/8	4 6/8	5 2/8	5	5	0	503	60
	Weber River / Desmond Shields / Desmond Shields / 1960										
191 1/8	26 5/8	24 6/8	24 3/8	28 5/8	4 7/8	4 7/8	5	5	0	532	62
	Uintah County / Robert B. Keel / Robert B. Keel / 1986										
191	25 4/8	25 1/8	25 1/8	31 4/8	5 6/8	5 2/8	6	6	3 5/8	535	63
	Kane County / Edward B. Franceschi, Jr. / Edward B. Franceschi, Jr. / 1990										
190 2/8	25 2/8	25 1/8	23	29 1/8	5	4 7/8	5	5	0	546	64
	Rich County / Troy Howard / Troy Howard / 1992										
190	24 1/8	24 2/8	19 5/8	25	5 2/8	5 1/8	5	6	1 7/8	548	65
	Rich County / Ernie Davis / Ernie Davis / 1992										
189 4/8	25 2/8	25 1/8	27 7/8	29 4/8	4 4/8	4 5/8	5	5	0	555	66
	Emery County / Marvin H. Christensen / Marvin H. Christensen / 1974										
189 3/8	24 7/8	25 1/8	24 3/8	27 2/8	5 1/8	5 3/8	5	5	0	556	67
	San Juan County / Keele Johnson / Keele Johnson / 1986										
188 2/8	23	23 2/8	16 2/8	26 6/8	4 7/8	4 7/8	5	5	0	572	68
	Daggett County / Roy D. Sessions / Roy D. Sessions / 1979										
188 1/8	26 1/8	25	27 3/8	32 6/8	5 2/8	5 4/8	6	8	11 2/8	574	69
	Garfield County / Johnny Parsons / Johnny Parsons / 1984										
187 6/8	23 6/8	23 6/8	23 1/8	29	5 5/8	5 3/8	5	6	7 1/8	581	70
	Kane County / Theo J. McAllister / Theo J. McAllister / 1985										
187 1/8	22 6/8	23 5/8	26 1/8	34 3/8	4 7/8	4 7/8	5	5	1 2/8	589	71
	Morgan County / Terry R. Bitton / Terry R. Bitton / 1989										

Score	Length of Main Beam R	L	Inside Spread	Greatest Spread	Circumference at Smallest Place between Burr and First Point R	L	Number of Points R	L	Total of Lengths Abnormal Points	All-Time Rank	State Rank
* Locality / Hunter / Owner / Date Killed											
186 7/8	25 6/8	25 5/8	25 3/8	28 3/8	4 6/8	4 7/8	5	5	0	593	72
♦ Washington County / Paul A. Stewart / Paul A. Stewart / 1994											
186 4/8	26 5/8	25 1/8	26 6/8	33	4 5/8	4 5/8	5	5	1 1/8	600	73
♦ Rich County / Mark P. Hodges / Mark P. Hodges / 1967											
186 1/8	24 6/8	26 4/8	25 1/8	32 2/8	5 6/8	5 5/8	7	5	10 6/8	603	74
♦ Sanpete County / Deland G. James / Emma James / 1935											
185 7/8	25 2/8	25	23 6/8	29 2/8	4 5/8	4 4/8	5	7	2 5/8	609	75
♦ Juab County / Chris J. Carter / Chris J. Carter / 1987											
181 5/8	24 6/8	24 4/8	24 3/8	27 1/8	5 5/8	5 6/8	5	5	0	627	76
♦ Washington County / Picked Up / Paul A. Stewart / PR 1994											
203 6/8	26 6/8	27 1/8	26	31 1/8	5 6/8	5 7/8	7	5	3 6/8	*	*
♦ Beaver County / John A. Dotson / John A. Dotson / 1989											

Photograph from Boone & Crockett Club Archives

UTAH STATE RECORD
NON-TYPICAL MULE DEER
SCORE: 330⅛
Locality: Box Elder Co.   Date: 1943
Hunter: Alton Hunsaker
Owner: Bob Howard

UTAH

NON-TYPICAL MULE DEER

Score	Length of Main Beam R	Length of Main Beam L	Inside Spread	Greatest Spread	Circumference at Smallest Place between Burr and First Point R	Circumference at Smallest Place between Burr and First Point L	Number of Points R	Number of Points L	Total of Lengths Abnormal Points	All-Time Rank	State Rank
♦ *Locality / Hunter / Owner / Date Killed*											
330 1/8	23 2/8	22	9 4/8	31	8 2/8	8 3/8	21	28	142 7/8	2	1
♦ *Box Elder County / Alton Hunsaker / Bob Howard / 1943*											
302	26 7/8	26 2/8	21 5/8	40 7/8	6 3/8	6 5/8	21	15	108 3/8	14	2
♦ *Iron County / Darwin Hulett / Don Schaufler / 1950*											
293 6/8	26 7/8	26 3/8	27 3/8	38 3/8	5 3/8	5 5/8	12	17	86 7/8	23	3
♦ *Garfield County / Lloyd Barton / Lloyd Barton / 1993*											
286 1/8	27	26 6/8	26 1/8	34 4/8	5 2/8	5 3/8	12	20	86	27	4
♦ *Utah County / Joe Allen / Todd L. Johnson / PR 1950*											
284 3/8	27 4/8	24 3/8	26	38 2/8	5 1/8	5 2/8	15	15	84 7/8	31	5
♦ *Duchesne County / Clyde Lambert / Lucy L. Back / 1935*											
284	25 7/8	26 3/8	24 1/8	43 6/8	5 2/8	5 4/8	15	15	82 1/8	32	6
♦ *Provo River / Melvin T. Ashton / Don Schaufler / 1961*											
283	28	29 2/8	24 3/8	37 1/8	8	7 7/8	14	13	69 5/8	34	7
♦ *Rose Creek / Verl N. Creager / Verl N. Creager / 1960*											
277 2/8	23 6/8	25 1/8	25 6/8	47 4/8	5 2/8	5 5/8	11	10	55 3/8	46	8
♦ *Morgan County / Jim Kilfoil / Gilbert Francis / 1938*											
274 1/8	28 3/8	28	23	36 6/8	5 4/8	5 7/8	10	4	53 5/8	59	9
♦ *Beaver / Murray Bohn / Parowan Rod & Gun Club / 1920*											
273 7/8	27 7/8	29 2/8	26 6/8	40 6/8	6 1/8	6	8	12	52 3/8	61	10
♦ *Kane County / Waldon Ballard / Alice Ballard / 1950*											
273 5/8	28 3/8	28 2/8	23 7/8	42 4/8	6	6 1/8	15	16	54 6/8	64	11
♦ *Morgan County / Harold B. Rollins / Harold B. Rollins / 1944*											
271 2/8	24 3/8	24 4/8	20	38 3/8	4 6/8	5 1/8	13	14	92 6/8	70	12
♦ *East Canyon / Joseph H. Greenig / Mrs. J.H. Greenig / 1947*											
266 7/8	22 5/8	22 7/8	18 6/8	37 5/8	5 1/8	5 1/8	8	8	67 3/8	87	13
♦ *Draper / Glenn W. Furrow / Glenn W. Furrow / 1962*											
265 6/8	25 6/8	25 6/8	24 1/8	41	5 1/8	5 4/8	11	13	79 5/8	96	14
♦ *Cache County / Jerry S. Wuthrich / Jerry S. Wuthrich / 1966*											
264 2/8	24 4/8	26 2/8	21	26 7/8	5 3/8	5 3/8	7	13	61 6/8	103	15
♦ *Southern Utah / Unknown / Earl Mecham / 1932*											
263 6/8	26 5/8	26 5/8	22 2/8	37	5	5	16	14	53 4/8	106	16
♦ *Sanpete County / Wayne Dwyer / Raymond R. Cross / 1974*											
262	25 7/8	23 7/8	21	37 7/8	4 7/8	5	14	15	71 2/8	116	17
♦ *Utah County / Michael D. Atwood / Michael D. Atwood / 1967*											

Score	Length of Main Beam R	L	Inside Spread	Greatest Spread	Circumference at Smallest Place between Burr and First Point R	L	Number of Points R	L	Total of Lengths Abnormal Points	All-Time Rank	State Rank
	♦ *Locality / Hunter / Owner / Date Killed*										
261 5/8	25	26 3/8	23 6/8	41 4/8	4 7/8	5	10	12	71 5/8	119	18
	♦ *Heber Mountain / DuWayne C. Bailey / DuWayne C. Bailey / 1963*										
260 1/8	26	27 2/8	24 3/8	37 1/8	4 6/8	5 1/8	16	20	75 4/8	129	19
	♦ *Newcastle / Unknown / Utah Div. of Wildl. Resc. / 1961*										
259 7/8	25 7/8	24	24 6/8	35 2/8	4 7/8	4 6/8	11	13	76 5/8	132	20
	♦ *Kanab / Arthur Glover / Arthur Glover / 1947*										
259 3/8	27 3/8	29 2/8	24 6/8	42	5 6/8	5 4/8	13	13	52 5/8	139	21
	♦ *Iron County / Mont Hunter / Mont Hunter / 1939*										
258 6/8	26	25 2/8	18 2/8	31 4/8	4 5/8	4 4/8	13	11	70 4/8	141	22
	♦ *Washington County / Brian A. Bowler / Brian A. Bowler / 1989*										
258 4/8	25 4/8	26 6/8	24 4/8	36	5 6/8	5 4/8	11	9	53 6/8	145	23
	♦ *Grand County / Vernon K. Heller / Vernon K. Heller / 1971*										
258 1/8	27 1/8	25 6/8	23 2/8	29 7/8	5 7/8	5 7/8	11	13	89 7/8	148	24
	♦ *Morgan County / Martin Harris / Rodney D. Layton / 1935*										
257 4/8	28 7/8	28 6/8	27 7/8	37 3/8	4 6/8	4 7/8	18	10	52 1/8	159	25
	♦ *Utah County / J. Clyde Burgess / Dave Burgess / 1949*										
257 4/8	23 6/8	24 1/8	20 2/8	29 5/8	5 6/8	5 4/8	12	10	49 6/8	159	25
	♦ *Sanpete County / Dan J. Keller / Dan J. Keller / 1986*										
257 1/8	25 2/8	24 7/8	19	31 6/8	5 6/8	5 3/8	10	8	49 7/8	164	27
	♦ *Juab County / P.L. Jones / Nelson L. Jones / 1949*										
257	26 7/8	26	24 2/8	31 6/8	5	4 7/8	12	12	57 6/8	165	28
	♦ *Cache County / Harold S. Shandrew / Harold S. Shandrew / 1958*										
256 1/8	23 7/8	24 7/8	25	33 5/8	4 7/8	5 1/8	12	13	54 2/8	175	29
	♦ *East Zion / Raymond Pocta / Raymond Pocta / 1963*										
256	24 4/8	26 7/8	25 1/8	34 2/8	5	4 6/8	13	10	62 1/8	178	30
	♦ *Garfield County / James D. Perkins / James D. Perkins / 1959*										
255 6/8	26 5/8	26 7/8	26 5/8	37 7/8	5 2/8	5 2/8	11	9	51 5/8	181	31
	♦ *Cache County / Roland Leishman / Roland Leishman / 1980*										
254 4/8	25 1/8	24 1/8	21 1/8	42 3/8	4 6/8	4 6/8	16	12	66 5/8	189	32
	♦ *Utah / Unknown / Dana J. Hollinger / PR 1960*										
253 3/8	20 1/8	22 1/8	22 6/8	28 5/8	5 2/8	5 3/8	15	22	90	195	33
	♦ *Utah County / Paul H. Mitchell / Paul H. Mitchell / 1953*										
252 1/8	25 1/8	24 1/8	21 5/8	31 5/8	4 6/8	4 7/8	11	10	54	208	34
	♦ *Salina Canyon / James C. Larsen / James C. Larsen / 1969*										
251 7/8	22	24 1/8	17 1/8	29 4/8	4 6/8	4 5/8	10	10	68 6/8	211	35
	♦ *Salem / John Vincent / John Vincent / 1956*										

Score	Length of Main Beam R	L	Inside Spread	Greatest Spread	Circumference at Smallest Place between Burr and First Point R	L	Number of Points R	L	Total of Lengths Abnormal Points	All-Time Rank	State Rank
251⁶⁄₈	25²⁄₈	25⁷⁄₈	23	40¹⁄₈	6³⁄₈	6	7	14	66⁶⁄₈	212	36
◆ *Washington County / Richard S. Mansker / Richard S. Mansker / 1990*											
251³⁄₈	26⁷⁄₈	26	31¹⁄₈	38⁴⁄₈	5⁵⁄₈	5³⁄₈	18	12	57⁴⁄₈	217	37
◆ *Wayne County / Chuck Simmons / Chuck Simmons / 1988*											
251¹⁄₈	28¹⁄₈	27⁷⁄₈	26³⁄₈	31⁵⁄₈	6	6¹⁄₈	10	9	42⁶⁄₈	218	38
◆ *Iron County / James C. Howard / James C. Howard / 1987*											
250⁵⁄₈	25³⁄₈	25³⁄₈	22²⁄₈	37⁶⁄₈	5¹⁄₈	5¹⁄₈	13	10	53⁷⁄₈	224	39
◆ *Millard County / Walter D. LeFevre / Walter D. LeFevre / 1968*											
247⁷⁄₈	25⁶⁄₈	26	25³⁄₈	36⁶⁄₈	5⁴⁄₈	5⁴⁄₈	19	17	71⁶⁄₈	259	40
◆ *Weber County / John Lindsay / Robert R. Donaldson / 1966*											
247⁶⁄₈	22⁶⁄₈	22⁵⁄₈	19²⁄₈	33⁴⁄₈	4³⁄₈	5	10	13	64	263	41
◆ *Grand County / Bruce M. Turnbow / Bruce M. Turnbow / 1967*											
247⁴⁄₈	22⁶⁄₈	27	31⁶⁄₈	37⁶⁄₈	6	6⁶⁄₈	14	13	56	268	42
◆ *Tooele County / Murray G. Loveless / Murray G. Loveless / 1949*											
247¹⁄₈	25⁷⁄₈	25	23⁷⁄₈	38⁵⁄₈	5⁶⁄₈	5⁴⁄₈	7	10	38	276	43
◆ *Carbon County / Ralph A. Sanich / Ralph A. Sanich / 1986*											
246⁷⁄₈	25⁵⁄₈	26²⁄₈	26⁵⁄₈	34¹⁄₈	5⁵⁄₈	5⁵⁄₈	10	7	36⁵⁄₈	282	44
◆ *Carbon County / Sherman R. Jensen, Jr. / Sherman R. Jensen, Jr. / 1965*											
245	26⁵⁄₈	26⁷⁄₈	24¹⁄₈	37⁴⁄₈	5³⁄₈	5²⁄₈	12	12	51⁵⁄₈	305	45
◆ *Kane County / Koyle T. Cram / Koyle T. Cram / 1966*											
244⁵⁄₈	27³⁄₈	29³⁄₈	26³⁄₈	36⁷⁄₈	4⁷⁄₈	4⁷⁄₈	8	12	51²⁄₈	310	46
◆ *Summit County / Dewey R. Saxton / Dewey R. Saxton / 1965*											
244²⁄₈	25¹⁄₈	24⁵⁄₈	22⁵⁄₈	37	5	5	12	13	69³⁄₈	316	47
◆ *Wasatch County / Unknown / Ted Clegg / 1938*											
244²⁄₈	25⁶⁄₈	26³⁄₈	22⁷⁄₈	29⁶⁄₈	5²⁄₈	5⁴⁄₈	12	13	53¹⁄₈	316	47
◆ *San Juan County / Phil Acton / Phil Acton / 1966*											
244	26⁴⁄₈	27¹⁄₈	24⁶⁄₈	31¹⁄₈	4⁶⁄₈	4⁶⁄₈	9	10	55	327	49
◆ *East Canyon / Ronald E. Coburn / Ronald E. Coburn / 1961*											
243⁷⁄₈	23⁶⁄₈	23⁷⁄₈	26	36³⁄₈	4⁶⁄₈	4⁶⁄₈	10	11	66	328	50
◆ *Utah County / Zenneth K. Chamberlain / Zenneth K. Chamberlain / 1956*											
243⁵⁄₈	23⁶⁄₈	23²⁄₈	26⁶⁄₈	37⁶⁄₈	4⁴⁄₈	4⁶⁄₈	7	9	42⁷⁄₈	335	51
◆ *Cache County / Albert C. Steffenhagen / A. Ladell Atkinson / 1924*											
241³⁄₈	27¹⁄₈	26⁷⁄₈	26¹⁄₈	32⁶⁄₈	5⁵⁄₈	5⁴⁄₈	13	11	37⁶⁄₈	372	52
◆ *Kane County / Aivars O. Berkis / Aivars O. Berkis / 1987*											
240⁴⁄₈	23⁶⁄₈	23⁵⁄₈	23²⁄₈	31⁴⁄₈	5¹⁄₈	5²⁄₈	11	14	57⁶⁄₈	386	53
◆ *Morgan County / Pietro De Santis / Pietro De Santis / 1982*											

Score	Length of Main Beam		Inside Spread	Greatest Spread	Circumference at Smallest Place between Burr and First Point		Number of Points		Total of Lengths Abnormal Points	All-Time Rank	State Rank
	R	L			R	L	R	L			
◆ *Locality / Hunter / Owner / Date Killed*											
230⅝	24⅛	25²⁄₈	27⁴⁄₈	34⅛	5	5⁴⁄₈	7	10	31⅞	417	54
◆ *San Juan County / Gregory S. Amaral / Gregory S. Amaral / 1988*											

Photograph Courtesy of Edward A. Leo

Edward A. Leo was hunting with Rodger Schroeder and Don Wedemeyer southwest of Chugwater, Wyoming, when he caught up with this high and wide typical mule deer buck that scores 188-2/8 points.

WASHINGTON STATE RECORD
TYPICAL MULE DEER
SCORE: 202
Locality: Chelan Co.   Date: Prior to 1970
Hunter: Unknown
Owner: James M. Brown

WASHINGTON
TYPICAL MULE DEER

Score	Length of Main Beam R	L	Inside Spread	Greatest Spread	Circumference at Smallest Place between Burr and First Point R	L	Number of Points R	L	Total of Lengths Abnormal Points	All-Time Rank	State Rank
					◆ Locality / Hunter / Owner / Date Killed						
202	27²⁄₈	27¹⁄₈	27⁵⁄₈	32²⁄₈	5⁴⁄₈	5⁵⁄₈	5	5	0	119	1
	◆ Chelan County / Unknown / James M. Brown / PR 1970										
200³⁄₈	27⁵⁄₈	27⁴⁄₈	27¹⁄₈	29⁷⁄₈	5⁴⁄₈	5²⁄₈	4	4	0	186	2
	◆ Okanogan County / E.R. Crooks / E.R. Crooks / 1939										
200²⁄₈	27⁵⁄₈	28⁵⁄₈	26	30⁶⁄₈	4⁷⁄₈	5	4	4	0	190	3
	◆ Asotin County / Grant E. Holcomb / Grant E. Holcomb / 1975										
200¹⁄₈	27³⁄₈	27⁶⁄₈	27³⁄₈	0	5³⁄₈	5⁴⁄₈	5	5	0	199	4
	◆ Cashmere / John F. Schurle / William H. Schott / 1913										
196⁵⁄₈	27²⁄₈	26⁶⁄₈	25⁵⁄₈	31⁵⁄₈	6	6	6	6	3⁵⁄₈	369	5
	◆ Chelan County / George Bolton / Welcome Sauer / 1930										
196	25¹⁄₈	25⁴⁄₈	25⁶⁄₈	34⁶⁄₈	5⁷⁄₈	6	5	5	0	414	6
	◆ Ferry County / Owen R. Burgess / Owen R. Burgess / 1982										
186¹⁄₈	28²⁄₈	28³⁄₈	25³⁄₈	29³⁄₈	6⁵⁄₈	6³⁄₈	5	5	0	603	7
	◆ Grant County / Keith A. Heldreth / Keith A. Heldreth / 1992										

Photograph Courtesy of Desiree Gillingham

WASHINGTON STATE RECORD (NEW)
NON-TYPICAL MULE DEER
SCORE: 283 4/8
Locality: Lewis Co.   Date: 1943
Hunter: Quinten R. Grow
Owner: Desiree Gillingham

WASHINGTON

NON-TYPICAL MULE DEER

Score	Length of Main Beam		Inside Spread	Greatest Spread	Circumference at Smallest Place between Burr and First Point		Number of Points		Total of Lengths Abnormal Points	All-Time Rank	State Rank
	R	L			R	L	R	L			
	Locality / Hunter / Owner / Date Killed										
283 $\frac{4}{8}$	26 $\frac{4}{8}$	27 $\frac{5}{8}$	28 $\frac{3}{8}$	37 $\frac{3}{8}$	5	5 $\frac{2}{8}$	14	14	76 $\frac{1}{8}$	33	1
◆ Lewis County / Quinten R. Grow / Desiree Gillingham / 1943											
266 $\frac{1}{8}$	22 $\frac{4}{8}$	22 $\frac{7}{8}$	16 $\frac{4}{8}$	32 $\frac{6}{8}$	5 $\frac{4}{8}$	5 $\frac{1}{8}$	16	13	94 $\frac{5}{8}$	92	2
◆ Stevens County / Joe C. Mally / Steve Mally / 1933											
265 $\frac{2}{8}$	25 $\frac{6}{8}$	24 $\frac{2}{8}$	18	38 $\frac{1}{8}$	5 $\frac{6}{8}$	5 $\frac{2}{8}$	22	18	88 $\frac{4}{8}$	99	3
◆ Blue Mts. / Frank Henriksen / Frank Henriksen / 1961											
261 $\frac{2}{8}$	25 $\frac{2}{8}$	26 $\frac{2}{8}$	24 $\frac{3}{8}$	35	4 $\frac{6}{8}$	5 $\frac{1}{8}$	13	19	90 $\frac{3}{8}$	121	4
◆ Iron Creek / Win Coultas / Win Coultas / 1924											
257 $\frac{6}{8}$	28 $\frac{3}{8}$	27 $\frac{1}{8}$	24 $\frac{2}{8}$	34 $\frac{2}{8}$	5 $\frac{4}{8}$	5 $\frac{4}{8}$	9	13	69 $\frac{4}{8}$	154	5
◆ Leclerc Creek / Ernest Fait / Ernest Fait / 1960											
250 $\frac{7}{8}$	26 $\frac{4}{8}$	27 $\frac{2}{8}$	24	29 $\frac{1}{8}$	5 $\frac{4}{8}$	6	19	13	54 $\frac{1}{8}$	221	6
◆ Chelan County / Ben R. Williamson / Vera T. Williamson / 1951											
250 $\frac{4}{8}$	26 $\frac{1}{8}$	27 $\frac{3}{8}$	28 $\frac{4}{8}$	35 $\frac{3}{8}$	5 $\frac{1}{8}$	5	12	10	53 $\frac{3}{8}$	225	7
◆ Washington / Unknown / Pat Redding / PR 1973											
248 $\frac{6}{8}$	27	25 $\frac{4}{8}$	28	39 $\frac{3}{8}$	5 $\frac{5}{8}$	5 $\frac{6}{8}$	9	14	62	247	8
◆ Okanogan County / Fred C. Heuer / Raymond R. Cross / 1940											
247 $\frac{7}{8}$	23 $\frac{6}{8}$	24	20 $\frac{7}{8}$	34 $\frac{5}{8}$	5	5	14	13	60 $\frac{2}{8}$	259	9
◆ Asotin County / David G. Bennett / David G. Bennett / 1971											
243	25	25 $\frac{5}{8}$	20 $\frac{4}{8}$	33	7 $\frac{1}{8}$	5 $\frac{2}{8}$	15	11	73	342	10
◆ Winthrop / Bruce Miller / Bruce Miller / 1941											

WYOMING STATE RECORD
TYPICAL MULE DEER
SCORE: 217
Locality: Hoback Canyon   Date: 1925
Hunter: Unknown
Owner: Jackson Hole Museum

WYOMING

TYPICAL MULE DEER

Score	Length of Main Beam R	L	Inside Spread	Greatest Spread	Circumference at Smallest Place between Burr and First Point R	L	Number of Points R	L	Total of Lengths Abnormal Points	All-Time Rank	State Rank
217	28⁴⁄₈	28²⁄₈	26⁶⁄₈	30⁶⁄₈	5⁵⁄₈	5⁶⁄₈	6	6	3	2	1

◆ Hoback Canyon / Unknown / Jackson Hole Museum / 1925

| 215⁵⁄₈ | 26⁷⁄₈ | 28¹⁄₈ | 29⁴⁄₈ | 36³⁄₈ | 5³⁄₈ | 5³⁄₈ | 5 | 7 | 5²⁄₈ | 3 | 2 |

◆ Uinta County / Gary L. Albertson / Don Schaufler / 1960

| 211⁶⁄₈ | 29⁷⁄₈ | 29⁶⁄₈ | 30³⁄₈ | 38⁴⁄₈ | 4⁵⁄₈ | 4⁵⁄₈ | 7 | 8 | 7³⁄₈ | 12 | 3 |

◆ Teton County / Robert V. Parke / Robert V. Parke / 1967

| 209³⁄₈ | 26¹⁄₈ | 25⁵⁄₈ | 23⁷⁄₈ | 29⁷⁄₈ | 5 | 4⁶⁄₈ | 5 | 5 | 0 | 21 | 4 |

◆ Lincoln County / L. Victor Clark / L. Victor Clark / 1992

| 207 | 31⁶⁄₈ | 27²⁄₈ | 27⁴⁄₈ | 31⁶⁄₈ | 7 | 7 | 6 | 6 | 15 | 37 | 5 |

◆ Split Rock / Herb Klein / Herb Klein / 1960

| 207 | 26⁷⁄₈ | 28 | 26⁵⁄₈ | 30⁴⁄₈ | 5³⁄₈ | 5³⁄₈ | 5 | 6 | 2⁷⁄₈ | 37 | 5 |

◆ Lincoln County / Al Firenze, Sr. / Al Firenze, Jr. / 1969

| 205⁴⁄₈ | 26⁶⁄₈ | 25⁷⁄₈ | 24⁶⁄₈ | 30¹⁄₈ | 5 | 5 | 5 | 5 | 0 | 57 | 7 |

◆ Lincoln County / John E. Myers / John E. Myers / 1968

| 205²⁄₈ | 27¹⁄₈ | 27⁶⁄₈ | 28¹⁄₈ | 32²⁄₈ | 4⁵⁄₈ | 5 | 5 | 5 | 0 | 63 | 8 |

◆ Carbon County / Shelly R. Risner / Shelly R. Risner / 1986

| 203²⁄₈ | 25³⁄₈ | 25⁷⁄₈ | 24⁶⁄₈ | 33¹⁄₈ | 4⁶⁄₈ | 4⁵⁄₈ | 6 | 7 | 3⁶⁄₈ | 89 | 9 |

◆ Crook County / Ora McGurn / Bob R. Butler / 1957

| 202⁷⁄₈ | 24⁵⁄₈ | 23 | 22¹⁄₈ | 27⁵⁄₈ | 5²⁄₈ | 5²⁄₈ | 5 | 5 | 0 | 98 | 10 |

◆ Lincoln County / Monte J. Brough / Monte J. Brough / 1968

| 202⁴⁄₈ | 29²⁄₈ | 29 | 29⁴⁄₈ | 33¹⁄₈ | 5²⁄₈ | 5¹⁄₈ | 5 | 7 | 4 | 106 | 11 |

◆ Park County / Paul M. Rothermel, Jr. / Paul M. Rothermel, Jr. / 1962

| 202³⁄₈ | 26¹⁄₈ | 27¹⁄₈ | 28³⁄₈ | 30²⁄₈ | 5³⁄₈ | 5⁴⁄₈ | 5 | 5 | 0 | 111 | 12 |

◆ Sublette County / Derek L. Kendrick / Derek L. Kendrick / 1992

| 202 | 26 | 24⁶⁄₈ | 27⁴⁄₈ | 32¹⁄₈ | 5 | 4⁷⁄₈ | 5 | 5 | 0 | 119 | 13 |

◆ Sweetwater County / Arnold A. Bethke / Arnold A. Bethke / 1976

| 201⁶⁄₈ | 26 | 26⁵⁄₈ | 21²⁄₈ | 27⁴⁄₈ | 5 | 5 | 5 | 4 | 0 | 132 | 14 |

◆ Afton / Bernard Domries / Bernard Domries / 1967

| 201³⁄₈ | 26⁵⁄₈ | 25⁷⁄₈ | 23³⁄₈ | 26 | 5²⁄₈ | 5²⁄₈ | 6 | 7 | 4²⁄₈ | 144 | 15 |

◆ Sublette County / Jerry C. Lopez / Jerry C. Lopez / 1985

| 200⁵⁄₈ | 25²⁄₈ | 25²⁄₈ | 25²⁄₈ | 30³⁄₈ | 5 | 5²⁄₈ | 6 | 5 | 2¹⁄₈ | 173 | 16 |

◆ Lincoln County / John Myers / John Myers / 1973

| 200²⁄₈ | 25 | 25¹⁄₈ | 22⁴⁄₈ | 37⁴⁄₈ | 5⁶⁄₈ | 5⁶⁄₈ | 6 | 6 | 2⁶⁄₈ | 190 | 17 |

◆ Battle Mt. / Ron Vance / Ronald Crawford / 1963

Score	Length of Main Beam R L	Inside Spread	Greatest Spread	Circumference at Smallest Place between Burr and First Point R L	Number of Points R L	Total of Lengths Abnormal Points	All-Time Rank	State Rank
	♦ *Locality / Hunter / Owner / Date Killed*							
200	25⅞ 25⁴⁄₈	21⅞	29⁴⁄₈	5⅝ 5⅝	5 7	3⅞	203	18
	♦ *Hot Springs County / Basil C. Bradbury / Basil C. Bradbury / 1977*							
199⅛	27 26²⁄₈	27²⁄₈	29⅝	5⅝ 5⁴⁄₈	5 6	1⅛	243	19
	♦ *Laramie County / David L. Shannon / David L. Shannon / 1981*							
199	25⅛ 26⅜	23⁴⁄₈	27²⁄₈	5⁴⁄₈ 5⅛	5 5	0	248	20
	♦ *Park County / Lois M. Pelzel / Lois M. Pelzel / 1965*							
198⅝	25⅛ 25²⁄₈	23⅛	27⅞	4⅞ 5	5 7	2⁴⁄₈	257	21
	♦ *Carbon County / M. Gary Muske / M. Gary Muske / 1968*							
198⁴⁄₈	28⅝ 28⁴⁄₈	24⅝	28⅝	5⅜ 5⅜	5 6	1⅝	262	22
	♦ *Afton / Ray M. Vincent / Ray M. Vincent / 1967*							
198⅛	25⁴⁄₈ 26⅛	26²⁄₈	34	5²⁄₈ 5²⁄₈	5 5	0	280	23
	♦ *Natrona County / Kerry J. Clegg / Kerry J. Clegg / 1983*							
197⁶⁄₈	27²⁄₈ 28	25²⁄₈	29⁶⁄₈	4⁶⁄₈ 4⁶⁄₈	5 5	0	302	24
	♦ *Encampment / Ralph E. Platt, Jr. / Ralph E. Platt, Jr. / 1936*							
197⁶⁄₈	26⅝ 27⅝	23⅞	33⁴⁄₈	4⁶⁄₈ 5	8 8	12⅜	302	24
	♦ *Teton County / John W. Farlow, Jr. / John W. Farlow, Jr. / 1971*							
197⁴⁄₈	26⅜ 25⅞	24⅞	30⅛	4⁶⁄₈ 4⅞	5 6	2⅝	317	26
	♦ *Uinta County / Ken L. Vernon / Ken L. Vernon / 1968*							
197⅜	24⅞ 24⅝	27²⁄₈	33⅛	4⅝ 4⁴⁄₈	5 4	1²⁄₈	324	27
	♦ *Lincoln County / Kim L. King / Kim L. King / 1990*							
197²⁄₈	27⅜ 27⅜	27⅛	36⅛	5²⁄₈ 5⁴⁄₈	6 5	1⅞	333	28
	♦ *Afton / Robert Williams / Robert Williams / 1960*							
196⅞	25⅜ 25²⁄₈	25⅜	31⁶⁄₈	5 5	5 5	0	357	29
	♦ *Lincoln County / William L. Lewis / William L. Lewis / 1990*							
196⅝	26 25⅞	22⁶⁄₈	27⅜	4⁴⁄₈ 4⁶⁄₈	6 5	2⅛	369	30
	♦ *Dubois / P.C. Alfred Dorow / P.C. Alfred Dorow / 1960*							
196⅝	23⅞ 24	22⅝	31⁴⁄₈	4⁶⁄₈ 4⅞	5 5	0	369	30
	♦ *Lincoln County / Chester P. Michalski / Chester P. Michalski / 1974*							
196⁴⁄₈	24⁴⁄₈ 25⅛	24	33⅜	4⅝ 4⅝	7 5	4	379	32
	♦ *Teton County / John C. Branca III / John C. Branca III / 1991*							
196⅜	26⅜ 27⅛	25⅛	31⁴⁄₈	5⁶⁄₈ 5⁴⁄₈	6 6	7	391	33
	♦ *Sublette County / S. Kim Bonnett / S. Kim Bonnett / 1978*							
196²⁄₈	27⅛ 27⅜	25⅛	31	5⅜ 5²⁄₈	5 6	2⅜	396	34
	♦ *Sweetwater County / Donald H. Pabst / Donald H. Pabst / 1962*							
196²⁄₈	24 25	20⁶⁄₈	27⁶⁄₈	4²⁄₈ 4⅝	5 5	0	396	34
	♦ *Big Horn Mts. / Ruth Davis / Ruth Davis / 1968*							

Score	Length of Main Beam		Inside Spread	Greatest Spread	Circumference at Smallest Place between Burr and First Point		Number of Points		Total of Lengths Abnormal Points	All-Time Rank	State Rank
	R	L			R	L	R	L			
♦ Locality / Hunter / Owner / Date Killed											
196	26 2/8	25 4/8	22	28 7/8	5	4 7/8	5	6	2 6/8	414	36
♦ Fremont County / Peter R. Ardlen / Peter R. Ardlen / 1992											
195 7/8	28	27 6/8	24 3/8	30 5/8	4 6/8	4 6/8	5	5	2 6/8	424	37
♦ Teton County / Lewis E. Sharp / Lewis E. Sharp / 1990											
195 7/8	25 2/8	23 5/8	19 1/8	27 1/8	5 5/8	5 3/8	5	5	0	424	37
♦ Teton County / Douglas L. Wynn / Douglas L. Wynn / 1994											
195 6/8	25 3/8	24 3/8	24 6/8	29 1/8	4 5/8	4 5/8	5	5	0	433	39
♦ Teton County / Joel M. Leatham / Joel M. Leatham / 1979											
195 3/8	27 3/8	26 7/8	26 5/8	29 7/8	4 6/8	4 6/8	5	5	0	464	40
♦ Natrona County / Richard Ullery / Richard Ullery / 1977											
195 2/8	28 5/8	29 7/8	29	31 5/8	5 5/8	5 7/8	5	5	0	472	41
♦ Niobrara County / David E. Pauna / David E. Pauna / 1976											
195 2/8	23 3/8	24 6/8	21 4/8	27 3/8	5 1/8	5 2/8	5	5	0	472	41
♦ Sublette County / John R. Birchett / John R. Birchett / 1981											
195	24 2/8	24 4/8	22 3/8	31 7/8	6 2/8	6 1/8	7	5	5 3/8	491	43
♦ Sublette County / Norm Busselle / Norm Busselle / 1977											
194	23 3/8	25 1/8	22 4/8	25 6/8	4 6/8	4 7/8	5	5	0	508	44
♦ Sublette County / James J. McBride / James J. McBride / 1979											
192 5/8	25	24 1/8	20 6/8	28 2/8	5 1/8	5 1/8	5	6	1 3/8	518	45
♦ Park County / LaVerne M. Nelson / LaVerne M. Nelson / 1992											
192	26 6/8	26 2/8	25 6/8	28 6/8	5	4 7/8	5	5	0	524	46
♦ Teton County / Steven G. Coy / Steven G. Coy / 1992											
190 3/8	25 4/8	25 1/8	21 5/8	24 1/8	4 4/8	4 6/8	5	8	6	543	47
♦ Lincoln County / Jerry A. McAllister / Jerry A. McAllister / 1990											
190	27 2/8	27 5/8	27 4/8	31	4 6/8	4 7/8	7	7	10	548	48
♦ Carbon County / Stephen M. Murnan / Stephen M. Murnan / 1990											
188 7/8	26 4/8	27	23 6/8	32 5/8	4 6/8	4 6/8	8	7	10 5/8	561	49
♦ Sublette County / George Shuleshko / George Shuleshko / 1986											
188 2/8	23 1/8	22 6/8	22	29	4 6/8	5	5	6	3	572	50
♦ Platte County / Edward A. Leo / Edward A. Leo / 1993											
186	25 2/8	26	28 4/8	30 4/8	5 2/8	5 1/8	5	5	0	606	51
♦ Park County / Darren W. Vorhies / Darren W. Vorhies / 1991											
185 7/8	24 3/8	24 3/8	22 1/8	29	4 5/8	4 7/8	6	5	1 4/8	609	52
♦ Lincoln County / James P. Speck / James P. Speck / 1987											
185	21 2/8	22 2/8	18 6/8	30 6/8	4 3/8	4 3/8	5	5	0	620	53
♦ Lincoln County / Edward D. Whitmore / Edward D. Whitmore / 1990											

Score	Length of Main Beam R	Length of Main Beam L	Inside Spread	Greatest Spread	Circumference at Smallest Place between Burr and First Point R	Circumference at Smallest Place between Burr and First Point L	Number of Points R	Number of Points L	Total of Lengths Abnormal Points	All-Time Rank	State Rank
♦ *Locality / Hunter / Owner / Date Killed*											
185	23	23 1/8	21 4/8	29 4/8	4 7/8	4 7/8	6	5	4	620	53
♦ *Sublette County / William P. Price / William P. Price / 1991*											
182	23 4/8	23 1/8	25	29 2/8	5	5	5	5	0	626	55
♦ *Lincoln County / Charlie Bridges / Lee Bridges / 1964*											

Photograph Courtesy of Stephen M. Murnan

Stephen M. Murnan and the typical mule deer buck he took near Baggs, Wyoming, in 1990 in a winter wonderland blanketed by six inches of fresh snow. Stephen's buck didn't make the all-time records book in 1990 as the minimum score in effect at that time was 195 points. The all-time minimum was lowered to 190 points in 1993.

Photograph by Paul Rock

WYOMING FOURTH PLACE
NON-TYPICAL MULE DEER
SCORE: 260 $\frac{2}{8}$
Locality: Pinedale   Date: 1965
Hunter: James H. Straley
Owner: Monte W. Straley

WYOMING

NON-TYPICAL MULE DEER

Score	Length of Main Beam R	L	Inside Spread	Greatest Spread	Circumference at Smallest Place between Burr and First Point R	L	Number of Points R	L	Total of Lengths Abnormal Points	All-Time Rank	State Rank
	Locality / Hunter / Owner / Date Killed										
293 7/8	26 4/8	24 6/8	27 6/8	39 1/8	5 6/8	5 4/8	18	16	99 1/8	22	1
	Wyoming / J.B. Marvin, Jr. / Unknown / PR 1924										
272 3/8	28 4/8	28 2/8	28 4/8	42 3/8	5 1/8	5 5/8	11	12	81 3/8	69	2
	Albany County / S.A. Lawson / Acad. Nat. Sci., Phil. / 1905										
266 7/8	26	25 1/8	22 4/8	33	6 4/8	6 1/8	13	15	73 3/8	87	3
	Wyoming / J.L. Kemmerer / Am. Mus. Nat. Hist. / 1905										
260 2/8	26 7/8	25	21 2/8	28 5/8	4 6/8	4 5/8	12	13	73 6/8	127	4
	Pinedale / James H. Straley / Monte W. Straley / 1965										
259 5/8	27 2/8	26 6/8	24 1/8	33 4/8	5 2/8	5 2/8	12	13	59 6/8	137	5
	Glendo / Rudolph B. Johnson / Rudolph B. Johnson / 1961										
258 6/8	21	22	16 2/8	30 4/8	10	5	18	18	86 2/8	141	6
	Sweetwater County / John A. Fabian / John A. Fabian / 1974										
257 4/8	24 5/8	23	19 2/8	35 3/8	5 4/8	5 4/8	11	11	57	159	7
	Encampment / Sam Whitney / Mrs. Sam Whitney / 1946										
256 6/8	24 6/8	26 4/8	20 4/8	33 1/8	5	5 1/8	12	15	60 2/8	170	8
	Hoback Basin / Buck Heide / Buck Heide / 1968										
253 3/8	24 4/8	24 3/8	20 4/8	34 3/8	5 3/8	5 3/8	11	11	52 7/8	195	9
	Rawlins / A.H. Henkel / A.H. Henkel / 1952										
253 1/8	24 2/8	23 2/8	24 6/8	37 2/8	5 4/8	5 1/8	16	12	67 7/8	200	10
	Sweetwater County / John C. Erickson / M. Painovich & J. Etcheverry / 1932										
250 1/8	23 4/8	22 7/8	17 7/8	37 6/8	4 5/8	4 6/8	14	14	80	232	11
	Sheridan County / Richard Legerski / Richard Legerski / 1976										
249 2/8	24 3/8	23 5/8	27	36 7/8	4 6/8	4 6/8	10	10	63 1/8	240	12
	Lincoln County / Robert J. Stallone / Robert J. Stallone / 1986										
248	26	27 1/8	22	36 1/8	5	5	12	9	45 4/8	256	13
	Pinedale / Lyle Rosendahl / Lyle Rosendahl / 1960										
246 4/8	26 2/8	27 2/8	30 4/8	38 4/8	4 4/8	4 5/8	9	9	36 6/8	288	14
	Lincoln County / Terry Barton / Dana J. Hollinger / 1989										
244 7/8	25 6/8	26 4/8	22 1/8	39 7/8	4 7/8	4 7/8	11	9	42 2/8	308	15
	Lincoln County / Brian H. Suter / Brian H. Suter / 1981										
244 5/8	25 5/8	24 2/8	22 1/8	40 6/8	5 6/8	5 6/8	13	14	54	310	16
	Teton County / Vern Shinkle / Vern Shinkle / 1968										
244 2/8	22 6/8	21 6/8	19 4/8	30 6/8	4 4/8	4 7/8	9	13	67 2/8	316	17
	Fremont County / Warren V. Spriggs / Warren V. Spriggs / 1962										

Score	Length of Main Beam R	L	Inside Spread	Greatest Spread	Circumference at Smallest Place between Burr and First Point R	L	Number of Points R	L	Total of Lengths Abnormal Points	All-Time Rank	State Rank
	◆ Locality / Hunter / Owner / Date Killed										
244 1/8	25	26 2/8	29 2/8	34	5 5/8	5 6/8	11	12	45 3/8	323	18
	◆ Split Rock / Herb Klein / Herb Klein / 1957										
244 1/8	24 1/8	24 2/8	28	34	4 4/8	4 4/8	9	10	75 5/8	323	18
	◆ Big Horn County / Picked Up / Henry D. Frey / 1978										
243 1/8	24 4/8	24 3/8	21 4/8	33 1/8	5	5	12	7	44 3/8	339	20
	◆ Converse County / William E. Goswick / William E. Goswick / 1968										
242 7/8	24 4/8	24 1/8	22 6/8	28 4/8	4 7/8	5	10	11	72 7/8	345	21
	◆ Sheridan / J.M. Blakeman / J.M. Blakeman / 1952										
241 6/8	24 7/8	23 5/8	21 6/8	32 7/8	5 6/8	6	17	19	57 2/8	366	22
	◆ Hot Springs County / Picked up / John A. Kotan, Jr. / 1983										
241 1/8	27 1/8	26 1/8	26 6/8	35 2/8	6 3/8	6 1/8	11	12	33 5/8	377	23
	◆ Lincoln County / Mark C. Lafferty / Mark C. Lafferty / 1994										
232 5/8	24 4/8	25 7/8	17 5/8	30 5/8	4 3/8	4 3/8	13	10	40 2/8	411	24
	◆ Teton County / Bruce K. McRae / Bruce K. McRae / 1986										
228 7/8	26	26 7/8	23 4/8	34 6/8	4 2/8	4 3/8	11	9	46 3/8	419	25
	◆ Sheridan County / Everette Spence / Gerald Combs / 1967										
262 7/8	27 4/8	27 5/8	25 1/8	34 6/8	5	4 7/8	12	15	68 2/8	*	*
	◆ Teton County / Thomas R. Ford / Thomas R. Ford / 1984										

Photograph Courtesy of Jeffrey S. Reichert

Alberta was experiencing an Indian summer in November 1989 when Jeffrey S. Reichert caught up with this typical mule deer on Teepee Creek. It scores 193-6/8 points.

Photograph Courtesy of Dale Ophus

ALBERTA PROVINCE RECORD (NEW)
TYPICAL MULE DEER
SCORE: 201⅝
Locality: Saddle Hills   Date: 1989
Hunter: Dale Ophus

ALBERTA

TYPICAL MULE DEER

Score	Length of Main Beam R	Length of Main Beam L	Inside Spread	Greatest Spread	Circumference at Smallest Place between Burr and First Point R	Circumference at Smallest Place between Burr and First Point L	Number of Points R	Number of Points L	Total of Lengths Abnormal Points	All-Time Rank	State Rank
♦ *Locality / Hunter / Owner / Date Killed*											
201 6/8	25 7/8	26 1/8	26 4/8	30 6/8	6 1/8	6 4/8	6	6	2 7/8	132	1
♦ *Saddle Hills / Dale Ophus / Dale Ophus / 1989*											
199 4/8	26 7/8	27 3/8	25 6/8	28 7/8	5 6/8	5 6/8	4	4	0	222	2
♦ *Medicine Hat / Duncan Baldie / D. Baldie & K.W. McKenzie / 1981*											
198 6/8	23 4/8	22 2/8	21 6/8	26 3/8	5 1/8	5 2/8	5	5	0	255	3
♦ *Hines Creek / Charles Lundgard / Charles Lundgard / 1960*											
193 6/8	25	26 2/8	22	27 3/8	4 4/8	4 5/8	6	5	2 4/8	510	4
♦ *Smoky River / Jeffrey S. Reichert / Jeffrey S. Reichert / 1989*											
191 7/8	25 2/8	24 7/8	23 5/8	31 2/8	4 7/8	5	5	5	0	527	5
♦ *Carbondale River / Michael Pearce / Michael Pearce / 1992*											
190 2/8	24 4/8	23 6/8	21	26	4 6/8	4 5/8	5	7	4 2/8	546	6
♦ *Sounding Lake / Brian J. Rehman / Brian J. Rehman / 1992*											
189 5/8	26 1/8	24 7/8	27 5/8	29 6/8	5 3/8	5 1/8	5	5	0	552	7
♦ *Forestburg / Ron Sinclair / Ron Sinclair / 1990*											
188 3/8	25 6/8	25 2/8	23 1/8	27 6/8	5	5	5	5	0	569	8
♦ *Tangent / David Hirsch / David Hirsch / 1990*											
186 4/8	25 6/8	25 1/8	24 5/8	31	5 2/8	4 7/8	8	7	16 7/8	600	9
♦ *Saddle Hills / Maurice Southmayd / Maurice Southmayd / 1989*											

Photograph from Boone & Crockett Club Archives

ALBERTA PROVINCE RECORD
WORLD'S RECORD
NON-TYPICAL MULE DEER
SCORE: 355 $\frac{2}{8}$
Locality: Chip Lake   Date: 1926
Hunter: Ed Broder

ALBERTA

NON-TYPICAL MULE DEER

Score	Length of Main Beam		Inside Spread	Greatest Spread	Circumference at Smallest Place between Burr and First Point		Number of Points		Total of Lengths Abnormal Points	All-Time Rank	State Rank
	R	L			R	L	R	L			
♦ Locality / Hunter / Owner / Date Killed											
355²⁄₈	26²⁄₈	26¹⁄₈	22¹⁄₈	38⁵⁄₈	5	4⁷⁄₈	22	21	147⁷⁄₈	1	1
♦ Chip Lake / Ed Broder / Ed Broder / 1926											
256⁷⁄₈	25⁵⁄₈	26¹⁄₈	22⁶⁄₈	27	5³⁄₈	5⁵⁄₈	10	15	59⁷⁄₈	167	2
♦ Moose Creek / Henry Thomas / Henry Thomas / 1993											
254⁴⁄₈	25¹⁄₈	24	18⁵⁄₈	30¹⁄₈	5⁴⁄₈	5²⁄₈	13	15	88⁵⁄₈	189	3
♦ Maloy / Otto Schmalzbauer / Otto Schmalzbauer / 1930											
252	22⁷⁄₈	22¹⁄₈	24⁶⁄₈	37	5⁴⁄₈	5⁴⁄₈	18	16	95¹⁄₈	209	4
♦ Grease Creek / Jack McCallum / J.H. Fry / PR 1940											
247⁵⁄₈	28⁴⁄₈	26⁷⁄₈	24⁴⁄₈	33	6	5⁷⁄₈	10	13	38⁷⁄₈	265	5
♦ Waterton Park / Eric Westergreen / Eric Westergreen / 1941											
245²⁄₈	23⁶⁄₈	24⁶⁄₈	24³⁄₈	34⁵⁄₈	5¹⁄₈	5	18	12	55¹⁄₈	302	6
♦ Lac Lariche / Julius Hagen / Olaf Hagen / 1945											
243⁶⁄₈	24¹⁄₈	27²⁄₈	27³⁄₈	36⁷⁄₈	5⁵⁄₈	5⁴⁄₈	16	18	70⁶⁄₈	331	7
♦ Slave Lake / R.W.H. Eben-Ebenau / R.W.H. Eben-Ebenau / 1930											
241⁵⁄₈	23⁴⁄₈	22³⁄₈	21⁷⁄₈	31¹⁄₈	6²⁄₈	6	15	16	61⁶⁄₈	367	8
♦ Red Deer River / Carl J. Peterson / Carl J. Peterson / 1993											
238²⁄₈	23⁶⁄₈	24¹⁄₈	26⁵⁄₈	31²⁄₈	5¹⁄₈	5	16	11	50¹⁄₈	403	9
♦ Walsh / Rick M. MacDonald / Rick M. MacDonald / 1987											

BRITISH COLUMBIA PROVINCE RECORD
TYPICAL MULE DEER
SCORE: 199$\frac{5}{8}$
Locality: Princeton   Date: 1979
Hunter: Buddy D. Baker

BRITISH COLUMBIA

TYPICAL MULE DEER

Score	Length of Main Beam R	Length of Main Beam L	Inside Spread	Greatest Spread	Circumference at Smallest Place between Burr and First Point R	Circumference at Smallest Place between Burr and First Point L	Number of Points R	Number of Points L	Total of Lengths Abnormal Points	All-Time Rank	State Rank
♦ *Locality / Hunter / Owner / Date Killed*											
199 5/8	27 5/8	26	21 5/8	25 3/8	5 5/8	5 6/8	5	5	0	220	1
♦ *Princeton / Buddy D. Baker / Buddy D. Baker / 1979*											
199 2/8	28 5/8	27 6/8	25	32	5 4/8	5 4/8	5	5	0	232	2
♦ *Gable Mt. / Jack V. Quiring / Jack V. Quiring / 1988*											
197 7/8	28 1/8	27 6/8	24 5/8	27 5/8	5 2/8	5 3/8	5	5	0	295	3
♦ *Rossland / Robert Simm / Robert Simm / 1968*											
197 6/8	26 6/8	24 7/8	23 6/8	31	5 3/8	5 4/8	5	5	0	302	4
♦ *Botanie Lake / Dennis R. Milton / Dennis R. Milton / 1991*											
197 5/8	28 6/8	27 4/8	23 1/8	27 4/8	5 1/8	5 1/8	5	5	0	308	5
♦ *Kootenay River / Raymond Carry / Raymond Carry / 1982*											
196 7/8	27 5/8	27	25 1/8	29 6/8	5 1/8	5 1/8	5	5	0	357	6
♦ *Scherf Creek / Manuela Selby / Manuela Selby / 1984*											
195 5/8	27 4/8	27 6/8	24 1/8	32 7/8	6	5 7/8	7	7	12	446	7
♦ *Slocan Valley / John Braun / John Braun / 1962*											
195 4/8	26 2/8	26 4/8	24 2/8	29 2/8	5 3/8	5 2/8	5	5	0	456	8
♦ *Princeton / Glen Stadler / Glen Stadler / 1958*											
195 1/8	27	29 5/8	29 1/8	31 7/8	5 7/8	6	5	5	0	482	9
♦ *Fruitvale / Allan Endersby / Allan Endersby / 1968*											
192 3/8	26 3/8	26 6/8	25 5/8	30 2/8	5 1/8	5 3/8	5	5	0	522	10
♦ *Williams Lake / Evan D. Howarth / Evan D. Howarth / 1994*											
188 1/8	25 1/8	27 1/8	25	31 2/8	4 4/8	4 3/8	5	5	1 5/8	574	11
♦ *East Pine River / Arthur L. Summers / Arthur L. Summers / 1993*											
187	25	24 5/8	22 2/8	27 1/8	4 5/8	4 5/8	6	5	2 4/8	590	12
♦ *Lone Prairie / Gordon J. Semenuk / Lorry Douglas / 1992*											
185 3/8	26	26 1/8	21 1/8	30 6/8	5 1/8	5 1/8	8	7	13 2/8	618	13
♦ *Harris Creek / Ian S. Mackenzie / Ian S. Mackenzie / 1992*											

BRITISH COLUMBIA PROVINCE RECORD
NON-TYPICAL MULE DEER
SCORE: 265 ³⁄₈
Locality: Tyaughton River   Date: 1970
Hunter: Terry E. Crawford

BRITISH COLUMBIA
NON-TYPICAL MULE DEER

Score	Length of Main Beam R	L	Inside Spread	Greatest Spread	Circumference at Smallest Place between Burr and First Point R	L	Number of Points R	L	Total of Lengths Abnormal Points	All-Time Rank	State Rank
Locality / Hunter / Owner / Date Killed											
265 3/8	25 6/8	25 1/8	21 5/8	29 4/8	5 3/8	5 3/8	13	14	73 4/8	98	1
◆ Tyaughton River / Terry E. Crawford / Terry E. Crawford / 1970											
258 2/8	29 5/8	30 5/8	29 3/8	39 1/8	6 6/8	6 7/8	15	14	47 7/8	147	2
◆ Rock Creek / George Whiting / B.C. Game Dept. / 1909											
256 1/8	26 2/8	27 4/8	21 6/8	34 1/8	4 6/8	4 5/8	15	13	64 5/8	175	3
◆ Summit Lake / Herald A. Friedenberger / Herald A. Friedenberger / 1988											
251 4/8	29 1/8	28 2/8	22 1/8	30 4/8	5 7/8	5 5/8	14	9	44 7/8	216	4
◆ Martha Creek / Charles J. McKinney / Charles J. McKinney / 1992											
250 4/8	26	27 2/8	27 3/8	33	5 4/8	6	11	9	54 4/8	225	5
◆ Quesnel / Picked Up / Paul W. Stafford / 1984											
245 7/8	23 1/8	24 5/8	17 6/8	28 2/8	4 7/8	5 2/8	14	16	83 5/8	297	6
◆ Tyee Lake / Harold Bartha / Harold Bartha / 1961											
244 5/8	26	25	18 6/8	28 6/8	5 5/8	5 4/8	15	20	63 7/8	310	7
◆ Rossland / Victor Mattiazzi / Victor Mattiazzi / 1970											
242	25 7/8	25 6/8	26 2/8	33 2/8	5 2/8	5 1/8	14	8	68 7/8	359	8
◆ Porcupine Ridge / Unknown / Rick Berreth / 1985											
241 3/8	19	24 6/8	20	31 6/8	6 2/8	6 4/8	12	15	63 7/8	372	9
◆ Nakusp / Frank Vicen / Frank Vicen / 1967											
241 1/8	24 3/8	24 5/8	24 6/8	32	5 7/8	5 7/8	16	13	59	377	10
◆ Bloom Creek / Ron Yerbury / Ron Yerbury / 1992											
240	28	28 2/8	25	32 3/8	5 4/8	5 4/8	7	10	42 2/8	396	11
◆ Kamloops / Ralph McLean / Ralph McLean / 1960											
237 5/8	25 4/8	26	21 7/8	32	4 7/8	4 6/8	8	9	51 2/8	405	12
◆ Lynx Creek / J. Gregory Simmons / J. Gregory Simmons / 1989											

Photograph Courtesy of Howard Jackle

SASKATCHEWAN PROVINCE RECORD (TIE)
TYPICAL MULE DEER
SCORE: 199 $\frac{2}{8}$
Locality: Great Sand Hills   Date: 1991
Hunter: Howard Jackle

SASKATCHEWAN
TYPICAL MULE DEER

Score	Length of Main Beam R	Length of Main Beam L	Inside Spread	Greatest Spread	Circumference at Smallest Place between Burr and First Point R	Circumference at Smallest Place between Burr and First Point L	Number of Points R	Number of Points L	Total of Lengths Abnormal Points	All-Time Rank	State Rank

♦ Locality / Hunter / Owner / Date Killed

199²⁄₈	27¹⁄₈	25⁴⁄₈	26	30¹⁄₈	5	5²⁄₈	7	5	5⁴⁄₈	232	1

♦ *Beechy / Marvin Taylor / Marvin Taylor / 1961*

199²⁄₈	26⁶⁄₈	26³⁄₈	25³⁄₈	27⁶⁄₈	5³⁄₈	4⁷⁄₈	5	6	2³⁄₈	232	1

♦ *Great Sand Hills / Howard Jackle / Howard Jackle / 1991*

197⁵⁄₈	22⁷⁄₈	22	22¹⁄₈	27⁴⁄₈	4⁵⁄₈	4⁴⁄₈	5	5	0	308	3

♦ *Major / Art Heintz / Art Heintz / 1961*

197⁵⁄₈	25⁶⁄₈	26¹⁄₈	19⁵⁄₈	22⁷⁄₈	5²⁄₈	5²⁄₈	5	5	0	308	3

♦ *Beechy / Brett E. Seidle / Brett E. Seidle / 1983*

197⁴⁄₈	28¹⁄₈	27³⁄₈	26¹⁄₈	34⁴⁄₈	5	5	9	5	13⁷⁄₈	317	5

♦ *Tompkins / Jim Hardin / Jim Hardin / 1994*

197²⁄₈	26⁴⁄₈	26⁴⁄₈	21⁶⁄₈	24⁴⁄₈	7	6⁶⁄₈	7	5	4	333	6

♦ *Beechy / Pete Perrin / Pete Perrin / 1947*

197	25⁷⁄₈	26⁴⁄₈	21⁷⁄₈	25³⁄₈	5²⁄₈	5	5	6	1¹⁄₈	347	7

♦ *Suffner Lake / Picked Up / Macklin Wildlife Federation / PR 1992*

195²⁄₈	26⁴⁄₈	25⁵⁄₈	26⁴⁄₈	32⁴⁄₈	4²⁄₈	4²⁄₈	5	5	0	472	8

♦ *Antelope Lake / Doug Westergaard / Doug Westergaard / 1977*

194⁵⁄₈	24⁷⁄₈	25²⁄₈	21³⁄₈	29⁵⁄₈	4⁵⁄₈	4⁵⁄₈	6	6	8⁴⁄₈	503	9

♦ *Cabri Lake / Dean R. Francis / Dean R. Francis / 1991*

186²⁄₈	26	25¹⁄₈	25³⁄₈	28⁶⁄₈	5	5¹⁄₈	5	6	1³⁄₈	602	10

♦ *Demaine / Bruce C. Brown / Bruce C. Brown / 1990*

Photograph Courtesy of Don Schaufler

SASKATCHEWAN PROVINCE RECORD
NON-TYPICAL MULE DEER
SCORE: 282⅝
Locality: Cabri   Date: 1962
Hunter: Robert Comba
Owner: Don Schaufler

SASKATCHEWAN
NON-TYPICAL MULE DEER

Score	Length of Main Beam R	L	Inside Spread	Greatest Spread	Circumference at Smallest Place between Burr and First Point R	L	Number of Points R	L	Total of Lengths Abnormal Points	All-Time Rank	State Rank
	◆ Locality / Hunter / Owner / Date Killed										
282 6/8	24 4/8	24 2/8	25 4/8	35 5/8	5 4/8	5 2/8	14	16	96	35	1
	◆ Cabri / Robert Comba / Don Schaufler / 1962										
282 2/8	25 3/8	25 6/8	24	31 5/8	7	6 2/8	17	13	71 2/8	37	2
	◆ Sasktchewan / Herman Cox / Herman Cox / 1947										
280 2/8	25 7/8	24 4/8	24 2/8	34 1/8	6	6	10	15	88 4/8	39	3
	◆ Otthon / Unknown / Don Schaufler / 1940										
275 6/8	25 4/8	26 3/8	19 2/8	31	5	5 2/8	20	16	82	51	4
	◆ Dahlton / Jim Hewitt / Jim Hewitt / 1932										
275 6/8	24 5/8	25 6/8	25 6/8	31 4/8	4 7/8	4 7/8	11	16	79 2/8	51	4
	◆ Red Deer River / K. Michael Weisbrod / K. Michael Weisbrod / 1992										
268 5/8	27	25 1/8	25 1/8	36	5	5 4/8	14	16	88 6/8	77	6
	◆ Leader / Cocks Brothers / Richard Jensen / 1954										
268 1/8	27 4/8	27 7/8	30 3/8	38 3/8	5 2/8	5 5/8	14	14	68 4/8	81	7
	◆ Elbow / Allan J. Selzler / Allan J. Selzler / 1986										
256 4/8	24	24 5/8	25 2/8	34 2/8	6	6 1/8	12	11	57 7/8	172	8
	◆ Portreeve / Mike Spies / Mike Spies / 1947										
253 4/8	25 6/8	26 5/8	30 2/8	34 6/8	4 6/8	4 6/8	11	11	58 5/8	193	9
	◆ East End / Henry Leroy / Henry Leroy / 1960										
248	23 3/8	22 4/8	23 2/8	33 1/8	5 6/8	5 6/8	12	14	57 6/8	256	10
	◆ Val Marie / J. Milton Brown / J. Milton Brown / 1958										
247 7/8	21 2/8	21 6/8	24 6/8	36 5/8	5 4/8	5 7/8	9	10	61 5/8	259	11
	◆ Cabri / Enos Mitchell, Jr. / Enos Mitchell, Jr. / 1960										
243 7/8	24 1/8	27	24 6/8	29 1/8	4 4/8	4 4/8	18	12	81 3/8	328	12
	◆ St. Cyr Hills / Raymond Jeancart / Raymond Jeancart / 1963										
243 6/8	22 6/8	25 7/8	26 3/8	33 2/8	5 4/8	5 4/8	12	11	50 7/8	331	13
	◆ Montrose / Gordon G. Pattison / Gordon G. Pattison / 1992										
242 3/8	23 1/8	22 3/8	17 3/8	29 2/8	4 7/8	5	12	12	61 4/8	352	14
	◆ Arborfield / Joseph Fournier / Joseph Fournier / 1930										
242 1/8	20 7/8	23 2/8	17 4/8	31 1/8	6	5 7/8	12	11	77 1/8	356	15
	◆ Cabri / Gordon Millward / Gordon Millward / 1960										
241 7/8	24	25 4/8	18 5/8	25	5 7/8	6	14	11	65 6/8	362	16
	◆ Great Sand Hills / A. Bruce LaRose / A. Bruce LaRose / 1989										
240 4/8	25 5/8	24 4/8	21 6/8	29 2/8	5 4/8	5 4/8	10	9	45 2/8	386	17
	◆ Great Sand Hills / Emile T. Paradis / Emile T. Paradis / 1989										

Score	Length of Main Beam		Inside Spread	Greatest Spread	Circumference at Smallest Place between Burr and First Point		Number of Points		Total of Lengths Abnormal Points	All-Time Rank	State Rank
	R	L			R	L	R	L			
	Locality / Hunter / Owner / Date Killed										
240	27⁶/₈	27⁷/₈	23²/₈	28	5⁶/₈	5⁵/₈	8	13	46²/₈	396	18
	◆ *Frenchman River / Edward J. Hardin / Edward J. Hardin / 1992*										
236	28⁶/₈	28²/₈	29⁴/₈	34⁷/₈	4⁷/₈	4⁶/₈	9	9	32⁶/₈	408	19
	◆ *Antelope Lake / Roland Joubert / Roland Joubert / 1993*										

Photograph Courtesy of Emile T. Paradis

Emile T. Paradis and his three hunting companions hunted 30 miles northwest of Swift Current, Saskatchewan, in 1989 and filled their tags with nice bucks by 10:30 a.m. on the first day of their hunt. Emile dropped this non-typical buck (scoring 240-4/8 points) at 225 yards with a single shot.

Photograph by Wm. H. Nesbitt

MEXICO RECORD
TYPICAL MULE DEER
SCORE: 204⅜
Locality: Sonora   Date: 1986
Hunter: David V. Collis

MEXICO
TYPICAL MULE DEER

Score	Length of Main Beam R	L	Inside Spread	Greatest Spread	Circumference at Smallest Place between Burr and First Point R	L	Number of Points R	L	Total of Lengths Abnormal Points	All-Time Rank	State Rank
	Locality / Hunter / Owner / Date Killed										
204 3/8	29 2/8	30 1/8	35	35 5/8	4 4/8	4 5/8	5	5	0	69	1
	Sonora / David V. Collis / David V. Collis / 1986										
198 2/8	25 6/8	25 5/8	24 3/8	32 5/8	5 1/8	5	5	6	3 1/8	274	2
	Sonora / Heinz G. Holdorf / Heinz G. Holdorf / 1966										
197	25 4/8	25 6/8	25	29	5 1/8	5 2/8	6	6	0	347	3
	Sonora / J.G. Cigarroa, Sr. / J.G. Cigarroa, Sr. / 1957										
189 6/8	23 5/8	24 2/8	27 6/8	29 6/8	4 7/8	4 6/8	5	5	0	551	4
	Sonora / Joseph J. Luterbach / Joseph J. Luterbach / 1986										
188 5/8	25	24 1/8	28 4/8	34 4/8	5 7/8	5 6/8	7	5	6 1/8	562	5
	Sonora / Roy V. Haskell / Roy V. Haskell / 1993										
188	25 5/8	25 7/8	27 1/8	33 5/8	4 7/8	4 7/8	5	6	8 3/8	576	6
	Sonora / George B. White / George B. White / 1992										

TOP 10 COLUMBIA BLACKTAIL DEER LISTINGS INDEX

TOP 10 SITKA BLACKTAIL DEER LISTINGS INDEX

Tabulations of Recorded Columbia and Sitka Blacktail Deer

The trophy data shown on the following pages are taken from score charts in the records archives of the Boone and Crockett Club. A comparison of the rankings of this book with those of the first edition of *Records of North American Elk and Mule Deer* will reveal many significant differences. This is primarily due to the addition of numerous trophies from the 21st (1989-1991) and the 22nd (1992-1994) Awards Programs, including two new Columbia blacktail and one new Sitka blacktail deer state/provincial records.

Columbia and Sitka blacktails are subspecies of the common mule deer, with smaller racks and body size. Found in the coastal areas of the Pacific states, geographic boundaries describe the areas from which trophies may be entered. (See the 10th Edition of the all-time records book for the detailed boundary descriptions.)

The scores and ranks shown are final, except for trophies shown with an asterisk (*). The asterisk identifies entry scores subject to final certification by an Awards Panel of Judges. The asterisk can be removed (except in the case of a potential World's Record) by the submission of two additional, independent scorings by Official Measurers of the Boone and Crockett Club. The Records Committee of the Club will review the three scorings available (original plus the two additional) and determine which, if any, will be accepted in lieu of the Judges' Panel measurement. When the score has been accepted as final by the records Committee, the asterisk will be removed in future editions of this book and the all-time records book, *Records of North American Big Game*. In the case of a potential World's Record, the trophy must come before a Judges' Panel at the end of an entry period. Only a Judges' Panel can certify a World's Record and finalize its score. Asterisked trophies are unranked at the end of their category.

279

Photograph by J.J. McBride

CALIFORNIA STATE RECORD
COLUMBIA BLACKTAIL DEER
SCORE: 166 2/8
Locality: Glenn Co.   Date: 1949
Hunter: Peter Gerbo
Owner: Dennis P. Garcia

COLUMBIA BLACKTAIL DEER

Score	Length of Main Beam R	Length of Main Beam L	Inside Spread	Greatest Spread	Circumference at Smallest Place between Burr and First Point R	Circumference at Smallest Place between Burr and First Point L	Number of Points R	Number of Points L	Total of Lengths Abnormal Points	All-Time Rank	State Rank
166 2/8	23 2/8	24 3/8	26 5/8	30 5/8	5 4/8	5 1/8	6	6	8 1/8	11	1
♦ Glenn County / Peter Gerbo / Dennis P. Garcia / 1949											
163 1/8	23 3/8	21 5/8	20 4/8	23	5	4 7/8	7	6	3 5/8	18	2
♦ Siskiyou County / Frank Barago / Frank Barago / 1945											
162 3/8	22	22 1/8	18 1/8	20 7/8	4 4/8	4 4/8	5	5	0	21	3
♦ Trinity County / Sidney A. Nystrom / Sidney A. Nystrom / 1961											
162 2/8	24 5/8	25 1/8	19 2/8	22 5/8	4 2/8	4 2/8	5	5	0	22	4
♦ Glenn County / Roger L. Spencer / Roger L. Spencer / 1956											
160 4/8	23 5/8	24 3/8	21	23 4/8	4 7/8	4 7/8	5	6	2	25	5
♦ Siskiyou County / John L. Masters / John L. Masters / 1967											
160 3/8	23 1/8	23 5/8	26 5/8	30	4	4	6	5	2	26	6
♦ Trinity County / A.H. Hilbert / Jack T. Brusatori / 1929											
160 1/8	25 1/8	24 7/8	24 7/8	25 5/8	5	5 5/8	5	4	0	28	7
♦ Trinity County / Lorio Verzasconi / Lorio Verzasconi / 1946											
159 7/8	22 2/8	21 7/8	16 3/8	20 4/8	4	4	5	5	0	29	8
♦ Siskiyou County / John C. Ley / E.R. Cummins / 1937											
159 7/8	22 5/8	22 3/8	21 7/8	23 4/8	4 5/8	4 4/8	5	5	0	29	8
♦ Siskiyou County / Francis M. Sullivan / Francis M. Sullivan / 1951											
159 6/8	21	21 1/8	12 3/8	17	5 4/8	5 5/8	5	6	1 3/8	31	10
♦ Humboldt County / Picked Up / D. & J. Phillips / 1968											
159 4/8	24 4/8	23 6/8	14 7/8	17	4 5/8	4 4/8	6	6	2 7/8	34	11
♦ Mendocino County / Russ McLennan / Russ McLennan / 1984											
159 1/8	21 5/8	22 1/8	19 1/8	23 5/8	4 6/8	4 6/8	5	5	0	38	12
♦ Trinity County / A.H. Hilbert / A.H. Hilbert / 1939											
158 4/8	24	24 4/8	22 5/8	24 5/8	4 5/8	4 5/8	6	6	4 5/8	40	13
♦ Trinity County / David Phillips / David Phillips / 1974											
158	21 7/8	21 7/8	18 2/8	20 6/8	4 4/8	4 4/8	5	5	0	43	14
♦ Trinity County / Charles A. Strickland / Charles A. Strickland / 1984											
157 5/8	22 6/8	23 3/8	21 5/8	25 4/8	4 2/8	4 3/8	5	5	0	45	15
♦ Shasta County / Richard L. Sobrato / Richard L. Sobrato / 1969											
157	24 7/8	26 1/8	24 1/8	28 6/8	5	5 1/8	5	7	10 5/8	47	16
♦ Santa Clara County / Brud Eade / Brud Eade / 1961											
156 6/8	23	23 7/8	16 6/8	21	4 6/8	4 6/8	7	6	8 4/8	48	17
♦ Trinity County / Picked Up / Charles Hageman / 1994											

CALIFORNIA COLUMBIA BLACKTAIL DEER *(continued)*

Score	Length of Main Beam R	L	Inside Spread	Greatest Spread	Circumference at Smallest Place between Burr and First Point R	L	Number of Points R	L	Total of Lengths Abnormal Points	All-Time Rank	State Rank
155 2/8	21 5/8	21 6/8	23 1/8	25 1/8	3 3/8	3 4/8	5	5	0	56	18
◆ Trinity County / Fred Heider / Fred Heider / 1927											
155 2/8	22 1/8	22 7/8	19 2/8	23 6/8	5 3/8	4 7/8	5	5	0	56	18
◆ Mendocino County / Gary Land / Gary Land / 1972											
155 1/8	21	21 6/8	18 5/8	22 7/8	4 3/8	4 3/8	4	4	0	60	20
◆ Shasta County / Vance Corrigan / Vance Corrigan / 1956											
154 6/8	20 4/8	20 3/8	20 4/8	23 6/8	4 5/8	4 5/8	4	4	0	62	21
◆ Mendocino County / W.A. McAllister / W.A. McAllister / 1968											
154 6/8	21 1/8	21 3/8	18 1/8	22	4 2/8	4 2/8	6	6	4 7/8	62	21
◆ Mendocino County / Andy Amerson / Andy Amerson / 1993											
154 5/8	24	22 7/8	23 3/8	25 1/8	4 3/8	4 4/8	5	5	0	65	23
◆ Humboldt County / Phillip Brown / Phillip Brown / 1962											
154 5/8	24 7/8	24 3/8	21	24 4/8	4 7/8	4 6/8	6	7	4 5/8	65	23
◆ Siskiyou County / Darrell R. Jones / Darrell R. Jones / 1984											
154 1/8	21 6/8	22 2/8	18 6/8	24 1/8	4 6/8	4 7/8	6	7	4 1/8	68	25
◆ Glenn County / Mitchell A. Thorson / Mitchell A. Thorson / 1969											
154	26 4/8	25 7/8	28 6/8	35 3/8	4 4/8	4 6/8	6	6	9 6/8	70	26
◆ Trinity County / A.H. Hilbert / A.H. Hilbert / 1930											
153 3/8	21 2/8	21 5/8	17 4/8	21 6/8	5	5	6	5	4 3/8	76	27
◆ Tehama County / James L. Carr / James L. Carr / 1979											
153	22 6/8	23 6/8	14 6/8	16 5/8	4 3/8	4 5/8	6	5	1 4/8	81	28
◆ Siskiyou County / John Carmichael / J.A. Brose / 1969											
152 5/8	22 1/8	22	19 5/8	22 7/8	4	4 3/8	5	5	0	82	29
◆ Mendocino County / Harold D. Schneider / H.D. & M.J. Schneider / 1979											
152 4/8	23	23	20	22 2/8	4	4	6	7	4	83	30
◆ Tehama County / Don Strickler / Don Strickler / 1979											
152 4/8	22	21 2/8	18 4/8	20 4/8	5 1/8	5	6	6	2	83	30
◆ Mendocino County / Richard C. Martin / Richard C. Martin / 1990											
152 1/8	22 4/8	21 4/8	17 7/8	20 3/8	4 2/8	4 1/8	5	5	0	86	32
◆ Trinity County / Robert V. Strickland / Robert V. Strickland / 1966											
152	23 3/8	22 7/8	21 6/8	23 2/8	4 4/8	4 4/8	5	5	0	89	33
◆ Yolo County / Herman Darneille / E.L. Gallup / 1943											
151 5/8	20 3/8	20 1/8	22 4/8	26 4/8	4 5/8	4 4/8	5	5	0	93	34
◆ Mendocino County / Bill L. Conn / Bill L. Conn / 1969											
151 5/8	22 1/8	21 7/8	22 5/8	24 2/8	4 6/8	4 6/8	5	5	0	93	34
◆ Siskiyou County / Jim A. Turnbow / Jim A. Turnbow / 1973											

282

CALIFORNIA COLUMBIA BLACKTAIL DEER *(continued)*

Score	Length of Main Beam R	Length of Main Beam L	Inside Spread	Greatest Spread	Circumference at Smallest Place between Burr and First Point R	Circumference at Smallest Place between Burr and First Point L	Number of Points R	Number of Points L	Total of Lengths Abnormal Points	All-Time Rank	State Rank
	♦ *Locality / Hunter / Owner / Date Killed*										
151	20 1/8	21	19 2/8	23 2/8	4 2/8	4 1/8	5	5	0	99	36
	♦ *Humboldt County / Elgin T. Gates / Elgin T. Gates / 1952*										
150 6/8	22	21 4/8	17	21	4 2/8	4 2/8	5	5	0	103	37
	♦ *Siskiyou County / Raymond Whittaker / Raymond Whittaker / 1978*										
150 4/8	24 1/8	24 2/8	19 5/8	21 6/8	5 1/8	5	6	6	2 7/8	105	38
	♦ *Trinity County / E.L. Brightenstine / E.L. Brightenstine / 1978*										
150 1/8	22 4/8	22	16 1/8	20 1/8	4 1/8	4 1/8	5	5	0	106	39
	♦ *Napa County / Robert G. Wiley / Robert G. Wiley / 1965*										
150 1/8	21	21	20 1/8	22 7/8	3 7/8	3 7/8	5	5	0	106	39
	♦ *Trinity County / Thomas L. Hough / Thomas L. Hough / 1969*										
150	24	25 1/8	24	26	4 5/8	4 4/8	4	4	0	110	41
	♦ *Napa County / W.C. Lambert / W.C. Lambert / 1957*										
150	20 7/8	20 2/8	20	22 6/8	5 3/8	5 3/8	4	4	0	110	41
	♦ *Lake County / Bruce Strickler / Bruce Strickler / 1970*										
150	20 4/8	21 7/8	16 6/8	19	4 2/8	4 2/8	5	5	0	110	41
	♦ *Tehama County / Marion F. Foster / Barbara J. Foster / 1971*										
149 7/8	23 2/8	22 5/8	17 3/8	20	4 2/8	4 1/8	6	5	2 6/8	115	44
	♦ *Siskiyou County / John R. Adams / John R. Adams / 1985*										
149 6/8	22 7/8	22	18 7/8	24 4/8	5	5	5	6	1 7/8	116	45
	♦ *Siskiyou County / Emit C. Jones / Emit C. Jones / 1961*										
149 5/8	20	21 3/8	17 7/8	22 2/8	4 4/8	4 4/8	5	5	0	117	46
	♦ *Humboldt County / Robert C. Stephens / Robert C. Stephens / 1961*										
149 4/8	22 5/8	21	20 6/8	23 2/8	5 1/8	5 2/8	5	5	0	119	47
	♦ *Glenn County / George Stewart, Jr. / George Stewart, Jr. / 1957*										
149 4/8	21 1/8	21 4/8	23	24 7/8	5 1/8	5	5	5	0	119	47
	♦ *Mendocino County / C.W. Bill King / C.W. Bill King / 1993*										
149 3/8	22 3/8	21 2/8	20 3/8	23 6/8	5 2/8	5 4/8	5	5	0	121	49
	♦ *Trinity County / Lyle L. Johnson / Lyle L. Johnson / 1979*										
149 3/8	23 7/8	26 5/8	20 5/8	23 2/8	4 5/8	4 4/8	5	5	0	121	49
	♦ *Tehama County / Bill F. Stevenson / Bill F. Stevenson / 1989*										
149 2/8	24 3/8	24 3/8	17 6/8	20 7/8	5 4/8	5 4/8	8	8	20 6/8	124	51
	♦ *Trinity County / Lauren A. Johnson / Lauren A. Johnson / 1964*										
148 7/8	22 1/8	21 3/8	18	21 4/8	4 7/8	4 7/8	6	5	1 1/8	128	52
	♦ *Humboldt County / F. Joe Parker / F. Joe Parker / 1946*										
148 4/8	23 2/8	22 7/8	20 6/8	25 3/8	4 3/8	4 5/8	5	5	0	132	53
	♦ *Mendocino County / N.D. Windbigler / N.D. Windbigler / 1969*										

Score	Length of Main Beam R	L	Inside Spread	Greatest Spread	Circumference at Smallest Place between Burr and First Point R	L	Number of Points R	L	Total of Lengths Abnormal Points	All-Time Rank	State Rank
\multicolumn{13}{l}{♦ Locality / Hunter / Owner / Date Killed}											
148 2/8	24	24 4/8	23 4/8	26	6 2/8	5 6/8	6	6	4 2/8	137	54
\multicolumn{13}{l}{♦ Shasta County / Jerry W. Sander / Jerry W. Sander / 1977}											
148 1/8	21 6/8	22 1/8	18 6/8	21	5	5 1/8	8	7	10 5/8	138	55
\multicolumn{13}{l}{♦ Trinity County / Dean Tackette / Dean Tackette / 1981}											
147 7/8	22	22 3/8	18 5/8	0	4 1/8	4 2/8	5	5	0	140	56
\multicolumn{13}{l}{♦ Glenn County / Emmet T. Frye / Emmet T. Frye / 1937}											
147 7/8	20 6/8	20 7/8	21 6/8	23	5	4 7/8	5	5	0	140	56
\multicolumn{13}{l}{♦ Trinity County / Chauncy Willburn / Chauncy Willburn / 1955}											
147 7/8	22 1/8	22 2/8	18 5/8	21 3/8	4 2/8	4 3/8	6	6	4 4/8	140	56
\multicolumn{13}{l}{♦ Humboldt County / Melvin H. Kadle / Melvin H. Kadle / 1979}											
147 5/8	23	23 6/8	19 5/8	22 7/8	4 4/8	4 3/8	5	4	0	143	59
\multicolumn{13}{l}{♦ Santa Clara County / Maitland Armstrong / Maitland Armstrong / 1944}											
147 5/8	22 3/8	22 7/8	22 3/8	25 3/8	4 5/8	4 5/8	4	4	0	143	59
\multicolumn{13}{l}{♦ Mendocino County / Richard Sterling / Richard Sterling / 1986}											
147 1/8	21 2/8	21	16 7/8	19 2/8	4 3/8	4 3/8	5	6	1 6/8	147	61
\multicolumn{13}{l}{♦ Trinity County / Craig L. Brown / Craig & Joy Brown / 1980}											
147 1/8	22 4/8	23 3/8	21 7/8	24 7/8	4 2/8	4 5/8	6	5	1	147	61
\multicolumn{13}{l}{♦ Trinity County / Barry D. Keyes / Barry D. Keyes / 1992}											
147	18	18 2/8	17	19 2/8	4 3/8	4 2/8	5	5	0	149	63
\multicolumn{13}{l}{♦ Siskiyou County / Ray Whittaker / Ray Whittaker / 1966}											
147	22 2/8	22 3/8	19 6/8	23 6/8	4 3/8	4 3/8	5	5	0	149	63
\multicolumn{13}{l}{♦ Mendocino County / David W. Wilson / David W. Wilson / 1993}											
146 6/8	20	20 4/8	18 4/8	22	4 3/8	4 3/8	5	5	0	153	65
\multicolumn{13}{l}{♦ Siskiyou County / Richard Silva / Richard Silva / 1958}											
146 4/8	21 2/8	21 2/8	17 2/8	19 1/8	4 6/8	4 7/8	5	5	0	157	66
\multicolumn{13}{l}{♦ Glenn County / Lawrence E. Germeshausen / Lawrence E. Germeshausen / 1983}											
146 3/8	23 4/8	23 6/8	24 6/8	26 3/8	4 5/8	4 5/8	5	5	1 1/8	159	67
\multicolumn{13}{l}{♦ Trinity County / Carroll E. Dow / Carroll E. Dow / 1962}											
146 2/8	21 6/8	22 3/8	13 6/8	15 4/8	5 6/8	5 6/8	5	5	0	160	68
\multicolumn{13}{l}{♦ Shasta County / William H. Taylor / William H. Taylor / 1971}											
146 2/8	21 7/8	21 6/8	16 2/8	20	3 7/8	3 7/8	5	5	0	160	68
\multicolumn{13}{l}{♦ Humboldt County / Charles R. Jurin / Charles R. Jurin / 1988}											
146 1/8	23 1/8	23 5/8	19 1/8	21 2/8	4 5/8	4	4	4	0	163	70
\multicolumn{13}{l}{♦ Trinity County / Kenneth M. Brown / Kenneth M. Brown / 1972}											
146 1/8	22 2/8	23 4/8	19 1/8	21 6/8	3 7/8	4 2/8	4	5	0	163	70
\multicolumn{13}{l}{♦ Mendocino County / Brad B. Pitt / Brad B. Pitt / 1994}											

CALIFORNIA COLUMBIA BLACKTAIL DEER *(continued)*

Score	Length of Main Beam R	L	Inside Spread	Greatest Spread	Circumference at Smallest Place between Burr and First Point R	L	Number of Points R	L	Total of Lengths Abnormal Points	All-Time Rank	State Rank
	◆ *Locality / Hunter / Owner / Date Killed*										
146	22⁶⁄₈	22²⁄₈	19²⁄₈	22²⁄₈	4⁴⁄₈	4⁵⁄₈	5	5	0	166	72
	◆ *Mendocino County / Brian E. Hornberger / Brian E. Hornberger / 1991*										
146	20⁵⁄₈	21⁵⁄₈	21⁴⁄₈	23¹⁄₈	4³⁄₈	4²⁄₈	5	5	0	166	72
	◆ *Mendocino County / Renaldo J. Marin / Renaldo J. Marin / 1993*										
145⁷⁄₈	23⁴⁄₈	23³⁄₈	22	27²⁄₈	5³⁄₈	5⁴⁄₈	6	8	12⁵⁄₈	169	74
	◆ *Lake County / Floyd Goodrich / Mrs. William Olson / 1926*										
145⁷⁄₈	22	23⁵⁄₈	16³⁄₈	19⁷⁄₈	4⁵⁄₈	4⁷⁄₈	5	5	0	169	74
	◆ *Napa County / C.H.N. Dailey / Tony Stoer / 1948*										
145⁷⁄₈	22⁶⁄₈	22⁶⁄₈	21⁷⁄₈	27³⁄₈	4³⁄₈	4⁵⁄₈	5	5	0	169	74
	◆ *Shasta County / Gary J. Miller / Gary J. Miller / 1968*										
145⁵⁄₈	22⁴⁄₈	23	18⁷⁄₈	20⁵⁄₈	4¹⁄₈	4¹⁄₈	6	5	1⁶⁄₈	176	77
	◆ *Humboldt County / Joe Dickerson / Jay Grunert / 1962*										
145⁵⁄₈	21²⁄₈	21¹⁄₈	19⁵⁄₈	21¹⁄₈	3⁷⁄₈	4	5	5	0	176	77
	◆ *Siskiyou County / Wallace D. Barlow / Wallace D. Barlow / 1985*										
145⁴⁄₈	21³⁄₈	21¹⁄₈	21³⁄₈	22⁶⁄₈	4⁵⁄₈	4⁷⁄₈	5	6	2¹⁄₈	178	79
	◆ *Mendocino County / Kenneth A. Bovero / Kenneth A. Bovero / 1993*										
145³⁄₈	22³⁄₈	21	23⁴⁄₈	26¹⁄₈	4⁵⁄₈	4⁶⁄₈	5	5	0	181	80
	◆ *Mendocino County / Paul M. Holleman II / Paul M. Holleman II / 1976*										
145²⁄₈	22⁴⁄₈	22⁵⁄₈	21	26	5³⁄₈	5¹⁄₈	7	9	15²⁄₈	182	81
	◆ *Tehama County / Clint Heiber / Clint Heiber / 1979*										
145¹⁄₈	23⁵⁄₈	23⁴⁄₈	23³⁄₈	24⁶⁄₈	5¹⁄₈	5²⁄₈	5	5	0	187	82
	◆ *Tehama County / Lamar G. Hanson / Lamar G. Hanson / 1972*										
145¹⁄₈	21⁴⁄₈	20⁷⁄₈	19⁴⁄₈	22⁴⁄₈	4³⁄₈	4³⁄₈	5	6	2⁵⁄₈	187	82
	◆ *Trinity County / Gene Shannon / Daniel M. Phillips / 1990*										
145	22²⁄₈	21⁴⁄₈	21²⁄₈	24⁴⁄₈	5¹⁄₈	5¹⁄₈	7	5	6⁴⁄₈	192	84
	◆ *Mendocino County / Ralph I. Sibley / Ralph I. Sibley / 1986*										
144⁶⁄₈	22²⁄₈	22⁴⁄₈	22⁴⁄₈	26⁵⁄₈	4⁴⁄₈	4⁶⁄₈	5	5	0	198	85
	◆ *Mendocino County / Richard Vannelli / Richard Vannelli / 1970*										
144⁴⁄₈	21⁴⁄₈	21³⁄₈	19⁴⁄₈	21⁵⁄₈	4³⁄₈	4²⁄₈	5	5	0	206	86
	◆ *Shasta County / Ernie Young / Chet Young / 1953*										
144³⁄₈	22¹⁄₈	23³⁄₈	21³⁄₈	23³⁄₈	5	5²⁄₈	5	4	0	212	87
	◆ *Santa Clara County / Maitland Armstrong / Maitland Armstrong / 1946*										
144³⁄₈	21	20⁷⁄₈	16⁵⁄₈	18²⁄₈	4⁷⁄₈	4⁵⁄₈	5	5	0	212	87
	◆ *Humboldt County / Gerald Wescott / Gerald Wescott / 1980*										
144³⁄₈	20¹⁄₈	22	19¹⁄₈	22⁴⁄₈	4⁴⁄₈	4⁴⁄₈	5	5	0	212	87
	◆ *Alameda County / Anthony S. Webb / Anthony S. Webb / 1990*										

Score	Length of Main Beam R	L	Inside Spread	Greatest Spread	Circumference at Smallest Place between Burr and First Point R	L	Number of Points R	L	Total of Lengths Abnormal Points	All-Time Rank	State Rank

♦ *Locality / Hunter / Owner / Date Killed*

Score	R	L	Inside Spread	Greatest Spread	R	L	R	L	Abnormal	All-Time	State
144³⁄₈	20⁴⁄₈	20⁷⁄₈	14⁷⁄₈	18⁶⁄₈	4⁴⁄₈	4⁵⁄₈	5	5	0	212	87
♦ *Humboldt County / Richard G. Van Vorst / Richard G. Van Vorst / 1990*											
144²⁄₈	21	22⁴⁄₈	20⁴⁄₈	24⁴⁄₈	4⁴⁄₈	4⁴⁄₈	5	5	0	217	91
♦ *Mendocino County / Frank Kester / Frank Kester / 1981*											
143⁷⁄₈	20⁵⁄₈	19⁵⁄₈	20³⁄₈	23	5	5¹⁄₈	5	5	0	224	92
♦ *Humboldt County / Lois C. Miller / Lois C. Miller / 1986*											
143⁶⁄₈	20⁵⁄₈	20²⁄₈	19⁷⁄₈	21³⁄₈	5²⁄₈	5²⁄₈	6	6	2¹⁄₈	227	93
♦ *Tehama County / Clint Heiber / Clint Heiber / 1978*											
143⁶⁄₈	19⁵⁄₈	19⁴⁄₈	15²⁄₈	19⁵⁄₈	4⁷⁄₈	4⁶⁄₈	5	6	2	227	93
♦ *Mendocino County / Mark Ciancio / Mark Ciancio / 1986*											
143⁶⁄₈	20⁶⁄₈	20³⁄₈	15⁴⁄₈	17²⁄₈	5²⁄₈	4⁷⁄₈	5	5	0	227	93
♦ *Humboldt County / Hartwell A. Burnett / Hartwell A. Burnett / 1988*											
143⁵⁄₈	20⁴⁄₈	20⁴⁄₈	18⁵⁄₈	22¹⁄₈	4⁴⁄₈	4⁴⁄₈	4	4	0	232	96
♦ *Siskiyou County / Emit C. Jones / Emit C. Jones / 1960*											
143⁵⁄₈	20⁵⁄₈	19³⁄₈	18⁵⁄₈	22⁷⁄₈	4¹⁄₈	4²⁄₈	5	5	0	232	96
♦ *Trinity County / Kenneth L. Cogle, Jr. / Kenneth L. Cogle, Jr. / 1985*											
143⁴⁄₈	21	20⁴⁄₈	17	19⁴⁄₈	4⁶⁄₈	4⁶⁄₈	5	5	0	235	98
♦ *Trinity County / Barry Griffin / Barry Griffin / 1983*											
143⁴⁄₈	22⁶⁄₈	22⁴⁄₈	20	22⁴⁄₈	4²⁄₈	4³⁄₈	5	5	0	235	98
♦ *Mendocino County / Arnold E. Dado / Arnold E. Dado / 1993*											
143³⁄₈	19²⁄₈	18⁷⁄₈	18³⁄₈	21⁴⁄₈	3⁴⁄₈	3⁴⁄₈	5	5	0	241	100
♦ *Mendocino County / Larry G. Miller / Larry G. Miller / 1978*											
143²⁄₈	22³⁄₈	22⁶⁄₈	21⁴⁄₈	23³⁄₈	4²⁄₈	4²⁄₈	5	5	0	243	101
♦ *Lake County / Mario Sereni, Jr. / Mario Sereni, Jr. / 1965*											
143²⁄₈	19⁵⁄₈	19⁴⁄₈	17²⁄₈	19⁷⁄₈	4	4	5	5	0	243	101
♦ *Humboldt County / Jack Stedman / Jack Stedman / 1965*											
143²⁄₈	26	26	25	30	4⁶⁄₈	4⁶⁄₈	5	6	9⁴⁄₈	243	101
♦ *Mendocino County / George W. Rogers / George W. Rogers / 1977*											
143²⁄₈	20	20²⁄₈	15⁶⁄₈	20	4²⁄₈	4	5	5	0	243	101
♦ *Shasta County / Ben Brackett / Ben Brackett / 1993*											
143¹⁄₈	22	22¹⁄₈	18¹⁄₈	19⁵⁄₈	4¹⁄₈	4	5	5	0	250	105
♦ *Humboldt County / Mitchell A. Thorson / Mitchell A. Thorson / 1965*											
143¹⁄₈	21⁶⁄₈	22²⁄₈	17¹⁄₈	20⁵⁄₈	4¹⁄₈	4¹⁄₈	5	5	0	250	105
♦ *Humboldt County / Eddie L. Mendes / Eddie L. Mendes / 1992*											
142⁷⁄₈	23¹⁄₈	22⁴⁄₈	17³⁄₈	19⁶⁄₈	4	4²⁄₈	5	5	0	253	107
♦ *Tehema County / Randy Croote / Randy Croote / 1993*											

Score	Length of Main Beam R	L	Inside Spread	Greatest Spread	Circumference at Smallest Place between Burr and First Point R	L	Number of Points R	L	Total of Lengths Abnormal Points	All-Time Rank	State Rank
142 5/8	20 2/8	20	16 5/8	22 4/8	4 1/8	4	5	5	0	259	108
◆ Santa Clara County / Picked Up / Ray & Neal Haera / PR 1966											
142 5/8	22 5/8	22 6/8	19 7/8	22 6/8	4 2/8	4 2/8	5	5	0	259	108
◆ Santa Clara County / Picked Up / Russel Rasmussen / PR 1966											
142 5/8	21 4/8	20 3/8	19 7/8	22 2/8	4 4/8	4 3/8	4	4	0	259	108
◆ Trinity County / Larry Brown / Larry Brown / 1979											
142 5/8	23 1/8	22 1/8	20 1/8	24	4 6/8	4 7/8	7	6	7	259	108
◆ Tehama County / Kenneth R. Hall / Kenneth R. Hall / 1979											
142 5/8	22	23	20 5/8	23 4/8	4	3 7/8	5	5	0	259	108
◆ Mendocino County / Warren F. Coffman / Warren F. Coffman / 1989											
142 5/8	20	20 6/8	17 7/8	20 5/8	4 2/8	4 1/8	5	5	0	259	108
◆ Trinity County / Robert T. Edwards / Robert T. Edwards / 1991											
142 4/8	22 2/8	22 6/8	13 3/8	15 3/8	4 6/8	4 6/8	4	5	1 3/8	268	114
◆ Trinity County / Jace Comfort / Jace Comfort / 1965											
142 4/8	21 1/8	20 4/8	15 4/8	18 7/8	4 6/8	4 6/8	5	5	0	268	114
◆ Mendocino County / Jerry C. Russell / Jerry C. Russell / 1993											
142 3/8	20 6/8	20 7/8	17 3/8	22	4 3/8	4 5/8	5	5	0	273	116
◆ Laytonville / Byron J. Rowland, Jr. / Byron J. Rowland, Jr. / 1964											
142 3/8	23	22	19 3/8	21 4/8	4	4	5	4	0	273	116
◆ Humboldt County / Darol L. Damm / Darol L. Damm / 1976											
142 3/8	20 6/8	20 5/8	19 1/8	20 7/8	4 6/8	4 5/8	5	5	0	273	116
◆ Humboldt County / James L. Sloan / James L. Sloan / 1992											
142 2/8	23 4/8	23 2/8	17	20 1/8	4 2/8	4 1/8	6	5	4 4/8	276	119
◆ Mendocino County / James A. Shelton / James A. Shelton / 1944											
142 1/8	21 3/8	22 3/8	19 7/8	22 6/8	5 1/8	5 1/8	5	4	0	278	120
◆ Shasta County / Richard R. Lowell / Richard R. Lowell / 1953											
142 1/8	22	22	20 3/8	22 1/8	4 3/8	4 1/8	4	4	. 0	278	120
◆ Siskiyou County / John T. Scheffler / John T. Scheffler / 1992											
141 7/8	21 4/8	21 2/8	17 7/8	20 6/8	4 7/8	5	5	5	0	288	122
◆ Trinity County / Pedro H. Henrich / Pedro H. Henrich / 1977											
141 7/8	21 6/8	21 4/8	17 6/8	22 2/8	3 7/8	4	6	5	1 1/8	288	122
◆ Trinity County / Melvin M. Clair / Melvin M. Clair / 1992											
141 5/8	19 7/8	19 6/8	20 3/8	25 1/8	4	4 2/8	5	5	0	296	124
◆ Trinity County / A.H. Hilbert / A.H. Hilbert / PR 1955											
141 5/8	21 1/8	21 6/8	18 5/8	22	3 6/8	3 6/8	5	5	0	296	124
◆ Mendocino County / Lanny G. King / Lanny G. King / 1992											

Score	Length of Main Beam R	L	Inside Spread	Greatest Spread	Circumference at Smallest Place between Burr and First Point R	L	Number of Points R	L	Total of Lengths Abnormal Points	All-Time Rank	State Rank

♦ *Locality / Hunter / Owner / Date Killed*

Score	R	L	Inside Spread	Greatest Spread	R	L	R	L	Abnormal	All-Time Rank	State Rank
141 4/8	21 2/8	21 1/8	16 2/8	18 6/8	4 2/8	4 2/8	5	5	0	299	126

♦ *Mendocino County / Greg Rocha / Greg Rocha / 1985*

141 4/8	20 7/8	20 4/8	20	22 3/8	4 4/8	4 4/8	5	5	0	299	126

♦ *Del Norte County / Les Johnson / Les Johnson / 1986*

141 3/8	22 1/8	21 5/8	18 7/8	22	4 7/8	4 5/8	5	4	0	303	128

♦ *Trinity County / Larry Brown / Larry Brown / 1980*

141 3/8	21 2/8	21 7/8	16 7/8	19 5/8	4 3/8	4 1/8	5	5	0	303	128

♦ *Mendocino County / Gene V. Bradley / Gene V. Bradley / 1988*

141 2/8	21 4/8	20 4/8	18	21 5/8	4 2/8	4 4/8	5	5	0	306	130

♦ *Trinity County / Barry D. Keyes / Barry D. Keyes / 1989*

141	21 3/8	21 1/8	17	20 3/8	3 7/8	4 1/8	5	5	0	312	131

♦ *Humboldt County / Allen Pierce, Jr. / Allen Pierce, Jr. / 1959*

141	21	20 2/8	19 4/8	25 5/8	4 4/8	4	5	4	0	312	131

♦ *Mendocino County / Richard Vannelli / Richard Vannelli / 1970*

141	23	24 4/8	22	24	5 4/8	5 4/8	7	6	8 4/8	312	131

♦ *Mendocino County / Gerald W. Whitmire / Gerald W. Whitmire / 1976*

141	22 4/8	21 3/8	20	22 2/8	4 3/8	3 6/8	5	4	0	312	131

♦ *Mendocino County / Richard L. Valladao / Richard L. Valladao / 1993*

140 7/8	21 1/8	20 1/8	21 1/8	24 4/8	4 3/8	4 4/8	5	5	0	317	135

♦ *Shasta County / Dave Swenson / Dave Swenson / 1968*

140 7/8	23 3/8	22	16 5/8	18 2/8	3 7/8	4	5	5	0	317	135

♦ *Mendocino County / Douglas W. Lim / Douglas W. Lim / 1981*

140 6/8	21	22 2/8	20 6/8	24 6/8	4	4	5	5	0	321	137

♦ *Mendocino County / Bill L. Conn / Bill L. Conn / 1968*

140 6/8	23 4/8	23	18 6/8	20 5/8	4 6/8	5 1/8	5	4	1 4/8	321	137

♦ *Mendocino County / Robert Lynch / Robert Lynch / 1971*

140 6/8	23	22 4/8	20	22	5 4/8	5 4/8	5	5	0	321	137

♦ *Mendocino County / Jerry D. Smith / Jerry D. Smith / 1978*

140 5/8	23	21 7/8	18 3/8	20 2/8	4 6/8	4 5/8	5	5	0	325	140

♦ *Shasta County / Luther Clements / R.H. Bernhardy / 1944*

140 4/8	19 4/8	20	17 2/8	21 2/8	4 4/8	4 4/8	5	5	0	327	141

♦ *Trinity County / Loran G. August / Larry Brown / 1980*

140 4/8	21 1/8	21 3/8	14 2/8	17 1/8	4 1/8	4 1/8	5	5	0	327	141

♦ *Mendocino County / Jay M. Gates III / Jay M. Gates III / 1986*

140 3/8	20 1/8	20 5/8	16 5/8	19 2/8	3 7/8	4 3/8	4	5	0	330	143

♦ *Humboldt County / George S. Johnson / Roy F. Johnson / 1934*

Score	Length of Main Beam R	L	Inside Spread	Greatest Spread	Circumference at Smallest Place between Burr and First Point R	L	Number of Points R	L	Total of Lengths Abnormal Points	All-Time Rank	State Rank
140³⁄₈	22	21	17⁷⁄₈	21²⁄₈	4	4	5	5	0	330	143

♦ *Siskiyou County / Rodney Irwin / Rodney Irwin / 1966*

| 140²⁄₈ | 21 | 20⁷⁄₈ | 19⁶⁄₈ | 23⁶⁄₈ | 5 | 4⁶⁄₈ | 5 | 5 | 0 | 333 | 145 |

♦ *Mendocino County / Harry S. Richardson / Harry S. Richardson / 1952*

| 140²⁄₈ | 21⁴⁄₈ | 21⁴⁄₈ | 19⁶⁄₈ | 21⁴⁄₈ | 3⁷⁄₈ | 3⁷⁄₈ | 5 | 5 | 0 | 333 | 145 |

♦ *Mendocino County / Earl E. Hamlow, Jr. / Earl E. Hamlow, Jr. / 1977*

| 140²⁄₈ | 22 | 21⁴⁄₈ | 23⁴⁄₈ | 26 | 4³⁄₈ | 4³⁄₈ | 4 | 5 | 3 | 333 | 145 |

♦ *Trinity County / Charles E. Davy / Charles E. Davy / 1983*

| 140¹⁄₈ | 21²⁄₈ | 21⁵⁄₈ | 15⁶⁄₈ | 18¹⁄₈ | 4²⁄₈ | 4²⁄₈ | 5 | 7 | 2⁷⁄₈ | 337 | 148 |

♦ *Mendocino County / Clarence W. Nelson / Clarence W. Nelson / 1948*

| 140¹⁄₈ | 20⁴⁄₈ | 19⁴⁄₈ | 16³⁄₈ | 20²⁄₈ | 4³⁄₈ | 4²⁄₈ | 4 | 4 | 0 | 337 | 148 |

♦ *Santa Clara County / Dick Sullivan / Dick Sullivan / 1977*

| 140¹⁄₈ | 21¹⁄₈ | 20²⁄₈ | 16³⁄₈ | 18¹⁄₈ | 3⁷⁄₈ | 4 | 4 | 4 | 0 | 337 | 148 |

♦ *Siskiyou County / Rickford M. Fisher / Rickford M. Fisher / 1986*

| 140¹⁄₈ | 21⁶⁄₈ | 21 | 17¹⁄₈ | 19²⁄₈ | 4 | 4⁴⁄₈ | 5 | 6 | 1²⁄₈ | 337 | 148 |

♦ *Trinity County / Wayne Sorensen / C.W. Sorensen / 1986*

| 140 | 20²⁄₈ | 20²⁄₈ | 16 | 22⁴⁄₈ | 4⁷⁄₈ | 4⁶⁄₈ | 7 | 5 | 4²⁄₈ | 345 | 152 |

♦ *Mendocino County / Roy Bergstrom / Roy Bergstrom / 1966*

| 140 | 22⁴⁄₈ | 22²⁄₈ | 18 | 20⁶⁄₈ | 5⁵⁄₈ | 5²⁄₈ | 5 | 5 | 0 | 345 | 152 |

♦ *Mendocino County / Nick Deffterios / Nick Deffterios / 1970*

| 140 | 22 | 21³⁄₈ | 17⁶⁄₈ | 21²⁄₈ | 4¹⁄₈ | 4¹⁄₈ | 5 | 5 | 0 | 345 | 152 |

♦ *Humboldt County / Carl A. Anderson / Carl A. Anderson / 1980*

| 140 | 21⁵⁄₈ | 22¹⁄₈ | 19 | 22¹⁄₈ | 3⁷⁄₈ | 4²⁄₈ | 4 | 5 | 0 | 345 | 152 |

♦ *Trinity County / William J. Olson / William J. Olson / 1981*

| 140 | 20⁴⁄₈ | 21⁴⁄₈ | 17²⁄₈ | 19⁷⁄₈ | 4 | 3⁶⁄₈ | 7 | 5 | 6⁶⁄₈ | 345 | 152 |

♦ *Siskiyou County / Doug Weinrich / Doug Weinrich / 1993*

| 139⁷⁄₈ | 19 | 18⁶⁄₈ | 15⁵⁄₈ | 19 | 4 | 4 | 4 | 5 | 0 | 351 | 157 |

♦ *Siskiyou County / Roy Eastlick / Roy Eastlick / 1954*

| 139⁷⁄₈ | 22¹⁄₈ | 20⁷⁄₈ | 21³⁄₈ | 24²⁄₈ | 5¹⁄₈ | 5 | 4 | 5 | 1²⁄₈ | 351 | 157 |

♦ *Trinity County / Craig L. Brown / Craig & Joy Brown / 1981*

| 139⁶⁄₈ | 21⁵⁄₈ | 22⁴⁄₈ | 16 | 18¹⁄₈ | 4¹⁄₈ | 4 | 5 | 5 | 0 | 354 | 159 |

♦ *Shasta County / Warren Hunter / Warren Hunter / 1964*

| 139⁶⁄₈ | 22²⁄₈ | 22⁵⁄₈ | 21⁴⁄₈ | 23²⁄₈ | 3³⁄₈ | 3⁵⁄₈ | 5 | 5 | 2⁶⁄₈ | 354 | 159 |

♦ *Trinity County / Andrew C. Hiebert / Andrew C. Hiebert / 1993*

| 139³⁄₈ | 19⁴⁄₈ | 19⁵⁄₈ | 20⁶⁄₈ | 22¹⁄₈ | 4⁷⁄₈ | 4³⁄₈ | 6 | 5 | 1 | 364 | 161 |

♦ *Mendocino County / Walter R. Schubert / Walter R. Schubert / 1952*

Score	Length of Main Beam R	L	Inside Spread	Greatest Spread	Circumference at Smallest Place between Burr and First Point R	L	Number of Points R	L	Total of Lengths Abnormal Points	All-Time Rank	State Rank
					◆ Locality / Hunter / Owner / Date Killed						
$139\frac{3}{8}$	$24\frac{5}{8}$	$23\frac{3}{8}$	$21\frac{5}{8}$	$23\frac{7}{8}$	$4\frac{7}{8}$	$4\frac{7}{8}$	5	5	$2\frac{6}{8}$	364	161
				◆ Trinity County / Andy Burgess / Andy Burgess / 1964							
$139\frac{3}{8}$	$21\frac{4}{8}$	$21\frac{5}{8}$	$22\frac{5}{8}$	$25\frac{1}{8}$	$4\frac{3}{8}$	$4\frac{1}{8}$	5	5	0	364	161
				◆ Siskiyou County / Loren L. Lutz / Loren L. Lutz / 1964							
$139\frac{3}{8}$	21	21	$19\frac{1}{8}$	$21\frac{4}{8}$	$4\frac{5}{8}$	$4\frac{7}{8}$	5	5	0	364	161
				◆ Mendocino County / Richard L. Moore / Richard L. Moore / 1992							
$139\frac{2}{8}$	$21\frac{3}{8}$	$21\frac{4}{8}$	$20\frac{1}{8}$	$22\frac{1}{8}$	$4\frac{1}{8}$	$4\frac{1}{8}$	5	4	$1\frac{3}{8}$	372	165
				◆ Humboldt County / Jeff Bryant / Jeff Bryant / 1964							
$139\frac{2}{8}$	$22\frac{5}{8}$	$21\frac{1}{8}$	$18\frac{6}{8}$	$22\frac{7}{8}$	$3\frac{3}{8}$	$3\frac{5}{8}$	4	6	$3\frac{6}{8}$	372	165
				◆ Trinity County / Gary L. Mayberry / Gary L. Mayberry / 1968							
$139\frac{2}{8}$	21	21	$16\frac{7}{8}$	$20\frac{7}{8}$	$3\frac{7}{8}$	$3\frac{7}{8}$	5	6	$3\frac{7}{8}$	372	165
				◆ Trinity County / Terry H. Walker / Terry H. Walker / 1986							
$139\frac{2}{8}$	$20\frac{5}{8}$	$20\frac{4}{8}$	20	$22\frac{6}{8}$	$4\frac{1}{8}$	4	4	4	0	372	165
				◆ Humboldt County / Daniel D. Zent / Daniel D. Zent / 1991							
$139\frac{2}{8}$	22	$21\frac{1}{8}$	$18\frac{6}{8}$	$22\frac{5}{8}$	$4\frac{4}{8}$	$4\frac{3}{8}$	6	6	$3\frac{4}{8}$	372	165
				◆ Siskiyou County / Thomas K. Higgs / Thomas K. Higgs / 1993							
$139\frac{1}{8}$	22	$21\frac{2}{8}$	$18\frac{5}{8}$	$20\frac{2}{8}$	$4\frac{2}{8}$	$4\frac{2}{8}$	5	5	0	379	170
				◆ Humboldt County / George E. Watson / George E. Watson / 1933							
$139\frac{1}{8}$	$22\frac{1}{8}$	22	$17\frac{5}{8}$	$20\frac{2}{8}$	4	$5\frac{6}{8}$	4	5	0	379	170
				◆ Mendocino County / John Winn, Jr. / John Winn, Jr. / 1972							
139	22	$21\frac{6}{8}$	$17\frac{2}{8}$	$19\frac{2}{8}$	4	$4\frac{1}{8}$	4	4	0	382	172
				◆ Trinity County / Roger J. Scala / Roger J. Scala / 1990							
$138\frac{7}{8}$	21	$22\frac{2}{8}$	$20\frac{5}{8}$	$22\frac{3}{8}$	$4\frac{5}{8}$	$4\frac{2}{8}$	4	4	0	389	173
				◆ Siskiyou County / Darrell Nowdesha / Darrell Nowdesha / 1961							
$138\frac{7}{8}$	$19\frac{1}{8}$	$20\frac{5}{8}$	$15\frac{3}{8}$	18	5	$4\frac{7}{8}$	6	5	$2\frac{2}{8}$	389	173
				◆ Trinity County / William O. Louderback / William O. Louderback / 1963							
$138\frac{7}{8}$	$21\frac{3}{8}$	$21\frac{7}{8}$	$19\frac{5}{8}$	$22\frac{2}{8}$	$4\frac{3}{8}$	$4\frac{5}{8}$	4	5	0	389	173
				◆ Mendocino County / Donald W. Biggs / Donald W. Biggs / 1992							
$138\frac{6}{8}$	$21\frac{3}{8}$	$20\frac{4}{8}$	16	$18\frac{5}{8}$	4	$4\frac{1}{8}$	5	5	0	395	176
				◆ Humboldt County / Larry Bowermaster / Larry Bowermaster / 1964							
$138\frac{6}{8}$	$22\frac{2}{8}$	$21\frac{1}{8}$	$22\frac{2}{8}$	$24\frac{2}{8}$	$4\frac{1}{8}$	4	5	5	0	395	176
				◆ Mendocino County / Gordon O. Hanson / Gordon O. Hanson / 1988							
$138\frac{6}{8}$	$18\frac{4}{8}$	18	$16\frac{2}{8}$	$18\frac{4}{8}$	$3\frac{6}{8}$	$3\frac{7}{8}$	5	5	0	395	176
				◆ Mendocino County / Richard L. Moore / Richard L. Moore / 1988							
$138\frac{6}{8}$	$22\frac{3}{8}$	$25\frac{2}{8}$	$20\frac{6}{8}$	$22\frac{6}{8}$	$3\frac{6}{8}$	$3\frac{6}{8}$	4	4	0	395	176
				◆ Mendocino County / Thomas R. Erasmy / Thomas R. Erasmy / 1993							

Score	Length of Main Beam R	L	Inside Spread	Greatest Spread	Circumference at Smallest Place between Burr and First Point R	L	Number of Points R	L	Total of Lengths Abnormal Points	All-Time Rank	State Rank
138 4/8	22 4/8	22 7/8	18 6/8	20 3/8	4	4	5	4	0	404	180
◆ Mendocino County / Jess Jones / Jess Jones / 1950											
138 4/8	21 1/8	20	18 2/8	21 2/8	4 3/8	4	5	5	0	404	180
◆ Siskiyou County / Bob Courts / Bob Courts / 1965											
138 4/8	19 4/8	19 4/8	17 2/8	20 2/8	4	4	5	6	1 2/8	404	180
◆ Siskiyou County / John Carmichael / John Carmichael / 1969											
138 3/8	22 4/8	22 2/8	18	21 4/8	4 4/8	4 1/8	5	5	11 1/8	407	183
◆ Humboldt County / Garry Hughes / Garry Hughes / 1968											
138 3/8	20 4/8	20 1/8	18 5/8	20 1/8	4 1/8	4 3/8	4	5	0	407	183
◆ Trinity County / Stanley A. Apuli / Stanley A. Apuli / 1991											
138 2/8	21 4/8	22	18 2/8	20 2/8	5 2/8	5 3/8	5	6	1 2/8	411	185
◆ Trinity County / E.G. Palmrose / Daniel M. Phillips / 1940											
138 2/8	21 3/8	21 3/8	15 6/8	17 3/8	4	3 7/8	5	5	0	411	185
◆ Tehama County / Robert L. Armanasco / Robert L. Armanasco / 1968											
138 2/8	21 5/8	22	17 6/8	19 2/8	3 6/8	3 6/8	5	5	0	411	185
◆ Trinity County / Thomas A. Pettigrew, Jr. / Thomas A. Pettigrew, Jr. / 1972											
138 2/8	18	18	14 4/8	17 4/8	4 4/8	4 1/8	5	5	0	411	185
◆ Mendocino County / Kenzia L. Drake / Kenzia L. Drake / 1985											
138 2/8	19 5/8	20 4/8	16 2/8	18 6/8	4 3/8	4 3/8	5	5	0	411	185
◆ Trinity County / Monte D. Matheson / Monte D. Matheson / 1990											
138	22 3/8	21 7/8	21 1/8	22 6/8	4 7/8	5	5	6	1 3/8	420	190
◆ Mendocino County / Brian K. Isaac / Brian K. Isaac / 1985											
137 7/8	20 4/8	19 4/8	18 6/8	23 4/8	4	4 2/8	6	5	1 1/8	423	191
◆ Shasta County / Paul G. Carter / Paul G. Carter / 1964											
137 7/8	18 4/8	17 5/8	17 3/8	19 6/8	4	4	5	5	0	423	191
◆ Trinity County / Picked Up / North Coast Tax. / 1965											
137 7/8	18	18 5/8	18 5/8	26 1/8	5	4 5/8	4	4	0	423	191
◆ Santa Clara County / Farber L. Johnston, Jr. / Farber L. Johnston, Jr. / 1967											
137 7/8	21	21	16	18 1/8	5	4 7/8	5	6	1 1/8	423	191
◆ Trinity County / Daniel M. Phillips / Daniel M. Phillips / 1993											
137 6/8	19 1/8	19 6/8	16 6/8	20 2/8	4	4	4	4	0	429	195
◆ Siskiyou County / Robert L. Miller / Robert L. Miller / 1985											
137 6/8	20 2/8	20 7/8	19 6/8	21 3/8	3 6/8	3 7/8	4	5	0	429	195
◆ Trinity County / Kevin Clair / Kevin Clair / 1986											
137 5/8	20 4/8	20 3/8	19 5/8	23 2/8	4 4/8	4 5/8	5	5	0	431	197
◆ Mendocino County / P.R. Borton / John R. Borton / 1965											

Score	Length of Main Beam		Inside Spread	Greatest Spread	Circumference at Smallest Place between Burr and First Point		Number of Points		Total of Lengths Abnormal Points	All-Time Rank	State Rank
	R	L			R	L	R	L			
◆ Locality / Hunter / Owner / Date Killed											
137⁵⁄₈	19⁷⁄₈	19⁵⁄₈	17⁵⁄₈	20⁴⁄₈	4⁴⁄₈	4⁶⁄₈	7	5	3²⁄₈	431	197
◆ Napa County / Bruce D. Ringsmith / Bruce D. Ringsmith / 1967											
137⁵⁄₈	20³⁄₈	21⅛	20⁷⁄₈	23⁴⁄₈	4⅛	4	4	4	0	431	197
◆ Trinity County / Kenzia L. Drake / Kenzia L. Drake / 1994											
137⁴⁄₈	19³⁄₈	19	17	18⁴⁄₈	4⅛	4⅛	5	5	0	435	200
◆ Trinity County / Philip Grunert / Philip Grunert / 1967											
137⁴⁄₈	21⅛	21⅛	19	22⅛	4⅛	4³⁄₈	5	5	0	435	200
◆ Trinity County / Picked Up / Craig & Joy Brown / 1982											
137³⁄₈	20⁴⁄₈	21⁷⁄₈	18⁷⁄₈	21⅛	4⁶⁄₈	4⁵⁄₈	5	5	0	438	202
◆ Mendocino County / Carlton C. White / Carlton C. White / 1983											
137³⁄₈	20⁶⁄₈	21²⁄₈	17⁶⁄₈	23	4⅛	4⅛	6	5	3⅛	438	202
◆ Trinity County / Robert E. Fulmer / Robert E. Fulmer / 1993											
137⅛	20	20⁵⁄₈	23²⁄₈	28	4³⁄₈	4³⁄₈	5	6	1⁴⁄₈	445	204
◆ Shasta County / Jack Floyd / Jack Floyd / 1957											
137⅛	23	22⁴⁄₈	22⁷⁄₈	24³⁄₈	5	4⁶⁄₈	5	4	0	445	204
◆ Tehama County / Clint Heiber / Clint Heiber / 1977											
137	20⁴⁄₈	21	21⁶⁄₈	24	3⁷⁄₈	3⁶⁄₈	5	5	0	450	206
◆ Siskiyou County / Shirley Eastlick / Shirley Eastlick / 1962											
136⁷⁄₈	20⅛	20³⁄₈	16⅛	18³⁄₈	4	4	5	5	0	454	207
◆ Humboldt County / Michael M. Golightly / Michael M. Golightly / 1991											
136⁶⁄₈	21⁶⁄₈	23	18²⁄₈	20²⁄₈	4⁷⁄₈	4⁶⁄₈	4	4	0	456	208
◆ Shasta County / Vance Corrigan / Vance Corrigan / 1957											
136⁴⁄₈	20³⁄₈	20⅛	18	20	4⁴⁄₈	4⁴⁄₈	5	5	0	464	209
◆ Ukiah / Charles Tollini / Charles Tollini / 1960											
136⁴⁄₈	22	22⅛	18⁴⁄₈	22⅛	5	4⁷⁄₈	5	4	0	464	209
◆ Mendocino County / Jeff P. Leyden / Jeff P. Leyden / 1993											
136²⁄₈	20⁶⁄₈	20⁴⁄₈	20²⁄₈	21⁷⁄₈	3⁶⁄₈	4⅛	4	5	0	471	211
◆ Covelo / David G. Cox / David G. Cox / 1967											
136²⁄₈	21⁶⁄₈	22	21⁴⁄₈	22⁶⁄₈	5	4⁷⁄₈	5	5	0	471	211
◆ Siskiyou County / Wayne G. Rose / Wayne G. Rose / 1977											
136	21⁶⁄₈	23	19	23	5⅛	5⅛	6	6	9⁶⁄₈	479	213
◆ Santa Clara County / Mrs. Maitland Armstrong / Mrs. Maitland Armstrong / 1956											
136	21⁴⁄₈	21	17	19⁶⁄₈	4⁴⁄₈	4³⁄₈	5	5	0	479	213
◆ Mendocino Natl. For. / Edward Q. Garayalde / Edward Q. Garayalde / 1966											
136	21⁴⁄₈	21	19²⁄₈	21⅛	4⁶⁄₈	4⁷⁄₈	4	5	0	479	213
◆ Tehama County / Robert L. Armanasco / Robert L. Armanasco / 1968											

Score	Length of Main Beam R	L	Inside Spread	Greatest Spread	Circumference at Smallest Place between Burr and First Point R	L	Number of Points R	L	Total of Lengths Abnormal Points	All-Time Rank	State Rank
136	23 1/8	23	21 6/8	23 6/8	4 7/8	4 6/8	3	4	0	479	213
			San Mateo County / Dan Caughey, Sr. / Dan Caughey, Sr. / 1973								
136	20 4/8	19 2/8	19	22 3/8	4 1/8	4 1/8	6	6	8 2/8	479	213
			Trinity County / Richard G. Shelton / Richard G. Shelton / 1973								
136	20 4/8	19 6/8	19 2/8	24 2/8	4	4	5	5	0	479	213
			Trinity County / John P. Morton / John P. Morton / 1987								
135 7/8	19 2/8	19 3/8	16 1/8	18 4/8	4 2/8	4 2/8	4	4	0	485	219
			Tehama County / John A. Crockett / John A. Crockett / 1982								
135 6/8	20 2/8	20 1/8	19 4/8	21 6/8	3 4/8	3 3/8	4	4	0	490	220
			Trinity County / Roy J. Renner / Roy J. Renner / 1965								
135 6/8	20 4/8	20 4/8	16	19 6/8	4 2/8	4 1/8	5	5	0	490	220
			Mendocino County / Phyllis W. Stevenson / Phyllis W. Stevenson / 1992								
135 5/8	20 2/8	21 2/8	15 1/8	17	4 1/8	4 1/8	5	5	0	497	222
			Humboldt County / Michael M. Golightly / Michael M. Golightly / 1990								
135 5/8	23 7/8	23 6/8	20 4/8	22 5/8	4 7/8	4 4/8	4	5	1 1/8	497	222
			Mendocino County / Ray D. MacDonald, Jr. / Ray D. MacDonald, Jr. / 1990								
135 4/8	20 1/8	20 6/8	17 4/8	20 2/8	4 3/8	4 3/8	5	5	0	501	224
			Trinity County / Robert T. Hammaker / Robert T. Hammaker / 1988								
135 2/8	19 6/8	20	15	17	3 4/8	3 3/8	4	4	0	506	225
			Trinity County / Andy Burgess / Andy Burgess / 1959								
135 2/8	19 1/8	19 4/8	13 2/8	16 6/8	3 4/8	3 4/8	4	4	0	506	225
			Humboldt County / Christopher A. Umbertus / Christopher A. Umbertus / 1981								
135	19	19 5/8	15 4/8	19 6/8	4 1/8	4 2/8	5	5	0	510	227
			Humboldt County / Edward F. Burgess / Edward F. Burgess / 1965								
135	18 6/8	18 6/8	15 6/8	17 4/8	4 3/8	4 2/8	5	5	0	510	227
			Trinity County / Andrew M. Felt / Andrew M. Felt / 1986								
135	22 6/8	23 2/8	20	21 6/8	4 4/8	4 3/8	4	4	0	510	227
			Mendocino County / Rodney E. Carley / Rodney E. Carley / 1989								
134 7/8	18 5/8	18 6/8	20 2/8	24 5/8	4 5/8	4 4/8	9	9	11 3/8	515	230
			Mendocino County / O.E. Schubert / Walter R. Schubert / 1917								
134 7/8	19 6/8	20 5/8	14 5/8	18	4 1/8	4 1/8	5	5	0	515	230
			Mendocino County / Jesse P. Foster, Jr. / Jesse P. Foster, Jr. / 1964								
134 7/8	22 3/8	22 2/8	18 3/8	21 5/8	4	4 2/8	4	5	0	515	230
			Tehama County / Mario Sereni, Jr. / Mario Sereni, Jr. / 1964								
134 7/8	21 1/8	21 5/8	14 4/8	17	4 1/8	4 2/8	5	6	3 5/8	515	230
			San Bernadino County / James Tacke / James Tacke / 1966								

Score	Length of Main Beam R	L	Inside Spread	Greatest Spread	Circumference at Smallest Place between Burr and First Point R	L	Number of Points R	L	Total of Lengths Abnormal Points	All-Time Rank	State Rank
				Locality / Hunter / Owner / Date Killed							
134⁷⁄₈	20⁴⁄₈	20³⁄₈	17³⁄₈	19⁷⁄₈	4¹⁄₈	4²⁄₈	5	5	0	515	230
◆ Siskiyou County / George L. Wilson / George L. Wilson / 1991											
134⁷⁄₈	17⁶⁄₈	17⁵⁄₈	15³⁄₈	17⁷⁄₈	4	4	5	5	0	515	230
◆ Mendocino County / Bette C. Hill / Bette C. Hill / 1993											
134⁶⁄₈	19⁴⁄₈	20	16³⁄₈	19⁷⁄₈	4⁴⁄₈	4⁴⁄₈	5	6	4⁷⁄₈	523	236
◆ Trinity County / Donald E. Stevens / Donald E. Stevens / 1979											
134⁶⁄₈	19⁷⁄₈	19⁶⁄₈	17²⁄₈	21	4⁶⁄₈	4⁷⁄₈	5	5	0	523	236
◆ Humboldt County / Bettie L. Lovie / Bettie L. Lovie / 1988											
134⁶⁄₈	20⁷⁄₈	21	18⁴⁄₈	20¹⁄₈	4¹⁄₈	4³⁄₈	4	4	0	523	236
◆ Trinity County / Leon T. Gemini / Leon T. Gemini / 1994											
134⁵⁄₈	20⁴⁄₈	20³⁄₈	15⁵⁄₈	18⁶⁄₈	4⁵⁄₈	4⁶⁄₈	5	5	0	530	239
◆ Siskiyou County / Roy Eastlick / Roy Eastlick / 1965											
134⁴⁄₈	21¹⁄₈	21²⁄₈	20²⁄₈	22¹⁄₈	4¹⁄₈	4³⁄₈	7	6	9²⁄₈	531	240
◆ Trinity County / William M. Longhurst / William M. Longhurst / 1951											
134⁴⁄₈	19⁴⁄₈	20	17	19	4⁴⁄₈	4²⁄₈	5	5	0	531	240
◆ Humboldt County / J.A. Phelps / J.A. Phelps / 1966											
134⁴⁄₈	22	21⁴⁄₈	18⁴⁄₈	21	5²⁄₈	5¹⁄₈	5	4	0	531	240
◆ Sonoma County / Richard O'Farrell / Richard O'Farrell / 1984											
134³⁄₈	22⁵⁄₈	21²⁄₈	22³⁄₈	24³⁄₈	4⁷⁄₈	4⁷⁄₈	5	4	0	537	243
◆ Tehama County / Bob C. Haase / Bob C. Haase / 1987											
134³⁄₈	21¹⁄₈	21⁶⁄₈	17⁷⁄₈	19³⁄₈	4²⁄₈	4¹⁄₈	5	5	0	537	243
◆ Humboldt County / Christopher L. Rudd / Christopher L. Rudd / 1991											
134²⁄₈	19⁴⁄₈	21	16	18³⁄₈	4	4³⁄₈	4	4	0	542	245
◆ Humboldt County / G.L. Dorris / G.L. Dorris / 1973											
134²⁄₈	24¹⁄₈	23⁶⁄₈	22⁴⁄₈	26⁶⁄₈	4³⁄₈	4⁴⁄₈	4	4	0	542	245
◆ Colusa County / Gregory R. Bonetti / Gregory R. Bonetti / 1983											
134²⁄₈	19³⁄₈	19⁶⁄₈	20²⁄₈	22	4⁷⁄₈	4⁶⁄₈	6	5	1⁶⁄₈	542	245
◆ Mendocino County / Sebastian D. Carrasco / Sebastian D. Carrasco / 1986											
134²⁄₈	18⁴⁄₈	19⁴⁄₈	13	16⁷⁄₈	4⁵⁄₈	4²⁄₈	5	5	0	542	245
◆ Mendocino County / Gary D. Powell / Gary D. Powell / 1990											
134¹⁄₈	19⁵⁄₈	20	16⁵⁄₈	19⁴⁄₈	4⁴⁄₈	4⁴⁄₈	5	5	0	550	249
◆ Mendocino County / Danny Pardini / Danny Pardini / 1976											
134¹⁄₈	18²⁄₈	18²⁄₈	14⁷⁄₈	17²⁄₈	4	4	6	5	1²⁄₈	550	249
◆ Trinity County / David Deininger / David Deininger / 1980											
134	19⁶⁄₈	19²⁄₈	16²⁄₈	18¹⁄₈	3⁶⁄₈	3⁴⁄₈	7	5	3	555	251
◆ Siskiyou County / Alicia Whittaker / Alicia Whittaker / 1970											

Score	Length of Main Beam R	L	Inside Spread	Greatest Spread	Circumference at Smallest Place between Burr and First Point R	L	Number of Points R	L	Total of Lengths Abnormal Points	All-Time Rank	State Rank
	Locality / Hunter / Owner / Date Killed										
134	18 4/8	19 3/8	17	19 4/8	4 6/8	4 6/8	5	5	0	555	251
	Glenn County / John Lohse / John Lohse / 1994										
133 7/8	20 4/8	21 3/8	13 5/8	16 5/8	3 6/8	3 5/8	5	5	0	558	253
	Siskiyou County / William E. Turner / William E. Turner / 1982										
133 7/8	19 4/8	21 3/8	20	24 6/8	4 4/8	4 4/8	6	4	6 1/8	558	253
	Contra Costa County / Howard F. Gardner / Howard F. Gardner / 1992										
133 6/8	21 2/8	21 5/8	17 2/8	21 3/8	4 3/8	4 3/8	5	4	0	560	255
	Mendocino County / Marvin DeAngelis / Marvin DeAngelis / 1978										
133 6/8	21 2/8	21 1/8	16	17 6/8	3 7/8	4	5	5	0	560	255
	Mendocino County / Terence K. Prechter / Terence K. Prechter / 1986										
133 5/8	19 1/8	18 3/8	15 7/8	21 3/8	3 4/8	3 7/8	6	4	5 4/8	564	257
	Siskiyou County / Edwin W. Masonheimer / Edwin W. Masonheimer / 1978										
133 5/8	21 3/8	21 2/8	21 5/8	24	4 4/8	4 3/8	4	4	0	564	257
	Shasta County / Mitchell A. Thorson / Mitchell A. Thorson / 1992										
133 4/8	21	22 4/8	17 4/8	20 4/8	4 6/8	5	6	5	5	571	259
	Trinity County / Barry Griffin / Barry Griffin / 1976										
133 4/8	22	20 4/8	20 4/8	24 4/8	4 6/8	4 4/8	5	6	1 4/8	571	259
	Trinity County / George M. Moxon / George M. Moxon / 1977										
133 4/8	22 1/8	22 1/8	18 1/8	27	4 6/8	4 6/8	7	6	15 3/8	571	259
	Mendocino County / Ryan McDonald / Ryan McDonald / 1991										
133 3/8	18 3/8	18 3/8	17 3/8	19 2/8	4 4/8	4 4/8	5	5	0	578	262
	Mendocino County / Richard L. Moore / Richard L. Moore / 1989										
133 3/8	20 2/8	20 3/8	19 3/8	22 4/8	4 1/8	4	4	4	0	578	262
	Trinity County / Reuben R. Tipton III / Reuben R. Tipton III / 1993										
133 2/8	19 1/8	18 5/8	16	21 7/8	3 2/8	3 2/8	5	5	0	584	264
	Trinity County / Kirk Finch / Kirk Finch / 1975										
133 2/8	20 2/8	20 7/8	17	19 2/8	4 2/8	4 2/8	5	5	0	584	264
	Trinity County / Ralph L. Perry / Ralph L. Perry / 1980										
133 1/8	22 7/8	22	21 1/8	23 3/8	4 5/8	5	5	5	0	591	266
	Trinity County / Hugh A. Dow / Hugh A. Dow / 1969										
133	20 4/8	20 4/8	19 4/8	21 6/8	4 4/8	5	4	4	0	597	267
	Napa County / Fred C. Framsted / Fred C. Framsted / 1966										
133	19 1/8	18 4/8	18 6/8	21 7/8	4 3/8	4 6/8	5	5	0	597	267
	Humboldt County / George B. Stiglich / George B. Stiglich / 1988										
132 7/8	21 6/8	23 3/8	19 4/8	22	4 5/8	4 4/8	6	5	1 3/8	603	269
	Tehama County / Joe McBrayer / Joe McBrayer / 1981										

Score	Length of Main Beam R	L	Inside Spread	Greatest Spread	Circumference at Smallest Place between Burr and First Point R	L	Number of Points R	L	Total of Lengths Abnormal Points	All-Time Rank	State Rank
132 7/8	19 1/8	19 3/8	16 5/8	19 3/8	4	4 3/8	5	5	0	603	269
◆ Mendocino County / Gregory C. Moore / Gregory C. Moore / 1985											
132 7/8	20 6/8	21 4/8	19 1/8	21 1/8	4 2/8	4 3/8	5	5	0	603	269
◆ Humboldt County / Dennis R. Lake / Dennis R. Lake / 1988											
132 7/8	21 1/8	22 5/8	17	20	3 2/8	3 2/8	5	5	0	603	269
◆ Mendocino County / John E. Coughlin / John E. Coughlin / 1988											
132 7/8	19 7/8	18 3/8	21 4/8	22 6/8	4 2/8	4 2/8	4	4	0	603	269
◆ Trinity County / Jim D. Odom / Jim D. Odom / 1989											
132 6/8	19 1/8	17 6/8	16 4/8	18	3 6/8	3 7/8	5	5	0	610	274
◆ Tehama County / Daniel E. Osborne / Daniel E. Osborne / 1956											
132 6/8	19 5/8	21	18 6/8	19 5/8	4 4/8	4 4/8	5	5	0	610	274
◆ Mendocino County / Mason Geisinger / Mason Geisinger / 1967											
132 6/8	22	22 6/8	21 6/8	23 1/8	4 4/8	4 6/8	5	4	2	610	274
◆ Mendocino County / Jay M. Gates III / Jay M. Gates III / 1984											
132 6/8	20 5/8	21 5/8	17 6/8	20 2/8	4 4/8	4 4/8	5	5	0	610	274
◆ Siskiyou County / Paul J. Bruno / Paul J. Bruno / 1985											
132 5/8	20 4/8	20 2/8	16 1/8	18 1/8	4 1/8	4 3/8	5	5	0	616	278
◆ Siskiyou County / Daniel A. Rich / Daniel A. Rich / 1990											
132 3/8	22 2/8	22	19	21	5 1/8	4 5/8	5	4	1 1/8	622	279
◆ Trinity County / David L. Matley / David L. Matley / 1981											
132 3/8	18 7/8	19 7/8	18 1/8	22 7/8	4	4 1/8	5	5	0	622	279
◆ Siskiyou County / Lawrence F. Weckerle / Lawrence F. Weckerle / 1982											
132 3/8	20 4/8	20 4/8	16 3/8	20 5/8	4 1/8	4 1/8	5	6	2 6/8	622	279
◆ Mendocino County / Richard L. Moore / Richard L. Moore / 1989											
132 3/8	22 7/8	21 6/8	16 1/8	18 1/8	4 1/8	4	5	5	0	622	279
◆ Siskiyou County / Edward P. Reardon / Edward P. Reardon / 1989											
132 2/8	19 5/8	18 7/8	18 2/8	24 7/8	4 5/8	4 1/8	5	4	0	629	283
◆ Mendocino County / P.R. Borton / William R. Borton / 1971											
132 2/8	21 3/8	19 3/8	14 6/8	17 2/8	4 6/8	4 1/8	5	4	0	629	283
◆ Humboldt County / Guy Hooper / Guy Hooper / 1977											
132 2/8	20	20	16 4/8	18 4/8	4 1/8	4 2/8	5	5	0	629	283
◆ Mendocino County / Richard L. Moore / Richard L. Moore / 1987											
132 1/8	20 6/8	20 4/8	15 1/8	17 1/8	5 2/8	5 1/8	4	4	0	637	286
◆ Trinity County / R.C. Kauffman / R.C. Kauffman / 1936											
132 1/8	20 6/8	19 6/8	19 1/8	22 1/8	3 2/8	3 2/8	4	4	0	637	286
◆ Mendocino County / Fred E. Borton II / Matthew E. Borton / 1971											

Score	Length of Main Beam R	L	Inside Spread	Greatest Spread	Circumference at Smallest Place between Burr and First Point R	L	Number of Points R	L	Total of Lengths Abnormal Points	All-Time Rank	State Rank
					♦ Locality / Hunter / Owner / Date Killed						
132 1/8	20	19 4/8	18 1/8	21 1/8	4	4	5	5	0	637	286
					♦ Trinity County / Ronald L. Schneider / Ronald L. Schneider / 1979						
131 7/8	22 3/8	21 6/8	18 5/8	20 1/8	4 3/8	4 3/8	4	4	0	642	289
					♦ Santa Clara County / Gary D. Thompson / Gary D. Thompson / 1994						
131 6/8	19 1/8	19 3/8	14	16 3/8	4	3 7/8	5	5	0	643	290
					♦ Siskiyou County / Sid E. Ziegler / Sid E. Ziegler / 1957						
131 6/8	21	19 4/8	18	20 3/8	5	5	5	5	0	643	290
					♦ Trinity County / Carter B. Dow / Carter B. Dow / 1961						
131 6/8	19 1/8	18 5/8	14 4/8	17 3/8	4 2/8	4 2/8	5	5	0	643	290
					♦ Humboldt County / Larry Wilson / Larry Wilson / 1978						
131 6/8	18 5/8	19 3/8	13 6/8	15 4/8	5 1/8	4 6/8	6	5	2 4/8	643	290
					♦ Trinity County / Melvin M. Clair / Melvin M. Clair / 1979						
131 6/8	20 2/8	20	18 2/8	21 7/8	3 6/8	4	5	5	0	643	290
					♦ Trinity County / Kenneth L. Cogle, Jr. / Kenneth L. Cogle, Jr. / 1981						
131 6/8	20 4/8	20 4/8	21 3/8	22 6/8	4 4/8	4 3/8	5	5	0	643	290
					♦ Lake County / Michael D. Keesee, Sr. / Michael D. Keesee, Sr. / 1982						
131 4/8	19 6/8	19 1/8	17 2/8	21	3 6/8	3 6/8	5	6	3 4/8	653	296
					♦ Mendocino County / James J. McBride / James J. McBride / 1982						
131 4/8	20 4/8	21 3/8	18 1/8	20 6/8	4 6/8	4 6/8	6	5	1 1/8	653	296
					♦ Trinity County / Robert E. Fulmer / Robert E. Fulmer / 1993						
131 2/8	19 6/8	19 6/8	17 4/8	19 6/8	4	3 7/8	5	5	0	664	298
					♦ Trinity County / L. Irvin Barnhart / L. Irvin Barnhart / 1986						
131 2/8	21 1/8	19 4/8	18 4/8	24 4/8	3 7/8	3 7/8	5	5	0	664	298
					♦ Tehama County / Richard D. Stillwell / Richard D. Stillwell / 1989						
131 1/8	20 3/8	20	21 6/8	23 2/8	5 4/8	5 1/8	4	5	0	669	300
					♦ Mendocino County / Richard L. Valladao / Richard L. Valladao / 1991						
131	18 4/8	17 4/8	15 6/8	20 4/8	3 7/8	4	5	5	0	670	301
					♦ Siskiyou County / George Quigley / George Quigley / 1971						
131	18 2/8	18 4/8	18 4/8	21	4 2/8	4 2/8	5	5	0	670	301
					♦ Siskiyou County / Raymond Whittaker / Raymond Whittaker / 1981						
131	21 4/8	21 7/8	21 4/8	22	6 1/8	5 7/8	8	6	8	670	301
					♦ Mendocino County / Betty L. Gidding / Betty L. Gidding / 1992						
130 7/8	20 7/8	20 4/8	16 5/8	19 4/8	3 7/8	3 7/8	5	5	0	676	304
					♦ Tehama County / James D. Fiske / James D. Fiske / 1956						
130 7/8	17 5/8	19 4/8	16 7/8	22	4	4 2/8	4	5	0	676	304
					♦ Mendocino County / John W. McGehee / John W. McGehee / 1989						

Score	Length of Main Beam R	L	Inside Spread	Greatest Spread	Circumference at Smallest Place between Burr and First Point R	L	Number of Points R	L	Total of Lengths Abnormal Points	All-Time Rank	State Rank
			◆ *Locality / Hunter / Owner / Date Killed*								
130 6/8	21 6/8	21 4/8	19 4/8	21 2/8	4	4 2/8	8	6	10 2/8	678	306
	◆ *Siskiyou County / Larry E. Richey / Larry E. Richey / 1956*										
130 6/8	20 5/8	19	19	21 2/8	4 3/8	4	5	4	0	678	306
	◆ *Mendocino County / Tom Enberg / Tom Enberg / 1970*										
130 5/8	18	20	17 1/8	19	5	5	6	6	3 4/8	687	308
	◆ *Lake County / Bernard Domries / Bernard Domries / 1940*										
130 5/8	24 2/8	23 3/8	23 2/8	25	4 3/8	4 4/8	4	5	1 1/8	687	308
	◆ *Siskiyou County / Vernon Sutherlin / Vernon Sutherlin / 1961*										
130 4/8	21 6/8	21 7/8	18 6/8	18 6/8	5 2/8	4 2/8	5	3	0	690	310
	◆ *Mendocino County / Mitchell A. Thorson / Mitchell A. Thorson / 1969*										
130 4/8	19	19 5/8	15 4/8	19 3/8	4 2/8	4 2/8	4	4	0	690	310
	◆ *Santa Cruz County / William J. McGrath / William J. McGrath / 1982*										
130 4/8	22 5/8	22 1/8	21 1/8	22 6/8	4 2/8	4 1/8	4	5	1 1/8	690	310
	◆ *Trinity County / Wayne Erickson / Wayne Erickson / 1985*										
130 4/8	21	21 1/8	19 4/8	22	3 6/8	3 5/8	5	5	0	690	310
	◆ *Trinity County / Robert T. Hammaker / Robert T. Hammaker / 1991*										
130 4/8	19	19 2/8	19 5/8	21 1/8	4 5/8	4 3/8	5	5	0	690	310
	◆ *Humboldt County / Jim Dervin / Jim Dervin / 1992*										
130 3/8	18 3/8	18 1/8	16 1/8	18 1/8	4 2/8	4 2/8	5	5	0	699	315
	◆ *Mendocino County / Helen F. Ornbaun / Helen F. Ornbaun / 1960*										
130 3/8	20	20	16 3/8	18 4/8	4	4	5	5	0	699	315
	◆ *Siskiyou County / John Carmichael / John Carmichael / 1970*										
130 2/8	19 6/8	19 4/8	17	19	4 4/8	4 4/8	4	4	0	703	317
	◆ *Santa Clara County / John J. Marino / John J. Marino / 1993*										
130 1/8	20 3/8	20 1/8	20 1/8	21 5/8	4 2/8	4 5/8	4	4	0	706	318
	◆ *San Mateo County / Dan Caughey III / Dan Caughey III / 1988*										
130	22 1/8	22 2/8	15 6/8	17 7/8	3 5/8	3 5/8	5	3	0	709	319
	◆ *Trinity County / Terry H. Walker / Terry H. Walker / 1979*										
130	20 2/8	19 6/8	19 2/8	20 3/8	4 3/8	4 4/8	5	5	0	709	319
	◆ *Mendocino County / Matt D. Mazzuca / Matt D. Mazzuca / 1994*										
129 5/8	19 6/8	20 2/8	18 3/8	21	4	3 6/8	5	5	0	712	321
	◆ *Trinity County / John P. Livingston / John P. Livingston / 1991*										
129	20	17 5/8	14 4/8	17 6/8	3 7/8	4 7/8	4	5	0	716	322
	◆ *Humboldt County / Stephen Walker / Stephen Walker / 1961*										
128 4/8	20	20 2/8	18 7/8	21 4/8	4 1/8	4 1/8	5	6	1 1/8	719	323
	◆ *Trinity County / Tony Stoer / Tony Stoer / 1979*										

CALIFORNIA COLUMBIA BLACKTAIL DEER *(continued)*

Score	Length of Main Beam R	L	Inside Spread	Greatest Spread	Circumference at Smallest Place between Burr and First Point R	L	Number of Points R	L	Total of Lengths Abnormal Points	All-Time Rank	State Rank
128²⁄₈	20	19³⁄₈	15²⁄₈	17²⁄₈	4²⁄₈	4⁴⁄₈	5	5	0	720	324
◆ Trinity County / Terry L. Barns / Terry L. Barns / 1991											
127⁷⁄₈	20⁴⁄₈	21²⁄₈	15³⁄₈	17⁴⁄₈	3³⁄₈	3³⁄₈	4	4	0	723	325
◆ Trinity County / Marlene L. Coats / Marlene & Johnny Coats / 1988											
127²⁄₈	21	21³⁄₈	21	23⁷⁄₈	4⁴⁄₈	4⁴⁄₈	4	5	0	728	326
◆ Mendocino County / Timothy Hickam / Timothy Hickam / 1991											
126⁵⁄₈	18¹⁄₈	19¹⁄₈	20¹⁄₈	21⁶⁄₈	4	4	5	5	0	730	327
◆ Sonoma County / William E. Soekland / William E. Soekland / 1989											
125⁶⁄₈	19⁴⁄₈	19⁴⁄₈	19²⁄₈	22	4	3⁷⁄₈	5	5	0	732	328
◆ Mendocino County / Jon McQueen / Jon McQueen / 1993											
125⁵⁄₈	18²⁄₈	19⁵⁄₈	22⁵⁄₈	23⁵⁄₈	3⁶⁄₈	3⁵⁄₈	4	4	0	733	329
◆ Humboldt County / Lodewijk J. Wurfbain / Lodewijk J. Wurfbain / 1986											
125³⁄₈	19⁷⁄₈	20⁴⁄₈	15³⁄₈	19⁴⁄₈	4¹⁄₈	4¹⁄₈	4	4	0	735	330
◆ Humboldt County / Michael Williams / Michael Williams / 1993											
125²⁄₈	19⁴⁄₈	19⁶⁄₈	16⁴⁄₈	18³⁄₈	3⁶⁄₈	3⁷⁄₈	5	5	0	736	331
◆ Humboldt County / Dan Noga / Dan Noga / 1991											
125	19⁴⁄₈	19³⁄₈	17	19⁴⁄₈	4¹⁄₈	4	4	5	0	737	332
◆ Sonoma County / Matthew R. Petersen / Matthew R. Petersen / 1993											
124²⁄₈	19³⁄₈	20³⁄₈	18	19⁵⁄₈	4	4	5	4	0	738	333
◆ Santa Cruz County / Warren D. Huber / William C. Huber / 1971											
123⁶⁄₈	21⁵⁄₈	20²⁄₈	18	20⁴⁄₈	3⁵⁄₈	4²⁄₈	3	4	0	739	334
◆ Trinity County / Joseph C. Cordonier / Joseph C. Cordonier / 1991											
123⁵⁄₈	18	18¹⁄₈	15⁵⁄₈	19¹⁄₈	4³⁄₈	4²⁄₈	5	5	0	740	335
◆ Trinity County / Monte D. Matheson / Monte D. Matheson / 1988											
123³⁄₈	18⁷⁄₈	17⁴⁄₈	19⁶⁄₈	20⁷⁄₈	4³⁄₈	4²⁄₈	5	5	0	742	336
◆ Mendocino County / Timothy Hickam / Timothy Hickam / 1990											
122⁶⁄₈	21⁷⁄₈	19⁶⁄₈	16	17³⁄₈	4⁴⁄₈	4⁴⁄₈	4	5	0	746	337
◆ San Mateo County / Daniel R. Caughey, Jr. / Daniel R. Caughey, Jr. / 1964											
122³⁄₈	19⁴⁄₈	21	16¹⁄₈	18⁶⁄₈	4³⁄₈	4¹⁄₈	4	4	0	749	338
◆ San Mateo County / Daniel R. Caughey, Jr. / Daniel R. Caughey, Jr. / 1986											
122²⁄₈	19	20	15⁴⁄₈	18	4⁴⁄₈	4¹⁄₈	5	5	0	752	339
◆ Humboldt County / Don L. Corley / Don L. Corley / 1982											
122²⁄₈	19	18⁵⁄₈	17	19⁶⁄₈	4²⁄₈	5	5	4	0	752	339
◆ Sonoma County / Richard O'Farrell / Richard O'Farrell / 1983											
122¹⁄₈	20²⁄₈	19⁶⁄₈	17⁷⁄₈	20	4	4	4	4	0	756	341
◆ Trinity County / Terry H. Walker / Terry H. Walker / 1976											

Score	Length of Main Beam R	L	Inside Spread	Greatest Spread	Circumference at Smallest Place between Burr and First Point R	L	Number of Points R	L	Total of Lengths Abnormal Points	All-Time Rank	State Rank
	♦ *Locality / Hunter / Owner / Date Killed*										
121³⁄₈	23⁴⁄₈	23¹⁄₈	15⁷⁄₈	17⁶⁄₈	4²⁄₈	4	4	4	0	759	342
	♦ *Mendocino County / Donald W. Biggs / Donald W. Biggs / 1993*										
121	18⁶⁄₈	18⁶⁄₈	18⁶⁄₈	20⁷⁄₈	4	4	4	4	0	761	343
	♦ *San Mateo County / Daniel R. Caughey, Jr. / Daniel R. Caughey, Jr. / 1971*										
120⁶⁄₈	17⁶⁄₈	18¹⁄₈	17²⁄₈	18⁶⁄₈	4⁴⁄₈	4⁴⁄₈	5	5	0	762	344
	♦ *Trinity County / Monte D. Matheson / Monte D. Matheson / 1988*										
120⁵⁄₈	19¹⁄₈	18⁴⁄₈	17⁷⁄₈	19⁶⁄₈	4	4	5	5	0	763	345
	♦ *Trinity County / Roger Baker / Roger Baker / 1993*										
173⁵⁄₈	21⁵⁄₈	21⁴⁄₈	17¹⁄₈	23²⁄₈	4⁵⁄₈	4⁶⁄₈	6	5	1²⁄₈	*	*
	♦ *Mendocino County / Clem Coughlin / D. & J. Phillips / 1981*										
154	22	23⁷⁄₈	22²⁄₈	25¹⁄₈	4³⁄₈	4⁴⁄₈	5	4	0	*	*
	♦ *Mendocino County / William E. Soekland / William E. Soekland / 1994*										
152⁵⁄₈	23⁶⁄₈	22⁷⁄₈	18⁵⁄₈	19⁴⁄₈	5	5²⁄₈	5	4	1²⁄₈	*	*
	♦ *Trinity County / Larry Brown / Larry Brown / 1979*										

Photograph Courtesy of Mary L. Hannah

Mary L. Hannah is one of a growing number of sportswomen who have taken and entered trophy animals in B&C's archives. Here she poses with the Columbia blacktail deer, scoring 154-2/8 points, that she took in 1988 in Jackson County, Oregon.

OREGON STATE RECORD (NEW)
COLUMBIA BLACKTAIL DEER
SCORE: 172 ⅜
Locality: Marion Co.   Date: 1969
Hunter: B.G. Shurtleff

OREGON

COLUMBIA BLACKTAIL DEER

Score	Length of Main Beam R	Length of Main Beam L	Inside Spread	Greatest Spread	Circumference at Smallest Place between Burr and First Point R	Circumference at Smallest Place between Burr and First Point L	Number of Points R	Number of Points L	Total of Lengths Abnormal Points	All-Time Rank	State Rank
♦ *Locality / Hunter / Owner / Date Killed*											
172 2/8	26 3/8	25 7/8	20 4/8	26 5/8	5 2/8	5 3/8	7	7	6 2/8	2	1
♦ *Marion County / B.G. Shurtleff / B.G. Shurtleff / 1969*											
170 6/8	23 1/8	24	21 4/8	25 3/8	5 3/8	5 4/8	5	5	0	4	2
♦ *Elk City / Clark D. Griffith / Clark D. Griffith / 1962*											
170 2/8	25 6/8	25 5/8	20 2/8	22 2/8	4 5/8	4 6/8	5	5	0	5	3
♦ *Jackson County / Dennis R. King / King Tax. Studios / 1970*											
170 1/8	23	22 6/8	19 5/8	24 1/8	5	4 6/8	5	5	0	6	4
♦ *Linn County / Woodrow W. Gibbs / Woodrow W. Gibbs / 1963*											
170	23 2/8	24	20 2/8	22 4/8	4 3/8	4 3/8	5	5	0	7	5
♦ *Jackson County / Wayne Despain / Wayne Despain / 1989*											
167 4/8	24 3/8	24 3/8	19 4/8	26	4 7/8	5	5	6	1 2/8	9	6
♦ *Marion County / Robert L. Brown / Robert L. Brown / 1980*											
165 6/8	22 6/8	23	20 6/8	22 3/8	4 6/8	4 6/8	5	5	0	12	7
♦ *Curry County / Si Pellow / Si Pellow / 1988*											
165 4/8	23 6/8	24 5/8	21 6/8	24 1/8	5 1/8	5 1/8	4	4	0	13	8
♦ *Yamhill County / Jim McKinley / Jim McKinley / 1971*											
165 1/8	21 4/8	21 7/8	18 5/8	23 5/8	4 4/8	4 4/8	5	5	0	14	9
♦ *Jackson County / Jay Walker / Jay Walker / 1983*											
163 7/8	21 7/8	21 7/8	19 5/8	25 6/8	4 4/8	4 4/8	5	5	0	16	10
♦ *Lincoln County / Picked Up / Bruce & Scott Wales / 1987*											
163 6/8	22 3/8	21 4/8	18	22 3/8	5	5	5	5	0	17	11
♦ *Jackson County / Donald G. Spence / Donald G. Spence / 1982*											
163 1/8	21 3/8	22 5/8	19 1/8	0	5 1/8	5	5	5	0	18	12
♦ *Eugene / Russell Thomas / Russell Thomas / 1964*											
160 7/8	23 3/8	23 3/8	19 3/8	24 6/8	4 6/8	4 5/8	6	5	5 6/8	23	13
♦ *Jackson County / G. Scott Jennings / G. Scott Jennings / 1972*											
160 5/8	20 5/8	21 4/8	16 5/8	23 1/8	4 5/8	4 5/8	4	4	0	24	14
♦ *Camas Valley / Bernard L. Den / Bernard L. Den / 1958*											
160 3/8	22 7/8	23 1/8	17 7/8	21 6/8	4 2/8	4 1/8	5	5	0	26	15
♦ *Jackson County / Mickey C. Haynes / Travis J. Harvey / 1989*											
159 6/8	25 6/8	24 4/8	22 4/8	26 7/8	4 6/8	4 4/8	6	6	3 4/8	31	16
♦ *Jackson County / Frank Chapman / Frank Chapman / 1965*											
159 6/8	24 3/8	24 1/8	16 1/8	18 5/8	4 5/8	4 6/8	5	8	3 5/8	31	16
♦ *Jackson County / Douglas L. Milburn / Douglas L. Milburn / 1985*											

Score	Length of Main Beam R	L	Inside Spread	Greatest Spread	Circumference at Smallest Place between Burr and First Point R	L	Number of Points R	L	Total of Lengths Abnormal Points	All-Time Rank	State Rank

♦ *Locality / Hunter / Owner / Date Killed*

159²⁄₈	22⁴⁄₈	22⁷⁄₈	19⁴⁄₈	24⁴⁄₈	4⁴⁄₈	4⁴⁄₈	5	5	0	35	18

♦ *Josephine County / Wayne Despain / Wayne Despain / 1979*

| 159²⁄₈ | 21⁷⁄₈ | 20⁷⁄₈ | 18²⁄₈ | 21⁵⁄₈ | 4³⁄₈ | 4³⁄₈ | 5 | 6 | 2⁶⁄₈ | 35 | 18 |

♦ *Jackson County / Jeffrey S. Sedey / Jeffrey S. Sedey / 1988*

| 158⁶⁄₈ | 22 | 22¹⁄₈ | 17⁴⁄₈ | 19 | 4³⁄₈ | 4⁴⁄₈ | 5 | 5 | 0 | 39 | 20 |

♦ *Marion County / Bradley M. Brenden / Bradley M. Brenden / 1973*

| 158²⁄₈ | 22⁴⁄₈ | 23⁷⁄₈ | 19⁶⁄₈ | 22¹⁄₈ | 4⁶⁄₈ | 4⁶⁄₈ | 5 | 5 | 0 | 41 | 21 |

♦ *Josephine County / James E. Brierley / James E. Brierley / 1983*

| 158 | 22⁷⁄₈ | 23²⁄₈ | 18⁴⁄₈ | 20³⁄₈ | 4⁶⁄₈ | 4⁶⁄₈ | 5 | 5 | 0 | 43 | 22 |

♦ *Camas Valley / Frank Kinnan / Frank Kinnan / 1968*

| 157⁴⁄₈ | 21²⁄₈ | 19⁴⁄₈ | 17²⁄₈ | 23¹⁄₈ | 4⁷⁄₈ | 5 | 5 | 5 | 0 | 46 | 23 |

♦ *Yamhill County / Henry Davenport / Henry Davenport / 1932*

| 156⁴⁄₈ | 19⁶⁄₈ | 19⁷⁄₈ | 16⁶⁄₈ | 22⁷⁄₈ | 4³⁄₈ | 4²⁄₈ | 5 | 6 | 3⁴⁄₈ | 50 | 24 |

♦ *Lincoln County / Bruce G. Wales / Bruce G. Wales / 1985*

| 156¹⁄₈ | 22²⁄₈ | 22 | 20²⁄₈ | 24³⁄₈ | 4⁴⁄₈ | 4⁴⁄₈ | 5 | 6 | 3⁷⁄₈ | 52 | 25 |

♦ *Lincoln County / Robert G. Biron / Robert G. Biron / 1963*

| 156 | 25 | 23²⁄₈ | 21 | 23¹⁄₈ | 4⁴⁄₈ | 4⁴⁄₈ | 6 | 5 | 1 | 53 | 26 |

♦ *Polk County / Wayne Bond / Wayne Bond / 1965*

| 155³⁄₈ | 26²⁄₈ | 25⁷⁄₈ | 25⁷⁄₈ | 28¹⁄₈ | 4⁴⁄₈ | 4⁴⁄₈ | 7 | 7 | 23⁶⁄₈ | 55 | 27 |

♦ *Jackson County / Gary B. Christlieb / Gary B. Christlieb / 1979*

| 155²⁄₈ | 22³⁄₈ | 23¹⁄₈ | 20⁶⁄₈ | 25²⁄₈ | 5³⁄₈ | 5 | 4 | 5 | 0 | 56 | 28 |

♦ *Jackson County / L.M. Morgan & L. Miller / Lewis M. Morgan / 1971*

| 154⁷⁄₈ | 22²⁄₈ | 20⁷⁄₈ | 19⁵⁄₈ | 23⁵⁄₈ | 4 | 4 | 4 | 4 | 0 | 61 | 29 |

♦ *Linn County / Don L. Twito / Don L. Twito / 1971*

| 154²⁄₈ | 20³⁄₈ | 20²⁄₈ | 17⁵⁄₈ | 22⁵⁄₈ | 5 | 5¹⁄₈ | 6 | 5 | 2¹⁄₈ | 67 | 30 |

♦ *Jackson County / Mary L. Hannah / Mary L. Hannah / 1988*

| 154¹⁄₈ | 20⁴⁄₈ | 20⁴⁄₈ | 18¹⁄₈ | 20³⁄₈ | 4⁴⁄₈ | 4⁴⁄₈ | 5 | 5 | 0 | 68 | 31 |

♦ *Lane County / Eldon Lundy / Eldon Lundy / 1943*

| 154 | 24⁴⁄₈ | 24³⁄₈ | 19⁵⁄₈ | 21⁶⁄₈ | 4⁷⁄₈ | 4⁴⁄₈ | 5 | 5 | 1¹⁄₈ | 70 | 32 |

♦ *Josephine County / Wayne H. Breeze / Wayne H. Breeze / 1986*

| 154 | 23³⁄₈ | 23³⁄₈ | 23³⁄₈ | 28⁶⁄₈ | 4¹⁄₈ | 4²⁄₈ | 6 | 6 | 3⁷⁄₈ | 70 | 32 |

♦ *Josephine County / Ryan Kinghorn / Ryan Kinghorn / 1989*

| 153⁴⁄₈ | 21³⁄₈ | 20⁷⁄₈ | 17⁶⁄₈ | 22³⁄₈ | 4⁶⁄₈ | 4⁷⁄₈ | 5 | 5 | 0 | 75 | 34 |

♦ *Linn County / Greg L. Anderson / Greg L. Anderson / 1983*

| 153³⁄₈ | 21⁵⁄₈ | 20⁵⁄₈ | 19¹⁄₈ | 23⁵⁄₈ | 5²⁄₈ | 5²⁄₈ | 6 | 7 | 6 | 76 | 35 |

♦ *Columbia County / J.H. Roberts / Oreg. Dept. Fish & Wildl. / 1946*

Score	Length of Main Beam R	L	Inside Spread	Greatest Spread	Circumference at Smallest Place between Burr and First Point R	L	Number of Points R	L	Total of Lengths Abnormal Points	All-Time Rank	State Rank
153 1/8	22 4/8	22	19 7/8	21 5/8	5 1/8	5 2/8	6	6	4 2/8	80	36
◆ Canton Creek / Marell Abeene / Marell Abeene / 1967											
152 2/8	20 7/8	21	20 2/8	24 2/8	4	4 1/8	4	4	0	85	37
◆ Douglas County / Ronald L. Sherva / Ronald L. Sherva / 1987											
152 1/8	22 2/8	21 4/8	22	24 4/8	4 3/8	4 3/8	5	6	1 3/8	86	38
◆ Josephine County / Bob Ferreira / Bob Ferreira / 1988											
152	20 6/8	21 7/8	15 2/8	20	4 6/8	4 7/8	6	6	6	89	39
◆ Clackamas County / Larry W. Peterson / Larry W. Peterson / 1980											
151 7/8	25	24 3/8	20 3/8	23	4 3/8	4 5/8	5	5	0	91	40
◆ Jackson County / David Ellefson / David Ellefson / 1972											
151 6/8	22 2/8	22 4/8	17 4/8	20 4/8	5 4/8	5 1/8	6	5	1 6/8	92	41
◆ Glide / William Cellers / William Cellers / 1947											
151 4/8	20 3/8	19 1/8	16 4/8	18 4/8	4 5/8	4 7/8	5	5	0	95	42
◆ Marion County / John Davenport / John Davenport / 1958											
151 4/8	22 7/8	21 3/8	17 5/8	21 6/8	4 1/8	4 2/8	5	6	3 1/8	95	42
◆ Douglas County / Robert Shrode / Robert Shrode / 1959											
151 3/8	23 1/8	22 6/8	19 4/8	22 3/8	5	5	5	6	1 3/8	97	44
◆ Josephine County / E.L. McKie & S.E. McKie / Ernie L. McKie / 1977											
151 1/8	21 5/8	21 5/8	16 1/8	19	4	4	4	4	0	98	45
◆ Josephine County / Jim Wineteer / Jim Wineteer / 1980											
150 7/8	21 7/8	22	19 5/8	23	4 4/8	4 5/8	5	5	0	102	46
◆ Jackson County / Darrell Leek / Darrell Leek / 1974											
150 5/8	21 4/8	20 7/8	16 5/8	19 6/8	5 4/8	5 6/8	5	5	0	104	47
◆ Yamhill County / Russell W. Byers / Russell W. Byers / 1961											
150 1/8	22 7/8	23 1/8	19 3/8	21 7/8	4 6/8	4 7/8	5	6	2 2/8	106	48
◆ Clackamas County / E. Clint Kuntz / E. Clint Kuntz / 1981											
150	20 5/8	21 5/8	16 6/8	20 4/8	5	4 7/8	5	5	0	110	49
◆ Douglas County / Norman Burnett / Norman Burnett / 1967											
149 5/8	22 7/8	22 4/8	17 1/8	19 1/8	4 3/8	4 5/8	5	5	0	117	50
◆ Clackamas County / Ray W. Bunnell / Ray W. Bunnell / 1970											
149 2/8	20 2/8	20 3/8	14 6/8	16 5/8	4 2/8	4	5	5	0	124	51
◆ Clackamas County / Lance V. Bentz / Lance V. Bentz / 1980											
149 2/8	21 6/8	22 6/8	19 4/8	22 3/8	4 4/8	4 2/8	5	5	0	124	51
◆ Lane County / Richard C. MacKenzie / Richard C. MacKenzie / 1983											
148 6/8	24 5/8	24 2/8	20 2/8	22 6/8	5	5 1/8	5	5	1	129	53
◆ Tillamook County / Fred Dick / Fred Dick / 1948											

Score	Length of Main Beam R	L	Inside Spread	Greatest Spread	Circumference at Smallest Place between Burr and First Point R	L	Number of Points R	L	Total of Lengths Abnormal Points	All-Time Rank	State Rank
	◆ Locality / Hunter / Owner / Date Killed										
148 5/8	21 3/8	21 5/8	18 5/8	20 6/8	3 7/8	4 1/8	5	5	0	130	54
	◆ Lane County / Bill Sparks / Bill Sparks / 1970										
148 5/8	20 6/8	20 2/8	17 3/8	21 4/8	3 6/8	4	6	6	2	130	54
	◆ Jackson County / Jay Walker / Jay Walker / 1975										
148 4/8	21 6/8	22 5/8	15 6/8	17 7/8	5 3/8	5 6/8	5	5	0	132	56
	◆ Linn County / Marlin D. Brinkley / Marlin D. Brinkley / 1982										
148 3/8	21 2/8	21	19 5/8	21 4/8	4 3/8	4 2/8	5	5	0	135	57
	◆ Douglas County / Unknown / Bud Jackson / 1929										
148 3/8	21 7/8	21 1/8	18 6/8	24 6/8	4 2/8	4 1/8	5	10	6 1/8	135	57
	◆ Marion County / Mike Fenimore / Mike Fenimore / 1961										
148 1/8	23 4/8	22 4/8	15 5/8	17 7/8	5 1/8	5 1/8	6	5	2	138	59
	◆ Clackamas County / Steven C. Oaks / Steven C. Oaks / 1986										
147 2/8	22 6/8	23 4/8	19 6/8	22 4/8	4 2/8	4 3/8	4	5	0	145	60
	◆ Jackson County / Mike Taylor / Mike Taylor / 1969										
147 2/8	27	26 5/8	21 3/8	0	5 4/8	5 6/8	0	0	4 3/8	145	60
	◆ Marion County / James C. Tennimon / James C. Tennimon / 1988										
146 6/8	21 4/8	21 5/8	18 4/8	22 6/8	4 7/8	5	6	5	1	153	62
	◆ Camas Valley / Adam J. Hipp / Adam J. Hipp / 1961										
146 5/8	21 6/8	21	16 3/8	18 4/8	4 3/8	4 3/8	5	5	0	155	63
	◆ Coos County / Pete Serafin / Pete Serafin / 1968										
146 5/8	20 1/8	20 2/8	18 1/8	20 7/8	4 2/8	4 2/8	5	5	0	155	63
	◆ Clackamus County / Stan K. Naylor / Stan K. Naylor / 1990										
146 2/8	20 7/8	21 4/8	14 2/8	17 4/8	4 4/8	4 4/8	5	5	0	160	65
	◆ Douglas County / Bernard H. Schum / Bernard H. Schum / 1966										
146	20 2/8	20 7/8	15 2/8	19 5/8	5	5	5	5	0	166	66
	◆ Little Fall Creek / Gene B. Johnson / Gene B. Johnson / 1963										
145 7/8	24 5/8	22 4/8	19	20 5/8	5 5/8	5 6/8	6	5	2 1/8	169	67
	◆ Linn County / Harold Tonkin / C. Vernon Humble / 1954										
145 7/8	21 7/8	21	14 5/8	19 7/8	4 2/8	4 1/8	6	5	3 4/8	169	67
	◆ Yamhill County / Dwight A. Homestead / Dwight A. Homestead / 1992										
145 4/8	20 1/8	20 4/8	14 2/8	17	4 2/8	4 1/8	6	5	1 4/8	178	69
	◆ Jackson County / Gary D. Kaiser / Gary D. Kaiser / 1967										
145 4/8	21 1/8	20	16 2/8	18 5/8	4 7/8	4 7/8	5	5	0	178	69
	◆ Douglas County / Daniel J. Fisher / Daniel J. Fisher / 1973										
145 2/8	22 4/8	21 2/8	16 2/8	18	4 4/8	4 7/8	5	5	0	182	71
	◆ Jackson County / Bill Hays / Bill Hays / 1968										

Score	Length of Main Beam R	L	Inside Spread	Greatest Spread	Circumference at Smallest Place between Burr and First Point R	L	Number of Points R	L	Total of Lengths Abnormal Points	All-Time Rank	State Rank

♦ Locality / Hunter / Owner / Date Killed

145²⁄₈	20²⁄₈	21	16⁴⁄₈	18⁶⁄₈	5⁴⁄₈	5²⁄₈	5	5	0	182	71

♦ Marion County / James J. Edgell / James J. Edgell / 1979

145²⁄₈	23	23⁶⁄₈	22⁷⁄₈	24⁴⁄₈	4³⁄₈	4⁴⁄₈	6	5	3³⁄₈	182	71

♦ Josephine County / Jim Breeze / Jim Breeze / 1986

145¹⁄₈	19⁶⁄₈	19⁵⁄₈	15¹⁄₈	17¹⁄₈	4⁶⁄₈	4⁵⁄₈	5	5	0	187	74

♦ Lane County / Boyd Iverson / Boyd Iverson / 1982

145¹⁄₈	21⁷⁄₈	21²⁄₈	16⁷⁄₈	19⁷⁄₈	4³⁄₈	4³⁄₈	5	5	0	187	74

♦ Lane County / Kevin M. Albin / Kevin M. Albin / 1990

145	19²⁄₈	19²⁄₈	19²⁄₈	21⁷⁄₈	4⁵⁄₈	4⁴⁄₈	5	5	0	192	76

♦ Douglas County / Larry E. Waller / Larry E. Waller / 1980

144⁷⁄₈	20⁶⁄₈	20⁴⁄₈	13³⁄₈	16³⁄₈	4	4¹⁄₈	5	5	0	195	77

♦ Clatsop County / Pravomil Raichl / Pravomil Raichl / 1959

144⁷⁄₈	22¹⁄₈	23¹⁄₈	22⁷⁄₈	26⁴⁄₈	4¹⁄₈	4¹⁄₈	5	5	0	195	77

♦ Lane County / Clair R. Thomas / Clair R. Thomas / 1959

144⁶⁄₈	21³⁄₈	22⁴⁄₈	19⁵⁄₈	24²⁄₈	6	6	5	4	2⁷⁄₈	198	79

♦ Lincoln County / William D. Harmon / Oreg. Dept. Fish & Wildl. / 1976

144⁵⁄₈	22⁶⁄₈	22⁴⁄₈	21⁵⁄₈	23⁵⁄₈	4⁴⁄₈	4⁴⁄₈	5	5	0	202	80

♦ Josephine County / Jerry C. Sparlin / Jerry C. Sparlin / 1963

144⁵⁄₈	20¹⁄₈	20	18¹⁄₈	21³⁄₈	4	4	5	5	0	202	80

♦ Jackson County / Dean P. Pasche / Dean P. Pasche / 1988

144⁵⁄₈	22⁵⁄₈	23¹⁄₈	19¹⁄₈	21⁴⁄₈	4⁴⁄₈	4⁴⁄₈	5	5	0	202	80

♦ Linn County / Donald J. Semolke / Donald J. Semolke / 1990

144⁵⁄₈	21⁵⁄₈	21²⁄₈	16¹⁄₈	18	4⁴⁄₈	4²⁄₈	5	5	0	202	80

♦ Benton County / Gerald L. Hibbs / Gerald L. Hibbs / 1990

144⁴⁄₈	21⁶⁄₈	21⁵⁄₈	16²⁄₈	18⁴⁄₈	4²⁄₈	4³⁄₈	5	5	0	206	84

♦ Clackamas County / John R. Vollmer, Jr. / John R. Vollmer, Jr. / 1960

144⁴⁄₈	21²⁄₈	20⁵⁄₈	17²⁄₈	20⁵⁄₈	4²⁄₈	4²⁄₈	5	5	0	206	84

♦ Powers / Ray A. Davis / Ray A. Davis / 1968

144⁴⁄₈	21	20⁷⁄₈	15⁴⁄₈	18¹⁄₈	4¹⁄₈	4³⁄₈	5	5	0	206	84

♦ Benton County / Lance M. Holm / Lance M. Holm / 1988

144²⁄₈	20³⁄₈	21⁶⁄₈	17²⁄₈	19	4⁴⁄₈	4⁵⁄₈	5	5	0	217	87

♦ Jackson County / Warren Pestka / Warren Pestka / 1974

144²⁄₈	20²⁄₈	19⁶⁄₈	20³⁄₈	26²⁄₈	3⁶⁄₈	3⁶⁄₈	6	5	4	217	87

♦ Josephine County / Clinton Moore / Clinton Moore / 1975

144²⁄₈	21⁶⁄₈	21³⁄₈	15⁶⁄₈	18⁴⁄₈	4⁶⁄₈	4⁶⁄₈	6	5	1	217	87

♦ Marion County / Arthur L. Schmidt / Arthur L. Schmidt / 1978

Score	Length of Main Beam R	Length of Main Beam L	Inside Spread	Greatest Spread	Circumference at Smallest Place between Burr and First Point R	Circumference at Smallest Place between Burr and First Point L	Number of Points R	Number of Points L	Total of Lengths Abnormal Points	All-Time Rank	State Rank
	♦ *Locality / Hunter / Owner / Date Killed*										
144 1/8	21 7/8	21 3/8	17 7/8	19 5/8	4 5/8	4 4/8	5	5	0	221	90
	♦ *Siskiyou Natl. For. / Dennis E. Bourn / Dennis E. Bourn / 1971*										
144	21 2/8	21 5/8	17	20 3/8	4 7/8	5 1/8	5	5	0	222	91
	♦ *Linn County / Ed A. Taylor / Ed A. Taylor / 1981*										
143 7/8	21 7/8	23	20 6/8	23 2/8	5	4 5/8	6	6	3 1/8	224	92
	♦ *Linn County / Clarence Howe / Clarence Howe / 1941*										
143 7/8	23 4/8	22 7/8	21 3/8	24	5	4 6/8	5	5	0	224	92
	♦ *Clackamas County / Richard G. Mathis / Richard G. Mathis / 1965*										
143 4/8	21 3/8	20 7/8	16 6/8	19 1/8	4 5/8	4 5/8	5	5	0	235	94
	♦ *Jackson County / Jay Walker / Jay Walker / 1978*										
143 4/8	22	23	16 4/8	18 4/8	3 7/8	4	5	5	0	235	94
	♦ *Josephine County / Virgil Welch / Virgil Welch / 1983*										
143 2/8	21 6/8	21 5/8	19	21	4 3/8	4 5/8	5	5	0	243	96
	♦ *Linn County / Basil C. Bradbury / Basil C. Bradbury / 1960*										
143 2/8	21 2/8	21 3/8	18 2/8	20 7/8	4 6/8	5 1/8	5	5	0	243	96
	♦ *Josephine County / Jaime L. Torres / Jaime L. Torres / 1990*										
143 1/8	21 4/8	20 7/8	17 3/8	20 3/8	4 4/8	4 4/8	6	5	1 2/8	250	98
	♦ *Benton County / A.C. Nelson / A.C. Nelson / 1957*										
142 7/8	20 1/8	22	16 3/8	19 1/8	4	4	4	4	0	253	99
	♦ *Clackamas County / Larry Tracy / Larry Tracy / 1965*										
142 7/8	23 5/8	23 6/8	21 1/8	23 4/8	5 1/8	5 6/8	5	6	1 2/8	253	99
	♦ *Clackamas County / Ross A. Gordon / Ross A. Gordon / 1989*										
142 6/8	21 2/8	21 7/8	19 4/8	22	4 6/8	5	5	4	0	256	101
	♦ *Linn County / R. Reid & D. Liles / R. Reid & D. Liles / 1982*										
142 6/8	23 2/8	22	17 2/8	20	3 7/8	4	4	4	0	256	101
	♦ *Linn County / Kenneth W. Wegner / Kenneth W. Wegner / 1982*										
142 6/8	20 4/8	20 1/8	20 7/8	23 5/8	4 4/8	3 7/8	5	4	0	256	101
	♦ *Josephine County / Reginald P. Breeze / Reginald P. Breeze / 1986*										
142 5/8	22	22 3/8	17 1/8	19 1/8	4 2/8	4 1/8	5	5	0	259	104
	♦ *Marion County / Robert E. Bochsler / Robert E. Bochsler / 1950*										
142 5/8	19 6/8	19 4/8	17 7/8	19 5/8	4 6/8	4 6/8	5	5	0	259	104
	♦ *Jackson County / Leonard B. Sequeira / Nancy Sequeira / 1959*										
142 4/8	21 6/8	22	16 6/8	21 5/8	4 3/8	4 3/8	6	5	2 2/8	268	106
	♦ *Clackamas County / Henry A. Charriere / Henry A. Charriere / 1970*										
142 4/8	22 4/8	22 7/8	21	24	4 3/8	3 7/8	4	3	0	268	106
	♦ *Jackson County / Donald G. Spence / Donald G. Spence / 1980*										

Score	Length of Main Beam R	Length of Main Beam L	Inside Spread	Greatest Spread	Circumference at Smallest Place between Burr and First Point R	Circumference at Smallest Place between Burr and First Point L	Number of Points R	Number of Points L	Total of Lengths Abnormal Points	All-Time Rank	State Rank
142²⁄₈	20⁷⁄₈	20⁴⁄₈	16²⁄₈	18¹⁄₈	4³⁄₈	4⁶⁄₈	5	5	0	276	108
◆ *Jackson County / Eileen F. Damone / Eileen F. Damone / 1976*											
142¹⁄₈	23⁵⁄₈	22²⁄₈	16⁷⁄₈	18⁷⁄₈	4⁵⁄₈	4⁴⁄₈	5	5	0	278	109
◆ *Linn County / Bob L. Brazeale / Jack V. Logozzo / 1972*											
142	24	23⁵⁄₈	16⁷⁄₈	20⁴⁄₈	5¹⁄₈	5⁶⁄₈	8	5	11¹⁄₈	282	110
◆ *Marion County / Hugh W. Gardner / Hugh W. Gardner / 1966*											
141⁷⁄₈	21⁴⁄₈	21⁴⁄₈	16⁵⁄₈	19	4²⁄₈	4¹⁄₈	5	5	0	288	111
◆ *Lincoln County / Roy A. Parks / Roy A. Parks / 1984*											
141⁶⁄₈	21³⁄₈	21³⁄₈	19²⁄₈	21⁷⁄₈	4⁴⁄₈	4⁴⁄₈	5	5	0	292	112
◆ *Lane County / Jerry Shepard / Jerry Shepard / 1954*											
141⁶⁄₈	20²⁄₈	20⁷⁄₈	18²⁄₈	20⁶⁄₈	4⁵⁄₈	4⁴⁄₈	5	5	0	292	112
◆ *Linn County / Eugene L. Wilson / Eugene L. Wilson / 1982*											
141²⁄₈	21⁴⁄₈	20⁶⁄₈	18²⁄₈	21⁴⁄₈	4³⁄₈	4²⁄₈	5	5	0	306	114
◆ *Marion County / Arthur L. Schmidt / Arthur L. Schmidt / 1986*											
141¹⁄₈	23³⁄₈	23²⁄₈	17⁵⁄₈	19⁶⁄₈	4²⁄₈	4⁴⁄₈	6	6	2²⁄₈	309	115
◆ *Jackson County / Harold R. Embury / Harold R. Embury / 1985*											
141	20²⁄₈	19⁶⁄₈	14	17²⁄₈	4	4	4	5	0	312	116
◆ *Lane County / Richard Porter / Ruel Holt / 1962*											
140⁷⁄₈	23⁷⁄₈	23⁷⁄₈	18⁶⁄₈	23	5	5	10	8	20³⁄₈	317	117
◆ *Polk County / Gale A. Draper / Gale A. Draper / 1984*											
140⁴⁄₈	21¹⁄₈	20⁷⁄₈	18²⁄₈	20¹⁄₈	4⁷⁄₈	4⁶⁄₈	6	5	4⁴⁄₈	327	118
◆ *Yamhill County / Richard Watts / Richard Watts / 1981*											
140³⁄₈	24³⁄₈	24²⁄₈	17³⁄₈	20¹⁄₈	4	4²⁄₈	4	4	0	330	119
◆ *Jackson County / John T. Mee / John T. Mee / 1974*											
140¹⁄₈	20⁷⁄₈	22¹⁄₈	16⁵⁄₈	19²⁄₈	4³⁄₈	4³⁄₈	5	5	0	337	120
◆ *Lincoln County / Darrel R. Grishaber / Darrel R. Grishaber / 1984*											
140¹⁄₈	22	21²⁄₈	19¹⁄₈	23²⁄₈	3⁵⁄₈	3⁶⁄₈	4	5	0	337	120
◆ *Jackson County / Ronald L. Sherva / Ronald L. Sherva / 1989*											
140	21	20¹⁄₈	17	23⁴⁄₈	5	4⁶⁄₈	6	8	9²⁄₈	345	122
◆ *Polk County / Harold E. Stepp / Harold E. Stepp / 1970*											
139⁷⁄₈	20⁷⁄₈	20¹⁄₈	18⁷⁄₈	21¹⁄₈	5²⁄₈	5	5	5	0	351	123
◆ *Jackson County / Dale E. Hoskins / Dale E. Hoskins / 1946*											
139⁶⁄₈	20⁶⁄₈	19⁶⁄₈	18¹⁄₈	20⁷⁄₈	4⁴⁄₈	4²⁄₈	5	6	4¹⁄₈	354	124
◆ *Josephine County / Richard H. Caswell / Richard H. Caswell / 1969*											
139⁴⁄₈	21⁷⁄₈	21⁵⁄₈	20⁴⁄₈	23	4¹⁄₈	4²⁄₈	5	5	0	360	125
◆ *Lane County / Gene Tinker / Gene Tinker / 1955*											

Score	Length of Main Beam R	L	Inside Spread	Greatest Spread	Circumference at Smallest Place between Burr and First Point R	L	Number of Points R	L	Total of Lengths Abnormal Points	All-Time Rank	State Rank
♦ Locality / Hunter / Owner / Date Killed											
139⁴⁄₈	21⁷⁄₈	21⅛	17²⁄₈	20	3⁴⁄₈	3⁴⁄₈	7	5	2⁶⁄₈	360	125
♦ Jackson County / Arthur A. Ekerson / Arthur A. Ekerson / 1966											
139⁴⁄₈	20⁷⁄₈	22³⁄₈	19⁴⁄₈	29⁶⁄₈	4⁷⁄₈	4⁵⁄₈	6	7	6⁴⁄₈	360	125
♦ Jackson County / Everett B. Music, Jr. / Everett B. Music, Jr. / 1985											
139³⁄₈	21⁴⁄₈	21⅛	17⁷⁄₈	19³⁄₈	4³⁄₈	4⁴⁄₈	5	5	0	364	128
♦ Monmouth / Roy W. Miller / Roy W. Miller / 1967											
139³⁄₈	19²⁄₈	19⁵⁄₈	19⁵⁄₈	21⁶⁄₈	3⁶⁄₈	3⁶⁄₈	5	5	0	364	128
♦ Marion County / Robert W. Hickman / Randall W. Hickman / 1974											
139³⁄₈	20⁷⁄₈	20⁶⁄₈	19⁵⁄₈	21⁶⁄₈	4⁶⁄₈	4⁵⁄₈	5	5	0	364	128
♦ Marion County / Richard A. Hart / Richard A. Hart / 1982											
139²⁄₈	21⁷⁄₈	23³⁄₈	17⅛	20⁴⁄₈	5⅛	4³⁄₈	7	4	7⅛	372	131
♦ Josephine County / David L. Teasley / David L. Teasley / 1986											
139²⁄₈	23⁷⁄₈	22³⁄₈	16⁴⁄₈	19²⁄₈	4	3⁷⁄₈	5	5	0	372	131
♦ Douglas County / Ken Wilson / Ken Wilson / 1992											
139⅛	21⁷⁄₈	21⁷⁄₈	18⁵⁄₈	21	3⁷⁄₈	4⅛	4	5	0	379	133
♦ Florence / Edwin C. Stevens / Warner Pinkney / 1928											
139	21⁷⁄₈	21⅛	15⁷⁄₈	20²⁄₈	4³⁄₈	4⁶⁄₈	6	6	4³⁄₈	382	134
♦ Lane County / Picked Up / Ruel Holt / 1964											
139	19³⁄₈	19³⁄₈	18²⁄₈	20⁵⁄₈	4⅛	4	5	5	0	382	134
♦ Douglas County / Richard Wigle / Richard Wigle / 1968											
139	21²⁄₈	21³⁄₈	16⁴⁄₈	19³⁄₈	3⁷⁄₈	3⁷⁄₈	5	5	0	382	134
♦ Marion County / Gene Collier / Gene Collier / 1983											
139	21²⁄₈	20⁷⁄₈	17²⁄₈	19⁷⁄₈	5	5⅛	5	5	0	382	134
♦ Polk County / Jimmy L. Smithey / Jimmy L. Smithey / 1990											
138⁷⁄₈	23⁷⁄₈	24²⁄₈	18⁴⁄₈	0	4⁴⁄₈	4⁴⁄₈	5	5	5⁵⁄₈	389	138
♦ Tiller / Ronald Elliott / Ronald Elliott / 1963											
138⁷⁄₈	20⁴⁄₈	20⁵⁄₈	16⁵⁄₈	19	4²⁄₈	4²⁄₈	5	5	0	389	138
♦ Tillamook County / Henry Naegeli / Henry Naegeli / 1970											
138⁵⁄₈	21	21	15⁵⁄₈	17⁷⁄₈	5²⁄₈	5	5	5	0	402	140
♦ Clatsop County / Russell L. Hemphill / Russell L. Hemphill / 1972											
138⁵⁄₈	19³⁄₈	19⁵⁄₈	14⁶⁄₈	18⁶⁄₈	5	4⁷⁄₈	5	6	1⁷⁄₈	402	140
♦ Linn County / Jeff B. Garber / Jeff B. Garber / 1987											
138³⁄₈	22⁵⁄₈	22	20⁵⁄₈	23	4⁷⁄₈	4⁵⁄₈	5	5	0	407	142
♦ Clackamas County / J.B. Mitts / Wes Mitts / 1896											
138²⁄₈	18⁶⁄₈	18⁶⁄₈	15⁶⁄₈	19⁷⁄₈	4⅛	4³⁄₈	5	5	0	411	143
♦ Marion County / Gene Collier / Gene Collier / 1974											

Score	Length of Main Beam R	L	Inside Spread	Greatest Spread	Circumference at Smallest Place between Burr and First Point R	L	Number of Points R	L	Total of Lengths Abnormal Points	All-Time Rank	State Rank
	◆ Locality / Hunter / Owner / Date Killed										
138²⁄₈	21¹⁄₈	21²⁄₈	17⁴⁄₈	19⁴⁄₈	5	5¹⁄₈	5	4	0	411	143
	◆ Linn County / Douglas J. Morehead / Douglas J. Morehead / 1984										
138¹⁄₈	18⁵⁄₈	20³⁄₈	17¹⁄₈	19³⁄₈	4²⁄₈	4³⁄₈	5	5	0	419	145
	◆ Columbia County / Virginia L. Brown / Steve Crossley / 1981										
138	19⁶⁄₈	19⁶⁄₈	16⁷⁄₈	19⁵⁄₈	4⁶⁄₈	4⁵⁄₈	5	6	1⁷⁄₈	420	146
	◆ Douglas County / Will H. Brown / Will H. Brown / 1948										
138	19³⁄₈	20¹⁄₈	15	18	4¹⁄₈	4²⁄₈	5	5	0	420	146
	◆ Marion County / Frank C. Bersin / Frank C. Bersin / 1977										
137⁷⁄₈	20⁴⁄₈	20³⁄₈	17	20⁴⁄₈	4⁴⁄₈	4⁵⁄₈	5	6	2¹⁄₈	423	148
	◆ Yamhill County / Wallace Hill / Wallace Hill / 1963										
137⁴⁄₈	22	21⁷⁄₈	19²⁄₈	21	4⁴⁄₈	4⁴⁄₈	5	5	0	435	149
	◆ Linn County / Manny M. Kurtz / Manny M. Kurtz / 1993										
137³⁄₈	20³⁄₈	20	21⁵⁄₈	23⁷⁄₈	3⁶⁄₈	3⁴⁄₈	5	4	0	438	150
	◆ Jackson County / Jay Walker / Jay Walker / 1981										
137²⁄₈	19³⁄₈	20⁷⁄₈	18	20⁷⁄₈	4²⁄₈	4¹⁄₈	5	5	0	441	151
	◆ Douglas County / Bernard L. Den / Bernard L. Den / 1934										
137²⁄₈	19⁶⁄₈	20	15	18³⁄₈	4³⁄₈	4¹⁄₈	5	5	0	441	151
	◆ Douglas County / Francis R. Young / Francis R. Young / 1972										
137²⁄₈	20⁵⁄₈	21⁴⁄₈	17⁶⁄₈	23²⁄₈	5²⁄₈	4⁷⁄₈	8	5	5	441	151
	◆ Jackson County / Michael E. Earnest / Michael E. Earnest / 1992										
137²⁄₈	21⁷⁄₈	21⁶⁄₈	16	17⁷⁄₈	3⁷⁄₈	3⁵⁄₈	5	4	0	441	151
	◆ Jackson County / Ernie MacKenzie / Ernie MacKenzie / 1992										
137¹⁄₈	21³⁄₈	19²⁄₈	15⁷⁄₈	21	4²⁄₈	4²⁄₈	5	5	0	445	155
	◆ Douglas County / Peter Serafin / Peter Serafin / 1932										
137¹⁄₈	20⁴⁄₈	20¹⁄₈	15⁵⁄₈	19⁷⁄₈	4⁵⁄₈	4⁶⁄₈	5	5	0	445	155
	◆ Tillamook County / Iola M. Pfaff / Iola M. Pfaff / 1940										
137¹⁄₈	20⁴⁄₈	21¹⁄₈	19²⁄₈	23¹⁄₈	4⁴⁄₈	4⁴⁄₈	5	7	3³⁄₈	445	155
	◆ Douglas County / Jerry A. Caster / Jerry A. Caster / 1989										
137	20	19⁵⁄₈	15⁶⁄₈	17⁷⁄₈	4⁶⁄₈	4⁶⁄₈	5	5	0	450	158
	◆ Polk County / Ralph Cooper / Ralph Cooper / 1978										
136⁵⁄₈	21⁵⁄₈	22¹⁄₈	19⁵⁄₈	22⁴⁄₈	4⁵⁄₈	4⁶⁄₈	5	5	0	460	159
	◆ Tillamook County / J.A. Aaron / J.A. Aaron / 1943										
136⁵⁄₈	21⁶⁄₈	21⁶⁄₈	15⁷⁄₈	17⁵⁄₈	4¹⁄₈	4	5	5	0	460	159
	◆ Marion County / Ronald A. Bersin / Ronald A. Bersin / 1978										
136⁵⁄₈	22⁴⁄₈	21¹⁄₈	20¹⁄₈	24⁴⁄₈	3⁴⁄₈	3⁶⁄₈	4	5	2⁴⁄₈	460	159
	◆ Jackson County / Alberto L. Garcia / Alberto L. Garcia / 1988										

Score	Length of Main Beam R	L	Inside Spread	Greatest Spread	Circumference at Smallest Place between Burr and First Point R	L	Number of Points R	L	Total of Lengths Abnormal Points	All-Time Rank	State Rank
	♦ *Locality / Hunter / Owner / Date Killed*										
136 3/8	20 2/8	20 1/8	19 1/8	20 7/8	4	4 1/8	4	5	0	468	162
	♦ *Douglas County / Gerry F. Edwards / Gerry F. Edwards / 1971*										
136 3/8	20 2/8	19 7/8	15 7/8	17 6/8	4 3/8	4 2/8	5	5	0	468	162
	♦ *Tillamook County / Guy L. Thompson / Guy L. Thompson / 1983*										
136 3/8	21 4/8	21	15 3/8	17 2/8	5 1/8	4 7/8	5	5	0	468	162
	♦ *Marion County / Albert F. Brundidge / Albert F. Brundidge / 1990*										
136 2/8	20 3/8	20 5/8	16	17 4/8	3 6/8	3 5/8	4	5	2 4/8	471	165
	♦ *Jackson County / Martin S. Durbin / Ellis A. Jones / 1921*										
136 2/8	20 3/8	21 3/8	17	19	4 7/8	5 2/8	5	5	0	471	165
	♦ *Yamhill County / Monty Dickey / Monty Dickey / 1967*										
136 2/8	19 1/8	19 2/8	16	18 4/8	4 3/8	4 2/8	5	5	0	471	165
	♦ *Coos County / Ken Wilson / Ken Wilson / 1985*										
136 2/8	20 7/8	20 3/8	16 5/8	19 1/8	4 7/8	5	5	6	3 7/8	471	165
	♦ *Clackamas County / Loren R. Schilperoort / Loren R. Schilperoort / 1990*										
136 1/8	20 4/8	20	15 1/8	17 1/8	4 3/8	4 2/8	5	5	0	477	169
	♦ *Jackson County / Nancy J. Eden / Nancy J. Eden / 1971*										
135 7/8	22 1/8	22 2/8	17 3/8	19	4 4/8	4 4/8	4	3	0	485	170
	♦ *Jackson County / Mrs. Ila B. Bethany / Mrs. Ila B. Bethany / 1972*										
135 7/8	20 1/8	20 4/8	16 5/8	19	4 5/8	4 5/8	5	5	0	485	170
	♦ *Lane County / Aaron D. Helfrich / Aaron D. Helfrich / 1992*										
135 6/8	21 2/8	20 4/8	18	23 1/8	4 4/8	4	4	4	0	490	172
	♦ *Linn County / Gene Collier / Gene Collier / 1966*										
135 6/8	16 4/8	20 6/8	16 3/8	22 2/8	5 1/8	5 1/8	6	5	4 1/8	490	172
	♦ *Marion County / Joseph V. Pileggi / Joseph V. Pileggi / 1988*										
135 4/8	20	21 5/8	15 4/8	18 1/8	4 3/8	4 3/8	5	6	1 4/8	501	174
	♦ *Benton County / Mark A. Morris / Mark A. Morris / 1990*										
135 2/8	21 6/8	21 4/8	14 3/8	16 3/8	4	4	6	5	2 1/8	506	175
	♦ *Lane County / Lorrie A. Nyseth / Lorrie A. Nyseth / 1992*										
135 1/8	20 2/8	20 1/8	15 3/8	18 2/8	3 6/8	3 6/8	5	5	0	509	176
	♦ *Jackson County / Valton G. Albert / Valton G. Albert / 1991*										
135	19 1/8	19 4/8	15 4/8	19 3/8	4 3/8	4 3/8	5	5	0	510	177
	♦ *Clackamas County / Ray W. Bunnell / Ray W. Bunnell / 1978*										
134 7/8	21 2/8	21 4/8	16 1/8	17	3 4/8	3 6/8	4	4	0	515	178
	♦ *Butte Falls / Bob Doan, Jr. / Bob Doan, Jr. / 1973*										
134 7/8	21 3/8	21 6/8	21 1/8	22 6/8	4 5/8	4 6/8	5	5	0	515	178
	♦ *Josephine County / Kevin N. Walch / Kevin N. Walch / 1991*										

Score	Length of Main Beam R	L	Inside Spread	Greatest Spread	Circumference at Smallest Place between Burr and First Point R	L	Number of Points R	L	Total of Lengths Abnormal Points	All-Time Rank	State Rank
134 6/8	21 7/8	21	16 6/8	19 5/8	4	4	6	5	1 2/8	523	180
◆ Clackamas County / Nolen R. Schoenborn / Nolen R. Schoenborn / 1951
134 6/8	20 6/8	22	19 2/8	21	4 4/8	4 3/8	5	5	0	523	180
◆ Clackamas County / Nolen R. Schoenborn / Nolen R. Schoenborn / 1960
134 3/8	21 3/8	21 6/8	19 5/8	21 3/8	4 2/8	4 2/8	5	5	0	537	182
◆ Benton County / John E. Peterson / John E. Peterson / 1965
134 2/8	20 3/8	19 6/8	16 4/8	18 6/8	4 2/8	4 3/8	5	5	0	542	183
◆ Douglas County / John R. Hughey / John R. Hughey / 1965
134 2/8	21	20 6/8	16 6/8	18 4/8	4 1/8	4	5	5	0	542	183
◆ Clackamas County / Daniel C. Bean / Daniel C. Bean / 1983
134 2/8	22 2/8	22 3/8	15 7/8	19 5/8	4	4 1/8	5	5	9 3/8	542	183
◆ Yamhill County / Gorman R. Green III / Gorman R. Green III / 1992
134 1/8	20 3/8	21 3/8	19 3/8	20 7/8	3 7/8	3 7/8	5	5	0	550	186
◆ Coos County / Dan Woolley / Dan Woolley / 1971
134 1/8	21 5/8	21 6/8	15 7/8	19 1/8	5 1/8	4 7/8	5	6	1 6/8	550	186
◆ Clackamas County / Gary R. Schoenborn / Gary R. Schoenborn / 1985
133 6/8	19 4/8	19 7/8	13 4/8	17	4 5/8	4 7/8	5	5	0	560	188
◆ Douglas County / Ronald L. Sherva / Ronald L. Sherva / 1990
133 5/8	21 1/8	19 5/8	15	17 5/8	4 6/8	4 7/8	6	5	2 3/8	564	189
◆ Columbia County / Duane M. Bernard / Duane M. Bernard / 1952
133 5/8	22 2/8	21 1/8	18 1/8	20	5 5/8	5 1/8	6	4	3 6/8	564	189
◆ Linn County / Richard L. Rounds / Richard L. Rounds / 1978
133 5/8	19	19 5/8	15 7/8	20 5/8	4 1/8	4 2/8	5	6	1 2/8	564	189
◆ Clackamas County / Richard K. Hughes / Richard K. Hughes / 1981
133 5/8	18 6/8	18 1/8	13 1/8	16 2/8	4 2/8	4 3/8	5	5	0	564	189
◆ Josephine County / Jack D. Chambers / Jack D. Chambers / 1985
133 5/8	21 1/8	21 7/8	17 7/8	19 6/8	4 6/8	4 7/8	6	5	1 6/8	564	189
◆ Clackamas County / Vick L. Ward / Vick L. Ward / 1990
133 4/8	20 4/8	19 6/8	15 2/8	17 2/8	5 6/8	4 4/8	5	5	0	571	194
◆ Clackamas County / C.A. Pond / C.A. Pond / 1940
133 4/8	18 7/8	19 3/8	18	20 4/8	3 7/8	4	6	6	7	571	194
◆ Josephine County / Randy L. Hansen / Randy L. Hansen / 1981
133 4/8	19 7/8	19 1/8	14 6/8	17 5/8	4 3/8	4 3/8	5	5	0	571	194
◆ Clackamas County / Scott J. Fuge / Scott J. Fuge / 1990
133 3/8	18 6/8	19 3/8	17 6/8	20 3/8	4 2/8	4	6	5	3 3/8	578	197
◆ Coos County / Frank Neal / Foster H. Thompson / 1924

Score	Length of Main Beam R	L	Inside Spread	Greatest Spread	Circumference at Smallest Place between Burr and First Point R	L	Number of Points R	L	Total of Lengths Abnormal Points	All-Time Rank	State Rank
133 3/8	19 3/8	19 6/8	18 5/8	20 6/8	4	3 7/8	5	5	0	578	197
◆ Lane County / John D. Woodmark / John D. Woodmark / 1969											
133 3/8	21 4/8	20 5/8	16 5/8	18 6/8	4 1/8	4 1/8	5	5	0	578	197
◆ Marion County / Gene Collier / Gene Collier / 1984											
133 2/8	20	19 7/8	14 6/8	17 4/8	4 1/8	4 2/8	5	5	0	584	200
◆ Linn County / Leon Plueard / Leon Plueard / 1965											
133 2/8	19	19 5/8	17	21 3/8	4 2/8	4	4	4	0	584	200
◆ Clackamas County / Mary A. Schoenborn / Mary A. Schoenborn / 1971											
133 2/8	20 2/8	20 1/8	18 2/8	19 7/8	4 7/8	4 7/8	5	5	0	584	200
◆ Polk County / Ron Zimmerdahl / Ron Zimmerdahl / 1988											
133 1/8	23 2/8	23	20 3/8	26 1/8	3 7/8	4 6/8	4	5	0	591	203
◆ Lane County / Picked Up / Wayne E. Everett / 1971											
133 1/8	19 4/8	19 2/8	15 5/8	19	4 2/8	4 2/8	5	5	0	591	203
◆ Josephine County / Michael J. Collins / Michael J. Collins / 1983											
133 1/8	21 3/8	21 1/8	17	21 1/8	4 7/8	4 7/8	4	6	2 7/8	591	203
◆ Jackson County / Picked Up / Brian K. Samuel / 1989											
133 1/8	20 5/8	20 5/8	15 3/8	17 3/8	4 3/8	4 4/8	5	5	0	591	203
◆ Marion County / Corinne B. Olson / Corinne B. Olson / 1990											
133	18 3/8	18 7/8	15 6/8	19 4/8	3 7/8	4	5	5	0	597	207
◆ Lane County / Karl R. Rymer / Karl R. Rymer / 1969											
132 7/8	18 4/8	19 4/8	18 1/8	20 2/8	4 7/8	4 6/8	5	5	0	603	208
◆ Clackamas County / Kerry L. Schoenborn / Kerry L. Schoenborn / 1978											
132 7/8	21 6/8	22 5/8	18 6/8	20 2/8	3 6/8	4 2/8	4	4	1 7/8	603	208
◆ Jackson County / Lorin C. Bosch / Lorin C. Bosch / 1986											
132 6/8	21 4/8	20 3/8	15 2/8	17 2/8	4	4	4	5	0	610	210
◆ Jackson County / Brad B. Brown / Brad B. Brown / 1985											
132 6/8	22	21 7/8	15	17 3/8	5 3/8	4 3/8	7	5	3 4/8	610	210
◆ Clatsop County / Kenneth W. Heil / Kenneth W. Heil / 1991											
132 4/8	19 5/8	20 7/8	16 2/8	18 5/8	4 2/8	4 4/8	5	5	0	619	212
◆ Linn County / Gene Collier / Gene Collier / 1964											
132 4/8	20 4/8	19 7/8	15 2/8	17 1/8	4	3 7/8	5	5	0	619	212
◆ Clackamas County / Katherine M. Searls / Katherine M. Searls / 1982											
132 3/8	21 4/8	22 4/8	15 1/8	17	4	3 7/8	4	4	3	622	214
◆ Tillamook County / Greg E. Myers / Greg E. Myers / 1977											
132 2/8	21 6/8	21 1/8	12 4/8	14 7/8	5 2/8	4 6/8	4	4	0	629	215
◆ Douglas County / William McCaleb / William McCaleb / 1963											

Score	Length of Main Beam		Inside Spread	Greatest Spread	Circumference at Smallest Place between Burr and First Point		Number of Points		Total of Lengths Abnormal Points	All-Time Rank	State Rank
	R	L			R	L	R	L			
	◆ *Locality / Hunter / Owner / Date Killed*										
132²⁄₈	18⁶⁄₈	19⁶⁄₈	15	19²⁄₈	4²⁄₈	4²⁄₈	5	5	0	629	215
	◆ *Linn County / Ric A. Bergey / Ric A. Bergey / 1992*										
131⁶⁄₈	19⁷⁄₈	20¹⁄₈	18⁶⁄₈	22¹⁄₈	4³⁄₈	4⁵⁄₈	5	7	5²⁄₈	643	217
	◆ *Clackamas County / Marvin Schoenborn / Gary R. Schoenborn / 1946*										
131⁵⁄₈	19⁷⁄₈	20²⁄₈	16⁵⁄₈	18²⁄₈	4³⁄₈	4⁴⁄₈	5	5	0	650	218
	◆ *Lincoln County / Lloyd W. Carver / Lloyd W. Carver / 1966*										
131⁴⁄₈	19⁵⁄₈	20⁴⁄₈	16⁴⁄₈	19	4³⁄₈	4³⁄₈	5	5	0	653	219
	◆ *Tillamook County / Ted Wolcott / Ted Wolcott / 1943*										
131⁴⁄₈	18	18³⁄₈	14²⁄₈	16	4³⁄₈	4⁴⁄₈	5	5	0	653	219
	◆ *Lane County / Helen Sanderlin / Helen Sanderlin / 1966*										
131⁴⁄₈	21²⁄₈	22⁴⁄₈	15⁴⁄₈	17⁴⁄₈	4³⁄₈	4²⁄₈	5	5	0	653	219
	◆ *Jackson County / Yannick Y. Watkins / Yannick Y. Watkins / 1990*										
131³⁄₈	19	19	16¹⁄₈	22	4²⁄₈	4²⁄₈	4	4	0	661	222
	◆ *Lincoln County / Bert Kessi / Bert Kessi / 1942*										
131³⁄₈	20	19⁶⁄₈	14⁴⁄₈	16⁶⁄₈	4	4	5	5	1¹⁄₈	661	222
	◆ *Linn County / Boyd Iverson / Boyd Iverson / 1985*										
131²⁄₈	24⁴⁄₈	24	19⁷⁄₈	22⁴⁄₈	4¹⁄₈	4²⁄₈	5	4	1³⁄₈	664	224
	◆ *Polk County / Ray Burtis / Ray Burtis / 1960*										
131²⁄₈	19¹⁄₈	17⁶⁄₈	13⁵⁄₈	16³⁄₈	4⁴⁄₈	4⁴⁄₈	5	5	0	664	224
	◆ *Estacada / Roy Tracy / Lamont Rumgay / 1967*										
131	17⁵⁄₈	17⁴⁄₈	14⁶⁄₈	17³⁄₈	4⁴⁄₈	4¹⁄₈	5	5	0	670	226
	◆ *Jackson County / Robert R. Maben / Robert R. Maben / 1963*										
130⁶⁄₈	22	22	16⁶⁄₈	18⁷⁄₈	4⁴⁄₈	4⁴⁄₈	5	5	0	678	227
	◆ *Linn County / Gene Collier / Gene Collier / 1967*										
130⁶⁄₈	19⁴⁄₈	20⁴⁄₈	16²⁄₈	24²⁄₈	4²⁄₈	4²⁄₈	5	6	3⁶⁄₈	678	227
	◆ *Jackson County / Roy D. Hugie / Univ. of Mont. Mus. / 1983*										
130⁶⁄₈	19⁴⁄₈	19³⁄₈	14⁴⁄₈	17¹⁄₈	4¹⁄₈	4³⁄₈	5	5	0	678	227
	◆ *Yamhill County / Picked Up / John N. Washburn / 1984*										
130⁶⁄₈	20⁷⁄₈	20⁵⁄₈	17⁶⁄₈	21²⁄₈	3⁶⁄₈	3⁷⁄₈	5	5	0	678	227
	◆ *Jackson County / Ann F. Pope / Ann F. Pope / 1989*										
130⁶⁄₈	20⁴⁄₈	21⁵⁄₈	16	19²⁄₈	4³⁄₈	3³⁄₈	5	4	0	678	227
	◆ *Jackson County / Valmire M. Albert / Valmire M. Albert / 1991*										
130⁶⁄₈	18⁶⁄₈	17⁶⁄₈	18²⁄₈	23²⁄₈	4³⁄₈	4⁴⁄₈	5	5	0	678	227
	◆ *Josephine County / Richard J. Darner / Richard J. Darner / 1993*										
130⁵⁄₈	19⁷⁄₈	20⁵⁄₈	14⁵⁄₈	16⁴⁄₈	4	4³⁄₈	5	5	0	687	233
	◆ *Josephine County / Raymond D. Dodge / Raymond D. Dodge / 1987*										

Score	Length of Main Beam R	L	Inside Spread	Greatest Spread	Circumference at Smallest Place between Burr and First Point R	L	Number of Points R	L	Total of Lengths Abnormal Points	All-Time Rank	State Rank

♦ Locality / Hunter / Owner / Date Killed

Score	R	L	Inside Spread	Greatest Spread	R	L	R	L	Abnormal	All-Time	State
130 4/8	21	21 5/8	17 2/8	19 6/8	5 1/8	4 7/8	6	4	5	690	234

♦ *Multnomah County / Dennis R. Thorud / Dennis R. Thorud / 1985*

| 130 4/8 | 17 4/8 | 19 2/8 | 16 | 20 6/8 | 4 1/8 | 4 | 5 | 5 | 0 | 690 | 234 |

♦ *Josephine County / Ernest F. Stoker / Ernest F. Stoker / 1993*

| 130 2/8 | 20 4/8 | 20 | 16 4/8 | 18 6/8 | 4 4/8 | 4 5/8 | 5 | 5 | 0 | 703 | 236 |

♦ *Clackamas County / Thomas A. Tremain / Robert G. Elliott / 1976*

| 130 2/8 | 18 6/8 | 19 6/8 | 17 2/8 | 19 | 3 3/8 | 3 3/8 | 5 | 5 | 0 | 703 | 236 |

♦ *Jackson County / Stephanie J. Bigman / Stephanie J. Bigman / 1991*

| 129 3/8 | 19 1/8 | 19 4/8 | 15 3/8 | 19 2/8 | 4 1/8 | 4 2/8 | 5 | 5 | 0 | 713 | 238 |

♦ *Columbia County / Renay F. Bernard / Renay F. Bernard / 1992*

| 129 2/8 | 20 5/8 | 20 2/8 | 19 1/8 | 21 1/8 | 4 6/8 | 4 6/8 | 6 | 4 | 2 3/8 | 714 | 239 |

♦ *Columbia County / Delbert E. Riggs / Delbert E. Riggs / 1994*

| 128 5/8 | 18 6/8 | 18 4/8 | 13 7/8 | 15 5/8 | 4 | 4 2/8 | 4 | 5 | 0 | 718 | 240 |

♦ *Lincoln County / Ken E. Bernet / Ken E. Bernet / 1986*

| 127 4/8 | 20 4/8 | 21 | 18 6/8 | 20 4/8 | 4 6/8 | 4 5/8 | 5 | 5 | 0 | 725 | 241 |

♦ *Clatsop County / Allan R. Maki / Allan R. Maki / 1966*

| 127 4/8 | 19 6/8 | 19 2/8 | 17 2/8 | 20 5/8 | 4 3/8 | 4 3/8 | 5 | 5 | 0 | 725 | 241 |

♦ *Coos County / Charles E. Tatum, Jr. / Charles E. Tatum, Jr. / 1991*

| 127 3/8 | 21 4/8 | 22 1/8 | 17 5/8 | 21 6/8 | 4 7/8 | 4 4/8 | 5 | 5 | 0 | 727 | 243 |

♦ *Linn County / Patrick H. Kessi / Patrick H. Kessi / 1993*

| 127 1/8 | 21 | 21 1/8 | 20 1/8 | 22 3/8 | 4 2/8 | 4 3/8 | 4 | 5 | 0 | 729 | 244 |

♦ *Marion County / John E. Williams / John E. Williams / 1974*

| 126 3/8 | 20 7/8 | 16 4/8 | 17 3/8 | 19 | 4 | 4 4/8 | 4 | 4 | 0 | 731 | 245 |

♦ *Columbia County / Charles Lindberg / Charles Lindberg / 1971*

| 125 5/8 | 21 3/8 | 20 7/8 | 16 1/8 | 17 6/8 | 3 6/8 | 3 1/8 | 4 | 5 | 0 | 733 | 246 |

♦ *Marion County / Douglas G. Ellis / Douglas G. Ellis / 1984*

| 123 2/8 | 19 1/8 | 18 3/8 | 16 2/8 | 17 6/8 | 4 2/8 | 4 | 5 | 5 | 0 | 744 | 247 |

♦ *Tillamook County / Fain J. Little / Fain J. Little / 1943*

| 122 3/8 | 21 3/8 | 21 2/8 | 15 5/8 | 17 4/8 | 4 3/8 | 4 3/8 | 4 | 4 | 0 | 749 | 248 |

♦ *Columbia County / Kelly P. Dering / Kelly P. Dering / 1990*

| 122 2/8 | 19 | 18 6/8 | 16 2/8 | 20 6/8 | 4 2/8 | 4 | 5 | 4 | 0 | 752 | 249 |

♦ *Yamhill County / Picked Up / Mike McQuaw / 1980*

| 121 7/8 | 19 6/8 | 19 6/8 | 16 3/8 | 18 | 4 2/8 | 4 2/8 | 4 | 4 | 0 | 757 | 250 |

♦ *Columbia County / Daniel J. Bernard / Daniel J. Bernard / 1992*

| 162 6/8 | 24 1/8 | 25 4/8 | 18 4/8 | 24 2/8 | 5 4/8 | 5 4/8 | 7 | 8 | 8 6/8 | * | * |

♦ *Clackamas County / Curtis A. Lee / Steve Crossley / 1981*

Score	Length of Main Beam		Inside Spread	Greatest Spread	Circumference at Smallest Place between Burr and First Point		Number of Points		Total of Lengths Abnormal Points	All-Time Rank	State Rank
	R	L			R	L	R	L			
	Locality / Hunter / Owner / Date Killed										
162²⁄₈	23⁶⁄₈	22⁴⁄₈	21	24	5²⁄₈	5²⁄₈	5	5	0	*	*
	◆ *Jackson County / Mickey Geary / Mickey Geary / 1973*										
161²⁄₈	24	23³⁄₈	19²⁄₈	22⁶⁄₈	4⁵⁄₈	4⁵⁄₈	5	5	0	*	*
	◆ *Clackamas County / Darrell Stewart / Darrell Stewart / 1977*										

Photograph by Wm. H. Nesbitt

WASHINGTON STATE RECORD
WORLD'S RECORD
COLUMBIA BLACKTAIL DEER
SCORE: 182 ⅞
Locality: Lewis Co.   Date: 1953
Hunter: Lester H. Miller

WASHINGTON

COLUMBIA BLACKTAIL DEER

Score	Length of Main Beam R	L	Inside Spread	Greatest Spread	Circumference at Smallest Place between Burr and First Point R	L	Number of Points R	L	Total of Lengths Abnormal Points	All-Time Rank	State Rank
182²⁄₈	24²⁄₈	24⁵⁄₈	20²⁄₈	22⁴⁄₈	5²⁄₈	5²⁄₈	5	5	0	1	1
◆ Lewis County / Lester H. Miller / Lester H. Miller / 1953											
171⁶⁄₈	24³⁄₈	24²⁄₈	22²⁄₈	25⁵⁄₈	5⁶⁄₈	5²⁄₈	5	6	1²⁄₈	3	2
◆ Skagit County / Harry M. Kay / Dan Heasley / 1939											
169³⁄₈	23²⁄₈	22⁷⁄₈	18³⁄₈	22¹⁄₈	5⁷⁄₈	6¹⁄₈	6	6	6	8	3
◆ Lewis County / Larry V. Taylor / Thomas Gogan / 1941											
167²⁄₈	24³⁄₈	26	16¹⁄₈	19	6	6	7	6	7⁵⁄₈	10	4
◆ Lewis County / Maurice D. Heldreth / Loaned to B&C Natl. Coll. / 1976											
164¹⁄₈	20⁵⁄₈	20⁴⁄₈	21²⁄₈	24⁴⁄₈	4⁶⁄₈	4⁵⁄₈	6	5	1⁴⁄₈	15	5
◆ Cowlitz County / Harold Melland / Harold Melland / 1962											
162⁶⁄₈	25	25²⁄₈	23²⁄₈	26⁴⁄₈	4⁵⁄₈	4⁶⁄₈	7	7	6⁴⁄₈	20	6
◆ Pierce County / Dick Allen / Craig Allen / 1952											
159²⁄₈	24⁷⁄₈	24	24⁴⁄₈	30	4⁴⁄₈	5²⁄₈	4	5	0	35	7
◆ Whatcom County / Paul A. Braddock / Paul A. Braddock / 1963											
158²⁄₈	22⁶⁄₈	24⁴⁄₈	18⁶⁄₈	21⁷⁄₈	5²⁄₈	4⁵⁄₈	5	5	0	41	8
◆ Lewis County / Keith A. Heldreth / Keith A. Heldreth / 1984											
156⁶⁄₈	22²⁄₈	21³⁄₈	20²⁄₈	24²⁄₈	4⁵⁄₈	4⁴⁄₈	5	5	0	48	9
◆ Pierce County / Horst A. Vierthaler / Horst A. Vierthaler / 1963											
156⁴⁄₈	22⁴⁄₈	21⁶⁄₈	17	21²⁄₈	3⁵⁄₈	3⁶⁄₈	5	5	0	50	10
◆ King County / Byron Gusa / Byron Gusa / 1980											
155⁷⁄₈	23¹⁄₈	23⁷⁄₈	16²⁄₈	19²⁄₈	4⁶⁄₈	4⁷⁄₈	5	6	3¹⁄₈	54	11
◆ Pierce County / J. Bennett & F. Duell / J. Bennett & F. Duell / 1983											
155²⁄₈	21⁷⁄₈	20²⁄₈	17⁶⁄₈	20⁴⁄₈	4²⁄₈	4²⁄₈	5	5	0	56	12
◆ King County / Horst A. Vierthaler / Horst A. Vierthaler / 1960											
154⁶⁄₈	22⁴⁄₈	23⁴⁄₈	18	20⁵⁄₈	4⁵⁄₈	4⁶⁄₈	5	6	4²⁄₈	62	13
◆ Cowlitz County / Bud Whittle / Bud Whittle / 1957											
153⁷⁄₈	22	22¹⁄₈	17	19⁶⁄₈	4⁵⁄₈	4⁵⁄₈	6	5	4³⁄₈	73	14
◆ Jefferson County / Picked Up / Wayne Brown / PR 1940											
153⁶⁄₈	22⁵⁄₈	23¹⁄₈	17⁷⁄₈	21⁴⁄₈	5⁴⁄₈	5⁵⁄₈	6	5	6¹⁄₈	74	15
◆ Thurston County / Denise A. George / Denise A. George / 1987											
153³⁄₈	24⁵⁄₈	24⁴⁄₈	18⁵⁄₈	20⁷⁄₈	4⁶⁄₈	4⁷⁄₈	5	5	0	76	16
◆ Clallam County / Picked Up / Lawrence J. Bourm / 1949											
153²⁄₈	20¹⁄₈	20⁴⁄₈	21¹⁄₈	23⁵⁄₈	4³⁄₈	4¹⁄₈	5	5	0	79	17
◆ Pierce County / Brooks Carmichael / Brooks Carmichael / 1971											

Score	Length of Main Beam R	Length of Main Beam L	Inside Spread	Greatest Spread	Circumference at Smallest Place between Burr and First Point R	Circumference at Smallest Place between Burr and First Point L	Number of Points R	Number of Points L	Total of Lengths Abnormal Points	All-Time Rank	State Rank
♦ *Locality / Hunter / Owner / Date Killed*											
151	20 4/8	21 6/8	17 2/8	24 6/8	4 6/8	4 6/8	6	6	5 6/8	99	18
♦ *Lewis County / Norman Henspeter / Norman Henspeter / 1941*											
151	23 2/8	24	17 4/8	20 2/8	5 3/8	5 3/8	7	6	13 6/8	99	18
♦ *Lewis County / Harold Gossard / George V. Bagley / 1967*											
150 1/8	20 3/8	21	14 1/8	17	5 2/8	5 2/8	5	5	0	106	20
♦ *Lewis County / Carroll H. Fenn / Carroll H. Fenn / 1959*											
150	22 5/8	22 7/8	19 4/8	24	5 6/8	5 5/8	5	5	0	110	21
♦ *King County / Roscoe Rainey / Roscoe Rainey / 1963*											
149 3/8	20 5/8	22 5/8	17 5/8	21 6/8	5	5	5	5	0	121	22
♦ *Cowlitz County / Milton C. Gudgell / Milton C. Gudgell / 1957*											
149 1/8	21 4/8	22 7/8	16 1/8	18 1/8	5	4 7/8	5	5	0	127	23
♦ *Clallam County / Otis Dahman / E.A. Dahman / 1943*											
148 4/8	22 5/8	22 1/8	16 5/8	18 2/8	4 4/8	4 4/8	6	5	1 1/8	132	24
♦ *Skamania County / Alan D. Borroz / Alan D. Borroz / 1978*											
147	20	20 4/8	21 4/8	24	5	5	5	5	0	149	25
♦ *King County / Robert B. Gracey / Robert B. Gracey / 1963*											
146 7/8	22 4/8	22 2/8	15 1/8	17 6/8	5 3/8	5 3/8	5	5	0	152	26
♦ *Clallam County / Charles W. Lockhart / Charles W. Lockhart / 1946*											
146 4/8	22 6/8	22 7/8	22	24 1/8	5 2/8	5 4/8	5	5	0	157	27
♦ *King County / Leo Klinkhammer / Leo Klinkhammer / 1961*											
146 1/8	22 1/8	22 4/8	14 5/8	18 6/8	4 5/8	4 3/8	0	0	0	163	28
♦ *Lewis County / Keith A. Heldreth / Keith A. Heldreth / 1988*											
145 6/8	22 2/8	20 5/8	17	21 4/8	4 2/8	4 2/8	5	5	0	174	29
♦ *King County / Terry Flowers / Terry Flowers / 1959*											
145 6/8	19 4/8	20 2/8	14 6/8	18 1/8	5 3/8	6	5	6	3	174	29
♦ *Whatcom County / Dennis Miller / Dennis Miller / 1970*											
145 1/8	21 6/8	22 6/8	16 3/8	18 1/8	5	5 3/8	6	5	1	187	31
♦ *Pierce County / Robert L. Armstrong / Robert L. Armstrong / 1978*											
145	24 2/8	23 7/8	14 4/8	17	4 3/8	4 2/8	5	6	1 4/8	192	32
♦ *Whatcom County / Harry E. Williams / Harry E. Williams / 1992*											
144 7/8	22 1/8	21 6/8	18 3/8	20 2/8	5 1/8	5 2/8	5	6	1 2/8	195	33
♦ *Skamania County / Fred W. Campbell / Fred W. Campbell / 1992*											
144 6/8	20	20 4/8	19 4/8	24 4/8	3 4/8	3 4/8	5	4	3	198	34
♦ *King County / R. Walter Williams / R. Walter Williams / 1956*											
144 6/8	22 2/8	22 1/8	17 7/8	19 5/8	4 4/8	4 3/8	6	6	2 3/8	198	34
♦ *Skamania County / Melvin D. Robertson / Melvin D. Robertson / 1983*											

Score	Length of Main Beam R	L	Inside Spread	Greatest Spread	Circumference at Smallest Place between Burr and First Point R	L	Number of Points R	L	Total of Lengths Abnormal Points	All-Time Rank	State Rank
144 4/8	21	21 7/8	17	24	3 7/8	3 6/8	4	4	0	206	36
◆ Snohomish County / Roy Shogren / Roy Shogren / 1979											
144 4/8	20 5/8	21 2/8	16 4/8	19	4 6/8	4 7/8	5	5	0	206	36
◆ Clark County / Raymond M. Gibson / Raymond M. Gibson / 1992											
144 3/8	22 3/8	24 4/8	18 3/8	20 5/8	5	5	6	6	4 4/8	212	38
◆ Jefferson County / John E. Shultz / John E. Shultz / 1991											
144	20 7/8	20 4/8	17 2/8	18 7/8	4 4/8	4 5/8	5	5	0	222	39
◆ Skamania County / Wayne Crockford / Wayne Crockford / 1960											
143 6/8	20 1/8	20 2/8	16 4/8	18 7/8	5	5	5	5	0	227	40
◆ Lewis County / Bill W. Latimer / Bill W. Latimer / 1974											
143 5/8	21 2/8	21 2/8	17 7/8	19 6/8	5 6/8	5 7/8	5	6	3	232	41
◆ Grays Harbor County / E. & R. Dierick / E. & R. Dierick / 1958											
143 4/8	21 4/8	22 5/8	16 2/8	0	4 1/8	4 3/8	5	5	0	235	42
◆ Clark County / A.W. Gerber / Earl Gerber / 1929											
143 4/8	21 4/8	21 1/8	21 4/8	23 2/8	4 4/8	4 4/8	5	4	0	235	42
◆ Snoqualmie / Milton L. James / Milton L. James / 1964											
142 1/8	20 4/8	19 5/8	15 5/8	19 3/8	4 4/8	4 3/8	5	5	0	278	44
◆ Lewis County / Michael H. Carle / Michael H. Carle / 1989											
142	20 1/8	20 6/8	17	19	4 3/8	4 2/8	5	5	0	282	45
◆ Cowlitz County / Harold C. Johnson / Harold C. Johnson / 1947											
142	21 6/8	22 5/8	20 2/8	22 1/8	4 5/8	4 6/8	6	5	2 4/8	282	45
◆ Mt. Sheazer / Joseph B. Wilcox / Joseph B. Wilcox / 1953											
142	24 6/8	24 6/8	17	19 1/8	5	5	4	5	2	282	45
◆ Skamania County / Ted Howell / Ted Howell / 1968											
142	25 3/8	24	18 3/8	21	7	6 4/8	7	4	2 5/8	282	45
◆ Doty / Leslie A. Lusk / Leslie A. Lusk / 1973											
142	23	20 7/8	21 4/8	23 5/8	4 4/8	4 4/8	5	5	0	282	45
◆ Skamania County / Herbert P. Roberts / Herbert P. Roberts / 1983											
141 7/8	20 7/8	21 3/8	18 1/8	22	5 5/8	5 5/8	4	4	0	288	50
◆ Whatcom County / Kjell A. Thompson / Kjell A. Thompson / 1963											
141 6/8	22 7/8	22 2/8	17 5/8	19 4/8	4 5/8	4 6/8	6	7	3 3/8	292	51
◆ Pierce County / Joseph Kominski / Joseph Kominski / 1954											
141 6/8	19 7/8	19 3/8	16 4/8	18 7/8	4 7/8	4 7/8	5	5	0	292	51
◆ Hobart / Donald R. Heinle / Donald R. Heinle / 1958											
141 5/8	23	22 5/8	15 7/8	18 4/8	5 2/8	4 7/8	5	5	0	296	53
◆ Skamania County / E. Gerald Tikka / E. Gerald Tikka / 1987											

Score	Length of Main Beam R	L	Inside Spread	Greatest Spread	Circumference at Smallest Place between Burr and First Point R	L	Number of Points R	L	Total of Lengths Abnormal Points	All-Time Rank	State Rank
	Locality / Hunter / Owner / Date Killed										
141 4/8	20 2/8	20 6/8	17 6/8	19 5/8	4 7/8	5	5	5	0	299	54
	Morton / Ralph W. Cournyer / Ralph W. Cournyer / 1962										
141 4/8	22	22 5/8	15 4/8	17 6/8	5 2/8	5 1/8	5	5	0	299	54
	Pierce County / Ron Dick / Ron Dick / 1965										
141 2/8	25 6/8	25 3/8	21 5/8	24 7/8	5 4/8	5 6/8	6	6	3 3/8	306	56
	Pierce County / John Streepy, Sr. / John Streepy, Sr. / 1956										
141 1/8	22 2/8	22 4/8	17 7/8	19 7/8	4 6/8	4 6/8	5	5	0	309	57
	Pierce County / Jerry E. Burke / Jerry E. Burke / 1980										
141 1/8	21	21	19 3/8	21 6/8	4 6/8	4 5/8	5	5	0	309	57
	Clallam County / David P. Sanford / David P. Sanford / 1989										
140 7/8	22 2/8	25 7/8	12 3/8	15 6/8	6 5/8	7 4/8	5	7	9 6/8	317	59
	Clallam County / Frank Foldi / Steven Crossley / 1958										
140 6/8	17 6/8	18 5/8	17 2/8	20 6/8	4 5/8	4 4/8	5	6	2 2/8	321	60
	Lewis County / Nick Nilson / Nick Nilson / 1944										
140 5/8	21	21	18 6/8	21 1/8	4 6/8	4 6/8	6	5	4 5/8	325	61
	Glacier / John J.A. Weatherby / John J.A. Weatherby / 1965										
140 2/8	20 4/8	21 3/8	16 2/8	18 2/8	4 7/8	4 5/8	5	5	0	333	62
	Lewis County / Randy J. Brossard / Randy J. Brossard / 1978										
140 1/8	23 7/8	22 7/8	18 1/8	19 6/8	5	4 4/8	6	6	8	337	63
	Lewis County / George Nichols / George Nichols / 1964										
140 1/8	19	19 6/8	16 5/8	19 4/8	4 5/8	4 6/8	5	5	0	337	63
	Snohomish County / Kenneth A. Peterson / Kenneth A. Peterson / 1985										
139 6/8	21 1/8	21 3/8	18 6/8	20 7/8	5	4 6/8	5	5	0	354	65
	Thurston County / Eric Anderson / Eric Anderson / 1937										
139 6/8	19 6/8	19 7/8	18 6/8	0	4	4	5	5	0	354	65
	Lewis County / Keith A. Heldreth / Keith A. Heldreth / 1989										
139 5/8	21 2/8	21 2/8	14 4/8	16 1/8	4 2/8	4 2/8	6	5	1 3/8	359	67
	Cowlitz County / David A. Martin / David A. Martin / 1962										
139 4/8	22 2/8	21 5/8	16	18 3/8	4 6/8	4 6/8	4	5	0	360	68
	Lewis County / Kevin Pointer / Kevin Pointer / 1972										
139 3/8	20 1/8	20 2/8	15 5/8	19	4 2/8	4 1/8	5	5	0	364	69
	Whatcom County / Kim S. Scott / Kim S. Scott / 1959										
139	21 1/8	22 3/8	16 2/8	19 6/8	4 5/8	4 5/8	5	5	0	382	70
	Jefferson County / Picked Up / Aubrey F. Taylor / 1947										
139	20	20 5/8	16 4/8	18 4/8	4 6/8	4 4/8	5	5	0	382	70
	Lewis County / Mike Cournyer / Mike Cournyer / 1964										

WASHINGTON COLUMBIA BLACKTAIL DEER *(continued)*

Score	Length of Main Beam		Inside Spread	Greatest Spread	Circumference at Smallest Place between Burr and First Point		Number of Points		Total of Lengths Abnormal Points	All-Time Rank	State Rank
	R	L			R	L	R	L			
◆ Locality / Hunter / Owner / Date Killed											
138 7/8	19 7/8	19 7/8	15 7/8	18 6/8	4 4/8	4 4/8	5	5	0	389	72
◆ Pacific County / Russell Case / Russell Case / 1956											
138 6/8	20 2/8	21 3/8	15 5/8	17 3/8	5 1/8	5 2/8	6	7	3 5/8	395	73
◆ Snohomish County / Walter J. Kau / Walter J. Kau / 1950											
138 6/8	23 3/8	23	15 6/8	17 6/8	4 4/8	4 5/8	5	6	1	395	73
◆ Pierce County / James Latimer / James Latimer / 1962											
138 3/8	23 7/8	22 4/8	16 3/8	18 2/8	5 3/8	5 4/8	5	6	8	407	75
◆ Pierce County / George W. Halcott / George W. Halcott / 1966											
138 2/8	19 4/8	21	16 2/8	19 2/8	5 2/8	4 4/8	5	5	0	411	76
◆ Snohomish County / James McCarthy / James McCarthy / 1961											
137 5/8	20 1/8	19 7/8	15 6/8	18 1/8	4 6/8	4 6/8	6	5	2 1/8	431	77
◆ Lewis County / Larry L. Larson / Larry L. Larson / 1978											
137	24	23 6/8	21 2/8	23 4/8	4 3/8	4 3/8	4	5	0	450	78
◆ King County / Douglas F. Dammarell / Douglas F. Dammarell / 1974											
137	20 1/8	21 2/8	16 6/8	18 7/8	4 7/8	4 6/8	5	5	0	450	78
◆ Pierce County / Glenn T. Litzau / Glenn T. Litzau / 1992											
136 7/8	21 3/8	20 7/8	17 5/8	20 5/8	4 2/8	4 4/8	4	5	0	454	80
◆ Lewis County / Allen J. Roehrick / Allen J. Roehrick / 1968											
136 6/8	21 3/8	21	14	16 3/8	5 2/8	5 2/8	5	5	0	456	81
◆ King County / Ed Lochus / George B. Johnson / 1930											
136 6/8	19 3/8	20	14 3/8	16 3/8	4 5/8	5	6	6	2 7/8	456	81
◆ Lewis County / Mark G. Frohmader / Mark G. Frohmader / 1969											
136 6/8	20 5/8	21 1/8	16	17 6/8	4 1/8	4 1/8	5	5	0	456	81
◆ Pierce County / Patrick M. Blackwell / Patrick M. Blackwell / 1971											
136 5/8	21 4/8	22 3/8	19	21	5 6/8	5 2/8	5	4	1 1/8	460	84
◆ Arlington / Ernest J. Kaesther / Ernest J. Kaesther / 1959											
136 4/8	20 2/8	20	18 4/8	20 6/8	4 7/8	4 5/8	5	5	0	464	85
◆ Grays Harbor County / Joseph S. Prohaska / Stephen H. Prohaska / 1952											
136 4/8	23 4/8	22 1/8	18 2/8	20 1/8	4 6/8	4 6/8	5	5	0	464	85
◆ Lewis County / Larry F. Smith / Larry F. Smith / 1964											
136 1/8	19	18 6/8	14 5/8	17 3/8	5	5 2/8	5	6	3 2/8	477	87
◆ Whatcom County / Dick Vander Yacht / Dick Vander Yacht / 1960											
135 7/8	20 3/8	21 1/8	16 7/8	19 3/8	5	5	5	5	0	485	88
◆ Snohomish County / Edmund L. Hurst / Edmund L. Hurst / 1984											
135 6/8	20 5/8	19 7/8	15	19 3/8	5 4/8	5 4/8	5	6	1 2/8	490	89
◆ Whatcom County / Jack R. Teeter / Jack R. Teeter / 1969											

Score	Length of Main Beam R	Length of Main Beam L	Inside Spread	Greatest Spread	Circumference at Smallest Place between Burr and First Point R	Circumference at Smallest Place between Burr and First Point L	Number of Points R	Number of Points L	Total of Lengths Abnormal Points	All-Time Rank	State Rank
135 6/8	20	20 2/8	17 2/8	19 2/8	4 6/8	4 6/8	5	5	0	490	89
◆ *Cowlitz County / William R. Gottfryd / William R. Gottfryd / 1986*											
135 5/8	19 6/8	19 3/8	17 5/8	20 6/8	4 3/8	4 1/8	4	4	0	497	91
◆ *Clallam County / Gary L. Smith / Gary L. Smith / 1956*											
135 5/8	22 4/8	23 2/8	20 1/8	22 2/8	4 4/8	4 3/8	4	4	0	497	91
◆ *Pierce County / Mark A. Dye / Mark A. Dye / 1987*											
135 4/8	20 4/8	20 1/8	16 6/8	18 4/8	3 6/8	3 7/8	5	5	0	501	93
◆ *Lewis County / Oren Layton / Oren Layton / 1977*											
135 3/8	21 5/8	21 2/8	17 6/8	22	4 6/8	4 5/8	6	6	3 7/8	504	94
◆ *Clark County / Francis E. Gillette / Francis E. Gillette / 1934*											
135 3/8	21 7/8	21 6/8	16 5/8	18 6/8	5 1/8	5	5	5	1 2/8	504	94
◆ *King County / Ernest Zwiefelhofer / Wayne Ferderer / 1941*											
135	20	19 7/8	16 2/8	19 7/8	4 1/8	4 1/8	5	5	0	510	96
◆ *Whatcom County / Dennis R. Beebe / Dennis R. Beebe / 1981*											
134 6/8	22 4/8	22 6/8	16	18 6/8	5 1/8	5 1/8	5	6	3 6/8	523	97
◆ *Thurston County / George W. Sharrow / George W. Sharrow / 1946*											
134 6/8	21 5/8	23 2/8	19 2/8	20 6/8	4 3/8	4 2/8	5	5	0	523	97
◆ *Cowlitz County / Kenneth D. Nicholson / Kenneth D. Nicholson / 1970*											
134 4/8	22 2/8	23 2/8	18 2/8	20 4/8	4 5/8	4 6/8	4	4	0	531	99
◆ *Thurston County / Joseph Kominski / Joseph Kominski / 1955*											
134 4/8	21 6/8	22 5/8	13	16 5/8	4 3/8	4 4/8	6	6	2 2/8	531	99
◆ *Lewis County / Douglas G. McArthur / Douglas G. McArthur / 1967*											
134 4/8	26	27 1/8	20 2/8	22 3/8	4 7/8	4 6/8	5	4	0	531	99
◆ *Lewis County / Daniel E. Longmire / Daniel E. Longmire / 1974*											
134 3/8	18	15	17 7/8	20 6/8	4 6/8	4 2/8	6	5	1 2/8	537	102
◆ *Lewis County / Melvin B. Henle / Melvin B. Henle / 1973*											
134 2/8	21 7/8	22 1/8	16	18 5/8	4 4/8	4 4/8	4	5	0	542	103
◆ *Pierce County / James B. August / James B. August / 1971*											
134 1/8	20 4/8	20 4/8	14 5/8	18	4 2/8	4 2/8	5	5	0	550	104
◆ *King County / Greg E. Connell / Greg E. Connell / 1979*											
134	21 2/8	20 5/8	16	19 1/8	4 4/8	4 4/8	4	5	0	555	105
◆ *Pierce County / William B. Bressler / William B. Bressler / 1987*											
133 6/8	20 6/8	21 5/8	18 1/8	21 2/8	4 7/8	5 2/8	6	6	3 3/8	560	106
◆ *Pierce County / K.S. Sheets / K.S. Sheets / 1966*											
133 4/8	21 3/8	20 2/8	13 6/8	16 2/8	4 7/8	5	5	5	0	571	107
◆ *Clallam County / Tony M. Rickel / Tony M. Rickel / 1987*											

WASHINGTON COLUMBIA BLACKTAIL DEER *(continued)*

Score	Length of Main Beam R	Length of Main Beam L	Inside Spread	Greatest Spread	Circumference at Smallest Place between Burr and First Point R	Circumference at Smallest Place between Burr and First Point L	Number of Points R	Number of Points L	Total of Lengths Abnormal Points	All-Time Rank	State Rank
◆ *Locality / Hunter / Owner / Date Killed*											
133 3/8	20 7/8	21 7/8	12 1/8	15	4 4/8	4 6/8	5	5	0	578	108
◆ *Clallam County / Glen W. Gooding / Glen W. Gooding / 1957*											
133 2/8	21 1/8	21 1/8	13 6/8	15 7/8	4 6/8	4 5/8	5	5	0	584	109
◆ *Skagit County / L.A. Willoughby / L.A. Willoughby / 1951*											
133 2/8	20 5/8	20 4/8	14 6/8	16 5/8	4 5/8	4 6/8	5	5	0	584	109
◆ *Pierce County / Lowell Apple / Lowell Apple / 1968*											
133	22 4/8	23 2/8	20 6/8	23 4/8	5 6/8	4 6/8	9	4	7 2/8	597	111
◆ *Lewis County / George Sevey / George Sevey / 1941*											
133	23	21 6/8	16 6/8	19 5/8	4 3/8	4 2/8	5	5	0	597	111
◆ *Snohomish County / Burl Champeaux / Burl Champeaux / 1959*											
133	20 1/8	19 7/8	16 2/8	18	5 2/8	5 2/8	5	5	0	597	111
◆ *Skamania County / Jeffrey M. Divine / Jeffrey M. Divine / 1993*											
132 5/8	20 5/8	19 6/8	16 5/8	19	5 4/8	6 2/8	5	5	0	616	114
◆ *Mason County / Fred E. Champlin / Fred E. Champlin / 1981*											
132 5/8	20 4/8	20 1/8	17 7/8	20	4 7/8	4 7/8	6	5	2 2/8	616	114
◆ *Mason County / Brian L. Martin / Brian L. Martin / 1984*											
132 4/8	19	18 2/8	14	17	4 7/8	4 7/8	4	4	0	619	116
◆ *Lewis County / Robert L. Peck / Robert L. Peck / 1964*											
132 3/8	19 6/8	19	15 5/8	18 5/8	5 2/8	5 1/8	5	5	0	622	117
◆ *Cowlitz County / James H. Wilson / James H. Wilson / 1959*											
132 3/8	21 2/8	21 5/8	16 3/8	20 1/8	4	4	5	5	0	622	117
◆ *Grays Harbor County / Jack A. Allen / Jack A. Allen / 1963*											
132 2/8	20 3/8	20 2/8	16 2/8	18 3/8	5 1/8	5	5	4	0	629	119
◆ *Island County / Bert Klineburger / Bert Klineburger / 1969*											
132 2/8	21 7/8	22	18 5/8	21 2/8	5 1/8	5 1/8	5	5	2 7/8	629	119
◆ *Skamania County / Ralph D. Ford / Ralph D. Ford / 1991*											
132 2/8	19 3/8	19 5/8	16 6/8	18 6/8	4 2/8	4 2/8	5	5	0	629	119
◆ *Skamania County / Carl R. Dugger / Carl R. Dugger / 1992*											
132 1/8	21 1/8	20 4/8	13 1/8	14 7/8	4 3/8	4 5/8	5	5	0	637	122
◆ *Lewis County / George W. Rodrick III / George W. Rodrick III / 1980*											
132 1/8	21 2/8	20 7/8	16 7/8	20 4/8	4 2/8	4 1/8	5	5	0	637	122
◆ *Lewis County / Gregory J. Goff / Gregory J. Goff / 1990*											
131 5/8	19 1/8	19 6/8	14 7/8	17 1/8	4 6/8	4 6/8	5	5	0	650	124
◆ *Whatcom County / C.H. Head / C.H. Head / 1972*											
131 5/8	22	21 6/8	17 1/8	19 3/8	4 2/8	4 2/8	4	5	0	650	124
◆ *Pierce County / Lyle O. Brateng / Lyle O. Brateng / 1984*											

Score	Length of Main Beam R	Length of Main Beam L	Inside Spread	Greatest Spread	Circumference at Smallest Place between Burr and First Point R	Circumference at Smallest Place between Burr and First Point L	Number of Points R	Number of Points L	Total of Lengths Abnormal Points	All-Time Rank	State Rank
					◆ Locality / Hunter / Owner / Date Killed						
131⁴⁄₈	18⁴⁄₈	18⁶⁄₈	16²⁄₈	19⁴⁄₈	5⁷⁄₈	5⅛	5	6	1	653	126
	◆ Lewis County / Ron N. Nilson / Ron N. Nilson / 1963										
131⁴⁄₈	18²⁄₈	17⁴⁄₈	14⁴⁄₈	18²⁄₈	4⁶⁄₈	5	5	5	0	653	126
	◆ Snohomish County / Philip C. Thompson / Philip C. Thompson / 1986										
131⁴⁄₈	18³⁄₈	19	15⁶⁄₈	18⅛	4²⁄₈	4	5	5	0	653	126
	◆ Skamania County / Fred R. Froehlich / Fred R. Froehlich / 1988										
131³⁄₈	21	20⅛	15⅛	17⁵⁄₈	4⅛	4	5	5	0	661	129
	◆ Pierce County / Dean A. Bender / Dean A. Bender / 1990										
131²⁄₈	21⅛	20⁷⁄₈	13⁵⁄₈	16²⁄₈	4⁶⁄₈	4⁶⁄₈	7	6	5⅛	664	130
	◆ Skamania County / Thomas E. Krebs / Thomas E. Krebs / 1977										
131	21⁶⁄₈	20⁵⁄₈	15²⁄₈	18⁵⁄₈	4⁵⁄₈	4⁴⁄₈	5	5	0	670	131
	◆ King County / J.A. Ryezek / George B. Johnson / 1935										
131	20⅛	20⁴⁄₈	15	17⁴⁄₈	4²⁄₈	4⁷⁄₈	4	5	0	670	131
	◆ Skamania County / John I. Borchert / John I. Borchert / 1992										
130⁶⁄₈	20⁵⁄₈	20⁴⁄₈	17⁶⁄₈	20²⁄₈	4³⁄₈	4³⁄₈	5	5	0	678	133
	◆ Lewis County / Bill K. Stoner / Bill K. Stoner / 1988										
130⁴⁄₈	21	20⁶⁄₈	17³⁄₈	19²⁄₈	4⁶⁄₈	4⁶⁄₈	6	5	1⁵⁄₈	690	134
	◆ Pierce County / Don Argo / Don Argo / 1950										
130⁴⁄₈	20⁴⁄₈	20²⁄₈	12⁴⁄₈	14²⁄₈	4³⁄₈	4³⁄₈	5	5	0	690	134
	◆ Cowlitz County / Michael A. Demery / Steven J. Hellem / 1978										
130³⁄₈	19⅛	18³⁄₈	15³⁄₈	20⁴⁄₈	4²⁄₈	4²⁄₈	5	5	0	699	136
	◆ Mt. Jupiter / Jack Dustin / Jack Dustin / 1946										
130³⁄₈	22⁵⁄₈	22⁵⁄₈	16³⁄₈	19⁴⁄₈	4⁶⁄₈	4⁶⁄₈	4	4	0	699	136
	◆ Cowlitz County / James L. Conner / James L. Conner / 1993										
130⅛	19²⁄₈	19⁵⁄₈	17⅛	22²⁄₈	4⁷⁄₈	5⅛	5	6	1²⁄₈	706	138
	◆ Thurston County / Gano S. Hayes / Gano S. Hayes / 1985										
130⅛	20³⁄₈	20	15⁷⁄₈	18⁵⁄₈	4	4³⁄₈	4	5	0	706	138
	◆ Clallam County / Larry Hanna / Larry Hanna / 1992										
130	17²⁄₈	17²⁄₈	16	19	4³⁄₈	4²⁄₈	5	5	0	709	140
	◆ Cowlitz County / Harold E. Koenig / Harold E. Koenig / 1949										
129⅛	19⁴⁄₈	21²⁄₈	16⁷⁄₈	19⅛	4⁵⁄₈	4⁶⁄₈	5	5	0	715	141
	◆ Lewis County / Kenneth J. Alwine, Sr. / Kenneth J. Alwine, Sr. / 1956										
128⁷⁄₈	17⅛	17⅛	13⁷⁄₈	17⅛	4⅛	4⅛	5	5	0	717	142
	◆ Snohomish County / Donald E. Thomsen / Donald E. Thomsen / 1991										
128²⁄₈	20⁴⁄₈	20²⁄₈	14⁶⁄₈	17³⁄₈	4⅛	4²⁄₈	5	5	0	720	143
	◆ Clallam County / James W. Fatherson / James W. Fatherson / 1983										

Score	Length of Main Beam R	L	Inside Spread	Greatest Spread	Circumference at Smallest Place between Burr and First Point R	L	Number of Points R	L	Total of Lengths Abnormal Points	All-Time Rank	State Rank
	Locality / Hunter / Owner / Date Killed										
128²⁄₈	19¹⁄₈	19³⁄₈	17⁴⁄₈	20	4²⁄₈	4³⁄₈	5	5	0	720	143
	◆ *Skamania County / Jeffrey M. Divine / Jeffrey M. Divine / 1994*										
127⁵⁄₈	20³⁄₈	21	19⁶⁄₈	22¹⁄₈	5¹⁄₈	5²⁄₈	6	7	6⁵⁄₈	724	145
	◆ *Clallam County / Harry E. Reed, Jr. / Harry E. Reed, Jr. / 1977*										
123⁵⁄₈	21³⁄₈	21⁶⁄₈	18¹⁄₈	21⁴⁄₈	3⁶⁄₈	3⁵⁄₈	3	3	0	740	146
	◆ *King County / Gene D. Collecchi / Gene D. Collecchi / 1987*										
123³⁄₈	20⁵⁄₈	21	18⁶⁄₈	22	4⁴⁄₈	4³⁄₈	7	8	20¹⁄₈	742	147
	◆ *Lewis County / Unknown / Robert E. Shirer / PR 1960*										
123¹⁄₈	22¹⁄₈	21²⁄₈	18³⁄₈	21⁴⁄₈	4³⁄₈	4²⁄₈	5	4	1²⁄₈	745	148
	◆ *Pierce County / Robert J. Keeley / Robert J. Keeley / 1968*										
122⁶⁄₈	19⁶⁄₈	20¹⁄₈	14⁴⁄₈	17¹⁄₈	3⁶⁄₈	3⁶⁄₈	4	5	0	746	149
	◆ *Jefferson County / Ralph E. Wean / Ralph E. Wean / 1987*										
122⁶⁄₈	19³⁄₈	19³⁄₈	14⁶⁄₈	17²⁄₈	4⁶⁄₈	4⁵⁄₈	5	6	2	746	149
	◆ *Grays Harbor County / Robert J. Babineau, Jr. / Robert J. Babineau, Jr. / 1991*										
122³⁄₈	18	16⁶⁄₈	14¹⁄₈	16⁷⁄₈	5	4⁶⁄₈	5	5	0	749	151
	◆ *Pierce County / Guy A. Hanson / Guy A. Hanson / 1984*										
122²⁄₈	22	21⁵⁄₈	16⁴⁄₈	18¹⁄₈	4¹⁄₈	4¹⁄₈	4	4	0	752	152
	◆ *King County / Russell L. McKinnon / Russell L. McKinnon / 1987*										
121⁷⁄₈	20⁵⁄₈	20⁶⁄₈	15⁷⁄₈	18⁷⁄₈	4²⁄₈	4³⁄₈	5	5	0	757	153
	◆ *Lewis County / Robert E. Hill / Robert E. Hill / 1988*										
121¹⁄₈	20	20⁷⁄₈	15⁶⁄₈	18	4³⁄₈	4⁴⁄₈	5	5	2³⁄₈	760	154
	◆ *King County / Kip Sanders / Kip Sanders / 1992*										

BRITISH COLUMBIA PROVINCE RECORD (NEW)
COLUMBIA BLACKTAIL DEER
SCORE: 152⅛
Locality: Pemberton   Date: 1968
Hunter: Jim Decker

BRITISH COLUMBIA
COLUMBIA BLACKTAIL DEER

Score	Length of Main Beam R	L	Inside Spread	Greatest Spread	Circumference at Smallest Place between Burr and First Point R	L	Number of Points R	L	Total of Lengths Abnormal Points	All-Time Rank	State Rank
152 1/8	20 4/8	21 1/8	17 4/8	23 1/8	5 5/8	5 7/8	7	6	8 3/8	86	1
♦ Pemberton / Jim Decker / Jim Decker / 1968											
145 2/8	22 5/8	17 5/8	17 2/8	20 6/8	4	4	4	4	0	182	2
♦ Lake Harrison / Lloyd L. Ward, Jr. / Lloyd L. Ward, Jr. / 1947											
143 6/8	19 3/8	20 2/8	16	18 2/8	4 6/8	4 7/8	5	5	0	227	3
♦ Squamish / B. Miller / B. Miller / 1962											
143 3/8	20	20 1/8	15 3/8	17 7/8	4 7/8	4 7/8	5	5	0	241	4
♦ Chehalis River / Clair A. Howard / Clair A. Howard / 1971											
143 2/8	20 6/8	19 6/8	19	23	4 7/8	6 2/8	7	6	7 2/8	243	5
♦ Jones Lake / James Haslam / James Haslam / 1967											
142 5/8	19 6/8	19 4/8	16 5/8	21 6/8	4 3/8	4 3/8	5	5	0	259	6
♦ Chilliwack Lake / Blair R. Houdayer / Blair R. Houdayer / 1992											
142 4/8	18 3/8	18 3/8	15	20 2/8	4 5/8	4 6/8	5	5	0	268	7
♦ Chilliwack / Frank Rosenauer / Frank Rosenauer / 1967											
141 3/8	19 6/8	19 7/8	17 6/8	22 5/8	4 7/8	4 6/8	7	6	4 3/8	303	8
♦ Harrison Lake / D. Harrison / D. Harrison / 1963											
138 6/8	20 2/8	21 3/8	15 4/8	18 5/8	4 5/8	4 5/8	5	5	0	395	9
♦ Chipmunk Creek / Larri H. Woodrow / Larri H. Woodrow / 1987											
137 7/8	20 5/8	20 5/8	16 6/8	20 2/8	4 5/8	4 6/8	6	5	2 3/8	423	10
♦ Vancouver Island / Gordie Simpson / Gordie Simpson / 1966											
135 7/8	18 5/8	19 1/8	15 7/8	18 6/8	4 2/8	4 2/8	5	5	0	485	11
♦ Langley / Charles R. Yeomans / James G. Hill / 1959											
135 6/8	21 1/8	21 1/8	18 2/8	20 7/8	4 7/8	4 7/8	5	5	0	490	12
♦ Powell River / Paddy Price / Duncan Formby / 1939											
134 3/8	21 3/8	21 2/8	19 7/8	22 3/8	4 5/8	4 7/8	5	5	0	537	13
♦ Toba Inlet / L. Mitchell / Peters Sport Shop / 1962											
133 1/8	18 2/8	18 5/8	13 5/8	16 3/8	4 2/8	4 1/8	5	5	0	591	14
♦ Langley / Frank Jackson / Brooke Whitelaw / 1935											

Photograph by Wm. H. Nesbitt

ALASKA STATE RECORD
WORLD'S RECORD
SITKA BLACKTAIL DEER
SCORE: 128
Locality: Kodiak Island   Date: 1985
Hunter: Unknown
Owner: Craig Allen

ALASKA
SITKA BLACKTAIL DEER

Score	Length of Main Beam R	L	Inside Spread	Greatest Spread	Circumference at Smallest Place between Burr and First Point R	L	Number of Points R	L	Total of Lengths Abnormal Points	All-Time Rank	State Rank
128	$19^6/_8$	19	$19^4/_8$	$21^3/_8$	$4^7/_8$	$4^7/_8$	5	5	0	1	1
♦ Kodiak Island / Unknown / Craig Allen / 1985											
$126^3/_8$	$18^5/_8$	$19^4/_8$	$14^5/_8$	$16^5/_8$	4	$4^1/_8$	5	5	0	2	2
♦ Sunny Hay Mt. / Harry R. Horner / Harry R. Horner / 1987											
$126^2/_8$	$19^6/_8$	$20^3/_8$	$16^3/_8$	$18^4/_8$	$4^5/_8$	$4^4/_8$	5	6	$3^5/_8$	3	3
♦ Control Lake / William B. Steele, Jr. / William B. Steele, Jr. / 1987											
$125^7/_8$	$17^7/_8$	$18^6/_8$	$13^5/_8$	$16^1/_8$	4	4	4	4	0	4	4
♦ Tenakee Inlet / Donald E. Thompson / Loaned to B&C Natl. Coll. / 1964											
$124^2/_8$	$19^1/_8$	$18^2/_8$	$14^4/_8$	$16^6/_8$	$4^3/_8$	4	5	5	0	5	5
♦ Exchange Cove / Daniel J. Leo / Daniel J. Leo / 1986											
$123^4/_8$	$21^4/_8$	$20^3/_8$	$17^6/_8$	$19^7/_8$	$3^6/_8$	$3^6/_8$	4	4	0	6	6
♦ Uganik Bay / Donna D. Braendel / Donna D. Braendel / 1983											
$123^2/_8$	$18^4/_8$	$18^3/_8$	$14^4/_8$	16	$4^3/_8$	$4^1/_8$	5	5	0	7	7
♦ Prince of Wales Island / Kenneth W. Twitchell / Kenneth W. Twitchell / 1987											
$120^4/_8$	$18^4/_8$	$16^1/_8$	$14^6/_8$	$17^5/_8$	$3^7/_8$	$4^1/_8$	5	5	0	8	8
♦ Cleveland Pen. / Dennis E. Northrup / Dennis E. Northrup / 1986											
$120^1/_8$	$17^6/_8$	$17^6/_8$	$16^3/_8$	$18^7/_8$	$4^5/_8$	$4^4/_8$	5	5	0	9	9
♦ Halibut Bay / James W. Bickman / James W. Bickman / 1987											
$118^5/_8$	17	$16^6/_8$	$15^1/_8$	$17^5/_8$	$3^7/_8$	$3^7/_8$	5	5	0	10	10
♦ Uganik Lake / Larry D. Leuenberger / Larry D. Leuenberger / 1985											
$118^3/_8$	19	$17^1/_8$	$14^7/_8$	$17^1/_8$	4	$4^1/_8$	5	5	0	11	11
♦ Prince of Wales Island / Johnnie R. Laird / Johnnie R. Laird / 1987											
$117^4/_8$	17	$16^6/_8$	$15^2/_8$	$16^7/_8$	$3^7/_8$	$3^7/_8$	5	5	0	12	12
♦ Shrubby Island / Alfred Oglend / Alfred Oglend / 1986											
$117^1/_8$	$16^4/_8$	$16^4/_8$	$13^1/_8$	$15^6/_8$	$4^1/_8$	$4^2/_8$	5	6	$2^2/_8$	13	13
♦ Baird Peak / William C. Dunham / William C. Dunham / 1984											
$117^1/_8$	$16^6/_8$	$17^4/_8$	$16^7/_8$	$18^4/_8$	$4^3/_8$	$4^4/_8$	5	4	2	13	13
♦ Mitkof Island / Andrew Wright / Andrew Wright / 1991											
116	$17^2/_8$	$16^5/_8$	16	$18^5/_8$	$4^1/_8$	$3^6/_8$	5	5	0	15	15
♦ Kiliuda Bay / Timothy Tittle / Timothy Tittle / 1984											
$115^6/_8$	$18^6/_8$	$18^6/_8$	$17^2/_8$	19	$4^2/_8$	4	5	5	0	16	16
♦ Kodiak Island / Daniel J. Folkman / Daniel J. Folkman / 1991											
$114^7/_8$	$15^7/_8$	$16^1/_8$	$14^3/_8$	$16^1/_8$	$3^7/_8$	4	5	6	$1^4/_8$	17	17
♦ Control Lake / Timothy C. Winsenberg / Timothy C. Winsenberg / 1985											

Score	Length of Main Beam R	L	Inside Spread	Greatest Spread	Circumference at Smallest Place between Burr and First Point R	L	Number of Points R	L	Total of Lengths Abnormal Points	All-Time Rank	State Rank
114 7/8	17 7/8	19 1/8	17 5/8	19 3/8	4 2/8	4	5	5	0	17	17
◆ Dall Island / Picked Up / Lynn W. Merrill / 1987											
114 3/8	17 4/8	18 3/8	15 3/8	17 6/8	4 4/8	4 2/8	5	5	0	19	19
◆ Hobart Bay / Terry LaFrance / Terry LaFrance / 1988											
114	15 7/8	16	13 6/8	17 3/8	4	3 7/8	5	5	0	20	20
◆ Olga Bay / Frank E. Entsminger / Frank E. Entsminger / 1986											
113 6/8	17 5/8	19 1/8	16 2/8	18 5/8	3 2/8	3 2/8	4	4	0	21	21
◆ Long Island / Picked Up / Allan C. Merrill / 1987											
113 4/8	18 4/8	18 1/8	15 4/8	19	3 5/8	3 4/8	4	4	0	22	22
◆ Viekoda Bay / Edward R. Hajdys / Edward R. Hajdys / 1980											
113 1/8	17 5/8	18 7/8	16 1/8	17 6/8	3 6/8	3 7/8	5	5	0	23	23
◆ Wadding Cove / Kurt W. Kuehl / Kurt W. Kuehl / 1984											
113	16 1/8	16 4/8	13 6/8	17	4 3/8	4 2/8	5	5	0	24	24
◆ Zarembo Island / Scott D. Newman / Scott D. Newman / 1993											
112 3/8	16 6/8	16 7/8	13 5/8	16	4	4 2/8	5	5	0	25	25
◆ Kodiak Island / Keith M. Nowell / Keith M. Nowell / 1986											
112 3/8	18 2/8	17 7/8	17 5/8	19 4/8	3 5/8	4	7	6	4 4/8	25	25
◆ Alder Creek / Richard L. Reeves / Richard L. Reeves / 1988											
112 3/8	19 4/8	19 7/8	17 5/8	19 5/8	4 1/8	4 1/8	4	4	0	25	25
◆ Prince of Wales Island / David L. Hahnes / David L. Hahnes / 1990											
112 2/8	19	19 2/8	16 4/8	18 2/8	4 3/8	4 2/8	4	4	0	28	28
◆ Olga Bay / John D. Frost / John D. Frost / 1987											
112 2/8	17 3/8	17	15 6/8	18	3 6/8	3 6/8	6	6	4 2/8	28	28
◆ Big Salt Lake / Roy Weatherford / Roy Weatherford / 1988											
112 1/8	17	16 2/8	15 5/8	18	4 1/8	4	5	5	0	30	30
◆ Alitak Bay / Dale J. Bunnage / Dale J. Bunnage / 1988											
111 7/8	18 5/8	18 6/8	15 5/8	18	4 2/8	4 1/8	4	5	0	31	31
◆ Uganik Bay / Jeff A. Buffum / Jeff A. Buffum / 1987											
111 3/8	18	17 6/8	16 3/8	18 4/8	4	3 7/8	5	5	0	32	32
◆ Spiridon Lake / David H. Raskey / David H. Raskey / 1986											
111 3/8	18	18 1/8	15 5/8	18	3 7/8	3 7/8	4	4	0	32	32
◆ Kodiak Island / Craig T. Boddington / Craig T. Boddington / 1992											
111	16 3/8	16 5/8	14 2/8	16 7/8	3 6/8	3 7/8	5	5	0	34	34
◆ Karluk Lake / Ted H. Spraker / Ted H. Spraker / 1983											
110 7/8	17 4/8	17	15 7/8	17 3/8	3 4/8	3 6/8	5	5	0	35	35
◆ Kodiak Island / Ronnie L. Aldridge / Ronnie L. Aldridge / 1989											

Score	Length of Main Beam R	Length of Main Beam L	Inside Spread	Greatest Spread	Circumference at Smallest Place between Burr and First Point R	Circumference at Smallest Place between Burr and First Point L	Number of Points R	Number of Points L	Total of Lengths Abnormal Points	All-Time Rank	State Rank
110 6/8	16 4/8	16 4/8	14 6/8	16 5/8	3 7/8	3 7/8	5	5	0	37	36
◆ Zarembo Island / Helen G. Keller / Helen G. Keller / 1993											
110 5/8	16 4/8	17 1/8	14 7/8	16 6/8	3 5/8	3 5/8	5	5	0	38	37
◆ Amook Island / Bob Price / Bob Price / 1990											
110 5/8	17 4/8	18 1/8	15 5/8	17 1/8	3 4/8	3 7/8	4	5	0	38	37
◆ Prince of Wales Island / Edward E. Toribio / Edward E. Toribio / 1992											
110 4/8	20 4/8	19	17 4/8	19 2/8	4 2/8	3 6/8	5	4	0	40	39
◆ Klawock Lake / Chris J. Blanc / Chris J. Blanc / 1983											
110 4/8	17 4/8	16 7/8	15 7/8	17 7/8	3 7/8	3 7/8	6	5	1 5/8	40	39
◆ Kodiak Island / William N. Krenz / William N. Krenz / 1988											
110 3/8	16 5/8	17	13 7/8	16 2/8	3 3/8	3 4/8	5	5	0	42	41
◆ Hidden Basin / Don J. Edwards / Don J. Edwards / 1987											
110 2/8	18 6/8	17 6/8	14 2/8	16 2/8	4 1/8	4	5	5	0	43	42
◆ Kodiak Island / R. Fred Fortier / R. Fred Fortier / 1988											
110 2/8	16 5/8	17 1/8	15	17 4/8	3 7/8	3 7/8	5	5	0	43	42
◆ Halibut Bay / Mike D. O'Malley / Mike D. O'Malley / 1993											
110 1/8	19	18 6/8	15 4/8	17 4/8	3 7/8	4	6	6	6 7/8	45	44
◆ Outlet Cape / Henry T. Hamelin / Henry T. Hamelin / 1981											
110 1/8	16 3/8	16 7/8	14 1/8	16 1/8	4 2/8	4 1/8	5	5	0	45	44
◆ Ratz Harbor / Gerald Hedges / Gerald Hedges / 1985											
110 1/8	18 1/8	17 6/8	15 5/8	17 6/8	4 1/8	3 7/8	6	4	2 4/8	45	44
◆ Deadman Bay / Donald W. Simmons / Donald W. Simmons / 1989											
110 1/8	18	17 3/8	15 3/8	16 6/8	4 5/8	4 6/8	5	5	0	45	44
◆ Mitkof Island / Joseph G. Doerr / Joseph G. Doerr / 1992											
109 7/8	16 5/8	17 5/8	14 2/8	16 2/8	3 5/8	3 4/8	6	6	9 3/8	49	48
◆ Kosciusko Island / Michael C. Fezatte / Michael C. Fezatte / 1983											
109 6/8	17 7/8	17 3/8	14 4/8	16 4/8	4 3/8	4 4/8	5	5	0	50	49
◆ Cleveland Pen. / Dennis E. Northrup / Dennis E. Northrup / 1983											
109 5/8	17 1/8	17	15 1/8	17 1/8	3 5/8	3 3/8	5	5	0	51	50
◆ Terror Bay / Christopher L. Linford / Christopher L. Linford / 1987											
109 5/8	18 2/8	18 2/8	14 7/8	17 4/8	3 5/8	3 6/8	4	5	0	51	50
◆ Olga Bay / Ronnie L. Aldridge / Ronnie L. Aldridge / 1988											
109 4/8	19	17 7/8	17 2/8	19 1/8	3 6/8	3 7/8	4	4	0	53	52
◆ Uganik Bay / Harvey D. Harms / Harvey D. Harms / 1982											
109 3/8	18 1/8	18 1/8	15 5/8	17 4/8	4	3 6/8	5	5	0	54	53
◆ Kodiak Island / Gary L. McKay / Gary L. McKay / 1991											

Score	Length of Main Beam R	L	Inside Spread	Greatest Spread	Circumference at Smallest Place between Burr and First Point R	L	Number of Points R	L	Total of Lengths Abnormal Points	All-Time Rank	State Rank
	◆ Locality / Hunter / Owner / Date Killed										
$109\,^2/_8$	$18\,^2/_8$	$18\,^2/_8$	$15\,^2/_8$	17	4	4	4	4	0	55	54
◆ *Olga Bay / David G. Kelleyhouse / David G. Kelleyhouse / 1987*											
$109\,^1/_8$	$18\,^4/_8$	$18\,^7/_8$	$14\,^7/_8$	$16\,^5/_8$	$3\,^7/_8$	$3\,^7/_8$	5	5	0	56	55
◆ *Kupreanof Pen. / John B. Murray / John B. Murray / 1982*											
$109\,^1/_8$	$18\,^3/_8$	18	$16\,^7/_8$	19	4	$3\,^6/_8$	5	5	0	56	55
◆ *Ugak Bay / Donald H. Tetzlaff / Donald H. Tetzlaff / 1984*											
109	$17\,^4/_8$	$16\,^6/_8$	$16\,^4/_8$	$19\,^7/_8$	4	4	5	5	0	58	57
◆ *Uganik Bay / Karl G. Braendel / Karl G. Braendel / 1982*											
109	17	$17\,^4/_8$	$15\,^2/_8$	$17\,^3/_8$	4	4	5	5	0	58	57
◆ *Kodiak Island / D. Roger Liebner / D. Roger Liebner / 1983*											
109	$17\,^7/_8$	18	15	$17\,^1/_8$	$4\,^1/_8$	4	5	5	0	58	57
◆ *Dall Island / Sharla L. Merrill / Sharla L. Merrill / 1985*											
109	$15\,^5/_8$	16	$15\,^6/_8$	$18\,^4/_8$	$3\,^6/_8$	$3\,^5/_8$	5	5	0	58	57
◆ *Terror Bay / John R. Odom III / John R. Odom III / 1985*											
$108\,^7/_8$	$17\,^5/_8$	$17\,^5/_8$	$15\,^7/_8$	18	$3\,^7/_8$	$3\,^7/_8$	5	5	0	62	61
◆ *Karluk Lake / Wayne J. Jalbert / Wayne J. Jalbert / 1993*											
$108\,^7/_8$	$17\,^3/_8$	$17\,^5/_8$	$14\,^7/_8$	$16\,^6/_8$	$3\,^7/_8$	$3\,^6/_8$	5	5	0	62	61
◆ *Granite Mt. / Johnnie R. Laird / Johnnie R. Laird / 1994*											
$108\,^6/_8$	$17\,^2/_8$	$17\,^3/_8$	$15\,^4/_8$	$17\,^4/_8$	$3\,^4/_8$	$3\,^6/_8$	5	5	0	64	63
◆ *Barling Bay / Guy C. Powell / Guy C. Powell / 1984*											
$108\,^4/_8$	$19\,^3/_8$	$19\,^6/_8$	15	$16\,^4/_8$	4	4	4	4	0	65	64
◆ *Cleveland Pen. / Dennis E. Northrup / Dennis E. Northrup / 1985*											
$108\,^4/_8$	$16\,^4/_8$	15	15	$17\,^7/_8$	$4\,^5/_8$	$4\,^6/_8$	5	6	$2\,^4/_8$	65	64
◆ *Cape Uyak / Richard H. Dykema / Richard H. Dykema / 1986*											
$108\,^4/_8$	$15\,^5/_8$	$16\,^2/_8$	$11\,^6/_8$	$13\,^7/_8$	$3\,^6/_8$	$3\,^5/_8$	5	5	0	65	64
◆ *Winter Harbor / Rocky C. Littleton / Rocky C. Littleton / 1988*											
$108\,^2/_8$	$18\,^7/_8$	$19\,^2/_8$	$15\,^7/_8$	$17\,^1/_8$	$4\,^4/_8$	$4\,^7/_8$	7	5	$8\,^3/_8$	68	67
◆ *Whale Passage / Howard W. Honsey / Howard W. Honsey / 1985*											
$108\,^1/_8$	$15\,^6/_8$	$15\,^1/_8$	$14\,^5/_8$	$16\,^5/_8$	$3\,^7/_8$	4	5	5	0	69	68
◆ *Kodiak Island / Kenneth G. Gerg / Kenneth G. Gerg / 1988*											
108	$16\,^6/_8$	$17\,^3/_8$	$14\,^4/_8$	$16\,^4/_8$	$3\,^6/_8$	$3\,^6/_8$	5	5	0	70	69
◆ *Kizhuyak Bay / Gene D. Carter / Gene D. Carter / 1987*											
$107\,^2/_8$	17	$17\,^1/_8$	16	$17\,^7/_8$	$3\,^7/_8$	4	4	5	0	71	70
◆ *Uganik Bay / Robert C. Jones / Robert C. Jones / 1987*											
$107\,^1/_8$	17	$16\,^7/_8$	$13\,^7/_8$	$16\,^1/_8$	4	4	5	5	0	72	71
◆ *Copper Mt. / Lynn W. Merrill / Lynn W. Merrill / 1985*											

ALASKA SITKA BLACKTAIL DEER *(continued)*

Score	Length of Main Beam R	L	Inside Spread	Greatest Spread	Circumference at Smallest Place between Burr and First Point R	L	Number of Points R	L	Total of Lengths Abnormal Points	All-Time Rank	State Rank
107	17	17	16⁶⁄₈	18	3⁶⁄₈	4	5	5	0	73	72

♦ Kodiak Island / Andrew G. Johnson / Andrew G. Johnson / 1986

| 107 | 17²⁄₈ | 17⁵⁄₈ | 15⁶⁄₈ | 18²⁄₈ | 4 | 4 | 4 | 6 | 3²⁄₈ | 73 | 72 |

♦ Red Lake / Terry J. Fike / Terry J. Fike / 1993

| 106⁵⁄₈ | 18²⁄₈ | 17⁵⁄₈ | 16⁷⁄₈ | 18⁵⁄₈ | 4¹⁄₈ | 4¹⁄₈ | 5 | 4 | 0 | 75 | 74 |

♦ Deadman Bay / James L. Kedrowski / James L. Kedrowski / 1989

| 106²⁄₈ | 18³⁄₈ | 17²⁄₈ | 14 | 16 | 3⁷⁄₈ | 4 | 4 | 4 | 0 | 76 | 75 |

♦ Kodiak Island / Jon L. Myer / Jon L. Myer / 1989

| 105⁷⁄₈ | 17⁴⁄₈ | 17²⁄₈ | 14¹⁄₈ | 15⁶⁄₈ | 3⁶⁄₈ | 3⁷⁄₈ | 4 | 5 | 0 | 77 | 76 |

♦ Port Lions / Dean F. Kalbfleisch / Dean F. Kalbfleisch / 1988

| 105⁶⁄₈ | 14⁶⁄₈ | 14⁴⁄₈ | 13⁶⁄₈ | 15³⁄₈ | 4 | 4 | 5 | 5 | 0 | 78 | 77 |

♦ Cordova Bay / James Castle / James Castle / 1993

| 105⁵⁄₈ | 17⁶⁄₈ | 17⁷⁄₈ | 16 | 18 | 3⁴⁄₈ | 3⁶⁄₈ | 5 | 5 | 1³⁄₈ | 79 | 78 |

♦ Whale Pass / Victor R. Poythress / Victor R. Poythress / 1988

| 105⁵⁄₈ | 18²⁄₈ | 17⁷⁄₈ | 14⁵⁄₈ | 16²⁄₈ | 3⁷⁄₈ | 4 | 6 | 5 | 3²⁄₈ | 79 | 78 |

♦ Kaiugnak Bay / Mark B. Sippin / Mark B. Sippin / 1989

| 104⁴⁄₈ | 16⁶⁄₈ | 15⁵⁄₈ | 15⁴⁄₈ | 17²⁄₈ | 3⁵⁄₈ | 3⁴⁄₈ | 5 | 4 | 1 | 81 | 80 |

♦ Malina Bay / Thomas A. Ray / Thomas A. Ray / 1981

| 104²⁄₈ | 15⁴⁄₈ | 15⁴⁄₈ | 15⁴⁄₈ | 17⁴⁄₈ | 4 | 3⁷⁄₈ | 5 | 5 | 0 | 82 | 81 |

♦ Uganik Bay / John A. Miller / John A. Miller / 1984

| 104¹⁄₈ | 17 | 17¹⁄₈ | 15¹⁄₈ | 16⁷⁄₈ | 3⁴⁄₈ | 3⁴⁄₈ | 5 | 5 | 0 | 83 | 82 |

♦ Raspberry Island / George L. Arrington / George L. Arrington / 1993

| 104 | 17³⁄₈ | 17²⁄₈ | 15⁶⁄₈ | 17⁴⁄₈ | 3³⁄₈ | 3⁵⁄₈ | 5 | 5 | 0 | 84 | 83 |

♦ Kodiak Island / Robert C. Jones / Robert C. Jones / 1987

| 103³⁄₈ | 18²⁄₈ | 17⁵⁄₈ | 17⁵⁄₈ | 19⁵⁄₈ | 3⁷⁄₈ | 4²⁄₈ | 4 | 4 | 0 | 85 | 84 |

♦ Red Lake / Darrell L. Smith / Darrell L. Smith / 1994

| 103 | 17⁴⁄₈ | 17⁶⁄₈ | 17⁶⁄₈ | 19⁴⁄₈ | 3⁷⁄₈ | 3⁵⁄₈ | 4 | 4 | 0 | 86 | 85 |

♦ Viekoda Bay / Forrest E. Weiant / Forrest E. Weiant / 1984

| 102⁶⁄₈ | 17 | 16⁷⁄₈ | 15⁴⁄₈ | 20²⁄₈ | 3⁵⁄₈ | 3⁶⁄₈ | 4 | 4 | 0 | 87 | 86 |

♦ Browns Lagoon / Charles R. Price / Charles R. Price / 1986

| 102⁴⁄₈ | 16⁵⁄₈ | 16⁴⁄₈ | 13⁶⁄₈ | 15⁵⁄₈ | 3³⁄₈ | 3³⁄₈ | 5 | 5 | 0 | 88 | 87 |

♦ Kodiak Island / Joyce B. Guth / Joyce B. Guth / 1991

| 102²⁄₈ | 16 | 16¹⁄₈ | 15⁴⁄₈ | 18⁷⁄₈ | 3⁴⁄₈ | 3⁴⁄₈ | 6 | 5 | 3 | 89 | 88 |

♦ Kodiak Island / John H. Saunby / John H. Saunby / 1983

| 101⁷⁄₈ | 15⁴⁄₈ | 16¹⁄₈ | 13¹⁄₈ | 16⁶⁄₈ | 3⁵⁄₈ | 3⁵⁄₈ | 5 | 5 | 0 | 90 | 89 |

♦ Kodiak Island / Stephen R. Grubb / Stepehn R. Grubb / 1989

Score	Length of Main Beam R	L	Inside Spread	Greatest Spread	Circumference at Smallest Place between Burr and First Point R	L	Number of Points R	L	Total of Lengths Abnormal Points	All-Time Rank	State Rank
101 6/8	18	17 3/8	15	17 4/8	3 5/8	3 5/8	5	4	0	91	90
♦ Karluk Lake / Randy S. Shumate / Randy S. Shumate / 1988											
101 4/8	11 7/8	12 4/8	13 4/8	15	3 6/8	3 4/8	7	5	3 6/8	92	91
♦ Prince of Wales Island / Louis M. Seltzer / Louis M. Seltzer / 1951											
101 3/8	16 7/8	17	16 5/8	18 1/8	3 7/8	4	4	4	0	93	92
♦ Kodiak Island / Roger G. Stewart / Roger G. Stewart / 1988											
100 1/8	16 3/8	16 5/8	13 5/8	15 6/8	4	4 3/8	4	4	0	94	93
♦ Viekoda Bay / Forrest E. Weiant / Forrest E. Weiant / 1985											
100	16 3/8	16 7/8	14	15 6/8	3 4/8	3 5/8	4	4	0	95	94
♦ Barabara Cove / Victor R. Poythress / Victor R. Poythress / 1988											
131 5/8	19 2/8	20 5/8	16 5/8	19 1/8	5	4 5/8	7	6	8 2/8	*	*
♦ Luck Lake / Picked Up / Ronald L. Sowards / 1982											
120 3/8	17 5/8	17 4/8	15 7/8	18 4/8	4 4/8	4 3/8	5	5	0	*	*
♦ Boulder Bay / Ronald D. Swingle / Ronald D. Swingle / 1983											
120 2/8	18 7/8	18 6/8	16	17 5/8	3 7/8	3 7/8	5	5	0	*	*
♦ Luck Lake / Ronald A. Littleton / Ronald A. Littleton / 1988											
119 5/8	18 7/8	19 6/8	14 7/8	16 7/8	3 6/8	4 2/8	4	5	0	*	*
♦ Coffman Cove / Gary R. Dilley / Gary R. Dilley / 1987											
118 5/8	19 1/8	19 2/8	14 6/8	16 6/8	4 1/8	4 3/8	6	5	3 7/8	*	*
♦ Prince of Wales Island / Gerald R. Hedges / Gerald R. Hedges / 1987											
118 3/8	17 5/8	19 2/8	17 3/8	19 4/8	4 1/8	4 2/8	5	5	0	*	*
♦ Uganik Lake / Robert D. Gilliland / Robert D. Gilliland / 1983											
118 1/8	16 7/8	17 2/8	14 1/8	16 1/8	4	4 2/8	5	5	0	*	*
♦ Long Island / Daniel G. Bowden / Daniel G. Bowden / 1981											
114	16 4/8	17 1/8	13 4/8	16 4/8	3 4/8	3 4/8	5	5	0	*	*
♦ Prince of Wales Island / Robert D. Steward / Robert D. Steward / 1991											
113 5/8	17 4/8	17 7/8	14 7/8	17	4 1/8	4 2/8	5	5	0	*	*
♦ Kodiak Island / William C. Hayes / William C. Hayes / 1991											
112 7/8	17	18	15 1/8	17 5/8	3 6/8	3 6/8	5	5	0	*	*
♦ Kodiak Island / Gene Coughlin / Gene Coughlin / 1984											
112 4/8	17 6/8	17 3/8	16	18 1/8	3 7/8	4 1/8	5	5	0	*	*
♦ Prince of Wales Island / William H. Welton / William H. Welton / 1988											
112 2/8	17 5/8	17 2/8	16 4/8	18 6/8	4 1/8	3 7/8	5	5	0	*	*
♦ Uganik Lake / George W. Gozelski / George W. Gozelski / 1983											
111 3/8	18	17 5/8	15 5/8	18 7/8	4	4 1/8	5	4	0	*	*
♦ Uyak Bay / Charlie W. Hastings / Charlie W. Hastings / 1986											

ALASKA SITKA BLACKTAIL DEER *(continued)*

Score	Length of Main Beam		Inside Spread	Greatest Spread	Circumference at Smallest Place between Burr and First Point		Number of Points		Total of Lengths Abnormal Points	All-Time Rank	State Rank
	R	L			R	L	R	L			

Score	Length of Main Beam		Inside Spread	Greatest Spread	Circumference R	L	Number of Points R	L	Total Abnormal	All-Time Rank	State Rank
110 5/8	19 1/8	18 2/8	15 5/8	17 4/8	3 6/8	3 7/8	4	5	0	*	*

♦ *Afognak Island / Dale W. Grove / Dale W. Grove / 1987*

| 109 2/8 | 16 | 17 6/8 | 15 2/8 | 18 4/8 | 3 6/8 | 3 5/8 | 6 | 5 | 1 | * | * |

♦ *Uyak Bay / Bradley A. Pope / Bradley A. Pope / 1986*

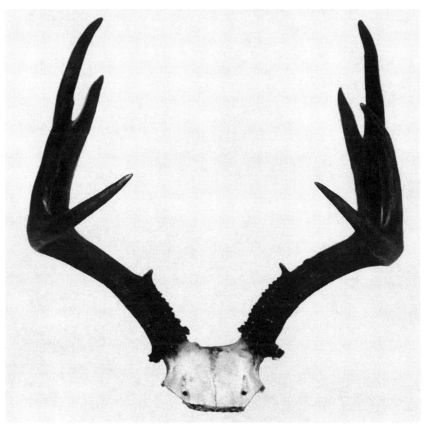

Photograph Courtesy of Gordon O. Tolman

BRITISH COLUMBIA PROVINCE RECORD (NEW)
SITKA BLACKTAIL DEER
SCORE: 110 7/8
Locality: Queen Charlotte Islands   Date: 1990
Hunter: Gordon O. Tolman

BRITISH COLUMBIA
SITKA BLACKTAIL DEER

Score	Length of Main Beam R	L	Inside Spread	Greatest Spread	Circumference at Smallest Place between Burr and First Point R	L	Number of Points R	L	Total of Lengths Abnormal Points	All-Time Rank	State Rank
◆ Locality / Hunter / Owner / Date Killed

110 7/8 17 6/8 17 6/8 12 3/8 14 2/8 3 5/8 3 7/8 4 4 0 35 1
◆ *Queen Charlotte Islands / Gordon O. Tolman / Gordon O. Tolman / 1990*

.

ISBN 0-940864-27-4

52495

9 780940 864276

RECORDS OF N AMERICAN ELK/MULE H